VICTORIAN CONFEDERATE POETRY

THE LOCHLAINN SEABROOK COLLECTION

AMERICAN CIVIL WAR
Abraham Lincoln Was a Liberal, Jefferson Davis Was a Conservative: The Missing Key to Understanding the American Civil War
Confederacy 101: Amazing Facts You Never Knew About America's Oldest Political Tradition
Confederate Blood and Treasure: An Interview With Lochlainn Seabrook
Everything You Were Taught About African-Americans and the Civil War is Wrong, Ask a Southerner!
Everything You Were Taught About the Civil War is Wrong, Ask a Southerner!
Give This Book to a Yankee! A Southern Guide to the Civil War For Northerners
Lincoln's War: The Real Cause, the Real Winner, the Real Loser
The Great Yankee Coverup: What the North Doesn't Want You to Know About Lincoln's War!
The Ultimate Civil War Quiz Book: How Much Do You Really Know About America's Most Misunderstood Conflict?

CONFEDERATE FLAG
Confederate Flag Facts: What Every American Should Know About Dixie's Southern Cross

SECESSION
All We Ask Is To Be Let Alone: The Southern Secession Fact Book

RECONSTRUCTION
Abraham Lincoln: The Southern View - Demythologizing America's Sixteenth President
Nathan Bedford Forrest and the Ku Klux Klan: Yankee Myth, Confederate Fact

SLAVERY
Everything You Were Taught About American Slavery is Wrong, Ask a Southerner!
Slavery 101: Amazing Facts You Never Knew About America's "Peculiar Institution"

CHILDREN
Honest Jeff and Dishonest Abe: A Southern Children's Guide to the Civil War
Saddle, Sword, and Gun: A Biography of Nathan Bedford Forrest For Teens

NATHAN BEDFORD FORREST
A Rebel Born: A Defense of Nathan Bedford Forrest - Confederate General, American Legend (winner of the 2011 Jefferson Davis Historical Gold Medal)
A Rebel Born: The Screenplay
Forrest! 99 Reasons to Love Nathan Bedford Forrest
Give 'Em Hell Boys! The Complete Military Correspondence of Nathan Bedford Forrest
Nathan Bedford Forrest and African-Americans: Yankee Myth, Confederate Fact
Nathan Bedford Forrest and the Battle of Fort Pillow: Yankee Myth, Confederate Fact
Nathan Bedford Forrest and the Ku Klux Klan: Yankee Myth, Confederate Fact
Nathan Bedford Forrest: Southern Hero, American Patriot - Honoring a Confederate Icon and the Old South
Saddle, Sword, and Gun: A Biography of Nathan Bedford Forrest For Teens
The Quotable Nathan Bedford Forrest: Selections From the Writings and Speeches of the Confederacy's Most Brilliant Cavalryman

QUOTABLE SERIES
The Alexander H. Stephens Reader: Excerpts From the Works of a Confederate Founding Father
The Quotable Alexander H. Stephens: Selections From the Writings and Speeches of the Confederacy's First Vice President
The Quotable Jefferson Davis: Selections From the Writings and Speeches of the Confederacy's First President
The Quotable Nathan Bedford Forrest: Selections From the Writings and Speeches of the Confederacy's Most Brilliant Cavalryman
The Quotable Robert E. Lee: Selections From the Writings and Speeches of the South's Most Beloved Civil War General
The Quotable Stonewall Jackson: Selections From the Writings and Speeches of the South's Most Famous General
The Unquotable Abraham Lincoln: The President's Quotes They Don't Want You To Know!

CONSTITUTIONAL HISTORY
The Articles of Confederation Explained: A Clause-by-Clause Study of America's First Constitution
The Constitution of the Confederate States of America Explained: A Clause-by-Clause Study of the South's Magna Carta

VICTORIAN CONFEDERATE LITERATURE
Rise Up and Call Them Blessed: Victorian Tributes to the Confederate Soldier, 1861-1901
The Old Rebel: Robert E. Lee As He Was Seen By His Contemporaries
Victorian Confederate Poetry: The Southern Cause in Verse, 1861-1901

ABRAHAM LINCOLN
Abraham Lincoln: The Southern View - Demythologizing America's Sixteenth President
Lincolnology: The Real Abraham Lincoln Revealed in His Own Words - A Study of Lincoln's Suppressed, Misinterpreted, and Forgotten Writings and Speeches
The Great Impersonator! 99 Reasons to Dislike Abraham Lincoln
The Unholy Crusade: Lincoln's Legacy of Destruction in the American South
The Unquotable Abraham Lincoln: The President's Quotes They Don't Want You To Know!

CIVIL WAR BATTLES
Encyclopedia of the Battle of Franklin - A Comprehensive Guide to the Conflict that Changed the Civil War
Nathan Bedford Forrest and the Battle of Fort Pillow: Yankee Myth, Confederate Fact

BIOGRAPHY
A Rebel Born: A Defense of Nathan Bedford Forrest - Confederate General, American Legend (winner of the 2011 Jefferson Davis Historical Gold Medal)
Nathan Bedford Forrest: Southern Hero, American Patriot - Honoring a Confederate Icon and the Old South
Saddle, Sword, and Gun: A Biography of Nathan Bedford Forrest For Teens

PARANORMAL
Carnton Plantation Ghost Stories: True Tales of the Unexplained from Tennessee's Most Haunted Civil War House!
UFOs and Aliens: The Complete Guidebook

FAMILY HISTORIES
The Blakeneys: An Etymological, Ethnological, and Genealogical Study - Uncovering the Mysterious Origins of the Blakeney Family and Name
The Caudills: An Etymological, Ethnological, and Genealogical Study - Exploring the Name and National Origins of a European-American Family
The McGavocks of Carnton Plantation: A Southern History - Celebrating One of Dixie's Most Noble Confederate Families and Their Tennessee Home

MIND, BODY, SPIRIT
Autobiography of a Non-Yogi: A Scientist's Journey From Hinduism to Christianity (Dr. Amitava Dasgupta, with Lochlainn Seabrook)
Britannia Rules: Goddess-Worship in Ancient Anglo-Celtic Society - An Academic Look at the United Kingdom's Matricentric Spiritual Past
Christ Is All and In All: Rediscovering Your Divine Nature and the Kingdom Within
Christmas Before Christianity: How the Birthday of the "Sun" Became the Birthday of the "Son"
Jesus and the Gospel of Q: Christ's Pre-Christian Teachings As Recorded in the New Testament
Jesus and the Law of Attraction: The Bible-Based Guide to Creating Perfect Health, Wealth, and Happiness Following Christ's Simple Formula
Seabrook's Bible Dictionary of Traditional and Mystical Christian Doctrines
The Bible and the Law of Attraction: 99 Teachings of Jesus, the Apostles, and the Prophets
The Book of Kelle: An Introduction to Goddess-Worship and the Great Celtic Mother-Goddess Kelle, Original Blessed Lady of Ireland
The Goddess Dictionary of Words and Phrases: Introducing a New Core Vocabulary for the Women's Spirituality Movement
The Way of Holiness: The Story of Religion and Myth From the Cave Bear Cult to Christianity

WOMEN
Aphrodite's Trade: The Hidden History of Prostitution Unveiled
Princess Diana: Modern Day Moon-Goddess - A Psychoanalytical and Mythological Look at Diana Spencer's Life, Marriage, and Death (with Dr. Jane Goldberg)
Women in Gray: A Tribute to the Ladies Who Supported the Southern Confederacy

Five-Star Books & Gifts From the Heart of the American South

SeaRavenPress.com

VICTORIAN CONFEDERATE POETRY

The Southern Cause In Verse, 1861-1901

COLLECTED, ARRANGED, & EDITED, WITH AN INTRODUCTION & NOTES, BY
"THE VOICE OF THE TRADITIONAL SOUTH," COLONEL

LOCHLAINN SEABROOK

JEFFERSON DAVIS HISTORICAL GOLD MEDAL WINNER

Diligently Researched and Generously Illustrated for the Elucidation of the Reader

2018
Sea Raven Press, Nashville, Tennessee, USA

VICTORIAN CONFEDERATE POETRY

Published by
Sea Raven Press, Cassidy Ravensdale, President
PO Box 1484, Spring Hill, Tennessee 37174-1484 USA
SeaRavenPress.com • searavenpress@gmail.com

Copyright © 2018 Lochlainn Seabrook
in accordance with U.S. and international copyright laws and regulations, as stated and protected under the Berne Union for the Protection of Literary and Artistic Property (Berne Convention), and the Universal Copyright Convention (the UCC). All rights reserved under the Pan-American and International Copyright Conventions.

1st SRP paperback edition, 1st printing: January 2018, ISBN: 978-1-943737-59-8
1st SRP hardcover edition, 1st printing: January 2018, ISBN: 978-1-943737-60-4

ISBN: 978-1-943737-59-8 (paperback)
Library of Congress Control Number: 2017958431

This work is the copyrighted intellectual property of Lochlainn Seabrook and has been registered with the Copyright Office at the Library of Congress in Washington, D.C., USA. No part of this work (including text, covers, drawings, photos, illustrations, maps, images, diagrams, etc.), in whole or in part, may be used, reproduced, stored in a retrieval system, or transmitted, in any form or by any means now known or hereafter invented, without written permission from the publisher. The sale, duplication, hire, lending, copying, digitalization, or reproduction of this material, in any manner or form whatsoever, is also prohibited, and is a violation of federal, civil, and digital copyright law, which provides severe civil and criminal penalties for any violations.

Victorian Confederate Poetry: The Southern Cause in Verse, 1861-1901, by Lochlainn Seabrook. Includes an index, endnotes, and bibliographical references.

Front and back cover design and art, book design, layout, and interior art by Lochlainn Seabrook.
All images, graphic design, graphic art, and illustrations copyright © Lochlainn Seabrook.
All images selected, placed, manipulated, and/or created by Lochlainn Seabrook.
Cover images & design copyright © Lochlainn Seabrook.

The views on the American "Civil War" documented in this book are those of the publisher.

PRINTED & MANUFACTURED IN OCCUPIED TENNESSEE, FORMER CONFEDERATE STATES OF AMERICA

Dedication

To the poets among my Confederate ancestors.

Epigraph

The public has been flooded for years with the triumphal praises of the victors. The noble sentiments of unity and freedom which animated the Northern troops have been sung into poetry time and time again, but in this instance, as in all accounts of great events, involving many passions and many phases of human feeling and emotion, the world has felt that there is another side of the affair to be spoken; another music, whose silence only waits a singer to become articulate.

For many reasons the Southern side of the great conflict is more pregnant with the soul of poetry than the other. The voice of sorrow is always more musical than the shout of victory. The tears that fall from eyes weeping for broken hearts are naturally elements of the tenderness that makes great poetry. Then, too, the South has gained a grander and later victory. She has taken the cypress garlands of mourning and made them into laurel wreaths. Through all the story the South is rich in pathos, in greatness, in heroism, and the time for the speaking of this music has come.

Sumner Archibald Cunningham, 1893

CONTENTS

Notes to the Reader 19
Introduction, by Lochlainn Seabrook 27

The Poems

DIXIE 33
CONFEDERATE SONG 35
TO THE CONFEDERATE GOVERNMENT 36
THE BONNIE BLUE FLAG 37
THE SOUTHERN CROSS 38
LAND OF KING COTTON 39
VICKSBURG—A BALLAD 40
IN MEMORY OF ALBERT SIDNEY JOHNSTON 42
PARODY ON BULL RUN 43
KENTUCKY STATE GUARD WAR SONG 44
MARYLAND, MY MARYLAND 45
A BATTLE CALL TO KENTUCKY 47
ALL QUIET ALONG THE POTOMAC TO-NIGHT 48
WHEN UPON THE FIELD OF GLORY 50
THE LONE SENTRY 51
MANASSAS 52
THE HEART OF LOUISIANA 53
THE SHADE OF THE TREES 54
MISSING 55
IN MEMORIAM OF COL. BENJAMIN F. TERRY 56
THE GIRLS OF THE MONUMENTAL CITY 58
THE TWO ARMIES 59
THE SOUTHERN CROSS 60
THE BATTLE RAINBOW 62
OUR LEFT 64
BEYOND THE POTOMAC 65
WE'LL BE FREE IN MARYLAND 67

A WORD WITH THE WEST	69
CHRISTMAS NIGHT OF '62	71
SOUTHERN SONG	73
CHICKAMAUGA	75
SOMEBODY'S DARLING	78
ODE TO JOHNSON'S ISLAND	79
THE BATTLE OF CHARLESTON HARBOR	80
FEDERAL NURSERY HYMN	82
DEATH OF STONEWALL JACKSON	84
THE BAND IN THE PINES	85
SOUTHLAND	86
MY LOVE & I, BY A PRISONER OF WAR	88
BEFORE RICHMOND	89
THE CAPTIVE'S DREAM	90
SONNET	91
OBSEQUIES OF JEB STUART	92
DREAMING IN THE TRENCHES	94
GENERAL LEE & TRAVELLER	95
SEVENTY-SIX & SIXTY-ONE	98
WOUNDED & SLAIN	99
REBELS	100
PROMETHEUS VINCTUS	101
THE FOE AT THE GATES	103
LINES ON A CONFEDERATE NOTE	104
OUR DIXIE	105
THE LAND WHERE WE WERE DREAMING	106
STACK ARMS	108
THE CONFEDERATE DEAD	109
THE DYING WORDS OF JACKSON	111
THE LAST WORDS OF GEN. STONEWALL JACKSON	112
RESULT OF THE WAR IN THE SOUTH	113
THE CONQUERED BANNER	114
OUR SACRED BANNER	116
TO OUR DEAD AT NEW HOPE CHURCH	117
THERE'S LIFE IN THE OLD LAND YET	118
THE REBEL'S RETURN	119
ONLY A PRIVATE	121
JOHN MARSHALL'S STATUE	122
TURNER ASHBY	124
MUSIC IN CAMP	125
MAGNOLIA CEMETERY ODE	127

THE PHANTOM HOST	128
A REBEL SOLDIER KILLED IN THE TRENCHES	131
BATTLE OF HAMPTON ROADS	132
THE SOUTHERN HOMES IN RUIN	134
THE SOLDIER IN THE RAIN	135
SACRIFICE	136
ONLY A SOLDIERS GRAVE	137
WILLIAM MUMFORD MARTYR OF NEW ORLEANS	138
ALBERT SIDNEY JOHNSTON	139
A LAMENT FOR DIXIE	141
MARSE ROBERT IS ASLEEP	143
DECORATING CONFEDERATE GRAVES	145
THE SOUTHERN FLAGS	146
MEMORIAL ODE	148
PASSING MANASSAS, 1892	149
BUILD THE MONUMENT	150
ROBERT E. LEE	151
THE SAME CANTEEN	152
PRAYER OF THE SOUTH	153
TO A CONFEDERATE BATTLE FLAG	156
JEFFERSON DAVIS' SECOND FUNERAL PROCESSION	158
IN THE SOUTH	159
MEMORIES	160
THE STARS & BARS	162
OUR BATTLE FLAG	164
IN MEMORIAM	165
THE DEATH OF STONEWALL JACKSON	166
SHERIDAN'S RAID IN THE JAMES RIVER VALLEY	167
A GEORGIA VOLUNTEER	169
THE BATTLE OF SHILOH	170
EXALTATION OF THE CONFEDERATE BANNER	172
THE SOUTHERN REPUBLIC	174
THE DEATH OF JEB STUART	176
TO SOUTH CAROLINA'S DEAD CONFEDERATE HEROES	178
A CONFEDERATE CAPTIVE ON LAKE ERIE	180
WILLIE PRESTON—DEAD	181
THE SOUTHERN CROSS	183
THE SOLDIER'S GRAVE	185
THE JACKET OF GRAY	186
STACK ARMS BOYS, ALL IS O'ER	187
MY SOUTH! MY SOUTH!	188

MY CONFEDERATE UNIFORM	189
ASHES OF GLORY	190
LEE AT APPOMATTOX	191
EPITAPH ON STONEWALL JACKSON	192
A RAINBOW FROM LOOKOUT MOUNTAIN	193
FLAG OF THE TWELFTH MISSISSIPPI REGIMENT	194
TO THE DEPARTING CONFEDERATE SOLDIERS	195
CONFEDERATE MEMORIAL DAY	196
MY LITTLE VOLUNTEER	197
THE HERO, STONEWALL JACKSON	198
LETTERS FROM VETERANS	199
TRIBUTE TO UNCROWNED HEROES	200
PRESIDENT DAVIS	201
WEARING THE GRAY	202
AN INCIDENT OF BATTLE	204
THE BROKEN BATTALIONS	206
MY SOUTHERN HOME	208
PELHAM AT FREDERICKSBURG	209
SAM DAVIS WAS TOO BRAVE TO DIE	210
HENRY T. STANTON'S POEM	212
THE DRUMMER BOY OF SHILOH	218
A JOHNNY REB ON PENSIONS TO YANKEES	219
A CONFEDERATE ACROSTIC	220
THE MEN WHO WORE THE GRAY	221
I'M CONSCRIPTED, SMITH, CONSCRIPTED	222
THE BUGLE CALL	223
CONFEDERATE CEMETERY	224
CONFEDERATE MONUMENT AT CHICAGO	225
TRUE TO THE SOUTH	226
MRS. MACLEAN'S ODE	227
AT REST—JEFFERSON DAVIS	228
JIM O'MERA'S RIDE	229
SAVANNAH FALLEN	230
THE STARS & BARS	231
SONGS OF THE CONFEDERACY	232
BARRIERS BURNED AWAY	233
THE SPIRIT OF 1861-1896	234
OUR DEAD	236
SAM DAVIS: THE CONFEDERATE MARTYR	238
OUR WOMEN & THE WAR	240
AN APPEAL TO THE SOUTH	242

A SOUTHERN ROSE	243
IN MEMORIAM	244
CALL IT NOT A "LOST CAUSE"	245
WE'VE FOUGHT AGAIN	246
THE CHARGE	247
AN HOUR IN HOLLYWOOD CEMETERY	250
OLD MAXCY'S SWORD	252
THEY HAVE DONNED THE GRAY AGAIN	254
CONFEDERATE MONUMENT AT WINCHESTER	255
NEC TEMERE, NEC TIMIDE	257
WHEN WILL PAPA COME?	259
THE SOUTHERN BATTLE FLAGS	261
OUR VETERANS AT RICHMOND	263
DAUGHTER OF THE CONFEDERACY	264
PRIVATE AT THE PLOW	265
REBEL OR LOYALIST (TO A YANKEE)	266
TO COMPANY B, TWELFTH VIRGINIA CAVALRY	269
THE BURIAL OF CAPTAIN WILLIAM LATANÉ	270
A SOLDIER IN GRAY	272
VIRGINIA	274
THE OLD SOUTH	275
VIRGE MOOSE	276
A CONFEDERATE MONUMENT	278
OUR VETERANS	279
THE CONFEDERACY	280
THOSE WHO CANNOT RALLY	281
THE GREAT CONFEDERATE REUNION AT RICHMOND	282
NASHVILLE'S INVITATION	285
HE'LL SEE IT WHEN HE WAKES	287
TO A STATUE OF SAM DAVIS	288
THE SONG "DIXIE" WILL NOT BE BANNED	289
DECKING SOUTHERN SOLDIERS' GRAVES	290
GENERAL ARCHIBALD GRACIE OF ALABAMA	291
THE RESCUE OF RYAN'S CONQUERED BANNER	293
TRIBUTE TO THE FALLEN	294
THE STRIFE IS O'ER	296
OUR GENERAL JOSEPH ORVILLE SHELBY	297
A COUNTRY MAIDEN'S "GENERAL" INVITATION	299
THE OLD CANTEEN	300
TO DIXIE LAND	301
THE BONNIE BLUE FLAG	302

SAM DAVIS	303
CLEBURNE'S BANNER	305
HER LETTER CAME TOO LATE	306
IN DIXIE LAND	308
THE UNKNOWN DEAD	309
THE SENTINEL & THE SCOUT	310
IN THE TRENCHES	311
HOOD'S TEXANS AT LITTLE ROUND TOP	314
SAM DAVIS	315
A SOLDIER OF ROBERT E. LEE	316
CONFEDERATE SOLDIERS: A MEMORIAL	317
AN OLD CONFED WHO MORGAN LED	318
WILMINGTON'S ROLL-CALL OF HONOR	319
CAROLINA, 1865	322
TO THE MEMORY OF THE BRAVE	323
AT REST	325
THE CONFEDERATE DEAD	326
TO AN OLD SABER	327
MEETING OF THE PICKETS	328
THE BOYS IN GRAY	330
THE SWORD OF LEE	332
WHEN THE ROLL IS CALLED UP YONDER	333
THE CONFEDERATE DEAD	334
A BALLAD OF EMMA SANSOM	335
OUR PAST	338
THE HOMESPUN DRESS	339
APPEAL FOR A SOLDIER'S HOME	341
GOD SPEED THE BRIGHT & GLORIOUS DAY	343
IN MEMORY OF JUDGE FARRAR	344
THE CONFEDERATE CABINET	346
THE BIVOUAC OF THE DEAD	347
TO THE SONS & DAUGHTERS OF VETERANS	349
WAR HYMN	350
THE OLD COAT OF GRAY	351
AT STONEWALL JACKSON'S TOMB	353
INVITATION TO THE VETERANS	354
FOR JUST A GLIMPSE OF SOUTHLAND	355
THE YANK & THE REB	356
REUNION HYMN	358
THE CONFEDERATE FLAG	359
LEAVE US OUR DEAD	361

THE SWORD OF THE SOUTH	362
THE MEN OF MOSBY'S COMMAND	364
THE OLD FLAG	365
DEATHLESS FAME	366
PRAYER FOR SUBMISSION IN A YANKEE PRISON	368
THE UNKNOWN DEAD	369
IN MEMORIAM—THE RAID, THE CHARGE, AT REST	370
THE SOUTHLAND	372
THE FELLOWS THAT TRAMPED IT WITH LEE	373
DEATH OF GENERAL BENJAMIN HARDIN HELM	375
THE GLORIOUS GHOST OF LEE	376
A RIDE WITH STUART	377
THE OLD JACKET OF GRAY	378
THE RECOMPENSE	380
OLD TIME CONFEDERATES	381
A REQUIEM	382
THE LAST WORDS OF STONEWALL JACKSON	383
TO OUR SACRED CONFEDERATE DEAD	384
THE SWORD OF CLEBURNE	385
SOUTHERN WOMEN—A TRIBUTE	386
THE BOY HERO OF THE WAR	387
TO THE ONLY CONFEDERATE MONUMENT IN GETTYSBURG	388
TRUEST, BRAVEST, & BEST	389
ABRAM JOSEPH RYAN, THE POET PRIEST	390
THE "BATTERED SCARECROWS"	391
A CONFEDERATE SPY	392
TO THE CONFEDERATE SURVIVORS OF THE WAR	395
IN MEMORIAM	397
THE ROAD TO IMMORTALITY	398
FORREST	400
CONFEDERATE CEMETERY, SPRINGFIELD, MISSOURI	402
CROSS OF HONOR	403
TRIBUTE POEM TO MAJOR PHILIP H. FALL	404
THE OLD SWORD ON THE WALL	405
SOMETIME	406
WOOING IN THE SIXTIES	407
HOME, SWEET HOME	410
THE RED, WHITE, & RED	411
THE CONFEDERATE CROSS OF HONOR	412
SCATTER SWEET FLOWERS O'ER THE DEAD	414
SOUTHERN MAIDEN'S LAMENT FOR HER COUNTRY	415

A MOTHER'S SORROW	416
MAJOR GENERAL PATRICK RONAYNE CLEBURNE	417
RABBI BEN-HISSAR	418
MEMORIAL ODE	420
SOUTHERN SENTIMENT	421
JUSTICE IS OUR PANOPLY	422
WAR SONG	423
A NEW RED, WHITE, & BLUE	424
SOUTHRONS	425
CHIVALROUS C.S.A.	426
THE SOLDIER'S HEART	428
MY WIFE & CHILD	429
THOUGHTS SUGGESTED BY A PICTURE	430
WOMAN'S WAR MISSION	431
HARP OF THE SOUTH, AWAKE!	434
O'ER THE TOMB	436
CLOUDS IN THE WEST	437
THE SOLDIER BOY	438
ROLL-CALL	439
THE VIRGINIANS OF THE VALLEY	441
THE BIVOUAC IN THE SNOW	442
STONEWALL JACKSON'S WAY	443
THE CONFEDERATE FLAG	445
LEE TO THE REAR	446
THE C.S.S. *ALABAMA*	449
GENERAL WORSELY TO GENERAL LEE	451
CHARLESTON	452
READING THE LIST	454
THE MEN	455
THE UNIFORM OF GRAY	456
THE BAREFOOTED BOYS	457
DIRGE FOR ASHBY	458
MISSING	460
I'M GWINE BACK TO DIXIE	461
THE OATH OF FREEDOM	462
UNDER ONE BLANKET	464
JOHN PELHAM	466
SUMTER IN RUINS	467
THE TWO ARMIES	468
SENTINEL SONGS	469
GATHERING SONG	471

LITTLE GIFFEN OF TENNESSEE	472
WE CONQUER OR DIE	473
ON THE DEATH OF GEN. LEONIDAS POLK	474
SONNET	475
STONEWALL JACKSON	476
THE COUNTERSIGN	477
HIGH TIDE AT GETTYSBURG	479
CALL ALL! CALL ALL!	481
GENERAL ALBERT SIDNEY JOHNSTON	482
FAREWELL TO JOHNSON'S ISLAND	483
FORT WAGNER	484
TO MY SOLDIER BROTHER	486
THE SOUTHRON MOTHER'S CHARGE	487
THE SOUTHERN PLEIADES	488
THE STARS & BARS	489
THE MARCH	491
THE SOUTH IN ARMS	492
MELT THE BELLS	493
GLORIOUS MEMORIES OF THE OLD SOUTH	494
OUR SOUTHERN WOMEN	495
ONLY A PRIVATE	496
THE GRAVE OF A SOUTHERN SOLDIER	497
SPRING IN WAR-TIME	500
OUR MARTYRS	502
CONFEDERATE MONUMENT INSCRIPTION	504
CAROLINA	505
COERCION: A POEM FOR THEN & NOW	507
HEROES OF THE SOUTH	509
GONE FORWARD	511
ADDRESS OF THE WOMEN TO SOUTHERN TROOPS	512
THE CAVALIERS OF DIXIE	513
SOUTHERN MARSEILLAISE	515
FROM THE SOUTH TO THE NORTH	517
THE CONFEDERATE FLAG	519
PATRIOTISM	520
THE CONFEDERATE FLAG	521
THE SOUTH	522
OLD BETSY	523
NO SURRENDER	524
THE DYING SOLDIER	525
VOICES OF THE FOUNDING FATHERS	526

HEART-VICTORIES	528
GOD SAVE THE SOUTH	530
THE BOY-SOLDIER	531
CONFEDERATE LAND	533
A CHRISTMAS OF LONG AGO	534
THE GUERILLAS	535
A CRY TO ARMS	537
THE TOURNAMENT	539
THE INVOCATION	540
Appendix A: Someone's Darlin' (poem)	543
Appendix B: Land of the South (poem)	544
Appendix C: Arm For the Southern Land (poem)	546
Notes	547
Bibliography	559
Index	568
Meet the Author	574

NOTES TO THE READER

"NOTHING IN THE PAST IS DEAD TO THE MAN WHO WOULD
LEARN HOW THE PRESENT CAME TO BE WHAT IT IS."

WILLIAM STUBBS, VICTORIAN ENGLISH HISTORIAN

THE TWO MAIN POLITICAL PARTIES IN 1860

ã In any study of America's antebellum, bellum, and postbellum periods, it is vitally important to understand that in 1860 the two major political parties—the Democrats and the newly formed Republicans—were the opposite of what they are today. In other words, the Democrats of the mid 19th Century were Conservatives, akin to the Republican Party of today, while the Republicans of the mid 19th Century were Liberals, akin to the Democratic Party of today.[1]

Thus the Confederacy's Democratic president, Jefferson Davis, was a Conservative (with libertarian leanings); the Union's Republican president, Abraham Lincoln, was a Liberal (with socialistic leanings).[2]

This is why, in the mid 1800s, the conservative wing of the Democratic Party was known as "the States' Rights Party."[3]

Hence, the Democrats of the Civil War period referred to themselves as "conservatives," "confederates," "anti-centralists," or "constitutionalists" (the latter because they favored strict adherence to the original Constitution—which tacitly guaranteed states' rights—as created by the Founding Fathers), while the Republicans called themselves "liberals," "nationalists," "centralists," or "consolidationists" (the latter three because they wanted to nationalize the central government and consolidate political power in Washington, D.C.).[4]

The author's cousin, Confederate Vice President and Democrat Alexander H. Stephens: a Southern Conservative.

Since this idea is new to most of my readers, let us further demystify it by viewing it from the perspective of the American Revolutionary War. If Davis and his conservative Southern constituents (the Democrats of 1861) had been alive in 1775, they would have sided with George Washington and the American colonists, who sought to secede from the tyrannical government of Great Britain; if Lincoln and his Liberal Northern constituents (the Republicans of 1861) had been alive at that time, they would have sided with King George III and the English monarchy, who sought to maintain the American colonies as possessions of the British Empire. It is due to this very comparison that Southerners often refer to their secession as the Second Declaration of Independence and the "Civil War" as the Second American Revolutionary War.

Without a basic understanding of these facts, the American "Civil War" will forever remain incomprehensible. For a full discussion of this topic see my book, *Abraham Lincoln Was a Liberal, Jefferson Davis Was a Conservative: The Missing Key to Understanding the American Civil War.*

THE TERM "CIVIL WAR"

As I heartily dislike the phrase "Civil War," its use throughout this book (as well as in my other works) is worthy of explanation.

Our entire modern literary system refers to the conflict of 1861 using the Northern term the "Civil War," whether we in the South like it or not. Of course, this is purposeful,

The American "Civil War" was not a true civil war as Webster defines it: "A conflict between opposing groups of citizens of the *same* country." It was a fight between two individual countries; or to be more specific, two separate and constitutionally formed confederacies: the U.S.A. and the C.S.A.

for America's book industry, which determines everything from how books are categorized and designed to how they are marketed and sold, is almost solely controlled by Liberals, socialists, globalists, and communists, individuals who will do anything to prevent the truth about Lincoln's War from coming out. An important aspect of this wholesale revisionism of American history is the use of the phrase "Civil War," which Yankee Liberals thrust into the public forum even as big government Left-winger Lincoln was diabolically tricking the Conservative South into firing the first shot at the Battle of Fort Sumter in April 1861.

The progressives' blatant American "Civil War" coverup continues to this day, one of the more overt results which pertains to how books are coded, indexed, and identified.[5] Thus, as all book searches by readers, libraries, and retail outlets are now performed online, and as all bookstores categorize works from or about this period under the heading "Civil War," honest book publishers and authors who deal with this particular topic have little choice but to use this deceptive term. If I were to refuse to use it, as some of my Southern colleagues have suggested, few people would ever find or read my books.

Add to this the fact that scarcely any non-Southerners have ever heard of the names we in the South use for the conflict, such as the "War for Southern Independence"—or my personal preference, "Lincoln's War." It only makes sense then to use the term "Civil War" in most commercial situations, distasteful though it is.

We should also bear in mind that while today educated persons, particularly educated Southerners, all share an abhorrence for the phrase "Civil War," it was not always so. Confederates who lived through and even fought in the conflict regularly used the term throughout the 1860s, and even long after. Among them were Confederate generals such as Nathan Bedford Forrest, Richard Taylor, and Joseph E. Johnston, not to mention the Confederacy's vice president, Alexander H. Stephens.

Confederate General James Longstreet was just one of many Southern officials who referred to the conflict of 1861 as the "Civil War."

In 1895 Confederate General James Longstreet wrote about his military experiences in a work subtitled, *Memoirs of the Civil War in America*. Even the Confederacy's highest leader, President Jefferson Davis, used the term "Civil War,"[6] and in one case at least, as late as 1881—the year he wrote his brilliant exposition, *The Rise and Fall of the Confederate Government*.[7] Authors writing for *Confederate Veteran* magazine sometimes used the phrase well into the early 1900s,[8] and in 1898, at the Eighth

Annual Meeting and Reunion of the United Confederate Veterans (the forerunner of today's Sons of Confederate Veterans), the following resolution was proposed: that from then on the Great War of 1861 was to be designated "the Civil War Between the States."⁹

A WORD ON EARLY AMERICAN MATERIAL

In order to preserve the authentic historicity of the antebellum, bellum, and postbellum periods, I have retained the original spellings, formatting, and punctuation of the early Americans I quote. These include such items as Old European and British-English spellings, long-running paragraphs, obsolete words, and various literary devices peculiar to the time. Bracketed words within quotes are my additions and clarifications, while italicized words within quotes are (where indicated) my emphasis.

POETS, ORDER, POEMS, & DATES

Some of my poets, such as Albert Pike and Margaret Junkin Preston, were not born in the South, but vigorously identified with and supported the South throughout Lincoln's War: Margaret as the wife of John Thomas Lewis Preston, Stonewall Jackson's aide-de-camp, and Pike as a brigadier general in the Confederate army. I count such individuals as Southerners and so have included them here.

As to my ordering sequence, generally speaking I have placed poems in chronological order, from oldest first (1861) to newest last (1901). Unfortunately, it is rare that a Victorian *Southern War* poem comes with an exact date attached. Typically even the year is not known with certainty. Thus in some cases educated guesswork was employed. Those poems whose birth years are "asserted" yet remain dubious—that is, several dates (and sometimes even authors) have been attributed to them over the past 150 years—I placed in the last 100 pages or so.

Note that the position of a poem in my book does not necessarily indicate even the approximate time of its creation. For example, a poem in the middle might seem to indicate a work created around 1881 (halfway between 1861 and 1901). However, it could just as likely point to the year it was published according to my source material—though even this could be decades after it was *first* actually published publicly. When *no date of origin* was provided and internal evidence indicated as much, I located such poems in the year in which their authors' words take place. For example, a poem about the Battle of Fort Sumter would be near the beginning, in the 1861 period; a poem about Lee's surrender would be in the 1865 period, etc.

Lastly: 1) I have included song lyrics, which, as a composer and lyricist myself, I consider poetry. 2) A number of individual poems have the same title, an inevitable outcome of a collection of poetry this size. 3) When a poem was absent a title (a not uncommon occurrence), I created my own, and note this where applicable. 4) Oddly, titles seem to have been somewhat arbitrary since, in many cases, the same poem is given different titles in different sources.

THE SO-CALLED "LOST CAUSE"

ಇ Some of my poets make reference to the "Lost Cause," a pessimistic term for what they perceived as the final death and ultimate extinction of the Southern Confederacy and all she stood for. Needless to say, I vehemently reject this view, as did most postwar Victorian Southerners (see, for example, Dargan's poem "Call It Not a 'Lost Cause'" on page 245). And with good reason.

As I have discussed at length in many of my other works, the Southern Cause, or Confederate Cause, as it is also known, was not a material thing. It was a principle or idea, and principles and ideas are impervious to harm, decay, or warfare. Bullets, bayonets, and cannon balls have no effect on them. Ideas are, in fact, imperishable and immortal, and none are more imperishable and immortal than the Southern Cause.

How can this be, South-loathers ask, if the Confederacy "lost the War"?

It is because the Southern Cause was (and still is) *conservatism*, also called Americanism, which Webster defines as an "attachment or allegiance to the traditions, interests, or ideals of the U.S.," as well as "the political principles and practices essential to American culture." This is conservatism in a nutshell, a political philosophy that has remained unchanged since it was inaugurated and embraced by our Conservative Founding Fathers some 250 years ago: Thomas Jefferson, George Mason, James Madison, and Patrick Henry, to name but a few.

In reality then, the American "Civil War" was nothing but a mid 19th-

Century battle between conservatism (Americanism) and liberalism (anti-Americanism), two irreconcilable enemies more commonly and misleadingly characterized today as "the South and the North," "the Gray and the Blue," "the Rebels and the Union," "the Confederates and the Yankees."

Throughout my numerous "Civil War" books I have exposed these fallacious labels for what they are: crude attempts to hide the truth about the War; namely, that the Democratic South (the Democrats then were Conservatives) were fighting for conservative principles; the Republican North (the Republicans then were Liberals) were fighting for liberal principles. This is the same political war that is going on in the U.S. today, and will continue for as long as humanity exists.

Thus, the Southern Cause was not "lost" as a result of the "Civil War." And it will never be "lost" as long as there are Conservatives. Indeed, 21st-Century Conservatives are the political descendants of 19th-Century Confederates. Both struggled for the same idea: the preservation of small-government principles, which includes self-government and states rights within the framework of a constitutionally formed "Confederate Republic," or "Confederate States of America," as the Founding Generation referred to the U.S.A.

Despite my position regarding the concept of the "Lost Cause," I have included the works of poets who espoused it in order to provide as broad a spectrum of views as possible. For a detailed discussion on the true foundation and results of the War for Southern Independence, see my book, *Lincoln's War: The Real Cause, the Real Winner, the Real Loser*.

PRESENTISM

As a historian I view *presentism* (judging the past according to present day mores and customs) as the enemy of authentic history. And this is precisely why the Left employs it in its ongoing war against traditional American, conservative, Southern, and Christian

Judging our ancestors by our own standards is unfair, unjust, misleading, and unethical.

values. By looking at history through the lens of modern day beliefs, they are able to distort, revise, and reshape the past into a false narrative that fits their ideological agenda: the liberalization *and* Northernization of America, the enlargement and further centralization of the national government, and total control of American political, economic, and social power, the same agenda that Lincoln championed.

This book rejects presentism and replaces it with what I call *historicalism*: judging our ancestors based on the values of their own time. To get the most from this work the reader is invited to reject presentism as well. In this way—along with casting aside preconceived notions and the fake "history" churned out by our left-wing education system—the truth in this work will be most readily ascertained and absorbed.

LEARN MORE

🕊 Lincoln's War on the American people and the Constitution can never be fully understood without a thorough knowledge of the South's perspective. As this book is only meant to be a brief introductory guide to these topics, one cannot hope to learn the complete story here. For those who are interested in additional material from Dixie's viewpoint, please see my comprehensive histories listed on pages 2 and 3.

Keep Your Body, Mind, & Spirit Vibrating at Their Highest Level

YOU CAN DO SO BY READING THE BOOKS OF

SEA RAVEN PRESS

There is nothing that will so perfectly keep your body, mind, and spirit in a healthy condition as to think wisely and positively. Hence you should not only read this book, but also the other books that we offer. They will quicken your physical, mental, and spiritual vibrations, enabling you to maintain a position in society as a healthy erudite person.

KEEP YOURSELF WELL-INFORMED!

The well-informed person is always at the head of the procession, while the ignorant, the lazy, and the unthoughtful hang onto the rear. If you are a Spiritual man or woman, do yourself a great favor: read Sea Raven Press books and stay well posted on the Truth. It is almost criminal for one to remain in ignorance while the opportunity to gain knowledge is open to all at a nominal price.

We invite you to visit our Webstore for a wide selection of wholesome, family-friendly, well-researched, educational books for all ages. You will be glad you did!

Five-Star Books & Gifts From the Heart of the American South

SeaRavenPress.com

INTRODUCTION

"AS CERTAIN EVEN OF YOUR OWN POETS HAVE SAID . . ." — SAINT PAUL

WHY A BOOK ON SOUTHERN Civil War poetry? Why devote years of my life to compiling the works of hundreds of Victorian poets dedicated to the so-called "Lost Cause"? What relevance do 19th-Century pro-South rhymes have for the 21st-Century reader, some over 150 years old?

I have written many dozens of both popular and scholarly books on Lincoln's War that thoroughly answer these questions. For those who are not familiar with my other titles, however, let me provide a brief explication.

As a 7th generation Kentuckian whose ancestors fought and died under the Confederate Flag, one of the primary motivations behind my work as a writer and historian is and always has been the preservation of *authentic* Southern history. For nearly 100 percent of what is being taught about the conflict in our schools today has been edited, revised, misinterpreted, rewritten, and even purposefully distorted by the victors.

Who were the victors? Since the platforms of the two major political parties were reversed in the 1860s, the "winners," Northern Republicans under Abraham Lincoln, were actually big government Liberals.[10] The so-called "losers," Southern Democrats under Jefferson Davis, were actually small government Conservatives.[11] As Liberals today are the self evident creators of fake political news, it should come as no surprise to anyone that they have been creating fake Civil War history since the day the first Southern state seceded in 1860. The unhappy result of this diabolical century and a half smear campaign against the Truth has been what I call "The Great Yankee Coverup": the total suppression of the facts about the War, mainly by Liberals, but sadly also by many uneducated Conservatives—the modern day political descendants of the Conservative Southern Confederacy.

But facts are not the only things missing from the mainstream version of the Civil War, the War for Southern Independence, as we call it here in Dixie. South-haters have also taken great care to expunge all traces of the emotional impetus which first prompted the South to take arms.

Fortunately for us this aspect was well documented in the many poems written by Southerners before, during, and shortly after the War—and these have *not* been edited, revised, misinterpreted, rewritten, and distorted by the victors. The importance of having a clean and clearly preserved record of Confederate poetry, untouched by the nefarious hands of enemies of the South, is incalculable. For facts alone, even genuine Southern facts, cannot communicate the full breadth and width of what lay at the heart of Southern secession, as well as her vigorous and deadly defense of hearth and home between 1861 and 1865. As one of my favorite Southern poets, William Gilmore Simms, wrote in 1866, just one year after war's end:

> The mere facts in a history do not always, or often, indicate the true animus of the action. But, in poetry and song, the emotional nature is apt to declare itself without reserve—speaking out with a passion which disdains subterfuge, and through media of imagination and fancy, which are not only without reserve, but which are too coercive in their own nature, too arbitrary in their influence, to acknowledge any restraints upon that expression, which glows or weeps with emotions that gush freely and freshly from the heart. With this persuasion, we can also forgive the muse who, in her fervor, is sometimes forgetful of her art.[12]

Even a few exceptional Yankees have recognized the need for chronicling Confederate poetry. One of these was Esther Parker Ellinger of Baltimore, Maryland, who in 1918 noted:

> *Southern* war poetry is worthy of preservation because it is an expression of vital appeal and of sentiment wrung from the heart of a people. For the most part, it was written under the stress of the moment. It was indeed the spontaneous overflow of powerful emotion, but only occasionally does it take its origin from emotion recollected in tranquillity. Nevertheless, it speaks the language of men and women, and in it we may read, as perhaps through no other medium, the true story of the development of Southern character, of national spirit, and of definite sectional consciousness.[13]

Having explained the significance of this book and my purpose in creating it, let us move onto the poets themselves, as well as their works.

My selection criteria had little to do with quality, but more with diversity. To put it another way, I focused on procuring the widest variety of individuals possible, to cover the broadest spectrum of views possible. To that end my poets include males and females, several foreign South-lovers, and even a number of admiring and respectful Yankees. The age span covers everyone from children to seniors, while talents range from amateurish and mediocre to professional and sublime (one of my poets made his living solely from writing pro-South poems). Many are soldiers ("lowly" privates), while a number of Confederate officers also make impressive contributions.

While naturally I could not include every Confederate or pro-South poet, I strove to incorporate most of Dixie's favorite bards: the aforementioned Simms, Sidney Lanier, Catherine Anne Warfield, Thomas Nelson Page, Olive Tully Thomas, James Ryder Randall, John Reuben Thompson, Ella Wheeler Wilcox, Henry Timrod, Jane T. H. Cross, Abram Joseph Ryan, Annie Chambers Ketchum, Francis Orray Ticknor, John Esten Cooke, and, of course, "the poet laureate of the South," Paul Hamilton Hayne—among others. One of the South's most beloved versifiers was Margaret Junkin Preston, a Yankee from Pennsylvania. Her beautiful pro-South poetry and ardent support for our region easily earned her a place between the covers of my book.

As a neo-Victorian Southern poet myself, *Victorian Confederate Poetry* has been a true labor of love, and I am proud to be associated with, and even related to, a number of individuals in this gifted group of "rebel" minstrels. The sentiments expressed in the 40 year period I have covered are indeed both extraordinary and poignant, and will transport my readers from laughter and tears to fascination and horror, and back again. Simultaneously, as most of my poets were eyewitnesses to the War (and so are, ultimately, the only credible sources of *authentic* Confederate history), this work will help further demolish the Left's massive and demonic corpus of fake Civil War history, fabricated to defame the Conservative Christian South while concealing the Liberal agnostic North's countless war crimes.

Yes, "The Great Yankee Coverup" remains alive and well. But with the publication of books such as this it is finally beginning to falter, and honorable Dixie—a political descendant of Conservative Founding Father Thomas Jefferson, the courageous progenitor of today's American Conservative movement—is beginning the long climb back up to her rightful place on the stage of world history. My poets would be overjoyed to see their words assisting in this noble process. God bless the South.

Lochlainn Seabrook
Nashville, Tennessee, USA
January 2018

THE POEMS

DIXIE

Southrons, hear your country call you!
Up, lest worse than death befall you!
   To arms! To arms! To arms, in Dixie!
Lo! all the beacon-fires are lighted,—
Let all hearts be now united!
   To arms! To arms! To arms, in Dixie!
     Advance the flag of Dixie!
        Hurrah! Hurrah!
For Dixie's land we take our stand,
  And live or die for Dixie!
     To arms! To arms!
   And conquer peace for Dixie!
     To arms! To arms!
   And conquer peace for Dixie!

Hear the Northern thunders mutter,
Northern flags in South winds flutter:
Send them back your fierce defiance!
Stamp upon the accursed alliance!

Fear no danger! Shun no labor!
Lift up rifle, pike, and saber!
Shoulder pressing close to shoulder,
Let the odds make each heart bolder!

How the South's great heart rejoices
At your cannons' ringing voices,
For faith betrayed, and pledges broken,
Wrongs inflicted, insults spoken!

Strong as lions, swift as eagles,
Back to their kennels hunt these beagles!
Cut the unequal bonds asunder:
Let them hence each other plunder!

Swear upon your country's altar
Never to submit or falter,
Till the spoilers are defeated,
Till the Lord's work is completed.

Halt not till our Federation
Secures among earth's powers its station:
Then at peace, and crowned with glory,
Hear your children tell the story!

If the loved ones weep in sadness,
Victory soon shall bring them gladness,—

>   To arms!
> Exultant pride soon banish sorrow,
> Smiles chase tears away to-morrow.
>   To arms! To arms! To arms, in Dixie!
>   Advance the flag of Dixie!
>   Hurrah! hurrah!
> For Dixie's land we take our stand,
>   And live or die for Dixie!
>   To arms! To arms!
>   And conquer peace for Dixie!
>   To arms! To arms!
>   And conquer peace for Dixie!¹⁴

CONFEDERATE GENERAL ALBERT PIKE

CONFEDERATE SONG

Rally round our country's flag!
Rally, boys, haste! do not lag;
Come from every vale and crag,
    Sons of liberty!

Northern Vandals tread our soil,
Forth they come for blood and spoil,
To the homes we've gained with toil,
    Shouting, "Slavery!"

Traitorous Lincoln's bloody band
Now invades the freeman's land,
Armed with sword and firebrand,
    'Gainst the brave and free.

Arm ye then for fray and fight,
March ye forth both day and night,
Stop not till the foe's in sight,
    Sons of chivalry.

In your veins the blood still flows
Of brave men who once arose—
Burst the shackles of their foes;
    Honest men and free.

Rise, then, in your power and might,
Seek the spoiler, brave the fight;
Strike for God, for Truth, for Right:
    Strike for Liberty![15]
CONFEDERATE CAPTAIN E. LLOYD WAILES

TO THE CONFEDERATE GOVERNMENT

Hath not the morning dawned with added light?
And shall not evening call another star
Out of the infinite legions of the night
To mark this day in heaven? At last we are
A nation among nations; and the world
Shall soon behold, in many a distant port,
    Another flag unfurled!
Now, come what may, whose favor need we court?
And, under God, whose thunder need we fear?
    Thank Him who placed us here
Beneath so kind a sky—the very sun
Takes part with us; and on our errands run
All breezes of the ocean; dew and rain
Do noiseless battle for us; and the year,
And all the gentle daughters in her train,
March in our ranks, and in our service wield
    Long spears of golden grain!
A yellow blossom as her fairy shield,
June flings her azure banner to the wind,
While in the order of their birth
Her sisters pass; and many an ample field
Grows white beneath their steps, till now, behold
    In endless sheets unrolled
The snow of Southern summers! Let the earth
Rejoice! Beneath these fleeces soft and warm
    Our happy land shall sleep
    In a repose as deep
    As if we lay intrenched behind
Whole leagues of Russian ice and Arctic snow.[16]
HENRY TIMROD

Confederate White House.

THE BONNIE BLUE FLAG

We are a band of brothers, and native to the soil,
Fighting for the property we gained by honest toil;
And when our rights were threatened the cry rose near and far
Hurrah for the bonnie blue flag that bears a single star!
Hurrah! hurrah! for the bonnie blue flag that bears a single star.

As long as the Union was faithful to her trust,
Like friends and like brothers, kind were we and just;
But now when Northern treachery attempts our rights to mar,
We hoist on high the bonnie blue flag that bears a single star.
Hurrah! hurrah! for the bonnie blue flag that bears a single star.

First gallant South Carolina nobly made the stand;
Then came Alabama, who took her by the hand;
Next, quickly, Mississippi, Georgia, and Florida—
All raised the flag, the bonnie blue flag that bears a single star.
Hurrah! hurrah! for the bonnie blue flag that bears a single star.

Ye men of valor, gather round the banner of the right:
Texas and fair Louisiana join us in the fight.
Davis, our loved President, and Stephens statesmen are
Now rally round the bonnie blue flag that bears a single star.
Hurrah! hurrah! for the bonnie blue flag that bears a single star.

And here's to brave Virginia, the Old Dominion State
With the young Confederacy at length has linked her Fate;
Impelled by her example, now other States prepare
I hoist on high the bonnie blue flag that bears a single star.
Hurrah! hurrah! for the bonnie blue flag that bears a single star.

Then here's to our Confederacy! Strong we are and brave;
Like patriots of old, we'll fight our heritage to save;
And rather than submit to shame, to die we would prefer,
So cheer for the bonnie blue flag that bears a single star.
Hurrah! hurrah! for the bonnie blue flag that bears a single star.

Then cheer, boys, cheer! Raise the joyous shout!
For Arkansas and North Carolina now have both gone out,
And let another rousing cheer for Tennessee be given!
The single star of the bonnie blue flag has grown to be eleven.
Hurrah! hurrah! for the bonnie blue flag that bears a single star.[17]
HARRY MCCARTHY

THE SOUTHERN CROSS

Oh! say can you see, through the gloom and the storm,
More bright for the darkness, that pure constellation?
Like the symbol of love and redemption its form,
As it points to the haven of hope for the nation.
How radiant each star, as the beacon afar,
Giving promise of peace, or assurance in war!
'Tis the Cross of the South, which shall ever remain
To light us to freedom and glory again!

How peaceful and blest was America's soil,
'Till betrayed by the guile of the Puritan demon,
Which lurks under virtue, and springs from its coil
To fasten its fangs in the life-blood of freemen.
Then boldly appeal to each heart that can feel,
And crush the foul viper 'neath Liberty's heel!
And the Cross of the South shall in triumph remain,
To light us to freedom and glory again!

'Tis the emblem of peace, 'tis the day-star of hope,
Like the sacred *Labarum* that guided the Roman;
From the shores of the Gulf to the Delaware's slope,
'Tis the trust of the free and the terror of foemen.
Fling its folds to the air, while we boldly declare
The rights we demand or the deeds that we dare!
While the Cross of the South shall in triumph remain,
To light us to freedom and glory again!

And if peace should be hopeless and justice denied,
And war's bloody vulture should flap its black pinions,
Then gladly "to arms," while we hurl, in our pride,
Defiance to tyrants and death to their minions!
With our front in the field, swearing never to yield,
Or return, like the Spartan, in death on our shield!
And the Cross of the South shall triumphantly wave,
As the flag of the free or the pall of the brave![18]
ST. GEORGE H. TUCKER

LAND OF KING COTTON

Oh! Dixie, the land of King Cotton,
    The home of the brave and the free;
A nation by Freedom begotten,
    The terror of despots to be;
Wherever thy banner is streaming,
    Base tyranny quails at thy feet,
And Liberty's sunlight is beaming,
    In splendor of majesty sweet.
        Chorus—Three cheers for our army so true,
        Three cheers for Price, Johnston, and Lee,
        Beauregard, and our Davis, forever;
        The pride of the brave and the free!

When Liberty sounds her war-rattle,
    Demanding her right and her due,
The first land who rallies to battle
    Is Dixie, the shrine of the true;
Thick as leaves of the forest in summer,
    Her brave sons will rise on each plain;
And strike, until each vandal comer
    Lies dead on the soil he would stain.
        Chorus—Three cheers for our army so true,
        Three cheers for Price, Johnston, and Lee,
        Beauregard, and our Davis, forever;
        The pride of the brave and the free!

May the names of the dead, that we cherish,
    Fill memory's cup to the brim;
May the laurels they've won never perish,
    Nor "star of their glory grow dim";
May the States of the South never sever,
    But champions of freedom e'er be;
May they flourish, Confed'rate forever,
    The boast of the brave and the free.
        Chorus—Three cheers for our army so true,
        Three cheers for Price, Johnston, and Lee,
        Beauregard, and our Davis, forever;
        The pride of the brave and the free![19]

JOSEPH AUGUSTINE SIGNAIGO

VICKSBURG—A BALLAD

For sixty days and upwards,
    A storm of shell and shot
Rained 'round us in a flaming shower,
    But still we faltered not!
"If the noble city perish,"
    Our grand young leader said,
"Let the only walls the foe shall scale
    Be the ramparts of the dead!"

For sixty days and upwards
    The eye of heaven waxed dim,
And even throughout God's holy morn,
    O'er Christian's prayer and hymn,
Arose a hissing tumult,
    As if the fiends of air
Strove to engulf the voice of faith
    In the shrieks of their despair.

There was wailing in the houses,
    There was trembling on the marts,
While the tempest raged and thundered,
    'Mid the silent thrill of hearts;
But the Lord, our shield, was with us,
    And ere a month had sped
Our very women walked the streets
    With scarce one throb of dread.

And the little children gambolled—
    Their faces purely raised,
Just for a wondering moment,
    As the huge bomb whirled and blazed!
Then turned with silvery laughter
    To the sports which children love,
Thrice mailed in the sweet, instinctive thought,
    That the good God watched above.

Yet the hailing bolts fell faster,
    From scores of flame-clad ships,
And about us, denser, darker,
    Grew the conflict's wild eclipse,
Till a solid cloud closed o'er us,
    Like a type of doom and ire,
Whence shot a thousand quivering tongues
    Of forked and vengeful fire.

But the unseen hands of angels
    Those death-shafts turned aside,
And the dove of heavenly mercy
    Ruled o'er the battle tide;
In the houses ceased the wailing,
    And through the war-scarred marts
The people trode with the step of hope,
    To the music in their hearts.[20]
PAUL HAMILTON HAYNE

IN MEMORY OF ALBERT SIDNEY JOHNSTON

Beyond this stone is laid,
for a season,
Albert Sidney Johnston,
A General in the Army of the Confederate States,
Who fell at Shiloh, Tennessee,
On the sixth day of April, A.D.,
Eighteen hundred and sixty-two;
A man tried in many high offices
And critical enterprises,
And found faithful in all.
His life was one long sacrifice of interest to conscience;
And even that life, on a woeful Sabbath,
Did he yield as a holocaust at his country's need.
Not wholly understood was he while he lived;
But, in his death, his greatness stands confessed in a people's tears
Resolute, moderate, clear of envy yet not wanting
In that finer ambition which makes men great and pure.
In his honor—impregnable;
In his simplicity—sublime.
No country e'er had a truer son—no cause a nobler champion.
No people a bolder defender—no principle a purer victim.
Than the dead soldier
Who sleeps here.
The cause for which he perished is lost—
The people for whom he fought are crushed—
The hopes in which he trusted are shattered—
The flag he loved guides no more the charging lines,
But his fame, consigned to the keeping of that time, which,
Happily, is not so much the tomb of virtue as its shrine,
Shall, in the years to come, fire modest worth to noble ends.
In honor, now, our great captain rests;
A bereaved people mourn him,
Three commonwealths proudly claim him
And history shall cherish him
Among those choicer spirits who, holding their conscience unmix'd with blame,
Have been, in all conjectures, true to themselves, their country and their God.[21]

JOHN B. S. DIMITRY

PARODY ON BULL RUN

At Bull Run, when the sun was low,
Each Southern face was pale as snow,
And loud as jackdaws rose the crow
Of Yankees boasting rapidly.

But Bull Run saw another sight
When, in the deepening shades of night,
Toward Fairfax Courthouse rose the flight
Of Yankees running rapidly.

Then broke each corps, with terror riven;
Then rushed the steed from battle driven;
The men of Battery number seven
Forsook their red artillery.

Still on McDowell's farthest left
The roar of cannon strikes one deaf,
Where furious Abe and fiery Jeff
Contend for death or victory.

The panic thickens; off, ye brave!
Throw down your arms, your bacon save;
Waive, Yankees, all your scruples waive,
And fly with all your chivalry.[22]
LONDON PUNCH

KENTUCKY STATE GUARD WAR SONG

Bring forth the flag, Kentucky's noble standard.
Wave it on high till the wind shakes each fold out:
Breezily it floats, nobly waving in the van-guard,
Then cheer up, boys, cheer, with a lusty, long bold shout.

CHORUS
Cheer, boys, cheer, we'll march away to battle—
cheer, boys, cheer, for our sweethearts and our wives—
Cheer, boys, cheer, we'll nobly do our duty,
And give Kentucky our hearts, our arms, our lives.

Although we march with heads all lowly bending,
Let us implore a blessing from on high;
Our Cause is just, the right from wrong defending,
And the God of battles will listen to our cry. (Chorus)

Though to our homes we never may return,
Ne'er press again our loved ones in our arms—
O'er our lone graves their faithful hearts will mourn,
Then cheer up, boys, cheer, such death has no alarms. (Chorus)

See, boys, see, the thunder clouds before us,
Hear the loud crash of musketry and gun.
Bring forth the flag and proudly wave it o'er us—
Then cheer up, boys, cheer, for the victory is won. (Chorus)[23]
UNKNOWN

Confederate Congress in session.

MARYLAND, MY MARYLAND

The despot's heel is on thy shore,
    Maryland!
His torch is at thy temple door,
    Maryland!
Avenge the patriotic gore
That flecked the streets of Baltimore,
And be the battle-queen of yore,
    Maryland, my Maryland!

Hark to an exiled son's appeal,
    Maryland!
My Mother-State, to thee I kneel,
    Maryland!
For life and death, for woe and weal,
Thy peerless chivalry reveal,
And gird thy beauteous limbs with steel,
    Maryland, my Maryland!

Thou wilt not cower in the dust,
    Maryland!
Thy beaming sword shall never rust,
    Maryland!
Remember Carroll's sacred trust,
Remember Howard's warlike thrust,
And all thy slumberers with the just,
    Maryland, my Maryland!

Come! 'tis the red dawn of the day,
    Maryland!
Come with thy panoplied array,
    Maryland!
With Ringgold's spirit for the fray,
With Watson's blood at Monterey,
With fearless Lowe and dashing May,
    Maryland, my Maryland!

Dear Mother I burst the tyrant's chain,
    Maryland!
Virginia should not call in vain,
    Maryland!
She meets her sisters on the plain,—
"Sic semper!" 'tis the proud refrain,
That baffles minions back amain,
    Maryland!
Arise in majesty again,

Maryland, my Maryland!

Come! for thy shield is bright and strong,
    Maryland!
Come! for thy dalliance does thee wrong,
    Maryland!
Come to thine own heroic throng
Walking with Liberty along,
And chant thy dauntless slogan-song,
    Maryland, my Maryland!

I see the blush upon thy cheek,
    Maryland!
For thou wast ever bravely meek,
    Maryland!
But lo! there surges forth a shriek,
From hill to hill, from creek to creek,
Potomac calls to Chesapeake,
    Maryland, my Maryland!

Thou wilt not yield the Vandal toll,
    Maryland!
Thou wilt not crook to his control,
    Maryland!
Better the fire upon thee roll,
Better the shot, the blade, the bowl,
Than crucifixion of the soul,
    Maryland, my Maryland!

I hear the distant thunder hum,
    Maryland!
The Old Line's bugle, fife, and drum,
    Maryland!
She is not dead, nor deaf, nor dumb;
Huzza! she spurns the Northern scum,—
She breathes! She burns! She'll come! She'll Come!
    Maryland, my Maryland![24]
JAMES RYDER RANDALL

A BATTLE CALL TO KENTUCKY

Arouse thee, Kentucky! the graves of thy sires
    Are pressed by the foot of the foe.
Has terror or avarice smothered the fires
    That were wont in thy bosom to glow?

Arise! shall the voice of Virginia in vain
    Call aloud to the child of her pride?
Thou should'st rush like a storm over mountain and plain.
    To conquer or die at her side.

Alas! shall the rifles thy forefathers bore
    Hang rusted and cold in their place?
Has the spirit that kindled their bosoms of yore
    Forever deserted their race?

Awake! there is scorn in the beautiful eyes
    Of thy maidens and mothers and wives:
"Have we given," they ask with indignant surprise,
    "To cowards our loves and our lives?"

Awake and redeem us! Arise in your might!
    Or forfeit to manhood the claim.
The arm that refuses to strike for the right,
    Let it wither and perish in shame.

And he who would hasten to cringe and to crawl
    At the feet of the ruthless invader,
A spirit so base it were flattery to call
    A craven, a serf, or a traitor![25]
MARY WALKER MERIWETHER

ALL QUIET ALONG THE POTOMAC TO-NIGHT

"All quiet along the Potomac," they say,
    "Except now and then a stray picket
Is shot, as he walks on his beat, to and fro,
    By a rifleman hid in the thicket.
'Tis nothing—a private or two, now and then,
    Will not count in the news of the battle;
Not an officer lost—only one of the men,
    Moaning out, all alone, the death-rattle."

All quiet along the Potomac to-night,
    Where the soldiers lie peacefully dreaming;
Their tents in the rays of the clear autumn moon,
    Or the light of the watch-fires, are gleaming.
A tremulous sigh, as the gentle night-wind
    Through the forest-leaves softly is creeping;
While stars up above, with their glittering eyes,
    Keep guard—for the army is sleeping.

There's only the sound of the lone sentry's tread,
    As he tramps from the rock to the fountain,
And thinks of the two in the low trundle-bed
    Far away in the cot on the mountain.
His musket falls slack—his face, dark and grim,
    Grows gentle with memories tender,
As he mutters a prayer for the children asleep—
For their mother—may Heaven defend her!

The moon seems to shine just as brightly as then,
    That night, when the love yet unspoken
Leaped up to his lips—when low-murmured vows
    Were pledged to be ever unbroken.
Then drawing his sleeve roughly over his eyes,
    He dashes off tears that are welling,
And gathers his gun closer up to its place
    As if to keep down the heart-swelling.

He passes the fountain, the blasted pine tree—
    The footstep is lagging and weary;
Yet onward he goes, through the broad belt of light,
    Toward the shades of the forest so dreary.
Hark! was it the night-wind that rustled the leaves?
    Was it moonlight so wondrously flashing?
It looked like a rifle—"Ah! Mary, good-bye!"
    And the life-blood is ebbing and plashing.

All quiet along the Potomac to-night,
    No sound save the rush of the river;
While soft falls the dew on the face of the dead—
    The picket's off duty forever.[26]
THADDEUS OLIVER

Lloyd Tilghman.

WHEN UPON THE FIELD OF GLORY

When upon the field of glory,
    'Mid the battle cry,
And the smoke of cannon curling
    Round the mountain high;
Then sweet mem'ries will come o'er me,
    Painting home and thee,
Nerving me to deeds of daring,
    Struggling to be free.
        Weep no longer, dearest,
        Tears are now in vain.
        When this cruel war is over
        We may meet again.

Oft I think of joys departed,
    Oft I think of thee;
When night's sisters throw around me,
    Their star'd canopy.
Dreams so dear come o'er my pillow,
    Bringing up the past,
Oh! how sweet the soldier's visions!
    Oh! how short they last!

When I stand a lonely picket,
    Gazing on the moon,
As she walks her starry pathway,
    In night's silent noon;
I will think that thou art looking
    On her placid face,
Then our tho'ts will meet together,
    In a heav'nly place.

When the bullet, swiftly flying
    Thro' the murky air,
Hits its mark, my sorrow'd bosom,
    Leaving death's pang there;
Then my tho'ts on thee will turn, love,
    While I prostrate lie.
My pale lips shall breathe, "God bless thee —
    For our cause I die!"
        Weep then for me, dearest,
        When I'm free from pain;
        When this cruel war is over,
        In heav'n we'll meet again.[27]

JOHN HILL HEWITT

THE LONE SENTRY

'Twas as the dying of the day,
    The darkness grew so still;
The drowsy pipe of evening birds
    Was hushed upon the hill.
Athwart the shadows of the vale
    Slumbered the men of might;
And one lone sentry paced his rounds
    To watch the camp that night.

A grave and solemn man was he,
    With deep and sombre brow;
The dreamful eyes seemed hoarding up
    Some unaccomplished vow.
The wistful glance peered o'er the plain,
    Beneath the starry light;
And, with the murmured name of God,
    He watched the camp that night.

The future opened unto him
    Its grand and awful scroll—
Manassas and the valley march
    Came heaving o'er his soul;
Richmond and Sharpsburgh thundered by,
    With that tremendous fight
That gave him to the angel host,
    Who watched the camp that night.

We mourn for him, who died for us,
    With one resistless moan,
While up the Valley of the Lord
    He marches to the Throne!
He kept the faith of men and saints
    Sublime, and pure, and bright;
He sleeps—and all is well with him
    Who watched the camp that night.

Brothers! the midnight of the cause
    Is shrouded in our fate—
The demon Goths pollute our halls
    With fire, and lust, and hate!
Be strong—be valiant—be assured—
    Strike home for Heaven and Right!
The soul of Jackson stalks abroad,
    And guards the camp to-night![28]
JAMES RYDER RANDALL

MANASSAS

They have met at last—as storm-clouds
    Meet in heaven;
And the Northmen back and bleeding
    Have been driven:
And their thunders have been stilled,
And their leaders crushed or killed,
And their ranks, with terror thrilled,
    Rent and riven!

Like the leaves of Vallambrosa
    They are lying;
In the moonlight, in the midnight,
    Dead and dying:
Like those leaves before the gale,
Swept their legions, wild and pale;
While the host that made them quail
    Stood, defying.

When aloft in morning sunlight
    Flags were flaunted,
And "swift vengeance on the Rebel"
    Proudly vaunted:
Little did they think that night
Should close upon their shameful flight,
And rebels, victors in the fight,
    Stand undaunted.

But peace to those who perished
    In our passes!
Light be the earth above them;
    Green the grasses!
Long shall Northmen rue the day
When they met our stern array,
And shrunk from battle's wild affray
    At Manassas![29]
CATHERINE ANNE WARFIELD

THE HEART OF LOUISIANA

Oh! let me weep, while o'er our land
    Vile discord strides, with sullen brow,
And drags to earth, with ruthless hand,
    The flag no tyrant's power could bow!

Trailed in the dust, inglorious laid,
    While one by one her stars retire,
And pride and power pursue the raid,
    That bids our liberty expire.

Aye, let me weep! for surely Heaven
    In anger views the unholy strife;
And angels weep that thus is riven
    The tie that gave to Freedom life.

I cannot shout—I will not sing
    Loud paeans o'er a severed tie;
And, draped in woe, in tears I fling
    Our State's new flag to greet the sky.

I can but choose, while senseless zeal
    And lawless hate are clothed with power,
The bitter cup; but still I feel
    The sadness of this parting hour!

I know that thousand hearts will bleed
    While loud huzzas the welkin rend;
The thoughtless crowd will shout, Secede!
    But ah! will this the conflict end?

Oh! let me weep and prostrate lie
    Low at the footstool of my God;
I cannot breathe one note of joy,
    While yet I feel His chastening rod.

Sure, we have as a nation sinned—
    Let every heart its folly own,
And sackcloth, as a girdle, bind,
    And mourn our glorious Union gone!

[Yankee] Sisters, farewell! You know not half
    The pain your pride, injustice, give;
You spurn our cause, and lightly laugh,
    And hope no more the wrong shall live.[30]
HARRIET STANTON

THE SHADE OF THE TREES
(Upon Stonewall Jackson's death)
What are the thoughts that are stirring his breast?
    What is the mystical vision he sees?
"Let us pass over the river and rest
    Under the shade of the trees."

Has he grown sick of his toils and his tasks?
    Sighs the worn spirit for respite or ease?
Is it a moment's cool halt that he asks
    Under the shade of the trees?

Is it the gurgle of waters whose flow
    Ofttime has come to him borne on the breeze.
Memory listens to, lapsing so low,
    Under the shade of the trees?

Nay—though the rasp of the flesh was so sore,
    Faith, that had yearnings far keener than these.
Saw the soft sheen of the Thitherward Shore,
    Under the shade of the trees;—

Caught the high psalms of ecstatic delight,—
    Heard the harps harping, like soundings of seas,—
Watched earth's assoiled ones walking in white
    Under the shade of the trees.

O, was it strange he should pine for release,
    Touched to the soul with such transports as these,—
He who so needed the balsam of peace,
    Under the shade of the trees?

Yea, it was noblest for him—it was best,
    (Questioning naught of our Father's decrees,)
There to pass over the river and rest
    Under the shade of the trees![31]
MARGARET JUNKIN PRESTON

MISSING

[On finding a dead Union soldier during the war]

Off duty near Malvern Hill,
Foraged one of Hampton's Legion,
In a glen with running rill,
'Twas In the Seven Days Battle region.

In a thicket, on grassy bank,
Grew summer flowers and berries sweet.
On Nature's couch the soldier sank
And slept in this retreat.

The battle rages in his dream.
Battalions charge and cannons thunder.
While beside him, near the stream,
Lies one down to death's dread slumber.

The soldier starts! before his eyes.
There on the sward with fruit and flowers,
The boney frame of a lost one lies,
Bleached to whiteness by sun and showers.

"A mother's son, a brother or lover,"
Mused the vet.; "from shot and shell hissing
Wounded, had crept to cover,
And this is how he came up missing."

Ah, the numbers on that sad list
Of "Missing"—Blue and Gray!
Let us hope they'll be first to "hist!"
When the roll is called on Judgment Day.[32]
B. H. TEAGUE

IN MEMORIAM OF COL. BENJAMIN F. TERRY

The war steed is champing his bit with disdain,
    And wild is the flash of his eye
As he waves to the wind his dark, flowing mane,
Starts, neighs, while the shouts and the bugler's refrain
    Proclaim that the battle is nigh!

Charge! charge! And the Ranger flies fast on his steed,
    Bold Terry! the fearless and brave;
His troops on his trail are moving with speed,
And each has crowned his name with a deed
    That story or song will engrave!

He swept to the field with an eye of delight,
    At the head of his brave, chosen band,
As a meteor's course, 'mid the storms of the night,
So splendidly shone his form in the fight,
    And sunk down with a glory as grand.

He fought for the land of his kindred and birth,
    Not for fame—though its laurels are won;
His thoughts had a higher, a holier worth
Than the trumpet's acclaim, which tells to the earth
    "Of the man!"—not the deeds he has done.

The lightning that burst on the warrior's head,
    From the foe that outnumbered his band,
Deterred not his course, as thro' columns he sped,—
And left on his pathway the dying and dead,
    That had yielded their breath to his brand.

The thunders of battle are hush'd on the plain,
    And the wild cry of carnage is o'er.
Dark vultures are gazing from high at the slain,
And the earth drank the blood from the dark purple vein
    That thrilled to life's passions before.

But tear-drops of grief dim the eyes of the brave,
    For their lion in death is laid low,
Their banners in sable above him they wave,
And muffle their drums in his march to the grave,
    To the music and language of woe.

The Magnolia City laments for the dead,
    Through whose streets his gay banners he bore

To a far distant land—but low lies his head,
Yet columns shall rise on the fields where he bled,
   And freemen his memory adore.

O calm in the tomb is the conqueror's rest!
   For his labors of life were well done,
And though quenched of the light of his generous breast,
With heroes immortal his spirit is blessed,
   Who o'er death have the victory won.³³
W. M. GILLELAND

THE GIRLS OF THE MONUMENTAL CITY
[Baltimore, Maryland]

Daughters of the sunny South,
    Where Freedom loves to dwell,
How rare your charms, how sweet your smiles,
    No mortal lips can tell;
Your native hills, the rippling rills,
    The echo wild and free,
Declare you born to hate and scorn
    All Northern tyranny.

Girls whose smiles are all reserved,
    The Southern youth to bless;
Whose hearts are kept for those who fight
    For Freedom's happiness;
Your spirits bold, so now unfold
    What willingly you would do,
Where Yankee spirit—the tyrants might
    Not wield against you.

For you your loving brothers rush
    To overthrow the invader's might—
On martial field the sword they wield,
    And Yankee cowards smite.
May heaven bless, with bright success,
    Each glorious Southern son;
Be this your prayer, O maidens fair!
    And our freedom will be won.

Southern girls, on this we've sworn,
    The South must—shall be free—
No Northern shackles will be worn;
    To them we'll bend no knee.
From hill to hill, exultant, shrill,
    Our battle-cry rings forth:
Freedom or death on every breath,
    And hatred to the North.

Confederate girls.

Cease not to smile, brave Southern girls,
    On our efforts to be free—
Whilst life remains, we'll struggle on,
    Till all the world shall see
That those who fight for home and right
    Can never be enslaved;
Their blood may stain the battle-plain;
    Our country must be saved.[34]
A CONFEDERATE PRISONER

THE TWO ARMIES

Two armies stand enrolled beneath
The banner with the starry wreath;
One, facing battle, blight and blast,
Through twice a hundred fields had passed;
Its deeds against a ruthless foe,
Stream, valley, hill, and mountain know,
Till every wind that sweeps the land
Goes, glory laden from the strand.

The other with a narrower scope,
Yet led by not less grand a hope.
Hath won, perhaps, as proud a place,
And wears its fame with meeker grace.
Wives march beneath its glittering sign,
Fond mothers swell the lovely line,
And many a sweetheart hides her blush
In the young patriot's generous flush.

No breeze of battle ever fanned
The colors of that tender band;
Its office is beside the bed,
Where throbs some sick or wounded head.
It does not court the soldier's tomb,
But plies the needle and the loom;
And, by a thousand peaceful deeds.
Supplies a struggling nation's needs.

Nor is that army's gentle might
Unfelt amid the deadly fight;
It nerves the son's, the husband's hand,
It points the lover's fearless band;
It thrills the languid, warms the cold,
Gives e'en new courage to the bold;
And sometimes lifts the veriest clod
To its own lofty trust in God.

When Heaven shall blow the trump of peace,
And bid this weary warfare cease,
Their several missions nobly done,
The triumph grasped, and freedom won,
Both armies, from their toils at rest,
Alike may claim the victor's crest.
But each shall see its dearest prize
Gleam softly from the other's eyes.[35]
HENRY TIMROD

THE SOUTHERN CROSS

In the name of God! Amen!
    Stand for our Southern rights!
Arm, ye Southern men,
    The God of Battle fights!
Fling the invaders far,
    Hurl back their work of woe,
The voice is the voice of a brother,
    But the hands are the hands of a foe.
They come with a trampling army,
    Invading our native sod—
Stand, Southrons! fight and conquer!
    In the name of the Mighty God!

They're singing our song of triumph[36]
    Which was made to make us free,
While they're breaking away the heartstrings
    Of our nation's harmony.
Sadly it floateth from us,
    Sighing o'er land and wave,
Till mute on the lips of the poet,
    It sleeps in his Southern grave.
Spirit and song departed!
    Minstrel and minstrelsy!
We mourn thee, heavy-hearted,
    But we will, we shall be free!

They are waving our flag above us,[37]
    With a despot's tyrant will;
With our blood they have stained its colors,
    And call it holy still.
With tearful eyes, but steady hand,
    We'll tear its stripes apart,
And fling them like broken fetters,
    That may not bind the heart;
But we'll save our stars of glory,[38]
    In the might of the sacred sign
Of Him who has fixed forever
    Our Southern Cross to shine.[39]

Stand, Southrons! stand and conquer!
    Solemn and strong and sure!
The strife shall not be longer
    Than God shall bid endure.
By the life which only yesterday
    Came with the infant's breath,

By the feet which ere the morn may
    Tread to the soldier's death!
By the blood which cries to Heaven!
    Crimson upon our sod!
Stand, Southrons! stand and conquer!
    In the name of the Mighty God![40]
MRS. ELLEN KEY BLUNT

THE BATTLE RAINBOW

The warm, weary day, was departing—the smile
    Of the sunset gave token the tempest had ceased;
And the lightning yet fitfully gleamed for a while
    On the cloud that sank sullen and dark in the east.

There our army—awaiting the terrible fight
    Of the morrow—lay hopeful, and watching, and still;
Where their tents all the region had sprinkled with white,
    From river to river, o'er meadow and hill.

While above them the fierce cannonade of the sky
    Blazed and burst from the vapors that muffled the sun,
Their "counterfeit clamors" gave forth no reply;
    And slept till the battle, the charge in each gun.

When lo! on the cloud, a miraculous thing!
    Broke in beauty the rainbow our host to enfold!
The centre o'erspread by its arch, and each wing
    Suffused with its azure and crimson and gold.

Blest omen of victory, symbol divine
    Of peace after tumult, repose after pain;
How sweet and how glowing with promise the sign,
    To eyes that should never behold it again!

For the fierce flame of war on the morrow flashed out,
    And its thunder-peals filled all the tremulous air:
Over slippery intrenchment and reddened redoubt,
    Rang the wild cheer of triumph, the cry of despair.

Then a long week of glory and agony came—
    Of mute supplication, and yearning, and dread;
When day unto day gave the record of fame,
    And night unto night gave the list of its dead.

We had triumphed—the foe had fled back to his ships—
    His standard in rags and his legions a wreck—
But alas! the stark faces and colorless lips
    Of our loved ones, gave triumph's rejoicing a check.

Not yet, oh not yet, as a sign of release,
    Had the Lord set in mercy his bow in the cloud;
Not yet had the Comforter whispered of peace
    To the hearts that around us lay bleeding and bowed.

But the promise was given—the beautiful arc,
    With its brilliant profusion of colors, that spanned
The sky on that exquisite eve, was the mark
    Of the Infinite Love overarching the land:

And that Love, shining richly and full as the day,
    Through the tear-drops that moisten each martyr's proud pall,
On the gloom of the past the bright bow shall display
    Of Freedom, Peace, Victory, bent over all.[41]
JOHN REUBEN THOMPSON

OUR LEFT

From dawn to dark they stood
    That long midsummer day,
        While fierce and fast
        The battle blast
    Swept rank on rank away.

From dawn to dark they fought,
    With legions torn and cleft;
        And still the wide
        Black battle tide
    Poured deadlier on "Our Left."

They closed each ghastly gap;
    They dressed each shattered rank;
        They knew—how well—
        That freedom fell
    With that exhausted flank.

"Oh, for a thousand men
    Like these that melt away!"
        And down they came,
        With steel and flame,
    Four thousand to the fray!

Right through the blackest cloud
    Their lightning path they cleft;
        And triumph came
        With deathless fame
    To our unconquered "Left."

Ye of your sons secure,
    Ye of your dead bereft—
        Honor the brave
        Who died to save
    Your all upon "Our Left."[42]
FRANCIS ORRAY TICKNOR

BEYOND THE POTOMAC

They slept on the fields which their valor had won,
But arose with the first early blush of the sun,
For they knew that a great deed remained to be done,
    When they passed o'er the river.

They rose with the sun, and caught life from his light—
Those giants of courage, those Anaks in fight—
And they laughed out aloud in the joy of their might,
    Marching swift for the river.

On! on! like the rushing of storms thro' the hills—
On! on! with a tramp that is firm as their wills—
And the one heart of thousands grows buoyant, and thrills,
    At the thought of the river!

Oh, the sheen of their swords! the fierce gleam of their eyes!
It seemed as on earth a new sunlight would rise,
And king-like flash up to the sun in the skies,
    O'er the path to the river.

But their banners, shot-scarred, and all darkened with gore,
On a strong wind of morning streamed wildly before,
Like the wings of death-angels swept fast to the shore,
    The green shore of the river!

As they march from the hillside, the hamlet, the stream,
Gaunt throngs whom the foeman had manacled teem,
Like men just aroused from some terrible dream,
    To pass over the river.

They behold the broad banners, blood-darkened, yet fair,
And a moment dissolves the last spell of despair,
While a peal as of victory swells on the air,
    Rolling out to the river.

And that cry, with a thousand strange echoings spread,
Till the ashes of heroes seemed stirred in their bed,
And the deep voice of passion surged up from the dead—
    Aye! press on to the river!

On! on! like the rushing of storms through the hills,
On! on! with a tramp that is firm as their wills,
And the one heart of thousands grows buoyant, and thrills,
    As they pause by the river.

Then the wan face of Maryland, haggard and worn,
At that sight lost the touch of its aspect forlorn,
And she turned on the foeman full statured in scorn,
    Pointing stern to the river.

And Potomac flowed calm, scarcely heaving her breast,
With her low-lying billows all bright in the west,
For a charm as from God lulled the waters to rest
    Of the fair rolling river.

Passed! passed! the glad thousands march safe through the tide.
(Hark, despot! and hear the dread knell of your pride,
Ringing weird-like and wild, pealing up from the side
    Of the calm flowing river!)

'Neath a blow swift and mighty the tyrant may fall,
Vain! vain! to his God swells a desolate call,
For his grave has been hollowed, and woven his pall,
    Since they passed o'er the river![43]
PAUL HAMILTON HAYNE

WE'LL BE FREE IN MARYLAND

The boys down South in Dixie's land,
The boys down South in Dixie's land,
The boys down South in Dixie's land,
    Will come and rescue Maryland.
        Chorus—If you will join the Dixie band,
        Here's my heart and here's my hand,
        If you will join the Dixie band;
        We're fighting for a home.

The Northern foes have trod us down,
The Northern foes have trod us down,
The Northern foes have trod us down,
    But we will rise with true renown.
        Chorus—If you will join the Dixie band,
        Here's my heart and here's my hand,
        If you will join the Dixie band;
        We're fighting for a home.

The tyrants they must leave our door,
The tyrants they must leave our door,
The tyrants they must leave our door,
    Then we'll be free in Baltimore.
        Chorus—If you will join the Dixie band,
        Here's my heart and here's my hand,
        If you will join the Dixie band;
        We're fighting for a home.

These hirelings they'll never stand,
These hirelings they'll never stand,
These hirelings they'll never stand,
    Whenever they see the Southern band.
        Chorus—If you will join the Dixie band,
        Here's my heart and here's my hand,
        If you will join the Dixie band;
        We're fighting for a home.

Old Abe has got into a trap,
Old Abe has got into a trap,
Old Abe has got into a trap,
    And he can't get out with his Scotch cap.
        Chorus—If you will join the Dixie band,
        Here's my heart and here's my hand,
        If you will join the Dixie band;
        We're fighting for a home.

"Nobody's hurt" is easy spun,
"Nobody's hurt" is easy spun,
"Nobody's hurt" is easy spun,
    But the Yankees caught it at Bull Run.
        Chorus—If you will join the Dixie band,
        Here's my heart and here's my hand,
        If you will join the Dixie band;
        We're fighting for a home.

We rally to Jeff Davis true,
Beauregard and Johnston, too,
Magruder, Price, and General Bragg,
    And give three cheers for the Southern flag.
        Chorus—If you will join the Dixie band,
        Here's my heart and here's my hand,
        If you will join the Dixie band;
        We're fighting for a home.

We'll drink this toast to one and all,
Keep cocked and primed for the Southern call.
The day will come, we'll make the stand,
Then we'll be free in Maryland.
        Chorus—If you will join the Dixie band,
        Here's my heart and here's my hand,
        If you will join the Dixie band;
        We're fighting for a home.[44]
ROBERT E. HOLTZ

Jefferson Davis.

A WORD WITH THE WEST

Once more to the breach for the Land of the West!
And a leader we give, of our bravest and best,
    Of his State and his army the pride;
Hope shines like the plume of Navarre on his crest,
    And gleams in the glaive at his side.

For his courage is keen and his honor is bright
As the trusty Toledo he wears to the fight,
    Newly wrought in the forges of Spain,
And this weapon, like all he has brandished for Right,
    Will never be dimmed by a stain.

He leaves the loved soil of Virginia behind,
Where the dust of his fathers is fitly enshrined,
    Where lie the fresh fields of his fame;
Where the murmurous pines, as they sway in the wind,
    Seem ever to whisper his name.

The Johnstons have always borne wings on their spurs,
And their motto a noble distinction confers,
    "Ever ready"—for friend or for foe—
With a patriot's fervor the sentiment stirs
    The large manly heart of our Joe.

We recall that a former bold chief of the clan
Fell, bravely defending the West, in the van
    On Shiloh's illustrious day;
And with reason we reckon our Johnston the man
    The dark bloody debt to repay.

There is much to be done: if not glory to seek,
There's a just and a terrible vengeance to wreak
    For crimes of a terrible dye,
While the plaint of the helpless, the wail of the weak
    In a chorus rise up to the sky.

For the Wolf of the North we once drove to his den,
That quailed in affright 'neath the stern glance of men,
    With his pack has returned to the spoil;
Then come from the hamlet, the mountain, the glen,
    And drive him again from the soil!

Brave-born Tennesseans, so loyal, so true,
Who have hunted the beast in your highlands, of you
    Our leader has never a doubt;

You will troop by the thousand the chase to renew
    The day when his bugles ring out.

But ye "Hunters" so famed "of Kentucky" of yore,
Where, where are the rifles that kept from your door
    The wolf and the robber as well?
Of a truth, you have never been laggard before
    To deal with a savage so fell.

Has the love you once bore to your country grown cold
Has the fire on the altar died out? Do you hold
    Your lives than your freedom more dear?
Can you shamefully barter your birthright for gold,
    Or basely take counsel of fear?

We will not believe it! Kentucky, the land
Of a Clay, will not tamely submit to the brand
    That disgraces the dastard, the slave;
The hour of redemption draws nigh—is at hand—
    Her own sons her own honor shall save!

Mighty men of Missouri, come forth to the call,
With the rush of your rivers when tempests appall,
    And the torrents their sources unseal;
And this be the watchword of one and of all—
    "Remember the butcher, McNeil!"

Then once more to the breach for the land of the West!
Strike home for your hearts—for the lips you love best—
    Follow on where your Leader you see!
One flash of his sword when the foe is hard pressed,
    And the Land of the West shall be free![45]
JOHN REUBEN THOMPSON

John R. Thompson.

CHRISTMAS NIGHT OF '62

The wintry blast goes wailing by,
    The snow is falling overhead;
      I hear the lonely sentry's tread,
And distant watch-fires light the sky.

Dim forms go flitting through the gloom;
    The soldiers cluster 'round the blaze,
      To talk of other Christmas days,
And softly speak of home and home.

My sabre swinging overhead
    Gleams in the watch-fire's fitful glow,
      While fiercely drives the blinding snow,
And memory leads me to the dead.

My thoughts go wandering to and fro,
    Vibrating 'twixt the Now and Then;
      I see the low-brow'd home agen,[46]
The old hall wreathed with mistletoe.

And sweetly from the far-off years
    Comes borne the laughter faint and low,
      The voices of the Long Ago!
My eyes are wet with tender tears.

I feel agen the mother-kiss,
    I see agen the glad surprise
      That lightened up the tranquil eyes
And brimmed them o'er with tears of bliss,

As, rushing from the old hall-door,
    She fondly clasp'd her wayward boy—
      Her face all radiant with the joy
She felt to see him home once more.

My sabre swinging on the bough
    Gleams in the watch-fire's fitful glow,
      While fiercely drives the blinding snow
Aslant upon my sadden'd brow.

Those cherished faces all are gone!
    Asleep within the quiet graves
      Where lies the snow in drifting waves,—
And I am sitting here alone.

There's not a comrade here to-night
    But knows that lov'd ones far away
    On bended knees this night will pray:
"God bring our darling from the fight."

But there are none to wish me back,
    For me no yearning prayers arise,
    The lips are mute and closed the eyes—
My home is in the bivouac.[47]
WILLIAM GORDON MCCABE

SOUTHERN SONG

Come, all ye sons of freedom,
    And join our Southern band,
We are going to fight the Yankees,
    And drive them from our land.
Justice is our motto,
    And Providence our guide,
So jump into the wagon,
    And we'll all take a ride.
        Chorus—So wait for the wagon, the dissolution wagon;
        The South is the wagon, and we'll all take a ride.

Secession is our watchword;
    Our rights we all demand;
To defend our homes and firesides
    We pledge our hearts and hands.
Jeff Davis is our President,
    With Stephens by his side;
Great Beauregard our General;
    He joins us in our ride.
        Chorus—So wait for the wagon, the dissolution wagon;
        The South is the wagon, and we'll all take a ride.

Our wagon is the very best;
    The running gear is good;
Stuffed round the sides with cotton,
    And made of Southern wood.
Carolina is the driver,
    With Georgia by her side;
Virginia holds the flag up,
    While we all take a ride.
        Chorus—So wait for the wagon, the dissolution wagon;
        The South is the wagon, and we'll all take a ride.

The invading tribe, called Yankees,
    With Lincoln for their guide,
Tried to keep Kentucky
    From joining in the ride;
But she heeded not their entreaties—
    She has come into the ring;
She wouldn't fight for a government
    Where cotton wasn't king.
        Chorus—So wait for the wagon, the dissolution wagon;
        The South is the wagon, and we'll all take a ride.

Old Lincoln and his Congressmen,

With Seward by his side,
Put old Scott in the wagon,
   Just for to take a ride.
McDowell was the driver,
   To cross Bull Run he tried,
But there he left the wagon
   For Beauregard to ride.
      Chorus—So wait for the wagon, the dissolution wagon;
      The South is the wagon, and we'll all take a ride.

Manassas was the battle-ground;
   The field was fair and wide;
The Yankees thought they'd whip us out,
   And on to Richmond ride;
But when they met our "Dixie" boys,
   Their danger they espied;
They wheeled about for Washington,
   And didn't wait to ride.
      Chorus—So wait for the wagon, the dissolution wagon;
      The South is the wagon, and we'll all take a ride.

Brave Beauregard, God bless him!
   Led legions in his stead,
While Johnson seized the colors
   And waved them o'er his head.
To rising generations,
   With pleasure we will tell
How bravely our Fisher
   And gallant Johnson fell.
      Chorus—So wait for the wagon, the dissolution wagon;
      The South is the wagon, and we'll all take a ride.[48]

M. C. FREER

CHICKAMAUGA

By many a peaceful valley home,
    In tranquil flow,
A river toward the sea doth come,
    Stealthy and slow.
In the day's of old, in the ages gone,
When the Indian claimed these lands his own,
He called the stream in a tongue unknown,
    "Chickamauga!"

Chickamauga, "River of Death,"
    O silent river,
What mystery through the ages hath
    Ever and ever
Haunted thy bed? Hath warrior bled
Upon thy banks, whose blood there shed,
His people looking on, have said,
    "Chickamauga?"

Was it for forests on thy shore,
    By vale and hill,
Silent e'en now, deathlike of yore,
    Somber and still?
Or for thy flow these trees beneath,
Feeble and sad as dying breath,
That thou wast called, O River of Death,
    "Chickamauga?"

Was it thy current's ceaseless flow
    Down toward the sea,
Constant as death, whose march, though slow,
    No man can flee,
Brought to the solemn Indian's mind
Grim Death, who all men stalks behind,
And he no better name could find,
    Chickamauga?

No, none of these. In ages gone—
    Ah! who can say
How oft to earth the leaves have flown
    Since that far-off day?—
When Lookout solitary stood,
And Pigeon knew not man's abode,
And nameless yet thy waters flowed,
    Chickamauga!

Upon thy shore a prophet stood
    That day of old—
A prophet of the Indian blood—
    And thus foretold:
"I see the red men vanish all,
I see these leafy forests fall,
I hear a stranger people call
    'Chickamauga!'

I see the smoke of wigwams rise—
    Not of my race;
For it hath sought 'neath other skies
    A resting place.
I see the white man's harvests wave,
I see the white man's home, his grave
Along the banks thy waters lave,
    Chickamauga.

I see adown yon mountain way
    (Countless they come),
The northmen marching many a day,
    From their far home.
With banners streaming on the gale,
Followed by widows', orphans' wail,
Ah! now they seek thy peaceful vale,
    Chickamauga.

Great Spirit! Hark! upon mine ears,
    Borne on the breeze,
What sounds come up from future years,
    What sounds are these,
As when the winds contend in heaven,
And cloud 'gainst cloud is thunder driven,
And all thy forests tempest riven,
    Chickamauga?

Great Spirit! As when burning brands,
    The opening year,
Prepare the pleasant hunting lands
    For nimble deer,
I see above the forest rise
Dread clouds of smoke—not to mine eyes
Like smoke of peace they seek thy skies,
    Chickamauga!

Great Spirit! hear! Great Spirit! see!
    Thy children die;

And thick as leaves 'neath wintry tree,
    In death they lie.
And—ah! no more! Upon my sight
Descends the future's viewless night.
The vision from thy shore takes flight,
    Chickamauga!

O limpid as thy native spring,
    Go take thy way,
Limpid still, till the ages bring
    That distant day,
When here within the somber wood,
Thy startled waves shall flow with blood—
Then will thy name be understood,
    Chickamauga!"

E'en now fulfilled, O "River of Death,"
    This dream of old,
Thy banks along, thy trees beneath,
    Mine eyes behold!
To northmen, who invading come,
To freemen fighting for their home,
To friend, to foe, thou art the tomb,
    Chickamauga![49]
JOSEPH B. CUMMING

SOMEBODY'S DARLING

Into a ward of the whitewashed halls
    Where the dead and the dying lay,—
Wounded by bayonets, shells, and balls,—
    Somebody's darling was borne one day.
Somebody's darling! so young and so brave:
    Wearing still on his pale sweet face—
Soon to be hid by the dust of the grave—
    The lingering light of his boyhood's grace.

Matted and damp are the curls of gold
    Kissing the snow of that fair young brow;
Pale are the lips of delicate mold,—
    Somebody's darling is dying now.
Back from the beautiful blue-veined brow
    Brush every wandering silken thread,
Cross his hands on his bosom now,—
    Somebody's darling is still and dead!

Kiss him once for somebody's sake;
    Murmur a prayer, both soft and low;
One bright curl from its fair mates take—
    They were somebody's pride, you know.
Somebody's hand has rested there
    Was it a mother's, soft and white?
Or have the lips of a sister fair
    Been baptized in those waves of light?

God knows best! He was somebody's love;
    Somebody's heart enshrined him there—
Somebody wafted his name above,
    Night and morn, on the wings of prayer.
Somebody wept when he marched away,
    Looking so handsome, brave, and grand;
Somebody's kiss on his forehead lay,
    Somebody clung to his parting hand.

Somebody's watching and waiting for him,
    Yearning to hold him again to her heart;
And there he lies—with his blue eyes dim,
    And the smiling, child-like lips apart.
Tenderly bury the fair young dead,
    Pausing to drop on his grave a tear;
Carve on the wooden slab o'er his head,
    "Somebody's darling slumbers here!"[50]

MARIE LA COSTE

ODE TO JOHNSON'S ISLAND
[Site of an infamous Yankee prison]

I love thee, green isle in Erie's great water,
For why should I hate thee, old Erie's bright daughter?
But how much I'd love thee, O how much the more.
Did the Colonel parole me to walk on thy shore!
I'd not be like "Selkirk" and boast thy domain;
The Colonel and all of his soldiers might reign
From thy tallest oak tree to thy most distant shore.
But if I could walk thee, I'd love thee the more.

It is not thy prison, 'tis thee that I love;
'Twas man made thy prison, but the great God above
Caused thee to spring forth in the midst of the flood.
Undisturbed by contention, unsprinkled by blood.
But yet for the captive thou art a sweet place.
When springtime and summer with flowery grace
Reign mild o'er the mainland, thyself and the lake,
I love thee alone for thy scenery's sake;
But if I could wander around thy wild shore,
I'd love thee, sweet island. I'd love thee the more.[51]
REV. J. M. GRANDIN

THE BATTLE OF CHARLESTON HARBOR

Two hours, or more, beyond the prime of a blithe April day,
The Northman's mailed "Invincibles" steamed up fair Charleston Bay;
They came in sullen file, and slow, low-breasted on the wave,
Black as a midnight front of storm, and silent as the grave.

A thousand warrior-hearts beat high as those dread monsters drew
More closely to the game of death across the breezeless blue,
And twice ten thousand hearts of those who watched the scene afar,
Thrill in the awful hush that bides the battle's broadening Star!

Each gunner, moveless by his gun, with rigid aspect stands,
The ready linstocks firmly grasped in bold, untrembling hands,
So moveless in their marbled calm, their stern heroic guise,
They looked like forms of statued stone with burning human eyes!

Our banners on the outmost walls, with stately rustling fold,
Flash back from arch and parapet the sunlight's ruddy gold—
They mount to the deep roll of drums, and widely-echoing cheers,
And then—once more, dark, breathless, hushed, wait the grim
    cannoneers.

Onward—in sullen file, and slow, low glooming on the wave,
Near, nearer still, the haughty fleet glides silent as the grave,
When sudden, shivering up the calm, o'er startled flood and shore,
Burst from the sacred Island Fort the thunder-wrath of yore![52]

Ha! brutal Corsairs! tho' ye come thrice-cased in iron mail,
Beware the storm that's opening now, God's vengeance guides the hail!
Ye strive the ruffian types of Might 'gainst law, and truth, and Right,
Now quail beneath a sturdier Power, and own a mightier Might!

No empty boast! for while we speak, more furious, wilder, higher,
Dart from the circling batteries a hundred tongues of fire.
The waves gleam red, the lurid vault of heaven seems rent above.
Fight on! oh! knightly Gentlemen! for faith, and home, and love!

There's not in all that line of flame, one soul that would not rise,
To seize the Victor's wreath of blood, tho' Death must give the prize—
There's not in all this anxious crowd that throngs the ancient Town,
A maid who does not yearn for power to strike one despot down.

The strife grows fiercer! ship by ship the proud Armada sweeps,
Where hot from Sumter's raging breast the volleyed lightning leaps;
And ship by ship, raked, overborne, 'ere burned the sunset bloom,
Crawls seaward, like a hangman's hearse bound to his felon tomb!

Oh! glorious Empress of the Main! from out thy storied spires,
Thou well mayst peal thy bells of joy, and light thy festal fires—
Since Heaven this day hath striven for thee, hath nerved thy dauntless sons,
And thou, in clear-eyed faith hast seen God's Angels near the guns![53]
PAUL HAMILTON HAYNE

FEDERAL NURSERY HYMN
[A Yankee newspaper mocks the Union's war efforts]

Sing a song of greenbacks,
    A pocket full of trash,
Over head and ears in debt,
    And out of ready cash;
Heaps of tax collectors,
    As busy as a bee—
Ain't we in a pretty fix,
    With gold at fifty-three?

Abe in the White House,
    Proclamations printing;
Meade on the Rapidan,
    Afraid to do the fighting;
Seward in the Cabinet,
    Surrounded by his spies;
Halleck with the telegraph,
    Busy forging lies;

Chase in the treasury,
    Making worthless notes;
Curtin at Harrisburg,
    Making shoddy coats;
Gillmore at Charleston,
    Lost in a fog;
Forney under Abe's chair,
    Barking like a dog;

Schenck down at Baltimore,
    Doing dirty work;
Butler at Norfolk,
    As savage as a Turk;
Sprague in Rhode Island,
    Eating apple sass;
Everett at Gettysburg.
    Talking like an ass;

Banks out in Texas,
    Trying to cut a figure;
Beecher in Brooklyn,
    Howling for the nigger;
Lots of abolitionists,
    Kicking up a yell;
In comes Parson Brownlow,
    And sends all to hell;

Burnside at Knoxville,
    In a kind of fix;
Dahlgren at Sumter,
    Pounding at the bricks;
Grant at Chattanooga,
    Trying Bragg to thrash—
Is it any wonder
    The Union's gone to smash?[54]
NEW YORK NEWS

DEATH OF STONEWALL JACKSON

Not 'mid the lightning of the stormy fight,
    Not in the rush upon the vandal foe,
Did kingly Death, with his resistless might,
    Lay the great leader low.

His warrior soul its earthly shackles broke
    In the full sunshine of a peaceful town;
When all the storm was hushed, the trusty oak
    That propped our cause went down.

Though his alone the blood that flecks the ground,
    Recording all his grand, heroic deeds,
Freedom herself is writhing with the wound,
    And all the country bleeds.

He entered not the Nation's Promised Land
    At the red belching of the cannon's mouth;
But broke the House of Bondage with his hand—
    The Moses of the South!

O gracious God! not gainless is the loss:
    A glorious sunbeam gilds thy sternest frown;
And while his country staggers with the Cross,
    He rises with the Crown.[55]
HARRY LYNDEN FLASH

Stonewall Jackson.

THE BAND IN THE PINES
[Heard after the death of John Pelham]

Oh, band in the pine wood cease!
    Cease with your splendid call;
The living are brave and noble,
    But the dead are bravest of all!

They throng to the martial summons,
    To the loud triumphant strain,
And the dear bright eyes of long dead friends
    Come to the heart again!

They come with the ringing bugle,
    And the deep drums' mellow roar;
Till the soul is faint with longing
    For the hands we clasp no more!

O band in the pine wood cease!
    Or the heart will melt with tears,
For the gallant eyes and the smiling lips,
    And the voices of old years.[56]
JOHN ESTEN COOKE

John E. Cooke.

SOUTHLAND

  They sing of the East,
  With its flowery feast,
And clime of the North, with its mountains of snow;
  But give me the land
  Where the breezes blow bland,
O'er realms of magnolia and myrtle below.
  The land of the South,
  The fair sunny South,
  The flower-crowned South,
  In its grandeur for me.

  Her sons are aye brave,
  And no chains can enslave,
Though countless the hordes of their foemen may be;
  Ah! see, even now,
  As with battle-stained brow,
They vanquish the Northmen on land and on sea!
  The land of the South,
  The young gallant South,
  The invincible South,
  In its valor for me.

  Her daughters are fair
  As the pure lilies there,
And cheer her brave soldiers for freedom to die;
  Their smiles are the light
  Of the war-clouded night,
Their tears are sweet dew-drops distilled from the sky.
  The land of the South,
  The sweet rosy South,
  The starry-gemmed South,
  In its beauty for me!

  In green blossomed dales,
  And in violet vales,
And fields white with cotton, its dwellings once stood;
  The spoilers now seek
  Their vile vengeance to wreak,
And darken this Eden with ashes and blood!
  The land of the South,
  The opulent South,
  The long-plundered South,
  In its richness for me!

  Oh, who would not stand

With his life in his hand,
To shield such a land from the feet of the foe?
God made it thus free,
And oh, perish must we,
Before it can be in bondage laid low!
The land of the South,
The proud sovereign South,
The God-shielded South,
In its freedom for me![57]
UNKNOWN

MY LOVE & I, BY A PRISONER OF WAR

My love reposes on a rosewood frame,
    A bunk have I,
A couch of feathery down fills up the same,
    Mine's straw, but dry;
She sinks to sleep at night, with scarce a sigh,
With waking eyes I watch the hours go by.

My love her daily dinner takes in state,
    And so do I
The richest viands flank her silver plate,
    Coarse grub have I.
Pure wine she sips at ease, her thirst to slake,
I pump my drink from Erie's crystal lake.

My love has all the world, at will to roam,
    Three acres I;
She goes abroad, or quiet stays at home,
    So cannot I.
Bright angels watch around her couch at night,
A Yank, with loaded gun keeps me in sight.

A thousand weary miles now stretch between
    My love and I,
To her, this winter night, calm, cold, serene.
    I waft a sigh.
And hope with all my earnestness of soul
To-morrow's mail may bring my parole.

There's hope ahead! We'll some day meet again,
    My love and I;
We'll wipe away all tears of sorrow then,
    Her love-lit eye,
Will all my many troubles then beguile,
And keep this wayward Reb from Johnson's Isle.[58]
ASA HARTZ

BEFORE RICHMOND

"Grant will hurl a thunderbolt
At the heart of the revolt;"
    We shall see!
Other men have tried and failed,
Other men have blenched and quailed,
    Forcing Lee.

What though Jackson, dear to God,
Lies beneath the battle sod,
    Dark and cold?
What though Stuart in earth is laid;
He who won in rapid raid
    Spurs of gold?

Longstreet in his anguish lies;
Tears are making soldiers' eyes
    Strangely dim;
And we hold our breath and say,
"Does Death's angel come this way,
    Seeking him?"

For the Lord of Hosts, who gave
These great men our land lo gave,
    Knoweth best.
We to the last man shall fight,
Doing battle for the right—
    His the rest.

On, then, Grant; we see the gray,
Kill your myriads that ye may
    Crush the free!
But here are great deeds to do,
Ere your mercenary crew
    Passes Lee.[59]
MORTIMER COLLINS

THE CAPTIVE'S DREAM

At midnight in his grated cell
Bright visions to the captive came,
And o'er his spirit sank a spell
As potent as the magic flame
In which the rapt disciple reads
The future's unaccomplished deeds.
He dreams his term of stay is done,
His dungeon doors are open thrown,
And the stern warden bids him go
Forth from the halls of crime and woe.
He dreams that Jeff at last relents,
To slacken up on Streight consents,
And by some apt negotiation
Redeems him from the yankee nation.
Then thick upon the captive's soul
Anticipated glories roll.
Beneath him his proud charger springs,
Defiantly his bugle rings;
Again in battle's stern parade
He sees their eager ranks arrayed;
Again in triumph and in pride
Kentucky sees the squadrons ride,
And every horse in Indiana
Is pressed to follow Morgan's banner.
But hark! he starts, he wakes, what sound
Here stills his heart's impetuous bound?
What awful sound with honor rife
Has backward turned the tide of life?
Upon his wakened hearing jars
The clash of those detested bars.
He hears his jailer's sullen tone
Which makes King Minion's mandates known;
And bids him straight away prepare
To lose his cherished beard and hair.
Great God! no hope, he must resign
His youth's fair pride, his manhood's sign.
What cheers the wretched captive now?
What "drives the shadows" from his brow?
His bosom, once with courage thrilled
Is now "chock up" with sausage filled,
And he who once the battles led
Attacks naught else but gingerbread.
I care no more, alas! my theme
Is anything now but a dream.[60]
CONFEDERATE GENERAL BASIL WILSON DUKE

SONNET

What right to freedom when we are not free?
    When all the passions goad us into lust;
    When, for the worthless spoil we lick the dust,
And while one-half our people die, that we
May sit with peace and freedom 'neath our tree,
The other gloats for plunder and for spoil:
Bustles through daylight, vexes night with toil,
Cheats, swindles, lies and steals!—Shall such things be
Endowed with such grand boons as Liberty
    Brings in her train of blessings? Should we pray
    That such as these should still maintain the sway—
These soulless, senseless, heartless enemies
Of all that's good and great, of all that's wise,
Worthy on earth, or in the Eternal Eyes![61]
UNKNOWN

OBSEQUIES OF JEB STUART

We could not pause, while yet the noon-tide air
    Shook with the cannonade's incessant pealing,
The funeral pageant fitly to prepare—
    A nation's grief revealing.

The smoke, above the glimmering woodland wide
    That skirts our southward border in its beauty,
Marked where our heroes stood and fought and died
    For love and faith and duty.

And still, what time the doubtful strife went on,
    We might not find expression for our sorrow;
We could but lay our dear dumb warrior down,
    And gird us for the morrow.

One weary year agone, when came a lull
    With victory in the conflict's storm closes,
When the glad Spring, all flushed and beautiful,
    First mocked us with her roses,

With dirge and bell and minute-gun, we paid
    Some few poor rites—an inexpressive token
Of a great people's pain—to Jackson's shade,
    In agony unspoken.

No wailing trumpet and no tolling bell,
    No cannon, save the battle's boom receding,
When Stuart to the grave we bore, might tell,
    With hearts all crushed and bleeding.

The crisis suited not with pomp, and she
    Whose anguish bears the seal of consecration
Had wished his Christian obsequies should be
    Thus void of ostentation.

Only the maidens came, sweet flowers to twine
    Above his form so still and cold and painless,
Whose deeds upon our brightest record shine,
    Whose life and sword were stainless.

They well remembered how he loved to dash
    Into the fight, festooned from summer bowers;
How like a fountain's spray his sabre's flash
    Leaped from a mass of flowers.

And so we carried to his place of rest
    All that of our great Paladin was mortal:
The cross, and not the sabre, on his breast,
    That opes the heavenly portal.

No more of tribute might to us remain;
    But there will come a time when Freedom's martyrs
A richer guerdon of renown shall gain
    Than gleams in stars and garters.

I hear from out that sunlit land which lies
    Beyond these clouds that gather darkly o'er us,
The happy sounds of industry arise
    In swelling peaceful chorus.

And mingling with these sounds, the glad acclaim
    Of millions undisturbed by war's afflictions,
Crowning each martyr's never-dying name
    With grateful benedictions.

In some fair future garden of delights,
    Where flowers shall bloom and song-birds sweetly warble,
Art shall erect the statues of our knights
    In living bronze and marble.

And none of all that bright heroic throng
    Shall wear to far-off time a semblance grander,
Shall still be decked with fresher wreaths of song,
    Than this beloved commander.

The Spanish legend tells us of the Cid,
    That after death he rode erect, sedately,
Along his lines, even as in life he did,
    In presence yet more stately:

And thus our Stuart, at this moment, seems
    To ride out of our dark and troubled story
Into the region of romance and dreams,
    A realm of light and glory;

And sometimes, when the silver bugles blow,
    That ghostly form, in battle reappearing,
Shall lead his horsemen headlong on the foe,
    In victory careering![62]
JOHN REUBEN THOMPSON

Jeb Stuart.

DREAMING IN THE TRENCHES

I picture her there in the quaint old room,
    Where the fading fire-light starts and falls,
Alone in the twilight's tender gloom
    With the shadows that dance on the dim-lit walls.

Alone, while those faces look silently down
    From their antique frames in a grim repose—
Slight scholarly Ralph in his Oxford gown,
    And staunch Sir Allan, who died for Montrose.

There are gallants gay in crimson and gold,
    There are smiling beauties with powdered hair,
But she sits there, fairer a thousand-fold,
    Leaning dreamily back in her low arm-chair.

And the roseate shadows of fading light
    Softly clear steal over the sweet young face,
Where a woman's tenderness blends to-night
    With the guileless pride of a haughty race.

Her hands lie clasped in a listless way
    On the old Romance—which she holds on her knee
Of Tristram, the bravest of knights in the fray,
    And Iseult, who waits by the sounding sea.

And her proud, dark eyes wear a softened look
    As she watches the dying embers fall—
Perhaps she dreams of the knight in the book,
    Perhaps of the pictures that smile on the wall.

What fancies I wonder are thronging her brain,
    For her cheeks flush warm with a crimson glow!
Perhaps—ah! me, how foolish and vain!
    But I'd give my life to believe it so!

Well, whether I ever march home again
    To offer my love and a stainless name,
Or whether I die at the head of my men,—
    I'll be true to the end all the same.[63]
WILLIAM GORDON MCCABE

GENERAL LEE & TRAVELLER

Behold that horse! A dappled gray!
I saw him in the month of May,
When wild flowers bloomed about his feet,
And sunshine was his mantle meet.

The shapely head he held up high.
And fire seemed flashing from his eye;
Arched grandly, too, his neck and mane,
And on them fell the slackened rein.

Down from the withers to the tail
The curve was perfect in detail.
While depth of chest, and haunch, and side,
Showed where his strength did most reside.

With limb, and hoof, and pastern small.
The body round and plump withal,
No pattern could be perfecter
Than was the form of "Traveler."

Rare model for an artist's skill!—
For brush, or chisel, or for quill!
For there, with muscles strained and tense,
His mould was sheer magnificence.

Bucephalus was not more gay
In ancient battle's stern array,
Than was that grand Virginia gray,
That mutely champed his bits that day.

A day of battle, truly, then!
A day of death to many men!
For war a gory drama played,
But "Traveler" was undismayed.

Dismounted, and quite near his head,
The right hand to the halter wed,
His rider stood—bold leader he!—
The great, the gallant—Robert Lee.

Broad shouldered, tall, stout, and straight.
The left hand down, his look sedate,
He wore a cap and suit of gray,
And gazed, but nothing had to say.

What courtliness in him was seen!
Aye, what nobility of mien!
As there, Horatius-like, he stood.
The honored, wise, and great, and good.

Great Chieftains had preceded him
With cups of glory to the brim,
But he among them all was Prince,
Unrivalled in the past, or since.

The battle raged around him near;
The clash of arms he saw, could hear,
But, dauntless, he stood out to view,
Though deadly missiles round him flew.

Brave Chief and Charger! Such were they.
In Dixie's hue of martial gray,
And such they will in memory be,
While time and sense remain to me.

Immortal Spottsylvania!
'Twas on that sacred hill of thine,
'Mid shouts of victory and huzzah,
We saw this picture from the line.

Ye artists! paint the signal scene,
Or fashion it in bronze, or stone,
That generations, yet unseen,
In all our Southland's sunny zone,—

May look upon Lee's noble form,
As there he stood amid the storm.
And did our Dixie Boys command,
Who fought for rights, and home, and land.

No need have we for Northern foe,
Living, or dead, above, below;
We honor those who wore the gray,
And weave for them our last bouquet.

We War's arbitrament accept,
And foemen leave in peace to rest,
But, when their graves are decked and wept,
The North must do it, and Northwest.

Away with sickly sentiment!
True Southrons never will repent;

For "Chartered Rights," they fought the fight.
And still they know their cause was right.

Had I but one, or even grant
That I'd ten thousand flowers to plant,
I'd put them all on Dixie's graves—
My Comrades, and our Southern braves.[64]
REVERAND ROBERT TUTTLE

General Lee and Traveller.

SEVENTY-SIX & SIXTY-ONE

Ye spirits of the glorious dead,
    Ye watchers in the sky,
Who sought the patriot's crimson bed
    With holy trust and high.
Come, lend your inspiration now,
    Come, fire each Southern son
Who nobly fights for freeman's rights
    And shouts for sixty-one.

Come teach them how on hill, in glade,
    Quick leaping from your side,
The lightning flash of sabers made
    A red and flowing tide;
How well ye fought, how bravely fell
    Beneath our burning sun;
And let the lyre in strains of fire
    So speak of sixty-one.

There's many a grave in all the land
    And many a crucifix
Which tells how that heroic band
    Stood firm in seventy-six.
Ye heroes of the deathless past.
    Your glorious race is run,
But from your dust springs freedom's trust
    And blows for sixty-one.

We build our altars where you lie,
    On many a verdant sod,
With sabers pointing to the sky
    And sanctified to God.
The smoke shall rise from every pile
    Till freedom's cause is won,
And every mouth throughout the South
    Shall shout for sixty-one.[65]
JOHN W. OVERALL

WOUNDED & SLAIN

The post has arrived, and most quickly is sought
    The news from the war which the papers contain;
They tell us another great battle's been fought.
    And thousands again have been wounded and slain.

'Tis said that another great victory's won,
    The foe has been humbled and vanquished again;
But dreadful, alas! is the work that is done,
    For many are wounded and many are slain.

There comes an old father, with care in his face,
    To hear the sad news, while he leans on his cane,
That the name of the son of his age has a place
    In the long and sad list of the wounded and slain.

"O tell me!" a fond, anxious mother exclaims,
    "Does that list the name of poor Willie contain?"
"Ah, yes," 'tis replied, "that is one of the names.
    Your Willie is wounded, your Willie is slain."

There comes a fair boy, through the wind and the sleet,
    To learn who was killed on the dark, bloody plain;
And homeward he hurries, with cold, shoeless feet,
    To tell his poor mother that father is slain!

O God! shall this red tide of war never cease?
    Wilt thou not hear the cries of the poor who complain?
O! span these dark clouds with the rainbow of peace!
    We are weary of hearing of "wounded and slain."[66]
P. H. BREWSTER

REBELS

Rebels! 'tis a holy name!
    The name our fathers bore,
When battling in the cause of Right,
Against the tyrant in his might,
    In the dark days of yore.

Rebels! 'tis our family name!
    Our father, Washington,
Was the arch-rebel in the fight,
And gave the name to us—a right
    Of father unto son.

Rebels! 'tis our given name!
    Our mother, Liberty,
Received the title with her fame,
In days of grief, of fear and shame,
    When at her breast were we.

Rebels! 'tis our sealed name!
    A baptism of blood!
The war—aye, and the din of strife—
The fearful contest, life for life—
    The mingled crimson flood.

Rebels! 'tis a patriot's name!
    In struggles it was given;
We bore it then when tyrants raved,
And through their curses 'twas engraved
    On the doomsday book of heaven.

Rebels! 'tis our fighting name!
    For peace rules o'er the land,
Until they speak of craven woe—
Until our rights receive a blow,
    From foe's or brother's hand.

Rebels! 'tis our dying name!
    For although life is dear,
Yet, freemen born and freemen bred,
We'd rather live as freemen dead,
    Than live in slavish fear.

Then call us Rebels if you will—
    We glory in the name;
For bending under unjust laws,
And swearing faith to an unjust cause,
    We count a greater shame.[67]

UNKNOWN

PROMETHEUS VINCTUS
[Concerning the imprisonment of Jefferson Davis]

Prometheus on the cold rock bound,
    The vulture at his heart,
In you, O Southern Chief, has found
    A fitting counterpart.

The Titan by his wondrous skill
    Fashioned a man from clay;
You formed a nation at your will,
And bent it to your sway.

He made a dull insensate thing,
    A form without a soul;
Your spirit, with life's stirring spring,
    Electrified the whole.

Like him, your greatness did you wrong,
    Your virtue was your bane;
Each soared above the common throng,
    Each found a prison chain!

Your aims alike were noble; well
    Ye battled, till at length
Each, having done his utmost, fell—
    Dragged down by Force and Strength!

Ye fell, but gained a height sublime,
    And more than mortal fame,
Binding upon the breast of Time
    An ever glorious name.

No farther may the semblance go.
    O'erwhelmed by Zeus' frown,
Prometheus with supernal woe
    In agony bowed down:

While you, O gentle sufferer, feel,
    Though bending 'neath the rod,
A holy joy, the sign and seal
    Of a sustaining God!

Within your grated prison cell
    A gracious guest abides,
And by the same low-spoken spell
    Which stilled the raging tides,

Of fierce Tiberias, he exerts
    As spirit-soothing calm,
And heals the sting of earthly hurts
    With heavenly peace and balm.

Around you in unending play
    The bounding billows roar,
And white with crests of seething spray
    Break thundering on the shore.

These ocean-surges well express
    The love, the hopes, the care,
Which to you in your loneliness
    Your faithful people bear.

Chains and a prison cannot wrest
    Your empire from its throne;
You find in every Southern breast
    A kingdom and a home!

The stately land you strove to save,
    In sable robes arrayed,
Majestic mourns beside the grave
    Where all her hopes are laid.

But though she weeps her cherished dead
    With sorrow deep and true,
No tears of bitterness are shed
    Like those that fall for you!

You hold her heart-strings in your hand,
    And every blow and slur
That strikes you as you helpless stand
    Falls doubly hard on her!

Heaven help us all! The New Year dawns
    Again with gladsome birth;
God grant, ere many smiling morns
    Have glorified the earth,

That one may break amid the stars,
    Which, by His blest decree,
Beaming across your prison bars,
    Shall shine upon you free![68]

FANNY DOWNING

THE FOE AT THE GATES
[of Charleston, South Carolina]

Ring round her! children of her glorious skies,
    Whom she hath nursed to stature proud and great;
Catch one last glance from her imploring eyes,
    Then close your ranks and face the threatening fate.

Ring round her! with a wall of horrent steel
    Confront the foe, nor mercy ask nor give;
And in her hour of anguish let her feel
    That ye can die whom she has taught to live.

Ring round her! swear, by every lifted blade,
    To shield from wrong the mother who gave you birth;
That never violent hand on her be laid,
    Nor base foot desecrate her hallowed hearth.

Curst be the dastard who shall halt or doubt!
    And doubly damned who casts one look behind!
Ye who are men! with unsheathed sword, and shout,
    Up with her banner! give it to the wind!

Peal your wild slogan, echoing far and wide,
    Till every ringing avenue repeat
The gathering cry, and Ashley's angry tide[69]
    Calls to the sea-waves beating round her feet.

Sons, to the rescue! spurred and belted, come!
    Kneeling, with clasp'd hands, she invokes you now
By the sweet memories of your childhood's home,
    By every manly hope and filial vow,

To save her proud soul from that loathed thrall
    Which yet her spirit cannot brook to name;
Or, if her fate be near, and she must fall,
    Spare her—she sues—the agony and shame.

From all her fanes let solemn bells be tolled;
    Heap with kind hands her costly funeral pyre,
And thus, with paean sung and anthem rolled,
    Give her unspotted to the God of Fire.

Gather around her sacred ashes then,
    Sprinkle the cherished dust with crimson rain,
Die! as becomes a race of free-born men,
    Who will not crouch to wear the bondman's chain.

So, dying, ye shall win a high renown,
    If not in life, at least by death, set free;
And send her fame through endless ages down—
    The last grand holocaust of Liberty.[70]

JOHN DICKSON BRUNS

LINES ON A CONFEDERATE NOTE

Representing nothing on God's earth now,
    And naught in the waters below it,
As the pledge of a Nation that's dead and gone,
    Keep it, dear friend, and show it.
Show it to those who will lend an ear
    To the tale that this trifle can tell,
Of a liberty born of the patriot's dream,
    Of a storm-cradled Nation that fell.

Too poor to possess the precious ones,
    And too much of a stranger to borrow,
We issued to-day our promise to pay,
    And hoped to redeem on the morrow.
The days rolled by and weeks and weeks became years,
    But our coffers were empty still;
Coin was so rare that the Treasury'd quake
    If a dollar should drop in the till.

But the faith that was in us was strong indeed,
    And our poverty well we discerned,
And this little check represented the pay
    That our suffering veterans earned.
We know it had hardly a value in gold,
    Yet as gold each soldier received it;
It gazed in our eyes with a promise to pay,
    And each southern patriot believed it.

But our boys thought little of price or of pay,
    Or of bills that were overdue;
We knew if it bought us our bread to-day,
    'Twas the best our poor country could do.
Keep it; it tells all our history over,
    From the birth of the dream to its last;
Modest, and born of the angel, Hope,
    Like our hope of success, it passed.[71]
S. A. JONAS

OUR DIXIE

I heard long since a simple strain;
It brought no thrill of joy or pain,
Nor did I care to hear again
    Of Dixie.

But time rolled on, and drum and fife
Gave token of a coming strife,
And called our youth to soldier life
    In Dixie.

And so our treasures, one by one,
All by the battlefield were won;
They heard at morn and setting sun
    Our Dixie.

Their blood flowed on the fresh green hill,
It mingled with the mountain rill,
And poured through vales once calm and still
    In Dixie.

The living rallied to their stand;
Their war cry was their "Native Land;"
But sadder from the lessening band
    Came Dixie.

Yet still it roused to deeds of fame,
And made immortal many a name;
It never caused a blush of shame,
    Our Dixie.

We may not hear that simple strain
Ever without a thrill of pain—
Our dead come back to live again
    With Dixie.

And if I were a generous foe,
I'd honor him whose heart's best throe
Leaped to that music soft and low,
    Our Dixie.[72]

A LADY OF AUGUSTA, GEORGIA

THE LAND WHERE WE WERE DREAMING

Fair were our nation's visions, and as grand
As ever floated out of fancy-land;
    Children were we in simple faith,
    But god-like children, whom nor death
Nor threat of danger drove from honor's path—
    In the land where we were dreaming.

Proud were our men as pride of birth could render,
As violets our women pure and tender;
    And when they spoke, their voice did thrill
    Until, at eve the whip-poor-will,
At morn the mocking-bird was mute and still,
    In the land where we were dreaming.

And we had graves that covered more of glory
Than over taxed the lips of ancient story;
    And in our dream we wove the thread
    Of principles for which had bled
And suffered long our own immortal dead,
    In the land where we were dreaming.

Our sleep grew troubled, and our dreams grew wild;
Red meteors flashed across our heaven's field,
    Crimson the moon, between the Twins
    Barbed arrows flew in circling lanes
Of light, red comets tossed their fiery manes
    O'er the land where we were dreaming.

A figure came among us as we slept—
At first he knelt, then slowly rose and wept;
    Then gathering up a thousand spears,
    He swept across the field of Mars,
Then bowed farewell, and walked among the stars,
    From the land where we were dreaming.

We looked again—another figure still
Gave hope, and nerved each individual will;
    Erect he stood, as clothed with power,
    Self-poised, he seemed to rule the hour
With firm, majestic sway—of strength a tower—
    In the land where we were dreaming.

As, while great Jove, in bronze, a warder god,
Gazed eastward from the Forum where he stood,
    Rome felt herself secure and free—

So, Richmond! we on guard for thee,
Beheld a bronzed hero, god like Lee,
    In the land where we were dreaming.

Woe! woe is us! the startled mothers cried;
While we have slept, our noble sons have died.
    Woe! woe is us! how strange and sad.
    That all our glorious visions fled
Have left us nothing real but our dead
    In the land where we were dreaming.

"And are they really dead, our martyred slain?"
No, dreamers! Morn shall bid them rise again
    From every plain, from every height
    On which they seemed to die for right;
Their gallant spirits shall renew the fight
    In the land where we were dreaming.[73]
DANIEL BEDINGER LUCAS

STACK ARMS

"Stack arms!" I've gladly heard the cry
    When, weary with the dusty tread
Of marching troops as night drew nigh,
    I sank upon my soldier's bed
And calmly slept, the starry dome
    Of heaven's blue arch my canopy,
And mingled with my dreams of home
    The thoughts of peace and liberty.

"Stack arms!" I've heard it when the shout
    Exulting rang along our line,
Of foes hurled back in bloody rout,
    Captured, dispersed; its tones divine
Then came to mine enraptured ear,
    Guerdon of duty nobly done,
And glistened on my cheek the tear
    Of grateful joy for victory won.

"Stack arms!" in faltering accents slow
    And sad it creeps from tongue to tongue,
A broken, murmuring wail of woe,
    From manly hearts by anguish wrung;
Like victims of a midnight dream,
    We move, we know not how or why,
For life and hope but phantoms seem,
    And it were a relief—to die.[74]

JOSEPH BLYTHE ALLSTON

Robert E. Lee.

THE CONFEDERATE DEAD

A simple board of rough, ill-shapen pine,
O'errun perchance by some tenacious vine,
Placed by some friendly hand above each head,
Is all that marks our brave Confederate dead.

No epitaph, save now and then "Unknown,"
Carved rudely on some unpretending stone;
No towering shaft, with flattering words inlaid,
Casts o'er our slain its proud, imperial shade.

But can the skillful hand of polished art
To worth unsullied one more charm impart,
Bequeath to hallowed dust a sweeter rest,
Or make their names more honored or more blest?

Though monumental stone should never rise,
To tell the world where fallen valor lies,
Each heart erects its own immortal shrine,
And there inscribes him attributes divine.

We need no piles of sculptured marble gray,
To tell us where the Southern soldier lay,
For roses cluster o'er his grassy bed,
And round the spot their sweetest fragrance shed.

Imbedded there by woman's virtuous hand,
Sweet emblems of our own bright, sunny land,
Could flowers fair for better purpose bloom
Than to adorn the Southern soldier's tomb?

Brave heroes of a "lost" but sacred cause,
Though now withheld their well-deserved applause;
Impartial history must in time grow bold,
Their virtues and their deeds will yet be told.

Poets will linger on the blood-dyed plains,
And chant above our lost their sweetest strains;
Confederate dead will yet survive in song,
Nor shall their glorious deeds be hidden long.

Fair daughters of our balmy clime will bring
Their floral offerings with each coming spring,
Entwine a wreath around each humble grave,
A loving tribute to our sleeping brave.

Though in the struggle triumph crowned the "strong,"
'Tis not to strength that honor should belong;
He most deserves it who most nobly gave
His life, his "all," his country's rights to save.

Who fought not through a selfish love of gain,
Spurned rank or "bounty," and shrunk not from pain;
'Twas but to save wife, children, home, and pride,
The Southern soldier battled, bled, and died.

Their cause was noble and their deeds sublime,
Their just reward is held in trust by time;
She must and will at last bestow the prize,
For worth immortal never, never dies![75]
MRS. C. O. DANNELLY

Confederate monument.

THE DYING WORDS OF JACKSON
[Stonewall died from wounds received by friendly fire]
"Order A. P. Hill to prepare for battle."
"Tell Major Hawks to advance the Commissary train."
"Let us cross the river and rest in the shade."

The stars of Night contain the glittering Day
And rain his glory down with sweeter grace
Upon the dark World's grand, enchanted face—
    All loth to turn away.

And so the Day, about to yield his breath,
Utters the stars unto the listening Night,
To stand for burning fare-thee-wells of light
    Said on the verge of death.

O hero-life that lit us like the sun!
O hero-words that glittered like the stars
And stood and shone above the gloomy wars
    When the hero-life was done!

The phantoms of a battle came to dwell
In the fitful vision of his dying eyes—
Yet even in battle-dreams, he sends supplies
    To those he loved so well.

His army stands in battle-line arrayed:
His couriers fly: all's done: now God decide!
—And not till then saw he the Other Side
    Or would accept the shade.

Thou Land whose sun is gone, thy stars remain!
Still shine the words that miniature his deeds.
O thrice-beloved, where'er thy great heart bleeds,
    Solace hast thou for pain![76]
SIDNEY LANIER

Sidney Lanier.

THE LAST WORDS OF GEN. STONEWALL JACKSON

"Over the river," a voice meekly said,
Whose clarion tones had thousands obeyed,
As in ranks upon ranks they grandly rushed on,
To battle for liberty, country and home.

"Over the river," immortality's plains,
In verdure eternal, where peace ever reigns,
Rejoice with their beauty his vision of faith,
As his spirit approaches the river of death.

"Over the river," Oh! glorious sight,
An escort celestial awaits with delight.
In the glittering armor of glory arrayed,
They welcome him over to rest in the shade.

"Over the river," no more to command
The drum-beat to arms in a war-stricken land;
No bugle call summons the brave to the fray,
Nor squadrons leap forth in battle array.

"Over the river," now a heavenly guest,
'Neath the shades of the trees forever at rest.
His memory and fame to ages belong,
And his lofty deeds live in story and song.[77]
D. S. MORRISON

Stonewall Jackson.

RESULT OF THE WAR IN THE SOUTH
Once it smiled like a garden, elate in the pride
Of a Beauty so peerless, the Sun called it Bride;
To endow it with jewels of gold and of green,
So resplendent, the stars were not grander in sheen.
All its gardens wore Eden's perennial bloom,
Ev'ry rain-drop that kissed it was coined to perfume;
While the rare skies above it, and rich soil below,
Bade the cotton plant whiten its valleys like snow;
And the hearts of its sons were the bravest in fight,
And the eyes of its daughters the darkest in light—
The darkest and sweetest, yet chaste as the beam
That illumines the love of an innocent dream.
But the Bride of the Sun shall enchant him no more;
All the pride of its green has been purpled with gore,
And its roses are sighing to shed their perfume
O'er a land where each turf hides a warrior's tomb;
And the hearts of its bravest are still as the stones
Of the battlefields, bleached with mouldering bones.
And so still they may heed not the call of the drum,
Or be startled by the thunder of cannon or bomb.
And the light in the eyes of its daughters is pale,
And the laugh of its children is turned into wail—
All are weeping alike for the dying or dead,
As they beg from their foemen a morsel of bread.
For the gaunt fiend of Famine now prowls in the sun
To accomplish the ruin that war had begun;
And the moans of the starving, in pitiless pain,
Pray for mercy, to God or their fellows, in vain.
There is peace, but such peace as the sepulchre knows,
In the desert of death—putrefaction's repose;
'Tis the peace of a wilderness wintry and fell,
The peace of a Paradise thrust into hell.[78]
A. W. ARRINGTON

THE CONQUERED BANNER

Furl that Banner, for 'tis weary;
Round its staff 'tis drooping dreary;
   Furl it, fold it, it is best;
For there's not a man to wave it,
And there's not a sword to save it,
And there's no one left to lave it
In the blood that heroes gave it;
And its foes now scorn and brave it;
   Furl it, hide it, let it rest!

Take that banner down! 'tis tattered;
Broken is its shaft and shattered;
   And the valiant hosts are scattered
Over whom it floated high.
O, 'tis hard for us to fold it;
Hard to think there's none to hold it;
Hard that those who once unrolled it
   Now must furl it with a sigh.

Furl that banner! furl it sadly:
Once ten thousands hailed it gladly.
   And ten thousands wildly, madly,
Swore it should forever wave;
Swore that foeman's sword should never
Hearts like theirs entwined dissever,
Till that flag should float forever
   O'er their freedom or their grave.

Furl it! for the hands that grasped it,
And the hearts that fondly clasped it,
   Cold and dead are lying low;
And the banner, it is trailing,
While around it sounds the wailing
   Of its people in their woe.
For, though conquered, they adore it,
Love the cold, dead hands that bore it,
Weep for those who fell before it.
Pardon those who trailed and tore it,
But, O! wildly they deplore it,
   Now who furl and fold it so.

Furl that banner! True, 'tis gory,
Yet 'tis wreathed around with glory,
And 'twill live in song and story,
   Though its folds are in the dust;

For its fame on brightest pages,
Penned by poets and by sages,
Shall go sounding down the ages,
    Furl its folds though now we must.
Furl that banner! softly, slowly,
Treat it gently—it is holy—
    For it droops above the dead;
Touch it not, unfold it never,
Let it droop there, furled forever,
    For its people's hopes are dead![79]
REVEREND ABRAM JOSEPH RYAN

OUR SACRED BANNER

[In response to the previous poem "The Conquered Banner"]

Gallant nation, foiled by numbers,
Say not that your hopes are fled;
Keep that glorious flag which slumbers,
One day to avenge your dead.
Keep it, widowed, sonless mothers,
Keep it, sisters, mourning brothers,
Furl it with an iron will;
Furl it now, but keep it still,
Think not that its work is done.
Keep it till your children take it,
Once again to hail and make it
All their sires have bled and fought for,
Bled and fought for all alone.

All alone! aye, shame the story,
Millions here deplore the stain;
Shame, alas! for England's glory,
Freedom called, and called in vain.
Furl that banner, sadly, slowly,
Treat it gently, for 'tis holy,
Till that day—yes, furl it sadly,
Then once more unfurl it gladly
Conquered banner, keep it still.[80]
SIR HENRY HOUGHTON (an Englishman)

TO OUR DEAD AT NEW HOPE CHURCH
[Occurrences from May 25, 1864, Georgia]
They sleep the deep sleep 'neath the sanctified sod
    Made holy with patriot gore;
They are resting for aye in the bosom of God.
    The bugle will wake them no more!

No more will they thunder their wrath on the foes,
    Nor smile on their friends as of yore,
By Honor's proud voice they were lulled to repose,
    Their knell was the fierce battle roar!

One died—he had sighted his gun ere he fell,
    That round was the Corporal's last:
His soul on the canister rushed with a yell
    And scattered the foe as it passed!

None braver in battle, in camp none more kind,
    On the march and bivouac none so gay;
Let him rest—in the hearts of his friends he's enshrined,
    And God Freedom's debt will repay.

Another was tending the trail—came the shot
    And buried itself in his head—
His brother stretched out the pale corpse—murmured not,
    And stern, took the place of the dead!

He also was struck, but unmoved he remained;
    At his post like a statue he stood,
Till his third brother came on the ground, crimson-stain'd
    By the flow of his own kindred blood!

'Twas then the young Spartan, on giving his place
    To the last of the heroic three,
Said, "Brother," then looking the dead in the face,
    "Give them one for revenge and for me!"

No more need we look in dead history's page.
    Our souls with devotion to fire,
For our eyes have beheld in this country and age
    How heroes and freemen expire!

All honor and fame to the good and the brave,
    The dead of our patriot band,
The martyrs who perished their country to save
    At Liberty's welcome command![81]
JOHN AUGUSTIN

THERE'S LIFE IN THE OLD LAND YET

By blue Patapsco's billowy dash
    The tyrant's war shout comes;
Along with the cymbals' fitful clash,
    And the growl of his sullen drums;
We hear it, we heed it, with vengeful thrills.
    And we shall not forgive or forget —
There's faith in the streams, there's hope in the hills
    There's life in the old land yet.

Minions! we sleep, but we are not dead;
    We are crushed, we are scourged, we are scarred;
We crouch—'tis to welcome the triumph tread
    Of the peerless Beauregard;
Then woe to your vile, polluting horde,
    When the Southern braves are met,
There's faith in the victor's stainless sword,
    There's life in the old land yet!

Bigots! ye quell not the valiant mind,
    With the clank of an iron chain—
The spirit of freedom sings in the wind,
    O'er Merryman, Thomas, and Kane;
And we, though we smite not, are not thralls,
    We are piling a gory debt.
While down by McHenry's dungeon-walls,
There's life in the old land yet!

Our women have hung their harps away,
    And they scowl on your brutal bands,
While the nimble poignard dares the day,
    In their dear, defiant hands;
They will strip their tresses to string our bows,
    Ere the Northern sun is set;
There's faith in their unrelenting woes—
    There's life in the old land yet!

There's life, though it throbbeth in silent veins,
    'Tis vocal without noise,
It is gushed o'er Manassas' solemn plains
    From the blood of the Maryland boys!
That blood shall cry aloud, and rise
    With an everlasting threat—
By the death of the brave, by the God in the skies.
    There's life in the old land yet![82]

JAMES RYDER RANDALL

THE REBEL'S RETURN

When wild war's deadly blast was blown,
    And Johnston did surrender,
When Dixie's cherished hopes had flown,
    And none now dared defend her,
I left the ditches poorly clad,
    Where long I'd been a lodger,
A C.S. mule was all I had,
    A poor and lousy sodger.

A heavy heart was in my breast,
    I had no load of plunder,
As from old Tishomingo's hills
    I weary on did blunder.
I thought upon the banks o' Possum,
    I thought upon my Sally,
I had sick feelings in my bosom,
    Jemina! Creminally!

At length I reached the Bigby hills,
    Where early life I sported,
I passed the lonely pine and mill,
    Where Sally oft I courted.
'Bout then I spied my own dear Sal,
    Down by her mamma's dwelling,
O how I longed to hug that gal,
    My heart with love was swelling!

With altered voice, "Sweel gal," I said,
    "Sweet honeysuckle blossom,
O, happy, happy is the Reb,
    That's dearest to thy bosom.
My purse is light, I've far to go,
    I'm hungry as the dead,
I've served my country long, you know,
    Take pity on a Rebel."

Then wistfully she gazed on me
    And lovelier seemed than ever:
Says she "I always like to see
    A Reb, but Yankee never!
Our pine-log hut and humble fare,
    You freely shall partake it,
A little bread we have to spare,
    As soon as I can bake it."

She gazed, then like a rose shone red,
    And jumping at me rudely,
She caught me in her arms, and said:
    "La sakes: if this ain't Hoodley!"
"Hurrah! I'm home! Luck's a die!
    My love is still regarded,
I am the very buck," says I,
    "A Rebel's thus rewarded.

"The war is o'er, and I've returned,
    To find you still so plucky,
'Tis true we're poor, but Sal I'm durned
    If I don't think we're lucky!"
Says she: "'Tis true we're poorly now,
    And scarcely worth a penny,
The Yankees killed the last old cow,
    And eat her, calf and any.

"Grim poverty and sorrow's here,
    Where once was joy and gladness,
But hearts are truer, Hoodley, dear,
    Where love is touched with sadness.
'Though blasting war has scorched the land,
    And we must toil the harder,
The willing heart and willing hand,
    With love, will stock the larder."

For greenbacks many bought and sold,
    And all their power exerted,
Betrayed their native land for gold,
    Their country's cause deserted.
And some the land did overrun
    And gained by spoil and plunder,
But glory, honor, love, and fun,
    Old webfoot's prize, by thunder![83]
CONFEDERATE CAPTAIN J. W. CARMACK

ONLY A PRIVATE

Only a private! his jacket of gray
    Is stained by the smoke and the dust;
As Bayard, he's brave; as Rupert, he's gay;[84]
Reckless as Murat in heat of the fray;
    But in God is his only trust.

Only a private! to march and to fight,
    To suffer and starve and be strong;
With knowledge enough to know that the might
Of justice and truth and freedom and right,
    In the end, must crush out the wrong.

Only a private! no ribbon or star
    Shall gild with false glory his name!
No honors for him in braid or in bar,
His Legion of Honor is only a scar,
    And his wounds are his roll of fame!

Only a private! one more hero slain
    On the field lies silent and chill!
And in the far South a wife prays in vain
One clasp of the hand she may ne'er clasp again,
    One kiss from the lips that are still.

Only a private! there let him sleep!
    He will need no tablet nor stone;
For the mosses and vines o'er his grave will creep,
And at night the stars through the clouds will peep
    And watch him who lies there alone.

Only a martyr! who fought and who fell
    Unknown and unmarked in the strife!
But still as he lies in his lonely cell
Angel and Seraph the legend shall tell—
    Such a death is eternal life![85]

CONFEDERATE CAPTAIN F. W. DAWSON

JOHN MARSHALL'S STATUE

We are glad to see you, John Marshall, my boy,
    So fresh from the chisel of Rodgers,
To take your stand on the monument there
    Along with the other old codgers.

With Washington, Jefferson, Mason, "and such,"
    Who sinned with a great transgression
In their old-fashioned notions of freedom and right
    And their hatred of wrong and oppression.

But you've come rather late to your pedestal, John;
    Things are very much changed since you've been here:
For the volume you hold is no longer the law,
    And this is no longer Virginia.

The "Marshall Law" you expounded of yore
    Is no longer at all to the purpose,
And the "martial law" of the new Brigadier
    Is stronger than *habeas corpus*.

So shut up the volume you hold with such care,
    For the days of the law are over;
And it needs all your brass to be holding it there,
    With "Justice" inscribed on the cover.

Could life awaken the limbs of bronze
    And blaze in the burnished eye.
What would you do with a moment of time,
    Ye men of the days gone by?
Would you chide us or pity us, blush or weep,
    Ye men of the days gone by?

Would Jefferson tear up the scroll he holds,
    Which time has proven a lie?
Would Marshall shut up the volume of law
    And lay it down with a sigh?

Would Mason roll up the "Bill of Rights"
    From a nation unworthy to scan it?
Would Henry dash down the patriot sword
    And clang it against the granite?

And Washington, seated in massy strength
    On his charger that paws the air.
Could he see his sons in deep disgrace,

Would he ride so proudly there?

He would get him down from his big brass horse,
    And cover his face with shame—
For the land of his birth is now "District One;"
    "Virginia" was once the name.[86]
INNIS RANDOLPH

John Marshall.

TURNER ASHBY

To the brave all homage render,
    Weep, ye skies of June!
With a radiance pure and tender,
    Shine, oh saddened moon!
        "Dead upon the field of glory,"
        Hero fit for song and story,
    Lies our bold dragoon!

Well they learned, whose hands have slain him,
    Braver, knightlier foe
Never fought with Moor nor Paynim—
    Rode at Templestowe;
        With a mien how high and joyous,
        'Gainst the hordes that would destroy us,
    Went he forth we know.

Never more, alas! shall sabre
    Gleam around his crest;
Fought his fight; fulfilled his labour;
    Stilled his manly breast;
        All unheard sweet Nature's cadence,
        Trump of fame and voice of maidens—
    Now he takes his rest.

Earth that all too soon hath bound him,
    Gently wrap his clay;
Linger lovingly around him,
    Light of dying day;
        Softly fall the summer showers,
        Birds and bees among the flowers
    Make the gloom seem gay.

There, throughout the coming ages,
    When his sword is rust,
And his deeds in classic pages;
    Mindful of her trust,
        Shall Virginia, bending lowly,
        Still a ceaseless vigil holy
    Keep above his dust.[87]
JOHN REUBEN THOMPSON

Turner Ashby.

MUSIC IN CAMP

Two armies covered hill and plain,
    Where Rappahannock's waters
Ran deeply crimsoned with the stain
    Of battle's recent slaughters.

The summer clouds lay pitched like tents
    In meads of heavenly azure;
And each dread gun of the elements
    Slept in its hid embrasure.

The breeze so softly blew, it made
    No forest leaf to quiver,
And the smoke of the random cannonade
    Rolled slowly from the river.

And now, where circling hills looked down
    With cannon grimly planted,
O'er listless camp and silent town
    The golden sunset slanted.

When on the fervid air there came
    A strain—now rich, now tender;
The music seemed itself aflame
    With day's departing splendor.

A Federal band, which, eve and morn.
    Played measures brave and nimble,
Had just struck up, with flute and horn
    And lively clash of cymbal.

Down flocked the soldiers to the banks.
    Till, margined by its pebbles,
One wooded shore was blue with "Yanks,"
    And one was gray with "Rebels."

Then all was still, and then the band,
    With movement light and tricksy,
Made stream and forest, hill and strand
    Reverberate with "Dixie."

The conscious stream with burnished glow
    Went proudly o'er its pebbles,
But thrilled throughout its deepest flew
    With yelling of the Rebels.

Again a pause, and then again
    The trumpets pealed sonorous,
And "Yankee Doodle" was the strain

> To which the shore gave chorus.

The laughing ripple shoreward flew,
  To kiss the shining pebbles;
Loud shrieked the swarming Boys in Blue
  Defiance to the Rebels.

And yet once more the bugles sang
  Above the stormy riot;
No shout upon the evening rang—
  There reigned a holy quiet.

The sad, slow stream its noiseless flood
  Poured o'er the glistening pebbles;
All silent now the Yankees stood,
  And silent stood the Rebels.

No unresponsive soul had heard
  That plaintive note's appealing,
So deeply "Home Sweet Home" had stirred
  The hidden founts of feeling.

Or Blue, or Gray, the soldier sees
  As by the wand of fairy,
The cottage 'neath the live-oak trees,
  The cabin by the prairie.

Or cold, or warm, his native skies
  Bend in their beauty o'er him;
Seen through the tear-mist in his eyes,
  His loved ones stand before him.

As fades the iris after rain
  In April's tearful weather,
The vision vanished, as the strain
  And daylight died together.

But memory, waked by music's art,
  Expressed in simplest numbers,
Subdued the sternest Yankee's heart,
  Made light the Rebel's slumbers.

And fair the form of music shines,
  That bright celestial creature,
Who still, 'mid war's embattled lines,
  Gave this one touch of Nature.[88]
JOHN REUBEN THOMPSON

MAGNOLIA CEMETERY ODE

Sleep sweetly in your humble graves.
    Sleep, martyrs of a fallen cause:
Though yet no marble column craves
    The pilgrim here to pause.

In the seeds of laurel in the earth
    The blossom of your fame is blown.
And somewhere, waiting for its birth,
    The shaft is in the stone.

Meanwhile behold the tardy years
    Which keep in trust your storied tombs.
Behold your sisters bring their tears
    And these memorial blooms.

Small tribute! but your shades will smile
    More proudly on these wreaths to-day
Than when some common-moulded file
    Shall overlook this clay.

Stoop, angels, hither from the skies!
    There is no nobler spot of ground
Than where defeated Valor lies
    By mourning beauty crowned.[89]
HENRY TIMROD

Henry Timrod.

THE PHANTOM HOST

My form was wrapped in the slumber
    That steals from the heart its cares.
For my very life was weary
    With its barren waste of years;
But my soul, with rapid pinions,
    Fled fast to the light that beams
From a phantom sun and planets,
    For the dreamer in his dreams.

I stood in a wondrous woodland,
    Where the sunlight nestled sweet
In the cups of snowy lilies
    Which grew about my feet;
And while the forest arches
    Stirred gently with the air,
The lilies underneath them
    Swung their censers, pale in prayer.

I stood, amazed and wondering
    And a grand memoriam strain
Came sweeping through the forest
    And died, then rose again;
It swelled in solemn measure
    'Till my soul, with comfort blest,
Sank down among the lilies,
    With folded wings to rest.

Then to that mystic music,
    Through the forest's twilight aisle,
Passed a Host with muffled footsteps,
    In martial rank and file;
And I knew those grey-clad figures,
    Thus slowly passing by,
Were the souls of Southern soldiers
    Who for freedom dared to die.

In front rode Sidney Johnston,
    With a brow no longer wrung
By the vile and senseless slanders
    Of a prurient rabble tongue;
And near him mighty Jackson,
    With placid front, as one
Whose warfare was accomplished,
    Whose crown of glory won.

There Hill, too, pure and noble,
    Passed in that spirit train,
For he joined the martyred army
    From the South's last battle plain
Then, next in order, followed
    The warrior priest, great Polk,
With joy to meet his master,
    For he had nobly borne his yoke.

There Stuart, the bold and daring,
    With matchless Pelham rode,
With earnest, chastened faces—
    They were looking up to God;
And Jenkins, glorious Jenkins,
    With his patient, fearless eyes,
And the brave, devoted Garnett,
    Journeyed on to Paradise.

Before a shadowy squadron
    Rode Morgan, keen and strong,
And I knew by his tranquil forehead
    He'd forgotten every wrong;
There peerless Pegram, matching
    With a dauntless, martial tread,
And I breathed a sigh for the hero
    The young, the early dead.

'Mid spectral Black Horse troopers.
    Passed Ashby's stalwart form,
With that proud, defiant bearing
    Which so spurned the battle storm;
But his glance was mild and tender,
    For in that phantom host
It dwelt with lingering fondness
    On the brother he had lost.

There strode the brave Malony,
    Kind, genial Adjutant;
And next him walked the truthful.
    The lion-hearted Gaunt.

There, to that mystic music,
    Passed triad of the brave—
Hayne, Taylor, Alfred Pinckney—
    All had found a soldier's grave;
They were young and gentle spirits,
    But they quaffed the bitter cup,

For their country's flag was falling,
    And they fell to lift it up.

Aye, there passed, in countless thousands,
    In that mighty Phantom Host,
True hearts and noble patriots,
    Whose names on earth are lost;
There the missing found their places
    Those who vanished from our gaze,
Like brilliant, flashing meteors.
    And were lost in Glory's blaze,

Yes, they passed that noble army—
    They passed to meet their Lord,
And a voice within me whispered,
    They but march to their reward.[90]
P. D. HAY

Ambrose P. Hill.

A REBEL SOLDIER KILLED IN THE TRENCHES

[Before Petersburg, Virginia, April 15, 1865]

Killed in the trenches! How cold and bare
    The inscription graved on the white card there.
'Tis a photograph, taken last Spring, they say,
    Ere the smoke of battle had cleared away—
Of a rebel soldier—just as he fell,
When his heart was pierced by a Union shell;
And his image was stamped by the sunbeam's ray,
As he lay in the trenches that April day.

Oh God! Oh God! How my woman's heart
    Thrills with a quick, convulsive pain,
As I view, unrolled by the magic of Art,
    One dreadful scene from the battle-plain:—
White as the foam of the storm-tossed wave,
Lone as the rocks those billows lave—
Gray sky above—cold clay beneath—
A gallant form lies stretched in death!

With his calm face fresh on the trampled clay,
    And the brave hands clasped o'er the manly breast
Save the sanguine stains on his jacket gray,
    We might deem him taking a soldier's rest.
Ah no! Too red is that crimson tide—
Too deeply pierced that wounded side;
Youth, hope, love, glory—manhood's pride—
Have all in vain Death's bolt defied.

His faithful carbine lies useless there,
    As it dropped from its master's nerveless ward;
And the sunbeams glance on his waving hair
    Which the fallen cap has ceased to guard—
Oh Heaven! spread o'er it thy merciful shield,
No more to my sight be the battle revealed!
Oh fiercer than tempest—grim Hades as dread—
On woman's eye flashes the field of the dead!

The scene is changed: In a quiet room,
    Far from the spot where the lone corpse lies,
A mother kneels in the evening gloom
    To offer her nightly sacrifice.
The noon is past, and the day is done,
She knows that the battle is lost or won—
Who lives? Who died? Hush! be thou still!
The boy lies dead on the trench-barred hill.[91]
A KENTUCKY GIRL

BATTLE OF HAMPTON ROADS

Ne'er had a scene of beauty smiled
    On placid waters 'neath the sun,
Like that on Hampton's watery plain,
    The fatal morn the fight begun.
Far toward the silvery Sewell shores,
    Below the guns of Craney Isle,
Were seen our fleet advancing fast,
    Beneath the sun's auspicious smile.

Oh, fatal sight! the hostile hordes
    Of Newport camp spread dire alarms:
The *Cumberland* for fight prepares—
    The fierce marines now rush to arms.
The *Merrimac*[92] strong cladded o'er,
    In quarters close begins her fire,
Nor fears the rushing hail of shot,
    And deadly missiles swift and dire;
But, rushing on 'mid smoke and flame,
    And belching thunder long and loud,
Salutes the ship with bow austere,
    And then withdraws in wreaths of cloud.

The work is done. The frigate turns
    In agonizing, doubtful poise—
She sinks, she sinks! along the deck
    Is heard a shrieking, wailing noise.
Engulfed beneath those placid waves
    Disturbed by battle's onward surge,
The crew is gone; the vessel sleeps,
    And whistling bombshells sing her dirge.

The battle still is raging fierce:
    The *Congress*, "high and dry" aground,
Maintains in vain her boasted power,
    For now the gunboats flock around,
With "stars and bars" at mainmast reared,
    And pour their lightning on the main,
While *Merrimac*, approaching fast
    Sends forth her shell and hotshot rain.

Meantime the *Jamestown*, gallant boat,
    Engages strong redoubts at land—
While *Patrick Henry* glides along,
    To board the *Congress*, still astrand.
This done, we turn intently on

The *Minnesota*, which replies,
With whizzing shell to *Teaser's* gun,
    Whose booming cleaves the distant skies.

The naval combat sounds anew;
    The hostile fleets are not withdrawn,
Though night is closing earth and sea
    In twilight's pale and mystic dawn.
Strange whistling noises fill the air;
    The powdered smoke looks dark as night,
And deadly, lurid flames, pour forth
    Their radiance on the missiles' flight;
Grand picture on the noisy waves!
    The breezy zephyrs onward roam,
And echoing volleys float afar,
    Disturbing Neptune's coral home.
The victory's ours, and let the world
    Record Buchanan's name with pride;
The crew is brave, the banner bright,
    That ruled the day when Hutter died.[93]
OSSIAN D. GORMAN

Franklin Buchanan.

THE SOUTHERN HOMES IN RUIN

Many a gray-haired sire has died,
    As falls the oak, to rise no more,
Because his son, his prop, his pride,
    Breathed out his last all red with gore.
No more on earth, at morn, at eve,
    Shall age and youth, entwined as one—
Nor father, son, for either grieve—
    Life's work, alas, for both is done!

Many a mother's heart has bled
    While gazing on her darling child,
As in its tiny eyes she read
    The father's image, kind and mild;
For ne'er again his voice will cheer
    The widowed heart, which mourns him dead;
Nor kisses dry the scalding tear,
    Fast falling on the orphans head!

Many a little form will stray
    Adown the glen and o'er the hill,
And watch, with wistful looks, the way
    For him whose step is missing still;
And when the twilight steals apace
    O'er mead, and brook, and lonely home,
And shadows cloud the dear, sweet face—
    The cry will be, "Oh, papa, come!"

And many a home's in ashes now,
    Where joy was once a constant guest,
And mournful groups there are, I trow,
    With neither house nor place of rest;
And blood is on the broken sill,
    Where happy feet went to and fro,
And everywhere, by field and hill,
    Are sickening sights and sounds of woe!

There is a God who rules on high,
    The widow's and the orphan's friend,
Who sees each tear and hears each sigh,
    That these lone hearts to Him may send!
And when in wrath He tears away
    The reasons vain which men indite,
The record book will plainest say
    Who's in the wrong, and who is right.[94]
R. B. VANCE

THE SOLDIER IN THE RAIN

Ah me! the rain has a sadder sound
    Than it ever had before;
And the wind more plaintively whistles through
    The crevices of the door.

We know we are safe beneath our roof
    From every drop that falls;
And we feel secure and blest, within
    The shelter of our walls.

Then why do we dread to hear the noise
    Of the rapid, rushing rain—
And the plash of the wintry drops, that beat
    Through the blinds, on the window-pane?

We think of the tents on the lowly ground,
    Where our patriot soldiers lie;
And the sentry's bleak and lonely march,
    'Neath the dark and starless sky.

And we pray, with a tearful heart, for those
    Who brave for us yet more—
And we wish this war, with its thousand ills
    And griefs, was only o'er.

We pray when the skies are bright and clear,
    When the winds are soft and warm—
But oh! we pray with an aching heart
    'Mid the winter's rain and storm.

We fain would lift these mantling clouds
    That shadow our sunny clime;
We can but wait—for we know there'll be
    A day, in the coming time,

When peace, like a rosy dawn, will flood
    Our land with softest light:
Then—we will scarcely hearken the rain
    In the dreary winter's night.[95]
JULIA L. KEYES

SACRIFICE

Another victim for the sacrifice!
    Oh! my own mother South,
      How terrible this wail above thy youth,
      Dying at the cannon's mouth,—
And for no crime—no vice—
No scheme of selfish greed—no avarice,
Or insolent ambition, seeking power;—
But that, with resolute soul and will sublime,
    They made their proud election to be free,—
To leave a grand inheritance to time,
    And to their sons and race, of liberty!

Oh! widow'd woman, sitting in thy weeds,
    With thy young brood around thee, sad and lone—
Thy fancy sees thy hero where he bleeds,
    And still thou hear'st his moan!
Dying he calls on thee—again—again!
    With blessing and fond memories. Be of cheer;
He has not died—he did not bless—in vain:
For, in the eternal rounds of God, He squares
The account with sorrowing hearts; and soothes the fears,
And leads the orphans home, and dries the widow's tears.[96]
UNKNOWN

ONLY A SOLDIERS GRAVE

Only a soldier's grave! Pass by,
For soldiers, like other mortals, die.
Parents he had—they are far away;
No sister weeps o'er the soldier's clay;
No brother comes, with a tearful eye:
It's only a soldier's grave—pass by.

True, he was loving, and young, and brave,
Though no glowing epitaph honors his grave
No proud recital of virtues known,
Of griefs endured, or of triumphs won;
No tablet of marble, or obelisk high;—
Only a soldier's grave—pass by.

Yet bravely he wielded his sword in fight,
And he gave his life in the cause of right!
When his hope was high, and his youthful dream
As warm as the sunlight on yonder stream;
His heart unvexed by sorrow or sigh;—
Yet, 'tis only a soldier's grave—pass by.

Yet, should we mark it—the soldier's grave,
Some one may seek him in hope to save!
Some of the dear ones, far away,
Would bear him home to his native clay:
'Twere sad, indeed, should they wander nigh,
Find not the hillock, and pass him by.[97]
S. A. JONES

WILLIAM MUMFORD MARTYR OF NEW ORLEANS

Where murdered Mumford lies,
Bewailed in bitter sighs,
Low-bowed beneath the flag he loved,
Martyrs of Liberty,
Defenders of the Free!
Come, humbly nigh,
And learn to die!

Ah, Freedom, on that day,
Turned fearfully away,
While pitying angels lingered near,
To gaze upon the sod,
Red with a martyr's blood;
And woman's tear
Fell on his bier!

O God! that he should die
Beneath a Southern sky!
Upon a felon's gallows swung,
Murdered by tyrant hand,—
While round a helpless band,
On Butler's name
Poured scorn and shame.

William B. Mumford.

But hark! loud paeans fly
From earth to vaulted sky,
He's crowned at Freedom's holy throne!
List! sweet-voiced Israfel[98]
Tolls far the martyr's knell!
Shout, Southrons, high,
Our battle cry!

Come, all of Southern blood,
Come, kneel to Freedom's God!
Here at her crimsoned altar swear!
Accursed for evermore
The flag that Mumford tore,
And o'er his grave
Our colors wave![99]
INA M. PORTER

ALBERT SIDNEY JOHNSTON

Honor to him who only drew
    In Freedom's cause his battle blade,
And 'round our Southern banners threw
    A halo that can never fade.
Honor to him, whose name sublime,
    Shall be the watchword of the free,
When yet the latest wave of time
    Shall break on far eternity.

In artless truth, a simple child;
    In valor, first of godlike men;
Who, tho' his countrymen reviled,
    Did ne'er revile again.
Like some lone rock, 'gainst which the flow
    Of Fickle passions foam and fret,
Unmoved our dear dead Captain stood,
    Firm-planted in his purpose yet.

What tho' detraction grieved the heart
    That bled but for his country's woe!
He recked but of his country's part
    To shield her weakness from the foe.
He gave his bosom to the storm,
    That rose in curses on the air,
Courting the shafts that might not harm
    His country, while they rankled there.

Slow falling back from Bowling Green,
    His crippled columns move along,
While flanking every side were seen
    The myriad hosts of human wrong.
Curtained beneath his clear, calm eye,
    The heroic impulse held in sway,
Till, turning in his path to die,
    The wounded lion stands at bay!

Ah! how he stood, and where he stood,
    Where strong men perished in their strength.
On Shiloh's field of death and blood
    His bolted thunders fell at length!
The fires of vengeance, hot and red,
    Far flashed where rode his knightly form;
And wreck, and rout, and ruin spread
    Where swept that day his battle storm.

Oh, peace to him who slumbers now
    Beneath the soil he died to save;
The wreath that decks his clay-cold brow,
    Shall blossom in the martyr's grave;
Shall blossom where, in after time,
    Our children's children bless the mold
Where Sidney Johnston sleeps sublime,
    Like some great mastodon of old.[100]
C. E. MERRILL

Albert S. Johnston.

A LAMENT FOR DIXIE

Southrons conquered, subjugated,
Mourn your country devastated:
    Mourn for hapless, hopeless Dixie—
Homes once happy, desolated;
Church and altar desecrated.
    Mourn for fallen, ruined Dixie.

CHORUS
Lament the fall of Dixie.
Alas! alas!
On Dixie's land we yet will stand,
And live or die for Dixie.
    Endure! endure!
All ills endure for Dixie!
    Endure! endure!
All ills endure for Dixie!

Bewail your dead, whose bones lie bleaching,
Courage to the living teaching;
    Mourn, but still be proud of Dixie.
Bewail your Southland, crushed and trampled,
Bearing sorrows unexampled;
    Mourn, but still be proud for Dixie.

Prey despoiled and victim bleeding,
Not to man for mercy pleading;
    Unto God alone cries Dixie.
Cross of anguish bravely bearing,
Crown of thorns submissive wearing,
    Patient and resigned Dixie.

All our States lie fainting, dying,
Each to each with sobs replying;
    Each still loving, honoring Dixie.
By the accursed scourge lacerated,
By her freed slaves ruled and hated,
    She is still our own dear Dixie.

Dear to us our conquered banners,
Greeted once with loud hosannas!
    Dear the tattered flags of Dixie;
Dear the fields of honor glorious,
Where, defeated or victorious,
    Sleep the immortal dead of Dixie.

Conquered, we are not degraded;
Southron laurels have not faded.
    Mourn, but not in shame, for Dixie.
Deck your heroes' graves with garlands
Till the echo comes from far lands:
    Honor to the dead of Dixie!

All is not yet lost unto us;
Baseness only can subdue us.
    Mourn—you cannot flush—for Dixie.
Kneeling at your country's altar,
Swear your children not to falter
    Till the right shall rule in Dixie.

If her fate be sealed, we'll share it,
By our shroudless dead, we swear it!
    Ours the life or death of Dixie.
By her past's all-glorious glory,
By her laureled martyr's glory,
    We will live or die for Dixie!

Shall there to our night of sorrow
Be no glad and bright to-morrow?
    Is hope ever lost to Dixie?
Every dark night has its morning,
Long though oft delayed its dawning.
    Wait be patient! pray for Dixie!

    Hope for dawn for Dixie.
        Endure! endure!
    On Dixie's land we yet will stand,
    And live or die for Dixie
        Endure! endure!
    All ills endure for Dixie!
        Endure! endure!
    All ills endure for Dixie![101]
CONFEDERATE GENERAL ALBERT PIKE

Albert Pike.

MARSE ROBERT IS ASLEEP

Had you heard the distant tramping
    On that glowing summer day!
Had you seen our comrades running
    To meet us on the way!
Oh! the wondrous, sudden silence,
    The unmilitary creep,
As down the line that caution ran,
    "Marse Robert is asleep!"

Give me your hand, Old Blue Coat,
    Let's talk of this awhile,
For the prettiest march of all the war
    Was this rank and file!—
Was the passing of that army,
    When 'twas hard, I ween, to keep
Those men from crying out, "Hurrah!
    Marse Robert is asleep!"

There lay that knightly figure,
    One hand upon his sword,
The other pressed above his heart,
    A vow without a word!
Two laurel leaves had fluttered down,
    For flowers their vigils keep,
And crown'd him, though I think they knew
    "Marse Robert was asleep!"

In glorious old Westminster,
    No monument of war,
No marble story half so grand
    As this our army saw!
Our leafy old Westminster—
    Virginia's woods—now keep
Immortal that low whisper,
    "Marse Robert is asleep!"

As we clasp hands, Old Blue Coat,
    List, brother of the North,
Had foreign foe assail'd your homes,
    You then had known his worth!
Unbroken vigil o'er those homes
    It had been his to keep:
Step lightly o'er the border then,
    "Marse Robert is asleep!"

He's yours and mine, is Robert Lee,
    He's yours and mine, Hurrah!
These tears you shed have sealed the past,
    And closed the wounds of war!
Thus clasping hands, Old Blue Coat,
    We'll swear by the tears you weep,
The sounds of war shall muffled be—
    "Marse Robert is asleep."[102]
UNKNOWN

DECORATING CONFEDERATE GRAVES
[at Charleston, South Carolina]

Sleep sweetly in your humble graves,
    Sleep, martyrs of a fallen cause;
Though yet no marble column craves
    The pilgrim here to pause.

In seeds of laurel in the earth
    The blossom of your fame is blown.
And somewhere, waiting for its birth,
    The shaft is in the stone!

Meanwhile, behalf the tardy years
    Which keep in trust your storied tombs.
Behold! your sisters bring their tears,
    And these memorial blooms.

Small tributes! but your shade will smile
    More proudly on those wreaths to-day
Than when some cannon-molded pile
    Shall overlook this bay.

Stoop, angels, hither from the skies!
    There is no holier spot of ground
Than where defeated valor lies,
    By mourning beauty crowned![103]
HENRY TIMROD

Victorian Southern women tending Confederate graves.

THE SOUTHERN FLAGS

Let those flags be furled forever,
    Just as when we laid them down,
Emblems of a vain endeavor,
    Duty done without its crown.
Covered as they are with glory,
    Let them molder into dust,
Emblematic of their story,
    Emblematic of our trust.

Let those braves who charged upon them,
    Men who met us in the fight
They who by their valor won them,
    Let them keep them—theirs by right.
Let them keep them, torn and tattered,
    Tokens of the tears they cost,
Symbols of a people scattered.
    Emblems of the cause they lost.

Emblems of a people dashing
    Down the tide of time to die;
Meteorlike, in splendor flashing,
    Flaming 'cross the Southern sky!
When before did such a nation,
    Born alone of hopes and prayers,
Freely offer such libation,
    Pouring out its blood and tears?

Not old Rome's heroic ages,
    Not e'en Greece's grandest days.
Not the world's historic pages,
    Furnish such a theme for praise.
Classic Greece yet tells the deeds of
    Heroes of her land and sea;
Wondering, all the world now reads of
    Raphael Semmes and Robert Lee.

Never marched men into battle,
    Braver men with firmer tread,
Spite of all the roar and rattle,
    Spite of dying and the dead.
Rest, ye warriors, from your labors:
    Rest your banners worn to rags;
Sheathed forever are your sabers;
    Furled forever be your flags.

Though in vain our brave endeavor,
    Though our skies lie overcast,
Appomattox meant "forever,"
    No repinings for the past.
Symbols of a grand oblation,
    Keep those flags forever furled;
Emblems of a vanished nation,
    Once the wonder of the world.[104]
DR. H. M. CLARKSON

Raphael Semmes.

MEMORIAL ODE

Our history is a shining sea
Locked in by lofty land,
And its great Pillars of Hercules,
Above the shifting sand
I here behold in majesty
Uprising on each hand.

These Pillars of our history,
In fame forever young,
Are known in every latitude
And named in every tongue,
And down through all the Ages
Their story shall be sung.

The Father of his Country
Stands above that shut-in sea,
A glorious symbol to the world
Of all that's great and free;
And to-day Virginia matches him—
And matches him with Lee.[105]
JAMES BARRON HOPE

PASSING MANASSAS, 1892

Here's where it thundered
From field to field, and through valley to valley.
    There, where the line was bluest,
    Crash, fell the volley truest!
Then broke the legions, then the grand rally,
    And day wept and wondered.

    Here's where the battle came,
The cannon and tumult, uproared to heaven;
    Then through the azure wall,
    As grey legions rise and fall;
There's wailing and triumph, the land in twain riven
    By shocks of Manassas' fame!

    There's where the sundered
And grand, stricken armies once wavered and fell;
    There's where the oriflame
    Of a new nation's birth came,
'Bove tumult and fires as if risen from hell;
    And the world gazed and wondered.

    Here now a pilgrim passed,
Pale from the terror and roar of life's battle!
    She's wept o'er the flying,
    The dead, lost, and dying;
And voices stilled ever by death's chilly rattle,
    While Hope was the last.

    Life-angel to leave her!
Long since faith, and love, as heroes inglorious,
    Fell in wrong's night-terror,
    Like Justice struck by Error;
But when the column breaks, comes one victorious!
    Death, the true victor, cannot deceive her.[106]

LILLIAN ROZELL-MESSENGER

BUILD THE MONUMENT

Build up a shaft to Davis! Let it tower to the skies.
Let those who fell in battle see the stately column rise.
'Twill represent the cause they loved, the cause they died to save,
And shadow forth our deep respect for every soldier's grave.
For right or wrong, our brethren fell on every bloody field,
They thought the cause they loved was just, and feeling so, to yield
Were baser than all baseness is, and greater to be feared
Than all the guns that ever roared since heaven's light appeared.

For Davis neither better was nor worse than those he led;
He simply represented all we did, or thought, or said.
He was the chieftain of our State, the leader of our band,
Duly chosen from amongst us, to assume and give command.
He erred? It was but human. Which of us that has not erred?
When we made him chief in power, we assumed his every word.
So far as it had bearing on the common cause, we knew;
And all his acts as chief of State were ordered in our view.

He failed to win the aim he sought? Why 'twas the State that failed.
They thrust him into dungeons—every man he led was jailed.
The irons that upon his weak and wasted limbs he wore
Were those that as their chief of State he for his people bore.
The criticism and abuse he silently endured,
Were only of the nature that his chieftaincy insured.
And shall we now forget the men who suffered in our stead?
Curst be the craven spirit who deserts his household dead!

We yet are in our father's house; we love our country's flag.
Long may its folds unchallenged fly on sea and mountain crag!
Long may Columbia's gonfalon float proudly to the breeze!
And let no man with angry hand the sacred emblem seize.
But let us grieve over every wound wherein our country bled.
We love the brave of every faith; we mourn our gallant dead.
Secure against fraternal hate they sleep beneath the sod,
The Lord of Hosts hath summoned them. Their fame is safe with God.[107]
WILLIAM C. FORSEE

ROBERT E. LEE
(In honor of the General's birthday)

He fought the fight to finish,
And his soldier work is done;
Lee ever stands immortal:
Freedom's model of a son.

As in the day of battle,
Or on his great retreat,
The center of attraction;
We come, our Lee to meet.

We've tried to mould his features,
To clothe him with a form;
To hold him up for men to see
How much he can adorn.

He came not home triumphant,
But a hero he did come;
With honor pure, unsullied,
And a love excelled by none.

No pathway strewn with flowers
Welcomed Lee back from the war,
But an anguish for his country
And the ruined homes he saw.

Robert E. Lee.

He, who could stand undaunted
'Midst the crash and clang of arms,
Grew grander when, disabled,
Leading comrades to their farms.

For he tread the path of duty,
And he won respect and fame,—
The proudest wreath of laurels
That a mortal man can claim.

'Tis not the smoke of battle,
The carnage, or the flame;
But we hold our Lee close to us,—
We love to call his name.

And we tell all we know of him;
And the nation yet unborn
Shall learn to know and love him
Like the fathers that have gone.[108]
R. H. DYKERS

THE SAME CANTEEN

There are bonds of all sorts in this world of ours,
Fetters of friendship and ties of flowers,
    And true lover's knots, I ween;
The girl and the boy are bound by a kiss,
But there's never a bond, old friend, like this,
We have drank from the same Canteen!

It was sometimes water, and sometimes milk,
And sometimes apple-jack "fine us silk;"
    But whatever the tipple has been
We shared it together in bane or bliss.
And I warm to you, friend, when I think of this,
We drank from the same Canteen!

The rich and great sit down to dine,
They quaff each other in sparkling wine,
    From glasses of crystal and green;
But I guess in their golden potations they miss
The warmth of regard to be found in this.
We drank from the same Canteen!

We have shared our blankets and tents together,
And have marched and fought in all kinds of weather,
    And hungry and full we have been;
Bad days of battle and days of rest.
But this memory I cling to and love the best,
We drank from the same Canteen!

For when wounded I lay on the center slope,
With my blood flowing fast and but little hope
    Upon which my faint spirit could lean;
Oh! then I remember you crawled to my side,
And bleeding so fast it seemed both must have died,
We drank from the same Canteen.[109]
UNKNOWN

PRAYER OF THE SOUTH

My brow is bent beneath a heavy rod;
    My face is wan and white with many woes;
But I will lift my poor chained hands to God
    And for my children pray, and for my foes.
Beside the graves where thousands lowly lie
    I kneel, and, weeping for each slaughtered son,
I turn my gaze to my own sunny sky,
    And pray, O Father, may thy will he done.

My heart is filled with anguish, deep and vast;
    My hopes are buried with my children's dust;
My joys have fled, my tears are growing fast—
    In whom save thee, our Father, shall I trust?
Ah! I forgot thee, Father, long and oft,
    When I was happy, rich and proud and free;
But, conquered now and crushed, I look aloft,
    And sorrow leads me, Father, back to thee.

Amid the wrecks that mark the foeman's path
    I kneel, and, wailing o'er my glories gone,
I still each thought of hate, each throb of wrath,
    And whisper, Father, let thy will be done.
Pity me, Father of the desolate;
    Alas, my burdens are so hard to bear;
Look down in mercy on my wretched fate,
    And keep me, guard me, with thy loving care.

Pity me, Father, for His holy sake
    Whose broken heart bled at the feet of grief
That hearts of earth, wherever they shall break,
    Might go to his and find a sure relief.
Ah me, how dark! Is this a brief eclipse?
    Or is it night, with no to-morrow's sun?
Father! Father! with my pale, sad lips
    And sadder heart, I pray, Thy will be done.

My homes are joyless; and a million mourn,
    Where many met, in joys forever flown;
Whose hearts are light, are burdened now and lorn;
    Where many smiled, but one is left to mourn.
And, ah, the widow's wails, the orphan's cries,
    Are morning hymn and vesper chant to me;
And groans of men and sounds of women's sighs
    Commingle, Father, with my prayer to thee.

Beneath my feet, ten thousand children dead!—
    Oh, how I loved each known and nameless one!
Above their dust I bow my crownless head
    And murmur, Father, still thy will be done.
Ah, Father, thou didst deck my own loved land
    With all bright charms, and beautiful and fair;
But the foeman came and, with ruthless hand,
    Spread ruin, wreck, and desolation there.

Girdled with gloom, of all my brightness shorn,
    And garmented with grief, I kiss thy rod,
And turn my face, with tears all wet and worn.
    To catch one smile of pity from my God.
Around me blight, where all was bloom;
    And so much lost, alas, and nothing won
Save this, that I can lean on wreck and tomb,
    And weep and, weeping, pray, Thy will be done.

And, oh, 'tis hard to say, but said, 'tis sweet;
    The words are bitter, but they hold a balm,
A balm that heals the wounds of my defeat
    And lulls my sorrows into holy calm.
It is the prayer of prayers—and how it brings,
    When heard in heaven, peace and hope to me!
When Jesus prayed it, did not angels' wings
    Gleam 'mid the darkness of Gethsemane.

My children, Father, thy forgiveness need
    Alas, their hearts have only room for tears—
Forgive them, Father, every wrongful deed,
    And every sin of those four bloody years.
And give them strength to bear their boundless loss,
    And from their hearts take every thought of hate;
And, while they climb their Calvary with their cross,
    O help them, Father, to endure it's weight.

And for my dead, Father, may I pray?
    Ah, sighs may soothe, but prayer shall soothe me more.
I keep eternal watch above their clay—
    O rest their souls, my Father, I implore.
Forgive my foes—they know not what they do—
    Forgive them all the tears they made me shed;
Forgive them, though my noblest sons they slew,
    And bless them, though they curse my poor, dear dead.

O may my woes be each a carrier dove,
    With swift white wings, that, bathing in my tears,

Will bear thee, Father, all my prayers of love,
    And bring me peace, in all my doubts and fears.
Father, I kneel, 'mid ruin, wreck, and grave—
    A desert waste where all was erst so fair—
And, for my children and my foes, I crave
    Pity and pardon: Father, hear my prayer.[110]
REVEREND ABRAM JOSEPH RYAN

TO A CONFEDERATE BATTLE FLAG

Whence comest thou, immortal rag?
Whose shapely hands so wondrous deft
Did fasten thee, beloved flag,
Mute witness of that cursed theft
Of nations' rights which hist'ry made?
What gallant lad, receiving thee
From her whom love and honor swayed,
Did bravely bear thee under Lee?
What spots be these upon thy face?
The blood of him whose trenchant blade
Defended from an alien race
The hearts and homes our fathers made?
Thou can'st not speak, and yet to me
A vivid picture of the past;
Its glories sufferings, agony,
Art thou, and wilt be to the last,
Till man forgets the deeds of men,
Who, conquering died, defeated bled
T' immortalize with brush and pen,
And fame and glory both are dead.
When first thy glories met the day—
Thy brilliant colors swept the sky,
Dread menace to invader's sway—
A careless, prattling child was I.
No heed gave I to sounds of strife.
Nor thought of what was just and right;
But now I know the glorious life
Of those who right, were crushed by might
And now, methinks, for one proud day
Of marching 'neath thy starry folds.
While matchless chieftains led the way.
I'd give the wealth that this earth holds.
Too brief for us thy glorious life,
Ah! far too long that struggle, rife
With scenes of carnage, women's woes,
Defeated heroes conq'ring foes.
'Twere better that thou should'st be furled—
While gazed enrapt a wond'ring world—
A dying nation's glorious shroud
Of which humanity is proud.
A million hearts which gladly gave
Their blood our country's flag to save
Still pulse on his'try's glowing page
The wonder of the present age.
Had'st thou survived those trying days

Thou mightest (thro' man's devious ways)
Have had thy laurels torn from thee,
For mankind's weaknesses, ah! me,
Permit no nation's color gage
To pass unsullied ev'ry age.
But now thy pure, unstained face,
Thou guerdon of a mighty race,
Doth speak to me the while I rue
The loss of valiant men and true;
Thou art to me an epic song
Of right and truth opposed to wrong.
Fear not that thou did'st live in vain,
No flag e'er fell more free from stain;
Thou art an emblem still to all
Who mourn thy too untimely fall;
Thy cross our faith, thy blue our skies,
Thy stars the wraith of woman's eyes,
Thy red the gore of gallant slain
Who died that o'er us peace might reign.[111]
ALBERT SIDNEY MORTON

JEFFERSON DAVIS' SECOND FUNERAL PROCESSION

Come, close ranks, comrades, round the bier
Where Davis lies, and let us rear
    His statue to the skies.
We'll rear it where the people pass,
And while the light of truth shall last
    His name shall lie revered.
In sculptured lines on stone we'll tell
The story of what since befell
The land we love and those who fell
    Defending all 'twas worth.
Where heroes of the "lost cause" dwell,
Where children list when matrons tell,
Where maidens sing the deeds of sires,
And virtue fans the patriot fires;
Where slopes Virginia's classic shore,
Where brawls the James at Richmond's door,
Where thousands sleep on fields of fame
We'll raise a shaft to Davis' name.
There he shall rest in phalanx deep
As heroes rest in one grand sleep;
There he shall rest in sweet accord
With those who dared to serve their God.
In Old Virginia's lap we lay
His sacred form of sacred clay.[112]
R. H. DYKERS

President Davis' funeral car.

IN THE SOUTH

In the South, a deeper crimson
    Comes upon the robin's breast,
And a grander opalescence
    Lingers in the fading west.

In the South, the soft winds whisper
    Love songs to the birds and flowers,
And responsive answers waken
    Echoes from the leafy bowers.

In the South, the rippling waters
    Softly chant fond lullabies,
To the nodding ferns and flowers
    Bending low in sweet surprise.

In the South, the grand orchestra
    Of the forest pines is heard,
When the low, sad misery
    Into trembling life is stirred.

In the South, the warm blood rushes
    Through the veins in faster streams,
Painting blushes on fair faces,
    Waking passion from its dreams.

In the South, love's chords are minors,
    Meant for hearts, not ears to hear,
Yet they sometimes tremble wildly,
    As if unseen hands were near.

In the South, my heart still lingers,
    Lingers loth to say farewell,
For, like rush of many waters,
    Memories come their loves to tell.

And I listen, fondly dreaming
    Of a past so wondrous bright,
That I start in wild amazement,
    Finding daylight turned to night.[113]
MRS. F. G. DÉ FONTAINE

MEMORIES

Never was step more steady as the "band-box soldiers" filed
Out from the famed "Camp Jackson," while the gods looked down and smiled
On troops so fair and graceful in their stainless garb of gray;
Each man ready, each man panting for the thickest of the fray.

They were leaving there in Portsmouth, in the city of her dead,
The first brave Georgia soldier who had bowed his gallant head
On the soil of old Virginia, pillowed on a spot so fair,
Where many a woman's tears had fallen above his golden hair.

He had yielded, ere the battle came, to "power none dare defy,"
And in a stranger's land, poor boy, had lain him down to die.
But he was sweetly sleeping in his calm, untroubled rest,
While fair hands strewed earth's loveliest flowers above his quiet breast.

And his comrades all were hasting to a fierce baptismal fire—
Not a laggard in the ranks, from sturdy boy to gray-haired sire;
Each with a picture in his heart of a dear Southern home—
O heaven, guard the homes till these brave wanderers shall come.

How they "illustrated Georgia" all along the well-fought front,
As 'mid the thickest of the fight they bore the battle's brunt.
How proudly waved the Southern Cross where'er their lot was cast.
Ah, Hill, the "band-box soldiers" are the fighting force at last!

The patrician was the private, high of soul and pure of blood,
And as if in armor clad, lo, how invincible he stood;
And on the weary road, anon, a soldier without peer,
He marched along with bleeding feet and sang a song of cheer.

Many moons had waxed and waned, yet they, on either stormy side
Of the classic old Potomac, sternly fought and bravely died.
Grim death had aimed his cruel shaft at many a shining mark,
And had crossed the Stygian river with his overladen barque.

Tongue of mortal ne'er can tell it, history can never show
Half the valor of the Southron as he met his Northern foe;
While nations gazed, awe-stricken, on the bitter, unmatched fray;
Marvelling the while they looked upon the troops who wore the gray.

O grand old uniform of gray, so faded, worn and old,
Yet covered many a princely form and many a heart of gold.
What if they wore the rough old jeans in the dark hour of need?
"A man's a man for a' that, and these be men indeed!"

On the fatal field, Cold Harbor, there their gallant leader fell,
And strong men looked their last upon the form they loved so well,
While pale lips whispered to sad hearts so full of grief and pride,
"He had lived long enough who in his country's cause had died."

Died at his post! O record meet for such exalted souls,
Who shall a bitter tribute ask for our beloved Doles?[114]
His life was o'er, mysterious fate denied him victory,
But blessed him at the last with glorious immortality.

Let us raise a fair white tablet o'er our honored chieftain's breast,
That shall tell in living words of him so early crowned and blest;
Of deathless love and memory, fresh from our hearts aglow,
And reverent passers by shall say, "Behold, they loved him so!"

There is no love like this, it fills his soldiers' hearts to-day;
Its height and depth be measured not, it fadeth not away;
'Twas born upon the battle-field where brave men's souls were tried,
It burns in every warrior's heart, whatever fate betide.

And sweet shall be his slumber in his own fair sunny clime,
For he sleeps in dear old Georgia, where for all the coming time
His flashing sword is sheathed, and with its wearer is laid down,
And the laurel wreath is but exchanged for the immortal crown.[115]
W. H. WILLIS

THE STARS & BARS

The stars and bars are fallen,
    And will never float again,
But bright on history's pages,
    It will live without a stain.

For proudest recollections
    Of battles fought and won,
And glorious deeds of valor,
    By Southern patriots done.

Will embalm in sacred memory
    That banner, bright and dear,
And sound it down the ages
    As the one without a peer.

'Twas born of stern oppression,
    And was cradled in the storm,
When retributive justice
    Rose demanding a reform,

And in the name of liberty
    Was christened in the blood
Of heroes and of patriots
    That flowed in crimson flood.

And thus endeared to freedom
    By every sacred tie,
Our hearts were rent with anguish
    When we saw it droop and die.

We held it in affection,
    And rejoiced to see it wave;
We loved the men who bore it,
    For they were true and brave.

We loved its holy cause,
    And the hopes that it inspired,
And we honor every martyr
    Who beneath its folds expired.

We reverence, too, the chieftains,
    Each and every separate name
Who 'neath that star-wreathed banner,
    Fought and won their glorious fame.

But supported not by nations
    Who beheld it from afar,
Alone it met the tempest
    On the fiery crest of war.

No nation recognized it,
    No arm was stretched to save;
But the world will ne'er forget it
    As the banner of the brave.

But now that flag is fallen,
    And will proudly float no more;
Our soldiers' tents are folded,
    And the din of war is o'er.

Our cannons' throats are silent,
    The sword is its sheath,
Our camps are all deserted
    Save the silent camps of death.

No sentinel now on duty
    Doth freedom's watch-words tell,
For liberty was ended
    When that glorious banner fell.[116]
O. T. DOZIER

First National Confederate Flag: the "Stars and Bars."

OUR BATTLE FLAG

Furl that flag, furl it gently,
    Touch sacredly its tattered shred;
Blackened and riddled, it speaks silently,
    Drooping and sad, of our honored dead.

It speaks of men who fought so valiantly,
    Now dead and forgotten, heroes unknown,
Who carried this flag, oh how bravely,
    Until death claimed them his own.

It speaks of the heroes still living,
    Who grasped this flag e'er it fell
From the clutch of a comrade falling,
    Bleeding and dying from the enemy's shell.

It speaks of moments when all seemed lost,
    From our ranks an unforgotten shout arose,
With maddened rush, at any cost.
    We wrenched our flag from the hand of foes.

It speaks of combats desperately fought
    From the dawn of day till the fall of night,
When in the darkness, with solemn thought,
    We prayed for souls that had taken flight.

It speaks of that pure and unequalled fame,
    And our hearts grow sad and proudest then,
As it utters that loved and cherished name
    Of heroines true, our Southern women.

It speaks of that awful and bitter day,
    Our hearts bowed down and broken asunder.
Unconquered we stood, standing at bay,
    When suddenly came the word, "Surrender."

For then did Lee, our grand old chieftain,
    Loving us well, he knew 'twas best
To bow to the will of God, not man,
    Our struggle was o'er history tells the rest.

Furl it, brave comrade, furl it with care.
    This dear old flag, for which we bled,
That the ravages of time may never wear
    This silent epitaph of a cause that is dead.[117]

H. L. BLANCHARD

IN MEMORIAM

To-day, though other lands rejoice,
We of the Smith, with lowered voice,
Bow at the shrine that shrouds our choice—
    The flag of the Confederacy.

To-day, out from the gloom of years,
Out from the sorrow and the tears
That flowed for heroes, there appears
    The peace of the Confederacy.

To-day, while Nature smiles all hues,
We of the South do not refuse
To don all colors—but we choose
    The gray of the Confederacy.

To-day, while songs of war and peace
Ring out, the battle now has ceased,
We still have "Dixie"—'tis at least
    The song of the Confederacy.

To-day, one day within the year,
They cannot bar our gath'ring here,
To lay fresh flowers on this bier—
    The bier of the Confederacy.

To-day, from out of mem'ry's wrecks,
We see the glory that bedecks
The hallowed mold the South protects—
    The graves of the Confederacy.

To-day, bejeweled by the light
Of many years, these deeds so bright
Still shine, all glorious in their right—
    The rights of the Confederacy.

For through all years this day we'll mark
With fair white stones, nor quench the spark
That burns on bright, in light or dark—
    The fame of the Confederacy.

Then lay sweet blossoms on their tomb
Mid tears and dew-drops—they shall bloom
Eternal in the world to come—
    Emblems of our Confederacy.[118]
RUTH CLIFFORD

THE DEATH OF STONEWALL JACKSON

We will rear for him the sacred fane,
    Who had a nation's tears;
No greater name is enwreathed with fame
    Than the one our Jackson wears.

He was the idol of our hearts,
    The champion of our cause;
He battled nobly for our rights,
    And gained the world's applause.

Our hearts were filled with gladness
    At the victories that he won
From Manassas to the Wilderness
    No cloud could dim his sun.

He cared for all with gentleness,
    He shared their common fate;
In cold and heat and weariness
    His goodness made him great.

The sun grew red with sorrow
    O'er Fredricksburg that even,
For on that sad to-morrow
    His last command was given.

In future years will linger
    Our youth beside his tomb,
And tell with pleasing wonder
    The fields his valor won.

At rest beyond the river.
    His marchings now are o'er;
By the tree of life forever,
    He dreams of strife no more.[119]
RUTH CLIFFORD

Stonewall Jackson.

SHERIDAN'S RAID IN THE JAMES RIVER VALLEY

Down thro' the heart of our beautiful land,
Swiftly and silently rode a strong band
Of Federal cavalry, spreading around,
And behind them the piteous sound
Of destruction, and burning, and miserable pain,
'Till even the echoes take up the refrain,
And all the bright, beautiful valley of James
Is blackened and ravaged with fury and flames.

Onward they come, relentless and strong,
Remorseless as fate, for to them shall belong
That cruelest, bitterest task in all war—
The bringing it home to the hearthstone and door,
The giving of homestead and barn to the torch,
The anguish of women and children, for such
An end fate decrees shall always attend
Brother's strife against brother, friend against friend.

Swiftly and silent, remorseless and strong,
The dark, blue thunder-cloud rolls along,
'Till the shades of evening begin to fall
Gently and calmly upon them all,
Victor and vanquished, friend and foe,
While the river murmurs in rhythmic flow,
And the breezes bring from the distant hill
God's own benison—"peace, be still."

"Halt!" the order runs down the line.
What sound is borne on the sleepy wind?
Nearer and nearer, distant and clear,
The tramping of horses comes to the ear,
And down a road to the left of their course
Quickly there comes a galloping horse,
Then another, 'till seeing the hostile train,
They turn and gallop the way they came.

Riding for life, while fuller and clearer
The sound of pursuit comes nearer and nearer;
Onward they dash in their desperate course;
Each man's life lies in the strength of his horse.
As they madly press on they well represent
The poor Southern Cause, so broken and spent—
A boy in his teens, a man war-worn and lame,
While fierce on their track a regiment came.

"Keep near!" groaned the man, with lips white and set;
"If I just keep the saddle we will distance them yet;
Your hand, quick, an instant, I'm slipping you see.
Oh God! if that shell had but left me my knee,
I'd still ride with the best. Hark, they gain on us fast.
I'd give life for a pistol, to have but one last
Good shot at the blue-coats, if just to requite
For the loss of my leg and this miserable flight."

"Don't turn your head," the boy eagerly cried;
"Speak not a word, for your life you must ride;
Down flat on your horse, I'll guide him all right;
Put your arms 'round his neck, quick, the leader's in sight.
How you reel in your saddle; don't try to look round.
Ho! steady, good horse—my God, he is down.
We are in for it now, they have us both fast;
I said I'd stand by him, and will to the last."

As a wild yell of triumph rings out on the air,
He springs from his horse, with the strength of despair;
Grasps the man in his arms, lifts him on to his steed,
Leaps back on his own and puts both to their speed;
But turns in his saddle to give a loud shout
Of mocking defiance. 'Tis vain to call out,
"Halt, or we fire!" As well to command
The outgoing tide to return to the strand.

"Stop, men," cried the officer; "not a step more;
So gallant an action I never before
Beheld in a lad of his years. Let them go;
To continue pursuit would serve but to show
Ourselves to be caitiffs, unworthy the name
Both of soldiers and men. I could hardly refrain
From cheering that brave 'little reb' on the spot.
We'll return to the main body; forward, then, trot."

'Tis many long years since the demon of war
Fled from our land. The grass grows o'er
Our ruins and graves. Still when memory turns
To review our dead past, then deeds like this boy's
Come to our remembrance, and bid us rejoice
That, tho' ruined and conquered, we're still not undone,
While our noble dead heroes yet live in their sons.[120]
MRS. M. G. MCCLELLAND

A GEORGIA VOLUNTEER

Death rode the field in hand with
Joyless fate, the unknown dead.
What mother, with long watching eyes,
And white lips cold and dumb,
Waits with appalling patience for
Her darling boy to come?
Her boy, whose grave swells up
But one of many a scar
Cut on the face of our fair land
By gory-handed war.

What fights he fought, what wounds he wore,
Are all unknown to fame;
Remember, on his lowly grave
There is not e'en a name!
That he fought well, and bravely, too,
And held his country dear,
We know, else he had not been
"A Georgia Volunteer!"

He sleeps—what need to question now
If he were wrong or right?
He knows ere this whose cause was just
In God the Father's sight.
He wields no warlike weapons now,
Returns no foeman's thrust.
Who but a coward would revile
An honest soldier's dust?

Roll, Shenandoah, proudly roll,
Adown the rocky glen,
Above thee lies the grave of one
of Stonewall Jackson's men!
Beneath the cedar and the pine,
In solitude austere,
Unknown, unnamed, forgotten lies
"A Georgia volunteer."[121]
FLORA ADAMS DARLING

THE BATTLE OF SHILOH

From its sources in the mountains,
    Gushing forth from many a glen,
With its many crystal fountains,
    Far beyond the haunts of men;
Swelling fast and roaring louder
    In its mighty power and glee,
Sweeping on by lonely Shiloh,
    Flows the grand old Tennessee.

Sunshine beams in tender glory,
    Springtime breezes softly blow
O'er the spot that soon in story
    A bloody name is doomed to know.
April showers fall like teardrops
    Where men's graves are soon to be,
On the grass-grown sod of Shiloh
    Near the shores of Tennessee.

Sunset shed its palling splendor
    O'er the landscape calm and still,
Stars come out and gaze in tender
    Pity o'er the death doomed hill;
Midnight falls, and white winged spirits,
    Flitting o'er the world in glee,
Pause and gaze on lovely Shiloh,
    Near the shores of Tennessee.

But with sunrise sounds a death note,
    E'en the cannon clear and loud,
And in fierce and deadly combat
    Face to face two armies crowd!
Louder, hotter grows the battle,
    As the men on both sides see
They must fight like men at Shiloh,
    On the shores of Tennessee!

And as noonday's lurid glory
    Once more gilds the southern sky,
On the field, upturned and gory,
    Many hearts all pulseless lie!
Johnston, with the rest, lies dying—
    What a grand, good man was he!
His brave soul takes flight at Shiloh—
    Shiloh on the Tennessee!

Once again night's peaceful curtain
    Falls around the death-strewn place,
Until morn it is not certain
    Which side victory's honors grace;
But with dawn the battle rages,
    And it shortly proves to be
That her own are doomed at Shiloh,
    Shiloh on the Tennessee!

Once more midnight's holy breezes
    Kiss the upturned faces there,
As many a manly bosom freezes,
    Many a death-groan cuts the air.
Many a wife is left a widow,
    Many a mother's heart will be
Broken as the news from Shiloh
    Is wafted down the Tennessee!

Angels through the air seem wailing
    O'er the world that faints in tears,
For in blood and dust lie trailing
    Hopes that once could feel no fears;
And they droop their wings in sadness
    As in blood they bend the knee,
Bow their heads and weep o'er Shiloh,
    Shiloh on the Tennessee.[122]
ANNIE JOHNSTON

EXALTATION OF THE CONFEDERATE BANNER

    Are those voices from the skies?
    Can the dead in truth arise?
    Who sees not that spirit band?
    Who hears not that chorus grand?
Or is it the lore of the sunset life?
With voices and visions the air is rife!

    On what mission have they come?
    Without bugle call or drum,
    Yet in serried lines they form,
    Rank on rank, and swarm on swarm!
And, circling, they wheel from Potomac's strand,
Traversing the whole of our Southern land.

    See what banner o'er them waves!
    Round it are the gray-clad braves,
    Now from hate and malice free,
    Type of all the noble Lee!
And gladly do all that gathering host
Assign unto them true glory's high post.

    Mingled are the blue and gray!
    Hostile no more in array,
    Now, united heart and hand,
    Form they but one brother-band!
And loudly they shout as they come to rest,
We hail thee, brave flag, thou purest and best!

    Spotless are thy gallant folds!
    Spirit pure thy staff upholds
    High above all mortal feet!
    Plucked from what seemed foul defeat,
Exalted art thou in thy Southern sky,
The proud oriflamme of each brave man's eye!

    Brightly shineth thy fair cross,
    Purged from all of human dross,
    Sit to guide each gallant eye
    That would nobly dare to die!
And round thee are gath'ring the bravest and best
Of those who through suff'ring have won their rest!

    All who have cross-bearers been
    In this world of grief and sin;

Who for right have borne defeat,
Who have walked with bleeding feet—
Assembling they come from each clime and age,
The martyr, the patriot, hero, sage!

    Fairest thou art, Southern land!
    Shineth brightest, thy true band!
    Comfort thee! thy children brave
    Thee will cherish, love and save!
And out of thine ashes thou'lt rise and soar,
Rejoicing, in triumph for evermore.

    Lands devoid of ruins, wrongs,
    Voiceless are of heroes' songs.
    Scars are on thy noble breast;
    Them they'll hide with love's rich rest.
Forgiving thy wrongs, thou wilt foes repay
With blessings free scattered along thy way!

    Had I Alston's magic brush,
    Painting visions as they rush,
    Lightning like, athwart the sky,
    Ere they fade from mortal eye.
Rejoicing, I'd show to our Southern youth
Their fathers' grand struggles for right and truth.

    Comrades, come, in love's pure zest!
    Vow, each one, with hand on breast,
    That our South again shall rise,
    Soaring upward to'ard the skies;
And, up as she mounts on bright, golden wing,
Rich blessings to all from her breast she'll fling!

    Hear, O God, our vows and pray'rs!
    Bottle up our bitter tears!
    Heal our land, by hatred rent!
    Save from wrathful discontent!
And, one by one, as we go, may we sing,
Departing in peace, "We are sons of the King."[123]
JOHN MANLY RICHARDSON

THE SOUTHERN REPUBLIC

In the galaxy of nations,
    A nation's flag's unfurled,
Transcending in its martial pride
    The nations of the world.
Though born of war, baptized in blood,
    Yet mighty from the time,
Like fabled phoenix, forth she stood—
    Dismembered, yet sublime.

And braver heart, and bolder hand,
    Ne'er formed a fabric fair
As Southern wisdom can command,
    And Southern valor rear.
Though kingdoms scorn to own her sway,
    Or recognize her birth,
The land blood-bought for Liberty
    Will reign supreme on earth.

Clime of the Sun! Home of the Brave!
    Thy sons are bold and free,
And pour life's crimson tide to save
    Their birthright, Liberty!
Their fertile fields and sunny plains
    That yield the wealth alone,
That's coveted for greedy gains
    By despots—and a throne!

Proud country! battling, bleeding, torn,
    Thy altars desolate;
Thy lovely dark-eyed daughters mourn
    At war's relentless fate;
And widow's prayers, and orphan's tears,
    Her homes will consecrate,
While more than brass or marble rears
    The trophy of her great.

Oh! land that boasts each gallant name
    Of Jackson, Johnston, Lee,
And hosts of valiant sons, whose fame
    Extends beyond the sea;
Far rather let thy plains become,
    From gulf to mountain cave,
One honored sepulchre and tomb,
    Than we the tyrant's slave!

Fair, favored land! thou mayst be free,
    Redeemed by blood and war;
Through agony and gloom we see
    Thy hope—a glimmering star;
Thy banner, too, may proudly float,
    A herald on the seas—
Thy deeds of daring worlds remote
    Will emulate and praise!

But who can paint the impulse pure,
    That thrills and nerves thy brave
To deeds of valor, that secure
    The rights their fathers gave?
Oh! grieve not, hearts; her matchless slain,
    Crowned with the warrior's wreath,
From beds of fame their proud refrain
    Was "Liberty or Death!"[124]
OLIVIA TULLY THOMAS

THE DEATH OF JEB STUART

Night wraps the slumb'ring camp about
    With fast increasing gloom,
When on the silence breaks a shout
    That speaks of pending doom.
Hoarse sentry's challenge, rude alarms
    Of cries and tramping feet;
The drowsy troopers fly to arms
    Expected foes to meet.
But see, a friend! the countersign
    Is given, picket passed,
And breathless, foaming, down the line
    He rushes, lightning fast:
"Ye Southern men, our city fair,
    The Mecca of our land.
Is doomed within a day to bear
    The weight of foeman's hand.
Phil Sheridan, the ruthless, rides
    With twenty thousand horse,
And, lest some accident betides
    To stop him in his course.
To-morrow's sun will set upon
    Our city given o'er
To foes whom even women shun.
    Remember Shenandoah!"
To Stuart thus the rider spake.
    Then turned and rode away,
While I they prepared the race to make
    Against the dawn of day.
The bugle sounds, and weary men
    Mount quick their jaded steeds;
No thought of sleep nor hunger then,
    They go where Stuart leads.
Their leader's face new life imparts
    In battle's fiery wrath;
Nor wounds nor death such rock-ribbed hearts
    Can fright from duty's path.
Oh, on! the dreaded foe doth knock
    At Richmond's very gates!
To-morrow brings the battle's shock,
    Scorn him who hesitates!
Day breaks; the battle gains apace,
    The sun is screened from sight,
While Stuart, 'gainst a kindred race,
    Does battle for the right.
Now strike for "Dixie," home and friends,

While "Stuart" is the cry
That to each arm uplifted lends
    The strength to do or die.
The serried ranks advance, retreat,
    The earth shakes 'neath their tread,
They trample 'neath their horses
    The corpses of the dead.
Sore pressed, the line of gray gives way
    Before the stronger blue.
Their chieftain dies; they hear him say,
    "Brave men, stand fast and true!"
While spurring hotly to the front
    Thro' hissing, leaden air,
He seeks the battle's very brunt
    To lead in person there.
He wins, but gives his precious life
    Our liberty to save;
This bitter, fratricidal strife
    Hath filled a hero's grave.
"Go back! each one your duty do
    As I mine own have done!"
Immortal words! Ye show how true
    This dying Southern son.
Our nation weeps with covered head
    While freedom's sadd'ning groan
Proclaims the peerless Stuart dead
    God taketh back his own,
But lives heroic, lives sublime,
    End not with fleeting breath;
They are as jewels set in Time,
    Whose luster o'ercometh death.
Forever thro' the years that lapse
    Shall ghastly banners wave,
While glory's bugle sounds the "taps"
    O'er deathless Stuart's grave.[125]
ALBERT SIDNEY MORTON

Jeb Stuart.

TO SOUTH CAROLINA'S DEAD CONFEDERATE HEROES

The heralds of eternal fame
    Of martyred dead should be
The voices of the glorious land
    And of the sadder sea.

Then we will woo the whispering winds
    To sing unto the sea
The saddened songs that ever bind
    Our ladened hearts to thee.

Great leaders of the hard-fought fights,
    Your battles o'er and done,
We'll give you praises through the night
    And 'neath the splendid sun.

To Barnard Bee, who named "Stonewall,"
    No immortelles we'll bring,
But 'mid the tall Palmetto's shade
    The mocking birds shall sing.

For Jenkins, best loved of his men,
    Who perished at their hands,
The sad sea waves, with moan and fret,
    Shall sing upon the sands.

Our Anderson, the Christian knight,
    Though "Fighting Dick" by name,
The fire flies, with flashing lights,
    Shall blazon forth his fame.

And Ripley, soldier brave, we'll praise
    With sea bird's weird-like call.
As fitting prelude to the tale
    Our wondering minds enthrall.

For Clement Stevens, Charleston's own,
    The "Iron Battery" sage.
All nature sings in unison,
    The world's book holds his page.

Heroic Elliott, Sumter's pride,
    The Bayard of his State—
The meteor, blazing through the sky,
    Portrays his most sad fate.

Of States Rights Gist, who fought and died
    Like knights of other days,
The whip-poor wills through summer's night
    Chant sweet but dirge-like lays.

Though Beauregard we may not claim
    By birthright as our own,
Yet when we sing our vesper hymns
    Our heart strings give the tone.

The sea, the seas, with ocean's roar,
    Doth pean Ingraham's glory;
The land, the lands reverberate
    This hero's famous story.

And Tom Huger, sublimely brave,
    Who fought his ship so well—
Go ask the spirits of the deep
    If still they feel his spell.

Our privates sleeping on the hills,
    Our sailors on the shore,
With graves moaning o'er their heads,
    At rest for evermore.

The God of peace above them all,
    Their flag forever furled,
We'll bow the knee in silent prayer,
    Poor fighters in the world.[126]
JAMES G. HOLMES

States Rights Gist.

A CONFEDERATE CAPTIVE ON LAKE ERIE

A captive on a lake-girt isle
    Looks o'er the waters sadly;
His thoughts on one whose blessed smile
    Would welcome him so gladly.
But that beneath a Northern sky,
    A sky to him so dreary,
He's doomed to pine and vainly sigh,
    Away out on Lake Erie.

The winds that waft to others bliss,
    But mock him with their tone,
The lips are pale they stoop to kiss,
    With yearning for his home;
The waves that dash upon the beach,
    Keep careless guard and weary,
They chant of joys beyond the reach
    Of him who looks on Erie.

They bear to him his mother's tone,
    His sister's mournful song,
Until he longs to be alone,
    Far from that captive throng;
And when he lays him down to sleep
    With aching heart and weary,
The winds and waves his vigils keep,
    Dear dreamer on Lake Erie.

But all who love him pray to God,
    To bless his precious life
With "patience" to endure the rod,
    With "faith" to close the strife;
And look beyond the dreary "now,"
    To brighter days and better,
When native winds shall fan his brow
    And only fond arms fetter.[127]

CONFEDERATE COLONEL C. W. FRAZER

WILLIE PRESTON—DEAD

Leave me to my speechless sorrow,
    Leave me to my pallid gloom,
Shut away the mocking sunlight,
    Take its burden from the room!

What are words but empty rattle,
    Words that murmur of relief,
In the deadly single-handed
    Struggle with the monster, grief.

Can I reason down my anguish?
    Can I talk my pain away?
Let the door be closed between us,
    Let me meet it as I may!

Dead! poor lips repeat, repeat it;
    Wrench from out that word of dread,
All the sharpest sting of meaning
    Wrapped within it, he is dead!

Dead! my Willie in his beauty,
    E'er the morning flush of joy
Yet had caught the chastening shadow
    Manhood flings around the boy.

Dead! my loving, gentle hearted,
    Noblest, bravest of the brave,
Fallen midst the rush of battle,
    Buried in a nameless grave!

He whose look and tone grew tender
    At a dear one's faintest moan,
All unwatched, unwept, unheeded,
    He to perish thus, alone!

Who can tell me of his longings?
    If he named his father's name,
If he softly murmured "sister,"
    When the ghastly struggle came?

If he breathed no parting message,
    As he pale and placid lay,
If his radiant smile still lingered
    When his soul had passed away?

If a consecrating calmness
    Kept upon his clay-cold brow?
None can tell me! These are secrets
    God hath in his keeping now.

All love's sweetest ministrations,
    All its needs for him are o'er.
Never will he cross the threshold
    Of the old familiar door.

Never will his ringing laughter
    Echo joyous through the hall,
Never will I answer gaily
    To his fond caressing call.

Never press his smooth white forehead,
    Never stroke his shining hair,
Never feel his arm about me,
    Never greet his smile so rare!

Ever miss the matchless kindness
    Strewn through every word he said,
Ever wail that blank of absence,
    Ever mourn my darling dead!

Dead! oh, grief has drowned my vision,
    Blotted all the gladness o'er,
Made me half forget "he liveth"
    As he never lived before.

That he was not all so lonely,
    Tho' no loved one closed his eye,
That the blessed Christ sustained him
    When he laid him down to die.[128]
M. J. P.

THE SOUTHERN CROSS

Freedom's blazing constellation,
Welcomed by the acclamation
Of a giant infant nation,
    Rose the Southern Cross.

Aye, to keep it where they found it,
In the heavens. Ne'er to ground it
Swore ten thousands madly 'round it—
    'Round the Southern Cross.

Matchless chiefs (a world admiring)
Wondrous deeds of valor firing,
'Neath its blazing light inspiring,
    Led the Southern Cross.

And our hopes grew higher, higher,
For the end seemed drawing nigher,
When above Manassas' fire
    Waved the Southern Cross.

'Mid the battle's lurid glaring,
Where the torch of war was flaring,
Ever where were deeds of daring,
    Gleamed the Southern Cross.

And the Northern heavens paling,
While the stoutest of them quailing
Watched in terror unavailing,
    Shone the Southern Cross.

O'er the dead and with the dying,
In the face of foemen flying,
"Down for aye with tyrants!" crying.
    Swept the Southern Cross.

Heroes bore it, proud to wave it,
Glad to give their blood to lave it,
Trusty swords were bared to save it—
    Save the Southern Cross.

Gallant lads, their faith defending,
Careless of the fate impending,
Sank to rest with angels tending
    'Neath the Southern Cross.

But 'twas fruitless immolation;
Over vandal desecration,
Over death and desolation,
　　Drooped the Southern Cross.

Lost was all for which we'd striven.
Like a bolt from heaven driven,
Like the oak by lightning riven,
　　Fell the Southern Cross.

Ages hence will tell the story
How, tho' tattered, torn and gory,
In a sea of blazing glory,
　　Set the Southern Cross.[129]
ALBERT SIDNEY MORTON

THE SOLDIER'S GRAVE

Tread lightly, 'tis a soldier's grave,
    A lonely, mossy mound;
And yet to hearts like mine and thine
    It should be holy ground.

Speak softly, let no careless laugh,
    No idle, thoughtless jest,
Escape your lips where sweetly sleeps
    The hero in his rest.

For him no reveille will beat
    When morning beams shall come;
For him, at night, no tattoo rolls
    Its thunders from the drum.

Tread lightly! for a man bequeathed,
    Ere laid beneath this sod,
His ashes to his native land,
    His gallant soul to God.[130]
PEARL RIVERS

THE JACKET OF GRAY

Fold it up carefully, lay it aside;
Tenderly touch it, look at it with pride;
For dear must it be to our hearts evermore,
The jacket of gray our loved soldier boy wore.

Can we ever forget when he joined the brave band,
Who rose in defense of our dear Southern land,
And in his bright youth hurried on to the fray—
How proudly he donned it—the jacket of gray?

His fond mother blessed him and looked up above,
Commending to Heaven the child of her love;
What anguish was her's, mortal tongue cannot say,
When he passed from her sight in the jacket of gray.

But her country had called, and she would not repine,
Though costly the sacrifice placed on its shrine;
Her heart's dearest hopes on its altar she lay,
When she sent out her boy in the jacket of gray.

Months passed and War's thunder rolled over the land,
Unsheathed was the sword, and lighted the brand;
We heard in the distance the sounds of the fray,
And prayed for our boy in the jacket of gray.

Ah! vain, all, all vain were our prayers and our tears,
The glad shout of victory rang in our ears;
But our treasured one on the red battlefield lay,
While the life-blood oozed out on the jacket of gray.

His young comrades found him, and tenderly bore
The cold lifeless form to his home by the shore;
Oh, dark were our hearts on that terrible day,
When we saw our dead boy in the jacket of gray.

Ah! spotted and tattered, and stained now with gore,
Was the garment which once he so proudly wore;
We bitterly wept as we took it away,
And replaced with death's white robe the jacket of gray.

We laid him to rest in his cold narrow bed,
And graved on the marble we placed o'er his head,
As the proudest tribute our sad hearts could pay,
He never disgraced the jacket of gray.

Then fold it up carefully, lay it aside.
Tenderly touch it, look on it with pride;
For dear must it be to our hearts evermore,
The jacket of gray our loved soldier boy wore![131]
CAROLINE AUGUSTA BALL

STACK ARMS BOYS, ALL IS O'ER

Ah, yes! this is the saddest day of all the blessed year,
For still the echo of those mournful words I seem to hear,
    "Stack arms, boys, all is o'er."

Though three decades have passed since then, I hear them still,
As through the portals of the past they come my soul to thrill,
    "Stack arms, boys, all is o'er."

They gave the death blow to our hopes, and left naught in their stead
Save love for those who guided us, and reverence for our dead.
    "Stack arms, boys, all is o'er."

As thus with heads low bowed we stood, a mist came o'er our eyes,
And something on our gray coats fell, that falls when loved one dies.
    "Stack arms, boys, all is o'er."

For through the vista of the future years looked grim despair,
And desolated homes, in which were vacant chairs stood there;
    "Stack arms, boys, all is o'er."

And now the old gray coat and hat must hang upon the wall,
For ne'er again shall wearer answer to the bugle call.
    "Stack arms, boys, all is o'er."

Aye, yes! this is the saddest day of all the blessed year,
For still the echo of those fatal words I seem to hear,
    "Stack arms, boys, all is o'er."[132]
MRS. F. G. DE FONTAINE

MY SOUTH! MY SOUTH!

Bend low, thou loved one, to my song of love,
    Thy child of battle, daughter of the storm,
Whose infant years were cradled on thy shield,
    Whose wondering eyes saw first thine armored form.

For I must sing thee, though thy fallen state
    Left but a sword gleam for a trusting smile,
And gave the first print of my baby feet
    Unto the prison earth of Johnson's Isle.

Yea, I will sing thee, though my pipes forget
    And voice sometime the strain thou knowest well;
Remember love, thou couldst not close my ears
    Against the music of the whizzing shell.

But if I pain thee with a martial prayer,
    Mine first in war, mine last, in mantling peace,
Lay thou thy soft hand on my throbbing heart,
    And bid the plaining of thy minstrel cease.

Thou art mine own, my beautiful, my love!
    I blame thee not, what cloud may come to me;
I give my faith into thy trustful arms;
    All that I am, or hope, I yield to thee!

Thy foot rests on the fairest spot of earth,
    Thine eyes are full of heaven's holy blue,
The sunlit kiss of peace is on thy brow,
    O thou, mine own, the beautiful, the true!

Let my right hand forget her tricks of art
    Ere I conceal the faith that lies in me,
And let my tongue forget to utter love
    If I pay homage unto aught but thee!

I trim my taper, but to seek the shrine—
    With thee I smile, with thee I breathe my sigh;
Yea, as thou goest, loved one, I will go,
    And when thou diest, Beautiful, I die![133]

VIRGINIA FRAZER BOYLE

MY CONFEDERATE UNIFORM

When first I put this uniform on,
    A hotspur of fifteen,
Mother and sister had I none;
Brothers? Hal was the only one;
I was the Benjamin—youngest son—
Sighing for victories to be won
    Ere I had turned sixteen,
As we marched proudly away.

At Petersburg my brother died,
    In the crater's awful zone;
In that red hell
Of flame and shell,
He breathed farewell,
As he foremost fell;
    I trod war's path alone,
And I marched sadly on.[134]
ONE OF "LEE'S MISERABLES"

ASHES OF GLORY

Fold up the gorgeous silken sun,
    By bleeding martyrs blest,
And heap the laurels it has won
    Above its place of rest.

No trumpet's note need hardly blare,
    No drum funereal roll,
Nor trailing sables drape the bier
    That frees a dauntless soul!

It lived with Lee, and decked his brow
    From Fate's empyreal Palm;
It sleeps the sleep of Jackson now,
    As spotless and as calm.

It was outnumbered, not outdone,
    And they shall shuddering tell
Who struck the blow; its latest gun
    Flashed ruin as it fell.

Sleep, shrouded Ensign! not the breeze
    That smote the victor tar
With death across the heaving seas
    Of fiery Trafalgar;

Not Arthur's knights, amid the gloom,
    Their knightly deeds have starred;
Not Gallic Henry's matchless plume,
    Nor peerless born Bayard.

Not all that antique fables feign,
    And Orient dreams disgorge;
Nor yet the silver cross of Spain,
    And Lion of St. George.

Can bid thee pale! Proud emblem, still
    Thy crimson glory shines
Beyond the lengthened shades that fill
    Their proudest kingly lines.

Sleep in thine own historic night,
    And be thy blazoned scroll;
A warrior's banner takes its flight
    To greet the warrior's soul![135]
JUDGE AUGUSTUS JULIAN REQUIER

LEE AT APPOMATTOX

The last gun was fired, the last roll was called,
Half starved, half naked, grim, gaunt, unappalled,
Stained with blood and powder the old army stood.
"I have done, my brave soldiers, all things for your good."

Thus spake their great leader, deep grief on his face,
While a halo of glory illumined the place.
Some trailed their muskets and some sheathed their swords.
They had smiled at Grant's cannon, they wept at Lee's words.

And Grant was as courteous as the grand knights of old;
No glad shouts were uttered, no loud drums were rolled.
And the victors saluted those gaunt men in gray,
And the fire-winged tempest died slowly away.[136]
J. A. BOOTY

EPITAPH ON STONEWALL JACKSON

This monument—
The gift of friends in England—
Was brought across the sea and raised
In the city of Richmond,
In the State of Virginia,
His mother,
To the memory of
Thomas Jonathan Jackson,
Who,
Living in an age of principle,
Chose what was a losing cause;
But to that cause
He gave a faith so true, a spirit so pure,
A genius so grand in a mold so heroic,
That his countrymen revered him,
Even his enemies honored him,
And a distant people, reading a lofty nature in lofty works,
Called him great!
His life was one of many and sharp contrastings,
Yet the meek simplicity that marked his character
Welded these into harmony.
A devout Christian, he was none the less a bold soldier;
In peace, tender of the humblest; in battle, his was a sword that
Conjured victory.
Strong in the qualities that shine most fitly in civil life—
A mild teacher gathering the peaceful harvest of youthful minds,
In war, approved of conscience, he towered a prayerful giant.
And, on historic fields, rivaled the choicest deeds of his
Most famous predecessors;
In every phase of his stainless career,
In his home, among men, with his pupils,
In his State's brightest hour, in her darkest,
He stood, ever, in himself,
The type of a noble race's noblest teachings;
And his fame,
Rounded in all, guarded from wrong by the verdict of his
    contemporaries,
Shall, when men's places come to be fixed by the recurrent generations,
Stand, before its judges, firm like a stone wall.[137]
JOHN B. S. DIMITRY

A RAINBOW FROM LOOKOUT MOUNTAIN

I stood on the cliff at twilight,
The cliff that o'erlooks the plain,
And I said: "There fought they the battle,
And there lie buried the slain."

And I gazed far over the valley
To the mountains that girdle the plain,
And I said: "Those mountains so lofty
Will ever stand guard o'er the slain."

Then I stood on the cliff at midnight,
But naught could I see of the plain,
For a soft sea of mist floated o'er it,
And enveloped the graves of the slain.

On this mist, so like a white ocean,
There floated a ship in the night,
It moved without sound or commotion,
So softly—I gazed in affright.

Then I heard mid the stillness a murmur
Borne gently across the white main:
"For the right we all fell in this battle,
For our country we fought on this plain."

I stood on the cliff as the rain fell,
A rainbow arched over the plain,
And its opaline tints made glorious
The spot where lie buried the slain.

I said: "'Tis a sign sent from heaven,
To tell us that never again
Will the hand of brother 'gainst brother
Be raised on this far-reaching plain."[138]
F. G. R.

FLAG OF THE TWELFTH MISSISSIPPI REGIMENT

Only a piece of bunting; soiled by the weather and torn,
Valueless, save to the worthy who followed where it was borne;
Dirty, a term most contemptuous! tattered and gone to decay:
No charm to present to the many; alas! it has served its day.

It's day was a time when heroes fought
Amid flashing of cannon, when the air was fraught
With the groans of the dying, and cries of pain
Of thousands of soldiers who lay 'mong the slain.

Only a star, dim and fallen, a star fast fading from sight—
One of a fair constellation—lost in the darkness of night;
A star, which forever has set, but whose history ever will tell
Of the deeds of "the boys in gray," who under its shadows fell.[139]
CONFEDERATE CAPTAIN FRED J. V. LECAND

TO THE DEPARTING CONFEDERATE SOLDIERS

One by one they pass away,
    Cross the river one by one;
And the shadows of to-day
    Darken the departing sun.
'Tis a hero falling, seeking
    In eternity sweet rest,
While his country's tears are reeking
    Sorrow's passion rends the breast
Of the chivalry and beauty
    South of Dixie's magic line.

One by one the ranks are thinning,
    And a comrade falls to sleep.
Death invades our sanctum, winning
    Jewels rare we fain would keep;
Jewels from the Southern cross,
    Tried by fires of deadly war,
Who shall recompense our loss?
    Will their spirits from afar
Whisper us some consolation,
    Minister at freedom's shrine?[140]
SMITH JOHNSON

CONFEDERATE MEMORIAL DAY

Memorial Day once more returns,
And in each loyal heart there burns
    A feeling sacred, pure.
It is to honor first our dead,
Who for us fought and for us bled,
    And for us did endure.

Young soldiers then who wore the gray,
Now old, yet stand barehead to-day
    Around their comrades' graves.
They come, with firm and solemn tread,
To pay heart tribute to the dead.
    These war-worn veteran braves.

With children's children hand in hand,
The young and old together stand
    Around our honored dead.
The young with fresh spring flowers appear;
The old bring but the gathering tear:
    With love each tribute's paid.

We also, in appropriate way,
Now celebrate the natal day
    Of our loved chief and head.
Beside the James he sweetly sleeps,
And Richmond's vigil ever keeps
    A guard around his bed.

Then let us through all future time
Keep green these memories sublime,
    All covered o'er with glory.
And let us to our children tell,
Of how they fought and how they fell,
    For 'tis a wondrous story.[141]

MRS. J. WILLIAM JONES

MY LITTLE VOLUNTEER

Say, have you seen my Harry, my little volunteer?
    As fine a lad as ever lived upon the Tennessee,
His voice so rich and cheery, his eye so bright and clear;
    Why has my darling ne'er come back to me?

He went to strike for freedom, to defend his State and home,
    When but sixteen at the birth of May;
None looked half so gay and bold, in garbs of gray and gold;
    But I never saw him after they marched away.

The whippoorwill is calling to her mate upon the hill,
    As they did the night he went away;
And my heart is just as lonely, and the sorrow rankles still,
    When I sit alone and listen to the mournful, heartsick lay.

Oft I reach my arms in yearning as I gaze toward the town,
    For he said he'd soon return to me;
But my heart is broke with longing—he is so long in coming
    To the dear ones waiting here upon the Tennessee.[142]
JOE BRENTWOOD

THE HERO, STONEWALL JACKSON

Thou image of a nation's pride,
    The star of hope amid our fears,
The hero among heroes tried,
    The noblest among noble peers:
To thee we bring, embalmed in tears,
A nation's love, a nation's cheers.

Our tears must fall that thou hast died,
    Our cheers will rise that thou didst live,
And those who battled by thy side
    Their tears and cheers together give.
O soldiers, battle-scarred and strong,
With moistened eye your cheers prolong!

Bring flowers to drape the hero's brow,
    Sweet flowers from soil his blood has stained.
He sleeps among those blossoms now:
    His war is passed, his victory gained.
Bring lily crowns and asphodel
To tell of climes where martyrs dwell.

Awake, ye cannon deep and long,
    The thunders that he knew so well!
Amidst your storm his soul was strong,
    'Tis meet that you his fame should swell!
To him your voice of power and might
Spoke but of deeds for truth and right![143]
MRS. MAY M. ANDERSON

Stonewall Jackson.

LETTERS FROM VETERANS

Not far ahead we all shall camp,
    Beyond life's battle lines,
With comrade true who marched in front
    And rest beneath the pines.

The reveille, the call to arms,
    For us no more shall sound,
Nor thundering arms disturb our sleep,
    Who bivouac under ground.

Let silent stars stand sentinel,
    No foe invades our grave;
The Captain of salvation comes
    To furlough home the brave.[144]
H. C. SIMMONS

TRIBUTE TO UNCROWNED HEROES

Let none declare that we are blind
    To bravery of friend or foe;
Though costly marble may not mark
    Each martyred brow that lieth low,
    We honor all.

The tears we shed o'er Southern graves,
    That fall upon each rose-gemmed bed,
Are for the private as the chief.
    There is no rank among the dead;
    God loves them all.

Salvation's starry helm is theirs,
    As bright for each as other;
The banner and the sword is cleansed,
    And Heaven, common mother,
    Hath crowned them all.[145]

RUBY BERYL KYLE

Confederate war heroes.

PRESIDENT DAVIS

The cell is lonely, and the night
    Has filled it with a darker gloom;
The little rays of friendly light,
    Which through each crack and chink found room
To press in with their noiseless feet,
All merciful and fleet,
And bring, like Noah's trembling dove,
God's silent messages of love—
      These, too, are gone,
      Shut out, and gone,
And that great heart is left alone.

Alone, with darkness and with woe,
    Around him Freedom's temple lies,
Its arches crushed, its columns low,
    The night-wind through its ruin sighs;
Rash, cruel hands that temple razed,
Then stood the world amazed!
And now those hands—ah, ruthless deeds!
Their captive pierce—his brave heart bleeds;
      And yet no groan
      Is heard, no groan!
He suffers silently, alone.

For all his bright and happy home,
    He has that cell, so drear and dark,
The narrow walls, for heaven's blue dome,
    The clank of chains, for song of lark;
And for the grateful voice of friends—
That voice which ever lends
Its charm where human hearts are found—
He hears the key's dull, grating sound;
      No heart is near,
      No kind heart near,
No sigh of sympathy, no tear!

Jefferson Davis.

Oh, dream not thus, thou true and good
    Unnumbered hearts on thee await,
By thee invisibly have stood,
    Have crowded through thy prison-gate;
Nor dungeon bolts, nor dungeon bars,
Nor floating "stripes and stars,"
Nor glittering gun or bayonet,
Can ever cause us to forget
      Our faith to thee,
      Our love to thee,
Thou glorious soul! thou strong! thou free![146]
JANE T. H. CROSS

WEARING THE GRAY

Wearing the gray, wearing the gray—
Struggling alone in the world of to-day,
Battling for bread in the battle of life
With courage as grand as they rode to the strife;
Marching to beat of toil's merciless drum;
Longing for comrades who never shall come,
Comrades who sleep where they fell in the fray,
Dead and immortal, in jackets of gray!
    Wearing the gray o'er the furrows of care—
    Mortality's banner that time planted there—
    Wearing a gray while the teams upward start,
    A gray that is buried down deep in the heart.

Wearing the gray, wearing the gray—
The old line marches in mem'ry to-day,
The old drums beat and the old flags wave—
How the dead gray jackets spring up from the grave!
They rush on with Forrest where young gods would yield!
They sweep with Cleburne the shell-harrowed field!
They laugh at the bolts from the batteries hurled,
Yet weep around Lee when the last flag is furled.
    Wearing the gray o'er the foreheads of white,
    Time's banner of truce for the end of the fight;
    Wearing a gray that was worn long ago,
    With their face to the front and their front to the foe.

Wearing the gray, wearing the gray—
Longing to bivouac over the way,
To rest o'er the river in the shade of the trees
And furl the old flag to eternity's breeze;
To camp by the stream of that evergreen shore,
And meet with the boys who have gone on before;
To stand at inspection mid pillars of light,
While God turns the gray into robings of white.
    Wearing the gray o'er the temples of snow
    The drum beat is quick, but the paces are slow!
    Wearing a gray for the camp of the blest
    When life's fight is o'er and the rebel shall rest.

Wearing the gray, wearing the gray—
Almost in the valley, almost in the spray,
Waiting for taps when the light shall go out,
Yet hoping to wake with a reveille shout!
Leaving to Heaven the right and the wrong,
Praying for strength in the old battle song,

Praying for strength in the last ditch to stay
When Death turns his guns on the old head of gray.
    Wearing the gray in the whiteness of death,
    For the angel has swept with a garnering breath,
    Wearing a gray when he wakes in the morn—
    The old rebel jacket our dead boy had on![147]
JOHN MOORE JR.

Stephen D. Lee.

AN INCIDENT OF BATTLE

A drummer boy fell in heat of battle,
    Only a lad in a suit of gray;
He heard the shouts and the musketry's rattle
    Over the field where the wounded lay.
No one could help while the guns were raking
    Meadow and wood with their leaden hail;
"The foe has charged and our lines are breaking!
    The day is lost!" was his bitter wail.

He closed his eyes while the shock and thunder
    Of awful carnage was opened anew,
Then fainted away. Was it any wonder,
    When another bullet had pierced him through?
He roused at last, and the tide of battle
    Again had changed, for he heard the fray
In the wood beyond, with the ceaseless rattle
    Of shot and shell in their deadly play.

His lips were parched and his throat was burning:
    "O for some water!" he faintly sighed.
He heard, at his feet, the labored turning
    Of a prostrate form, while a clear voice cried:
"My canteen's full, but my arms are broken;
    See, you can reach, if you bend this way."
He moved and groaned, and with thanks unspoken
    Reached for the water, then shrank away.

He saw, with a start and a sudden quiver,
    The youth at his feet wore a suit of blue,
And he marked the frown and the creeping shiver
    Which mastered and held him, and thrilled him through,
At sound of the yell from the rebel forces
    Which told the tale that the fight was done.
To the Southern lad, how the fresh life courses
    Along his veins, for the day is won

"See, here is the water!" The youth had rallied,
    And moved still nearer the form in gray;
It cost him much, for his face grew pallid;
    He gasped, yet struggled to faintly say:
"I'd reach you the can, but my arms are shattered."
    Then closed his eyes in a deathlike swoon.
He had given his all to a foe! What mattered,
    When all would be ended so swift and soon?

With a sob in his throat for the hero before him,
    The drummer boy turned, and with tremulous touch
On the pale face sprinkled the water, and o'er him
    Murmured a prayer. That was all; not much
Not much, yet methinks when the sorrow and anguish
    For soldier and drummer boy ended that night,
Mid horrors, around where faith seemed to languish,
    The darkness was spanned by a rift of light.[748]
MRS. MAY M. ANDERSON

THE BROKEN BATTALIONS

The sounds of the tumults have ceased to ring,
    And the battles sun has set,
And here in the peace of a newborn spring
    We would fain forgive and forget.

Forget the rage of hostile years,
    And the scars of a wrong unshriven;
Forgive the torture that thrilled to tears
    The angels, calm in heaven.

Forgive and forget? Yes! be it so,
    From the hills to the broad sea waves;
But mournful and low are the winds that blow
    By the slopes of a thousand graves.

We may scourge from the spirit all thought of ill,
    In the midnight of grief held fast;
And yet, O brothers! be loyal still
    To the sacred and stainless Past!

She is glancing now from the vapor and cloud,
    From the waning mansion of Mars,
And the pride of her beauty is wanly bowed,
    And her eyes are misted stars.

And she speaks in a voice that is sad as death:
    "There is duty still to be done,
Though the trumpet of onset has spent its breath,
    And the battle been lost and won."

And she points with a trembling hand below,
    To the wasted and worn array
Of the heroes who strove in the morning glow
    For the grandeur that crowned "the gray."

O God! they come not as once they came,
    In the magical years of yore;
For the trenchant sword and the soul of flame
    Shall quiver and flash no more.

Alas! for the broken and battered hosts;
    Frail wrecks from a gory sea;
Though pale as a band in the realm of ghosts,
    Salute them! they fought with Lee.

And gloried when dauntless Stonewall marched
    Like a giant o'er field and flood,
When the bow of his splendid victories arched
    The tempest whose rain is blood!

Salute them those wistful and sunken eyes
    Flashed lightnings of sacred ire,
When the laughing blue of the Southland skies
    Was blasted with cloud and fire.

Salute them! their voices, so faint to-day,
    Were once the thunder of strife,
In the storm of the hottest and wildest fray.
    That ever has mocked at life!

Not vanquished, but crushed by a mystic fate;
    Blind nations against them hurled
By the selfish might and the causeless hate
    Of the banded and ruthless world.

Enough; all fates are the servants of God,
    And follow his guiding hand;
We shall rise some day from the Chastener's rod,
    Shall waken and—understand!

But hark to the Past as she murmurs: "Come,
    There's a duty still to be done;
Though mute is the drum, and the bugle dumb,
    And the battle is lost and won!"

No palace is here for the heroes' needs,
    With its shining portals apart;
Shall they find the peace of their "Invalides,"
    O South in your grateful heart?

A refuge of welcome with living halls,
    And love for its radiant dome;
Till the music of death's reveille calls
    The souls of the warriors home![149]
UNKNOWN

MY SOUTHERN HOME

To my far away home where the laurel tree blooms.
    My heart ever turns with a sigh,
'Tis the land of my birth where my ancestors' tombs
    Point up to the clear Southern sky.
'Tis the land of the rose, of the myrtle and vine,
    Its carpet the moss covered sod;
'Tis the land which with pride I may ever call mine,
    A land richly blessed by our God.

'Tis the land of the sun, where the feathery hosts
    Sing sweet in their Creator's praise,
'Tis the land from whose glens rise the tangible ghosts,
    The memories left of past days.
'Tis the home of the pure and the land of the brave,
    The faithful, the true and the just,
'Tis the land on whose breast I would make me my grave,
    To rest my inanimate dust.

'Tis the land of the hero, the theme of the bard,
    Tho' true that her flag has been furled.
Yet the deeds of her sons and her face battle scarred
    Have challenged the praise of the world.
'Tis the land which hath reared in the temple of fame.
    The loftiest pile that we see,
And her sons ever thrill at the sound of that name—
    Immortal, invincible Lee!

There a father doth rest where the soft breezes play,
    The willows droop over his tomb,
There it mother still grieves for the son far away,
    'Mid winter and withering gloom.
Take me back, let me fly to the land of my birth,
    To rest—never more will I roam,
Let me hold evermore to the dearest on earth,
    My mother, my country, my home![150]

ALBERT SIDNEY MORTON

PELHAM AT FREDERICKSBURG

Into the hurtling storm of shell,
Into the gaping mouth of hell,
Pelham the dauntless dashed—
Out from the meager line of gray.
Out to the bloody fringe of fray,
Where thousand thunders crashed.

Lashes to straining horses plied,
Cheers of defiance as they ride
Under the eyes of Lee.
Out of the day and into night,
Clouded in smoke they ride to fight,
Glorious sight to see!

Out of that bedlam Freedom speaks
Hear it in Pelham's Parrot's shrieks,
Pelham! 'tis bravely done!
In the concentrating, deadly hail,
Daring to die but not to fail,
Pelham still fights his gun!

What is that, sound? 'Tis not a cheer—
There, yet again—list! comrades, hear!
Hark, 'tis the hymn of France!
Rising the lofty anthem swells,
Over the din of countless hells
Freedom defiance chants!

Never was witnessed braver deed,
Bringing of praise its richest meed,
Making a deathless name—
"Courage sublime in one so young!"—
Words from the heart of Lee he wrung,
Crown of immortal fame![151]
ALBERT SIDNEY MORTON

John Pelham.

SAM DAVIS WAS TOO BRAVE TO DIE

A fitful dream of dying light,
The herald of a gloomy night
    Illumed the thrilling scene—
A silent group of men at arms,
A guard inured to war's alarms,
    A captive scout between!

"Your life I give," the leader said,
"For traitor's name, to honor dead.
    Who gave you this design?"
A flush o'erspread the captive's cheek,
    "My life is yours, your vengeance wreak.
But honor still is mine.

"A soldier I, this dress of gray
Proclaims the truth of that I say;
    This life I hate to yield,
But you have asked too great a price,
    Dishonor ne'er was the device
Emblazoned on my shield."

"He chooses death, your orders, men,"
The captor grimly said, and then
    The fatal noose was brought.
"Again I offer, soldier, free,
Your life if but you name to me
    The traitor you have bought."

The loop of death was 'round his throat,
The captive smiled, nor seemed to note
    The moments' fleeting speed.
"I scorn to buy the life you take
At price of faith," 'twas thus he spake—
    "It were a coward's deed."

With curling lips and flashing eye,
His knightly head uplifted high,
    As tho' 'twould death defy,
He spoke the noblest words e'er penned—
"Before these lips betray a friend,
    I tell you I will die."

From flashing eye the tears now start—
Those tears for mother's broken heart;
    He tears his buttons loose.

"I pray you these my mother bear."
A moment spared for silent prayer,
    He dangles at the noose.

That fatal noose is glorified,
For thro' its port the deified,
    Heroic soul did fly.
His proudest epitaph the vain
Remorse of him who judged the slain—
    "Too brave, too brave to die."[152]
ALBERT SIDNEY MORTON

Sam Davis.

HENRY T. STANTON'S POEM
[To the Yankees who raised a Confederate monument]

Within this closed and darkened earth
    All seeds of being lie,
That in good time find light and birth,
    To blossom and to die—
To blossom and to fruit and turn
    Again to whence they came;
To give their ashes to an urn
    Where ash comes back to flame.

Such is the law of life and death,
    The law that nature gives—
Man comes from earth to one short breath,
    And dies while yet he lives;
For in this universe of parts
    One part completes the whole—
With varied minds—with varied hearts,
    There's one unvaried soul.

In all our stages of being here,
    From summer's dawn to frost;
From dark to light, from birth to bier,
    No part of soul is lost;
A system grand goes on and on,
    With true untiring wheels.
And that which in our night is gone
    Our morrow's sun reveals.

There is no finite mind that solves
    This problem of God's plan—
We know not if our life evolves
    From mollusk up to man;
We cannot trace an atom's course
    Above or under earth;
We cannot find in vital force,
    Its secret springs of birth.

Mayhap a thousand million years
    Have been since human kind
Came crowding on the sphere of spheres.
    With mastery of mind:
We may not tell, we cannot know,
    What space has been since then.
Though buried ages rise to show
    Their prehistoric men.

A monolith left here and there,
    In isolation stands.
An obelisk that spears the air,
    Gleams out of drifted sands;
On ancient Egypt's fruitless waste
    Vast pyramids are piled,
That prove how perished races graced
    A spot that one time smiled.

Throughout this thousand million years,
    That may, perhaps, have sped,
At intervals some mark appears
    Above their honored dead;
Some mark of issues lost or won
    With great men stricken down;
Some proof of sanguine war-work done,
    For subject or for crown.

That martial pulse which men now feel
    Throbbed in the cycles gone,
And battle waged with stone and steel
    For human pride went on—
We look not back from this new day
    For good or ill so wrought.
Sufficient that their granites say:
    "Here rest the men who fought."

Whilst yet our Arian race is young
    To these long lines of stone,
New hills and vales and plains among,
    We proudly add our own—
We leave our marks of contests red,
    Of battle fought too well,
And rear our piles to heroes dead
    The same sad tale to tell.

Where bright Potomac, in the sun,
    A plate of silver lies.
Our marble shaft to Washington
    Goes out to pierce the skies.
An obelisk that stands and waits
    New centuries of sun,
Compiled of stones from sovereign states
    He molded into one.

There stands a mark at Bunker Hill
    On grand, historic ground.

That proves how in the rebel still
    The patriot is found;
And everywhere about this land,
    These summer sunbeams slant
On polished marble stones that stand
    To Lincoln, Lee and Grant.

For men who fought in all our wars,
    And gave their valiant blood
To glow in after-time like Mars,
    O'er life's enduring flood;
For noble men on every field
    To honor's cause allied,
Whose truth and glory stand revealed
    In that they fought and died.

That after years and after man
    May find a stone-mark here,
Of strife 'twix northern Puritan
    And southern Cavalier;
That centuries anon may see
    How man to-day was brave.
This speaking pile is placed to be
    A guide-post to his grave.

This granite stands for men who fought
    As man heroic must.
Who loves his land and has no thought
    But that his cause is just;
This mark is such as valor plans
    For spirit such as hers.
Set up by victor Puritans
    For vanquished Cavaliers.

It may not be that deathless pile
    Of Egypt's brazen clime:
Nor yet that needle of the Nile,
    From out the sands of time.
But it will stand while men believe
    That glory fits the brave:
While flowers bloom, while women grieve,
    Beside the hero's grave.

Six thousand men lie buried here,
    Who, from their prison close,
Were borne upon a soldier's bier
    To rest among their foes:

No mother's tears, nor wife's bewail,
    Nor child's pathetic cry;
No home-friend near to list his tale,
    Or watch the soldier die.

At martial hands their graves were made,
    Their coffins rudely drest.
And valiant soldiers gently laid
    Their foeman down to rest:
And thus the brotherhood of man
    Is grandly proven here.
It puts aside the Puritan,
    Blots out the Cavalier.

This kinship of the hero lives,
    Estrange it how you will;
The soldier to the soldier gives
    His meed of honor still:
No matter what the cause may be.
    If wrongful, or if just,
Chivalric foeman only see,
    True valor in the dust.

The coward puts his spurning feet
    Upon a foeman's grave:
That base-blood cry: "Revenge is sweet!"
    Came never from the brave;
And truer manhood noblest shows
    Among ignoble hordes.
When victors to their vanquished foes
    Hand back the yielded swords.

This honor done on northern soil
    To southern soldier dead,
In days to come shall prove a foil
    To blood by brothers shed:
Shall stand before our children's eyes,
    A proof that courage shows
The best where it can recognize
    The manhood of its foes.

When faction lives and heat begins,
    And naught save war avails.
Comes revolution where it wins,
    Rebellion where it fails:
And from this rule of wrathfulness,
    Where blood-bound people meet,

The patriot is in success,
    The traitor in defeat.

When from proud England's iron sway
    Our liberties we tore,
Her stigma, "rebel," died away,
    Her "traitors" lived no more.
With man to man in conflict met,
    And war's great havoc done,
There came an end to epithet,
    And rebel-traitors won.

With fast subsiding passion here
    From internecine strife,
The Puritan and Cavalier
    Are lost in newer life;
Our days of perfect peace are on,
    Our compact made anew.
And every shade of gray has gone
    To mingle with the blue.

No more reproach, the end has come,
    The argument is o'er;
In north and south the call of drum
    Shall be for us no more—
The banner of St. Andrew's cross
    In silent dust is lain;
And what has been a section's loss
    Shall prove a nation's gain.

While yon unbelted soldier bends
    Above this granite base,
Our land shall be the home of friends
    Where peace upholds its mace;
Where martial lines shall never stand
    With gleaming sword and gun.
Until in service of our land
    We march to fight as one.

Nor Puritan, nor Cavalier,
    A home grown strife shall see.
While o'er the soldiers resting here
    This granite shaft shall be.
With all of bitterness forgot,
    With all of taunting done,
Columbia is freedom's spot,
    Its sovereign states are one.

We've had our change from life to death,
    And back from death to life:
The law of nature gave us breath,
    And with it pride and strife.
We came from earth to bloom and fruit,
    With mastery of mind;
We've held our kingdom o'er the brute,
    As gracious God designed.

And still we keep the atom's place
    In this grand system here;
We die and live again through grace.
    Immortal in our sphere.
We fall and find our rest in earth,
    Where seeds in darkness lie.
Where all things fall and come to birth
    And seem again to die.

And granite monuments that stand
    Through time's untiring roll,
Are only guide-posts on the land,
    To show the course of soul;
For human substance goes to earth,
    Whence human passions rise,
But soul with God himself had birth,
    And lives and never dies.[153]
CONFEDERATE COLONEL HENRY THOMPSON STANTON

Confederate monument.

THE DRUMMER BOY OF SHILOH

On Shiloh's dark and bloody ground
    The dead and wounded lay;
Amongst them was a drummer boy,
    Who beat the drum that day.
A wounded soldier held him up,
    His drum was by his side,
He clasped his hands, then raised his eyes.
    And prayed before he died.

"Oh, Mother" said the dying boy,
    "Look down from heaven on me;
Receive me to thy fond embrace.
    Oh, take me home to thee.
I've loved my country and my God,
    To serve them both I've tried."
He smiled, shook hands. Death seized the boy,
    Who prayed before he died.

Each soldier wept then like a child,
    Stout hearts were they and brave;
The flag his winding sheet, God's Book
    The key into his grave.
They wrote upon a single board,
    These words: "This is a guide
To those who mourn the drummer boy,
    Who prayed before he died."

Ye angels 'round the throne of grace,
    Look down upon the braves
Who fought and died on Shiloh's plain,
    Now slumbering in their graves.
How many homes made desolate,
    How many hearts have sighed.
How many like the drummer boy,
    Who prayed before he died.[154]
UNKNOWN

A JOHNNY REB ON PENSIONS TO YANKEES

I can truthfully say, that the C.S.A.,
    Those who dwell in the land of the living,
Begrudge not the pay you get every day,
    Which this nation so freely is giving—

That is, to the wounded, or whose sickness was founded
    On exposure incurred thro' the strife,
And thus were disabled, for to labor unable—
    Provide for them well thro' their life.

But the hale, hearty fellow, who for pensions yet bellows,
    Let him hustle as we Johnnies do;
For many got bounties from their States and counties.
    And for ducats alone wore the blue.

Then think for a minute, you know we ain't in it,
    When scattered around is the swag;
So tell Gen. Palmer, to try to keep calmer,
    When he sees that tattered old flag.

'Tis just like a story of heroes whose glory
    Will shine on history's pages;
But your flag is now ours 'gainst all foreign powers.
    And united we stand through all ages.[155]
UNKNOWN

A CONFEDERATE ACROSTIC

This is the day we celebrate,
Honoring both the small and great—
Every dead Confederate.

Causes which once were lost are won,
On southern lands, by southern sons.
Nobly righting side by side,
For us they fought, and bled, and died,
Every veteran true and tried.
Dead tho' they be, they did not die in vain:
Each hero's mem'ry has come again.
Right here on Bentonville battle plain,
As heroes they fell without a stain.
True to the cause for which they fought,
Each soldier's life was dearly bought.

Veterans, we who wore the gray—
Each were clad in battle array,
That met the foe from day to day,
Erect a monument to stay.
Round which we all have met to-day
A mound, indeed, which is no trifle
Nobly done by Goldsboro's Rifles.[156]
B. B. RAIFORD

THE MEN WHO WORE THE GRAY

Oh, "The Men Who Wore the Gray,"
Oh, the men who dared the fray,
Upholding the grand principles for which our fathers fought;
Fame's resounding voice shall tell
How they strove and how they fell—
A monument of glory their high sacrifice hath wrought!

Let inspired pens portray
How these "Men Who Wore the Gray"
Came back, the struggle ended, every hope of justice fled;
All the future dark and void,
Maimed and poor, their homes destroyed.
Their wives and children weeping o'er the memories of their dead!

But affliction could not stay
Those brave "Men Who Wore the Gray"
From gathering up courageously their broken ends of life;
As they battled, so they worked—
Never yet had Southron shirked
The field where love and honor gave command to face the strife!

They are victors in that fray;
Now these "Men Who Wore the Gray"
Exult in their achievements for the land they love so well;
It has vanquished many foes—
It has blossomed like the rose—
The story of their proud success, its smiling homes can tell.

May God's mercy, day by day,
Bless "The Men Who Wore the Gray"—
Those fearless, peerless heroes, who waxed stronger as they strove;
While the people, heart and soul,
Grant to their decreasing roll
A Patriot's best recompense, the country's reverent love.[157]
UNKNOWN

I'M CONSCRIPTED, SMITH, CONSCRIPTED

I'm conscripted, Smith, conscripted—
    Ebbs the subterfuges fast,
And the sub-enrolling marshals
    Gather with the evening blast—
Let thine arms, O! Smith, support me,
    Hush your gab, and close your ear,
Conscript-grabbers close upon you,
    Hunting for you—far and near.

Though my scarred, rheumatic "trotters"
    Bear me limping short no more;
And my shattered constitution
    Won't exempt me as before;
Though the provost guard surround me,
    Prompt to do their master's will,
I must to the "front" to perish,
    Die the great conscripted still.

Let not the seizer's servile minions,
    Mock the lion thus laid low—
'Twas no fancy drink that "slewed" him—
    Whisky straight-out struck the blow.
Here, then, pillowed on thy bosom,
    Ere he's hurried quite away.
Him, who, drunk with bust-head whisky,
    Madly threw himself away.

Should the base, plebeian rabble
    Dare assail me as I roam,
Seek my noble squaw, Octavia,
    Weeping in her widowed home;
Seek her, say the guards have got me
    Under their protecting wings.
Going to make me join the army.
    Where the shell and minie sings.

I'm conscripted, Smith, conscripted—
    Hark! you hear that grabber's cry—
Run, old Smith, my boy, they'll catch you—
    Take you to the front to die.
Fare thee well! I go to battle.
    There to die, decay and swell
Lockhart and Dick Taylor guard thee,
    Sweet Octavia—Smith!—farewell.[158]
JOHN HAPPY

THE BUGLE CALL

I love to feel on my bridle bit
    The champ of a thoroughbred,
When the bugle call and the ringing hoof
    Tell of a charge ahead.
There is no sound, there is no song,
That stirs a soldier's soul.
Like the bugle call and the ringing hoof
    In the charge of his Brigade.

Refrain:
There is no sound, there is no song.
    That stirs a soldier's soul,
Like the bugle call and the ringing hoof
    In the charge of his Brigade.

In squadron front, with closed ranks.
    Together side by side,
With bounding steed and sabre raised,
    Straight to the front we ride.
There is no fear, there is no doubt.
But every man responds
To the bugle call and the ringing hoof
    In the charge of his Brigade.

When the battle's o'er, and the roll is called,
    As in the ranks we stand,
There's many a horse that finds his place
    Without a guiding hand.
His rider's gone, and all alone
He rushes to respond
To the bugle call and the ringing hoof
    In the charge of his Brigade.

There's many a horse, and many a man,
    Who, charging in-the fray,
Together tight, together fall,
    Together pass away.
In years to come the mem'ry of these scenes
Will still remain,
Of the bugle call and the ringing hoof
    In the charge of our Brigade.[159]
UNKNOWN

CONFEDERATE CEMETERY

With one bright lane of native pines
    Mild art is here content;
A simple slab each grave defines—
    No more has beauty lent.

But someone, filled with southern pride,
    Among the rest has led
A shaft with this sweet thought supplied:
    "To the unknown dead."

The soldier who this grove supplied,
    That buried here might be
The southern dead, now sleeps beside
    His "buried chivalry."[160]
UNKNOWN

Confederate cemetery, Covington, Georgia.

CONFEDERATE MONUMENT AT CHICAGO
Where the golden sheaves are garnered near the modest violets blue,
Where the wheat, the oats and apples, glisten in the morning dew,
Where the prairie soil, productive, grows the grain, the fruit, the men,
Where the genius of the Northland glows a brilliant diadem;
Where the school house, white and sacred, nigh the church's steeple raised,
Where with broadest Christ-like teaching, hymns of home „ and love are praised,
By the fresh lake and its waters, with the breath of all their breeze,
Stands the glory crown of Christian, in a shaft beneath the trees.

Since the days men went to battle, and their coming home with spoil,
Grew reminders of the vict'ry snatched in death and sad turmoil;
Since they raised in vain self glory, skull and thigh and things of stone,
As a monument of vict'ry o'er their fallen foes alone,
Where the golden sheaves are garnered, near the modest violets blue,
Where the genius of the Northland keeps the words of Christ most true,
For the first time in all ages, since the sun did come and go,
Do the mighty victors, praising, raise a monument to foe.

Not to false hopes, nor false prophets, not to treason nor unrest,
But to manly men and brothers, fighting as they thought was best;
Not to argue now that battle shots have ceased for many a year,
For the White-winged Peace has folded round about the foeman's bier.
Not to fan the fading embers, with the fiendish breath of hate,
But to lay our Northern tributes on the silent wards of State;
Where the golden sheaves are garnered, near the modest violets blue,
Lie the gray in mercy gathered in a Christian land and true.

And as Christ himself hath taught it, "Love thy neighbor as thyself,"
Stands the shaft by Northmen builded, in their City with its pelf;
Rich and proud, the great Chicago, heart of Commerce, seat of Trade,
But its sons, and aye its daughters, of a better clay are made.
"God is love, and love is godly," so they thought this sunlit day,
As they dedicate to mem'ry noble deeds of boys in gray;
And their soldier boys with dirges, being the flower of City's pride,
Lay the laurel and the lily o'er the men who fought and died.

And the bugle sounds out softly, "Taps" for nevermore to cease,
And the rolling volleys thunder, "Men of gray now rest in peace,"
And but one flag waves above them, dead and living, old and new,
Where the golden sheaves are garnered, near the modest violets blue.[161]
LAWRENCE M. ENNIS

TRUE TO THE SOUTH

True to the South, they offered, free from stain,
Courage and faith; vain faith and courage vain.
For her they threw lands, honors, wealth away.
And one more hope that was more prized than they;
For her they languished in a foreign clime.
Gray-haired with sorrow in their manhood's prime:
Beheld each night their homes in fevered sleep,
Each morning started from their dreams to weep;
Till God, who saw them tried too sorely, gave
The resting place they asked—an early grave.
Oh, then forget all feuds and shed one manly tear
O'er Southern dust—for broken hearts lie there.[162]
UNKNOWN

MRS. MACLEAN'S ODE

Mother of men! thou liest in solemn state
Upon the bier of many faithful hearts,
All mule and cold, pierced thro' with many darts,
A queen discrowned by Fate.
Bring here the frankincense of loyal vows,
And myrrh, the meed of grief too deep for tears,
The precious spice of love, t' embalm thro' years,
And gold for royal brows.

We shall not wake thee from thy dreamless sleep,
With murmuring moan disturb thy deep repose;
No blatant tongue shall travesty thy woes,
As silent here we weep.
Yet we remember! Aye, nor can forget,
Those deeds of splendor, those heroic days,
When thy leal sons rode forth thro' bloody ways
Where Death and Honor met.

O dream of glory past! Of high resolve,
To teach the world how brave it is to dare,
And daring, do—tho' costing lives so rare,
A nation to evolve.
Roll drums, and sound across the utmost seal
Blow bugles, in one long majestic strain!
Tho' she is dead, she dieth not in vain,
Whose death hath made us free.

Free to live on and learn to suffer wrong,
Nor vengeance seek, nor feel ignoble fear;
Free to see truly and to grandly bear,
And grow thro' suffering strong.
Mother of Men! we gather round thy grave,
And pledge thy pure name ne'er shall be belied;
A martyr thou hast lived, a martyr died,
The South's best self to save.

Yes, we will bury thee with pomp and pride,
And leave thee sleeping in thy sacred shroud:
For we behold thee far above the cloud,
Transfigured, glorified!
Sound we a paean, then, and not a knell,
Sing we a Jubilate not a dirge;
For lo! the South holds Victory's noblest verge!
God is in Heaven! All's well![63]
MRS. CLARA DARGAN MACLEAN

AT REST—JEFFERSON DAVIS

Full of grief-laden years, he has passed to his tomb:
    But see! as its portals unfold.
Immortality's lamp shines bright 'mid the gloom,
And memory as sentinel watches his tomb,
And the laurel beside it bursts forth into bloom,
    And Peace breathes "At Rest" to his soul.

At rest from the battle-field's fearful array,
    Where he bled for the Union he loved;
At dread Buena Vista, and fierce Monterey,
His genius and prowess won for us the day,
And wreathed round his temples a chaplet of bay,
    His slanderings ne'er have removed.

At rest from the Cabinet's council of State,
    Where he faithfully served thro' the strife
In the Halls of the Nation, where heated debate,
And partisan rancor, and sectional hate,
Drove the Southron to arm for the Rights of his State,
    And Liberty, dearer than life.

When the cloud-burst of battle overwhelmed our land,
    With unfaltering devotion to right.
Our chieftain pledged all to our patriot band,
And after defeat, in the dungeon enchained.
He patiently suffered at Power's fell hand,
    A victim to fate, and to might.

For our "Lost Cause" he suffered, and so will his name,
    Embalmed in our memories dwell;
And his tomb prove a Mecca, at whose holy fane,
The sons of the South inspiration will gain,
And History write of his glorious fame,
    Of all he hath done, "It is well."[164]
SALLIE JONES

Jefferson Davis.

JIM O'MERA'S RIDE

"Send me a man who is brave and true."
    This message the General sent,
And over the roll in quick review
    The Captain, in fancy, went.

"No lion's more brave than the Irishman,
    Aye, brave, nor is steel more true;
Nor fears he loss of life or limb,
    Yes, Jim O'Mera'll do."

His orders received, to horse Jim leapt,
    To the General's side he sped,
Then checked his steed and doffed his cap.
    "Well, Gin'ral, I'm here," he said.

Sure, never a shell more rough and rude,
    Covered a soul more brave and true,
And the General thought, "The Captain's right.
    Yes, Jim O'Mera'll do."

The orders were brief: "Ride parallel
    To the breastworks of the Yanks
And see if they're manned." O'Mera bowed
    And smote his good steed's flank.

He galloped amain, till parallel
    The piled-up breastworks lay
Fully manned, he saw without thought of fear,
    Not seventy yards away.

A cocking of rifles; a sudden flash,
    And the forest rang again.
O'Mera escaped, but his horse was hit
    And plunged and reared in pain.

Undaunted by the heavy fire,
    O'Mera drew his rein.
And coolly fired his trusty gun
    And then rode on again.

Ah, he rode for life! The foam on his horse
    Was flecked with bloody red.
The breast works passed, the lines regained,
    "They're there yit, Gin'ral," he said.[165]
HENRIETTA HENDERSON DANGERFIELD (11 years old)

SAVANNAH FALLEN

Bowing her head to the dust of the earth,
    Smitten and stricken is she,
Light after light gone out from her hearth,
    Son after son from her knee.
Bowing her head to the dust at her feet,
    Weeping her beautiful slain,
Silence! keep silence, for aye in the street,
    See! they are coming again.

Coming again, oh! glorious ones,
    Wrapped in the flag of the free;
Queen of the South! bright crowns for thy sons,
    Only the cypress for thee!
Laurel, and banner, and music, and drum,
    Marches, and requiems sweet;
Silence! keep silence! alas, how they come,
    Oh! how they move through the street!

Slowly, ah! mournfully, slowly they go,
    Bearing the young and the brave,
Fair as the summer, but white as the snow
    Bearing them down to the grave.
Some in the morning, and some in the noon,
    Some in the hey-day of life;
Bower nor blossom, nor summer nor June,
    Wooing them back to the strife.

Some in the billow, afar, oh! afar,
    Staining the waves with their blood;
One on the vessel's high deck, like a star,
    Sinking in glory's bright flood.[166]
Bowing her head to the dust of the earth,
    Humbled but honored is she,
Lighting the skies with the stars from her hearth,
    Who shall her comforter be?

Bring her, oh! bring her the garments of woe,
    Sackcloth and ashes for aye;
Winds of the South! oh, a requiem blow,
    Sighing and sorrow to-day.
Sprinkle the showers from heaven's blue eyes
    Wide o'er the green summer lea,
Rachel is weeping, oh! Lord of the skies,
    Thou shalt her comforter be![167]

ALETHEA S. BURROUGHS

THE STARS & BARS

There's not beneath the gilded stars
    An ensign or a fallen banner,
Which like the glorious Stars and Bars,
    Is held in such a sacred manner.

It rose upon the wings of peace
    To wave for equal right and glory,
But every year saw hopes decrease
    To end its short eventful story.

It had a valorous, youthful might,
    It conquered only to surrender;
Now memories of its honor bright
    Are all that wounded hearts remember.

O may the memory of its dead
    Forever linger round above us,
The virtues of the ones it led
    Fill well our lives, that others love us.

We do not ask for it to wave,
    That rising might restore it;
But that, we all revere the brave
    Who till their death, so nobly bore it![168]

ANDREW M. MCCONNELL

SONGS OF THE CONFEDERACY

When falls the soldier brave
    Dead at the feet of wrong,
The poet sings—and guards his grave
    With Sentinels of Song.

"Go Songs,"—he gives command—.
    "Keep faithful watch and true;
The living and dead of the Conquered Land
    Have now no guards save you."

"And ballads! Mark ye well,
    Thrice holy is your trust;
Go out to the fields where warriors fell,
    And sentinel their dust."[169]
DANIEL BOND

BARRIERS BURNED AWAY
[A postwar reunion of Confederates and Yankees]
A Blue and Gray commingling was in successful swing;
The fraternizing "boom" was on, and all that sort of thing—
When, as it chanced, an old Confed fell chinning with a Yank
Who proved, in sooth, a caution as a reminiscence "crank."

"How pleasant 'tis," the latter cried, "to grasp the hand of him
That through four long and bloody years faced us in battle grim!
And, by the way, was it your luck to fight at Franklin? eh!"
"Well, I should smile," quoth Stars and Bars; "I lost an ear that day."

"Ah ha! in that event I know 'twill please you much to hear
That 'twas a rooster of my size who scooped your missing ear.
I shot it off; it all comes back;" but ere he could conclude,
The Confed loomed before his gaze in no uncertain mood.

"And 'twas you that did the job, you wretched little Yank!
I've often wondered if I'd meet the man I had to thank
For this depletion—as at length I see your form once more,
Take that, and that, and that, for what you did in Sixty-four!"[170]
CHARLES EDGEWORTH JONES

THE SPIRIT OF 1861-1896

We've met again, comrades bold,
    To grasp each other's hands,
And talk of times that tried each soul
    All o'er these Southern lands;
We've closer grown thro' fleeting years
    Since we together stood,
And bared our breasts to leaden storms
    On fields baptized with blood.

Our land's been filled with widow's weeds;
    We've heard the orphan's sigh—
While comrades long since disappeared
    Are marching through the sky.
We'll write their names on fame's proud scroll,
    As heroes in the strife.
And cherish those they loved and left
    As long as we have life.

Our banner, with its triple bars,
    No more 'mongst flags is seen;
The battlefields once drenched in gore,
    With waving grass are green—
Nor rude commands resounding now
    Disturb the warriors' rest;
Their forms asleep in camps of death.
    Their souls are with the blest.

But though our flag lies folded now,
    To kiss the breeze no more,
And though no more we grasp the arms
    We once so proudly bore,
We walk again with freemen's tread
    The land that gave us birth;
And glory in the Sunny South,
    The grandest spot of earth.

And when all hate shall ease to burn,
    And truth shall grasp the pen
To write our country's history down
    She'll say this of our men:
That truer patriots never lived.
    Nor filled more honored graves,
Than those who fell in Freedom's cause—
    Our own Confederate braves.

We're not ashamed of what we did,
    We battled for the right;
And though by numerous foes o'erwhelmed,
    We yielded to their might.
We walk again with freemen's tread
    The land that gave us birth;
And glory in our Sunny South,
    The grandest spot of earth.

And while we do not brag or boast
    Of how our comrades fought—
The pension rolls you know full well
    The facts of this have taught;
And if these pension rolls be true,
    And none have proved they lied,
We must have crippled all the world
    And half the Coons beside.

My song I'll close with homely phrase
    That has a statement true,
Of how the light ended and—
    I'll prove it by the blue.
The Yankees didn't whip us, boys.
    No—let that ne'er be said;
We wore ourselves out whipping them;
    Then stopped for want of bread.

Then let us sing till Heaven shall sing
    To our departed braves,
And let us pray each passing day,
    Among their silent graves.
That when our time to fall shall come,
    And we must pass away,
We'll rise with them to reign
    In one eternal day.[171]

J. B. K. SMITH

OUR DEAD

We bury our dead,
We lay them to sleep
With the earth for their bed,
With stones at their head:
We leave them and weep
When we bury our dead.

We bury our dead,
We lay them to sleep,—
On our Mother's calm breast
We leave them to rest—
To rest while we weep.

We bury our dead,
We lay them to sleep—
They reck not our tears,
Though the sad years creep—
Through our tears, through the years
They tranquilly sleep.

We bury our dead,
We lay them to sleep;
We bury the bloom
Of our life,—all our bloom
In the coffin we fold;
We enfold in the tomb:
We reenter the room
We left young,—we are old.

We bury our dead,
We lay them to sleep;
The cold Time-tides flow
With winter and spring,
With birds on the wing,
With roses and snow,
With friends who beguile
Our sorrow with pity—
With pity awhile.
Then weary and smile,
Then chide us, say, "Lo!
How the sun shines,—'tis May."
But we know 'tis not so—
That the sun died that day
When we laid them away,
With the earth for a bed—

When we buried our dead.

We bury our dead,
We lay them to sleep;
We turn back to the world;
We are caught,—we are whirled
In the rush of the current—
The rush and the sweep
Of the tide, without rest.
But they sleep—they the blest—
The Blessed dead sleep:
They tranquilly rest
On our Mother's calm breast.[172]
THOMAS NELSON PAGE

Thomas N. Page.

SAM DAVIS: THE CONFEDERATE MARTYR

Before his foes the captive stood.
    And many a pitying eye
Bent on him, when they knew that he,
    So young, so brave, must die.
And many a heart responsive beat,
    While gazing on that face,
Where dauntless courage blended with
    A soldier's youthful grace.

"I offer," thus the leader spoke,
    "Thy life and liberty;
The traitor tell, to honor dead,
    Who gave these notes to thee.
Knowest thou not a direful death
    Awaits thee as a spy?
And thou art young; a soldier brave
    More gloriously should die."

Deep sadness for one moment fell
    Upon the captive's face;
Then firm resolve, and courage high,
    And valor look its place.
"The life you'd give is far too dear
    That would involve a friend;
I spurn an offer that would bring
    So infamous an end.

"I thought to serve my native land,
    When from the oppressor free;
In colors fair, I hoped to write
    My name in history.
But honor is more dear to me
    Than is this fleeting breath.
And ere I would betray a friend,
    I'd ten times suffer death."

When ready for the dreadful doom
    That waited him that day,
A courier swift was seen to ride
    This message to convey.
"Our General sends me still to say
    It is not yet too late;
He grieves that one so young must die;
    Too brave for such fate!"

With flushing cheek, and kindling eye,
    The captive turned to say,
"I thank your leader for the care
    He's shown for me this day;
Tell him, had I a thousand lives,
    I'll bow to duty's call;
Before these lips betray a friend,
    I'd freely give them all."

Then to the waiting Chaplain, said,
    "I'm ready; pray you send
These tokens to my mother her dear,
    When my brief life shall end.
And write her that her boy's last thought
    Was of his childhood's home;
And that lie hopes to meet her in
    A brighter world to come."

He ceased; the sun's last parting ray
    Played round his knightly head,
And glorified the thrilling scene;
    But not a radiance shed
So bright, as that which illumes,
    And shall unto the end,
The name of that young martyr who
    Would not betray a friend.

"Too brave to die!" his captors said:
    And it is even so;
The glory of his sacrifice
    Through coming years shall grow.
The brave die not—a prouder fate
    Succeeds dread Azreal's dart;
They but exchange their country's arms
    For more—their country's heart,
And on the roll of honor, shall
    His name emblazoned be
With glory that is due to him
    In his country's history.[173]
SALLIE JONES

Sam Davis House.

OUR WOMEN & THE WAR

They bid us tell the story
    Of our nation's golden past,
And sing her hymns of conquest
    And chant her dirge at last.
But when the wounds are fresh and quiv'ring,
    Is there any place for art?
Can we print the stories graven
    On the tablets of the heart?

Women hide their dearest treasures
    From the public's curious gaze;
When her thoughts are of her lover
    Does a maiden speak his praise?
Nay, the brown lark hides her secret
    In her faithful frightened breast,
And she flutters farthest from it
    When the school boy seeks her nest.

So we sing of other nations
    And the glories they have known,
But our pride is in our Southland
    And our hearts speak of our own.
When we sing of lofty courage
    And of knightly chivalry,
We may write the name of Sidney
    But we think the name of Lee.

We may write of reckless Roland
    As he led his gallant band.
But we think of dashing Morgan,
    In our peerless Southern land.
When we praise all England's Stuarts.
    'Tis our own we fain would sing—
There was none so gay and gallant.
    There was none more truly king.

We laud the bold crusader
    With the red cross on his breast,
Who sought the Holy City
    From the Moslems grasp to wrest.
But a knighthood no less noble
    Claims now our pride and love—
The gray-clad ranks of Southrons
    With their red cross high above.

It may be a woman's folly
    That she guards her treasures so,
But shall History's page be blotted
    By our tears so quick to flow?
Let our children tell the story
    Of the cause their fathers led.
For our sorrow seals our utterance,
    And our silence shrines our dead.[174]
UNKNOWN

Confederate women.

AN APPEAL TO THE SOUTH

Aye, rear a monument, Tennessee,
    To the soldier-boy whose life
Was laid bravely down to make you free,
    In those dark years of strife.
But not you alone—let the Southland
    In the glorious task unite,
And each Southron give, with a willing hand.
    To the sacred cause, his mite.

There were many as young and brave as he,
    Who for Dixie gladly died;
Who left home and friends to follow Lee,
    And with Stuart and Hampton ride:
Under Stonewall Jackson's lead to fight.
    Or advance to meet the foe,
'Neath Beauregard, our-gallant Knight.
    Or the soldiers' friend, "Old Joe."

In the battle's shock they bravely fell,
    With their comrades close beside;
With the music of the Rebel yell
    For their requiem, they died.
No nobler death could a patriot crave,
    Than to yield, in fearless strife,
Back to our God the gift He gave,
    A brave and stainless life.

But this hero boy died all alone,
    In the midst of that cruel band;
With no farewell word, no loving tone,
    No grasp of a friendly hand;
With no gun or sword, on the battle plain,
    With no comrade at his side,
For he, whose life had been free from stain,
    On the shameful gallows died.

Aye, rear to brave Davis' memory
    A lofty burial stone.
Type of our Southern chivalry,
    We build, not to him alone,
But sacred to honor, truth, and right.
    Let it point from Dixie's breast,
Up to God's Home of eternal light,
    Where the hero found his rest.[175]

ANNIE BARNWELL MORTON

A SOUTHERN ROSE

Beneath the sky
    Where you and I
Were born; where beauty grows,
    Up from the sod,
        At touch of God,
There sprang a stately rose.

It grew, and men in wonderment
    Beheld the beauteous thing
Alas, for Hope which wooing went.
    And Love which sorrowing,
Learns that the flower it loves the best.
    The one it guards the tenderest,
    The hand of Fate transplants!
    Our Southern rose
        Now sweetly grows
Among the hills of France!

Go search the gardens of Vendee—
    Which poets long have sung—
Go cull the flowers that blush the hills
    Of Picardie among,
        Land of romance!
        Fair land of France!
With all your glorious flowers,
    Lilies of old
        And cloth of gold
We needs must lend you ours!
    Right well, I guess,
    For loveliness.
        For beauty in repose,
There is no Lily in all France
    Can match our Southern Rose![176]
DR. JOHN ALLAN WYETH

John A. Wyeth.

IN MEMORIAM

Southland's great heroes are passing away—
Southland is mourning their absence to-day;
Southland is weeping great tears of regret;
Southland is striving her wrongs to forget.

Scatter bright flowers bedewed with the tears
Of loved ones whose hearts have been lonely for years;
And scatter them, too, on this hallowed day,
Over the blue, as well as the gray.

Brothers in death, and brothers in life,
Help us forget the unnatural strife;
But memory silently weeps by the urn
Of buried hopes that can never return.

The glory that gladdened the land of their birth
Is wanting the lustre they lent to our earth;
But God, in His wisdom, permitted the blight,
And faith in His love will reveal what is right.

And now, after three long decades have fled,
We meet here to weep o'er our glorified dead.
And wreath with bright flowers their mouldering clay—
The heroes who once wore the blue and the gray![177]
MRS. MARY WARE

Confederate veteran.

CALL IT NOT A "LOST CAUSE"

Call not the Cause they fought for "Lost"!
That silent, ghostly, hero-host.
That sleep upon the eternal plains
Where sound the silver trumpet-strains
Of Angels at their post!

The laurel wreath the warrior wears
Is often wet with widow's tears;
And silent Forms float o'er the field
And give the wreath to them that yield.
While Victory crowns her dears!

There's but one cause, and they who fight
To set their conscience in the right,
Tho' Hell sent forth her friends to aid
The foe unconquerable is made
The dying patriot's might!

With God the issues ever lie,
He sounds to us the battle-cry;
For us, 'tis but to meet the foe
In bloody fray, nor ask or know,
And as the hero die!

But they ne'er fight in vain who fall
In answer to that battle call,
Though broken be their shield, and torn
The flag that shook defiant scorn
And now a death-shroud pall!

Aye! say not that they fought in vain!
Who fell without dishonor's stain—
On their cold brows the victor wreath
By unseen Hands is fixed in death—
Oh, hail victorious slain!

Heroic deeds are victories!
He always wins who never flies—
And they, our hero-dead, are gone
To reap the meed of victory won,
Beyond the weeping skies!

Then harbor not that leper thought—
That they that silent host—who sought
In vain to stay their Country's Sun—
Did fail, for they have nobly Won
The Cause for which they fought![178]
PEGRAM DARGAN

WE'VE FOUGHT AGAIN

Though years have passed away since that sad day
    When Southern arms were stacked, and tears like rain
Coursed down the Southern cheeks, I've heard them say,
    The veterans scarred and old, "We've fought again!"

The saddest day has come—and it has passed.
    What tongue can tell the heart-break and the pain?
Though then we stood through war, not first, but last,
    Have we done ill since then? We've fought again!

Though three decades have passed since war did cease,
    We have not idle stood upon the plain;
We've won our old-time place through arts of peace,
    But not through lethargy. We've fought again!

The death blow to our hopes left Hope alive,
    And though we love our dead, who would complain?
They live a better life, while we, who strive,
    Keep green their memory—though we've fought again.

The world is ours yet, and who the cur
    Would treat our Southern land with such disdain
As not to make our Union see in her
    The surest anchor—when we've fought again?

Oh, Comrades of the Gray! though laid aside
    The arms and banners, can you not explain
When asked, "How have you stemmed ill-fortune's tide?"
    By saying, "We had faith and—fought again?"[179]

JACK LE BRUNI

THE CHARGE

Sublime beyond description is the scene:
Two armies are in conflict. The stern crash
Of muskets rises from within the screen
Of mingled dust and smoke; the vivid flash
Of the incessant cannon plays like a lash
Of lurid lightning o'er an angry cloud.
The sounds that tell when hostile legions clash
Combine to raise an uproar fierce and loud,
Of which contending fiends in hell might well be proud.

Beyond yon wooded hillside's sheltering curve.
Along whose front the storms of battle play,
A picked brigade is stationed in reserve,
Who take, as yet, no portion in the fray,
But wait to watch the fortunes of the day.
They may at any moment hear the call
To hold the too successful foe at bay
And for their wearied comrades form a wall,
When on their shattered ranks o'erwhelming numbers fall.

In thoughtful silence they await their task,
While bleeding sufferers from the front pass by,
Of whom, with anxious brow, they sometimes ask
News from the doubtful conflict raging nigh.
But few the words they speak—the stifled sigh
Reveals what solemn thoughts their bosoms fill;
Remembrances of loved ones dim the eye
And cause the overburdened heart, to thrill,
While prayers ascend from earnest souls whose lips are still.

For what prophetic tongue can now make known
Who of their number shall go unharmed hence,
When yon death-laden cloud has overblown,
Or who must martyr fall in home's defence.
Approaching action quickens every sense;
They long, yet dread, their fate at once to try
And end the torpor of their forced suspense,
While overhead the lingering sun hangs high
As though some Joshua held it spell-bound in the sky

The sun at length sinks slowly towards the West,
The wavering battle surges to and fro,
Like tempest-troubled sea that cannot rest,
And nearer still its blasts of fury blow
To those who next their fearful power must know.

And now begins to fall the leaden spray
Of war's advancing tide, whose swelling glow
How threatens seriously to sweep away
The sadly broken barriers which resist its sway.

Now the expected trial hour draws near;
From mouth to mouth is passed the quick command,
Above the rising din distinct and clear,
And soon in battle's solemn line they stand
To strike or suffer for their native land
Could not that land they serve so well forgive
A faltering now in this devoted band.
If they but share the common wish to live
And shrink before the storm which others fail to drive?

Not so—but, without pause or backward glance,
Loud rings the joyous Southern battle cry,
Which ever hailed the star-cross flag's advance,
As on they spring the combat to defy.
Like some huge meteor on a midnight sky
Their line of bayonets flashes into sight,
Reflecting back the sunset's golden dye.
Which bathes the hillside in a flood of light,
Then swiftly sweeps towards the point of fiercest fight.

Stern is the greeting they receive from grape,
From whistling bullet and from screaming shell;
Death comes—and pain—in many a ghastly shape,
To strew the ground with mangled frames, that tell
Their track across the bloody vale too well.
A banner falls—it scarcely strikes the plain
Before another band uplifts the magic spell
And bears it onward through the fiery rain;
For that must never drop till the last man be slain.

But see, the hostile ranks begin to break,
And one by one the cannons cease to roar,
Stilled by the shouts which now the echoes wake,
Because their banners float in triumph o'er
The lines where other banners waved before.
They have achieved another glorious name
To write upon their standards, where a score
Of other names are clustered, which may claim
A place among the highest on the scroll of fame.

But warm and loving hearts must soon be chilled,
When the proud story of this charge is told,

And distant homes with aching grief be filled
For some who charged to-day with footstep bold,
Whose fevered pulse is now forever cold.
This hour of fame cost many a house its heir
And broke the staff of many a helpless fold.
The crutch, the empty sleeve, the vacant chair
Will tell for weary years the price of victory there.[180]
JAMES E. WILSON

Confederate ware heroes.

AN HOUR IN HOLLYWOOD CEMETERY

The haze of Indian summer lay
    Across the dreamy hills.
And plaintive murmurs filled the air
    From Nature's hidden rills.
A mourner clad in sombre black.
    With proud, but gentle face,
Stood by three narrow grass-grown graves,
    With thoughtful, tender grace.
She strewed white blossoms o'er the mounds,
    Then turned her tearful eyes
Where thirty thousand brave ones slept;
    Beneath the sun-lit skies.

"The dear South gave her bravest, best,
    And gave them all in vain!"
She sighed, as bitter memories woke
    A tide of grief and pain.
A human rosebud, fair and sweet,
    Her Hubert's wilful Rose,
Ran gayly up and clasped her hand.
    "Oh, grandma, see! He knows
Just how dear grandpa fell! He saw
    The awful charge that day!"
She cried, and pointed down the path,
    Her young voice blithe and gay.

The mourner turned, then caught her breath;
    A soldier, clad in blue,
With silvered hair and stately tread,
    Had met her startled view.
He drew more near. She turned her eyes
    Upon each grass-grown grave
Where slept her dead. The soldier paused.
    "Here rest three warriors brave,"
He gently said, and on the mounds
    Laid rosebuds pure and white.
She turned and faced him, then, her eyes
    With bitter memories bright.

He read her heart—the sorrow there,
    The suffering and the pride—
And to his eyes a tear-drop sprang
    He did not care to hide.
Sweet, wilful Rose, with childish grace,
    Reached upward, and he stooped

And raised her to his stalwart breast
    The mourner's eyelids drooped.
And sudden tears ran down her cheeks,
    For in that simple act
She saw the bitter past was dead!
    Could she accept the fact?

She trembled, wavered, saw the child
    Smile in the stranger's face;
Then watched him stroke her sunny hair
    Till tears to smiles gave place
Her smiles were sadder than her tears.
    The soldier reached across.
And o'er the mounds their hands were clasped;
    The gold was freed from dross.
She never saw his face again,
    But o'er her shadowed way
The tide of universal love
    Holds calm and peaceful sway.[181]
MRS. MAY M. ANDERSON

Confederate cemetery.

OLD MAXCY'S SWORD

What thoughts within my heart are stirr'd
    As on "Old Maxcy Gregg's" sword I gaze!
I seem to hear, as l have heard
    In past, but unforgotten days.
The hero's voice ring clear and high,
    In tones of brief and stern command;
I mark the flashing of his eye—
    I seem to see his lifted hand.

His gallant bearing I recall—
    A soldier to the core was he;
Alas, tis still the noblest fall,
    O dear-bought liberty, for thee!
I see him, and my soul is fill'd
    With fervors time can never quell;
I see him, and my heart is thrill'd,
    Down to its inmost, deepest cell.

The sword he bore in Mexico—
    That trusty sword is with him still;
A soldier of the long ago,
    Our Gregg a soldier's grave must fill.
For strife is raging fiercely round,
    And brave men freely shed their blood;
And every inch of Southern ground,
    Drinks up, in streams, the glorious flood.

Our Southern flag floats free and fair,
    It floats beneath the skies so blue,
And they who gave it to the air—
    They were the best the Southland knew.
Than Maxcy Gregg none better fought—
    Than Maxcy Gregg none braver fell;
The love of country in him wrought,
    And burned with fire unquenchable.

And looking on the sword he wore,
    A host of feelings in me rise;
The long years part my gaze before,
    And give the hero to my eyes,
In all the calmness of his faith,
    The simple grandeur of his soul,
In all the glory of his death,
    Where flames of battle fiercely roll.

I am a soldier for the time—
    In life's wild fret there comes a pause,
Again I rise to hopes sublime—
    Again I fight for our Lost Cause!
The dream is gone—I wake once more,
    To face the present with its need;
The flag is furl'd—the strife is o'er—
    And all the past is dead indeed![182]
NINA MANDEVILLE ROGERS

Maxcy Gregg.

THEY HAVE DONNED THE GRAY AGAIN

At the Great Commander's order,
    Though no war clouds lower to-day,
The veterans of the stars and bars
    Again have donned the gray;

And they now are marching on,
    As the swift winged years speed by,
To the camp of the battalions
    Who are tenting in the sky.

There'll be hailing of old comrades
    Some day in a brighter sphere,
There'll be welcome from the boys agone
    For the boys still tarrying here.

And those who wait their coming—
    When life's mists shall break away—
Will wonder that the old reserve
    Appears with locks of gray;

For those to whom the summons came
    Mid battles roar and grime,
Went down a glorying in the strength
    Ol' manhood's youth and prime.

We're putting on the gray again,
    Though peace its victory claims,
And the tattered banners on the wall
    Are but memory's oriflammes:

We're wearing it adown the slant,
    The hills are all behind us,
And every day a link is lost
    In the chain that seemed to bind us.

The phalanx dwindling to a squad,
    The serried line still closes
To fill the gaps that time has made,
    As one by one reposes

Close up, old boys, let elbows touch,
    The march will soon be past;
On, steady, on! ye'll wear the gray
    As long as life shall last.

If this be treason, then to Him
    Who gave and took away,
Must be the plea of the old "Coated,"
    Who again has donned the gray.[183]
S. A. JONAS

CONFEDERATE MONUMENT AT WINCHESTER

From out the ground the blood of heroes cried;
   Remembrance, hearing, would not be denied,
   And from her heartbeats loyal, pure, divine,
Rose Heavenward, stone on stone, this sacred shrine.

Long have these silent slumberers been pressed,
   Beloved Virginia! to thy faithful breast;
   And Louisiana, through her grateful tears,
Hails thee, staunch guardian of her soldiers' biers!

The buglers' notes, the drummers' calls are stilled—
   Mute all the martial hearts once battle thrilled;
   But as a banner, which the broad earth heeds,
Above them floats the splendor of their deeds!

Here rest the peerless riders of a time
   When valley campaigns rung with feats sublime;
   Here sleep the gunners who have fought the fight,
And bled and died for that they deemed the right.

Here are the hands that held undaunted swords;
   Here, men who kept our mountain gaps and fords—
   Men of the musket who could die—and smile;
Heroes and martyrs of the rank and file!

To these is reared—but not alone to these—
   This noble meed to noble memories;
   It stands above the dust it shuts within
For attributes which make all brave men kin!

It stands a monument beneath the skies
   To honest creeds, to grand self-sacrifice;
   To zeal that leaped to meet the opposing flood,
With lavish torrents of intrepid blood.

It stands for resolute purpose ne'er dismayed;
   For sacred trusts, for honor unbetrayed;
   For fearless fervor facing any fate,
For human greatness that makes nations great!

It stands for heroism; hearts to dare,
   For heights of hope, the valleys of despair;
   For stern convictions—for such soul-felt fires
As stirred our Revolutionary sires!

It stands for courage that unswerved could be
    By scourging surges of adversity;
    It stands for deeds unknown to song or story—
For Duty done alone for Duty's glory!

Farewell, ye brave who sleep beneath this stone!
    Who dies for her is e'er his country's own:
    Heir to a place upon her proudest page,
Co-heir to all her holiest heritage.

No more for you the battle nor retreat—
    This pillar, rising o'er your last defeat,
    Points, like a lifted finger, past all these
Up yonder, toward Eternal Victories![184]
MARY ASHLEY TOWNSEND

NEC TEMERE, NEC TIMIDE
["Not Rashly, Nor Timidly"]

Gentlemen of the South,
    Gird on your glittering swords!
Darkly along our borders fair
    Gather the Northern hordes.
Ruthless and fierce they come
    At the fiery cannon's mouth,
To blast the glory of our land,
    Gentlemen of the South!

Ride forth in your stately pride,
    Each bearing on his shield
Ensigns our fathers won of yore
    On many a well-fought field!
Let this be your battle-cry,
    Even to the cannon's mouth,
Cor unum via una![185] Onward,
    Gentlemen of the South!

Brave knights of a knightly race,
    Gordon, and Chambers, and Gray,
Show to the minions of the North
    How Valor dares the fray!
Let them read on each stainless crest
    At the belching cannon's mouth,
Decori decus addit avito,[186]
    Gentlemen of the South!

Morrison, Douglas, Stuart,
    Erskine, and Bradford, and West,
Your gauntlets on many a bloody field
    Have stood the battle's test!
Animo non astutia![187]
    March to the cannon's month,
Heirs of the brave dead centuries! Onward,
    Gentlemen of the South!

Call forth your stalwart men,
    Workers in brass and steel!
Bid the swart artisans come forth
    At sound of the trumpet's peal!
Give them your war-cry, Erskine!
    Fight! to the cannon's mouth!
Bid the men Forward! Douglas, Forward!
    Yeomanry of the South!

Brave hunters! Ye have met
    The fierce black bear in the fray;
Ye have trailed the panther night by night,
    Ye have chased the fox by day!
Your prancing chargers pant
    To dash at the gray wolf's mouth,
Your arms are sure of their quarry! Onward!
    Gentlemen of the South!

Fight! that the lowly serf
    And the high-born lady still
May bide in their proud dependency,
    Free subjects of your will!
Teach the base North how ill,
    At the fiery cannon's mouth,
He fares who touches your household gods,
    Gentlemen of the South!

From mother, and wife, and child,
    From faithful and happy slave,
Prayers for your sakes ascend to Him
    Whose arm is strong to save!
We check the gathering tears,
    Though ye go to the cannon's mouth;
Dominus providebit![188] Onward,
    Gentlemen of the South![189]
ANNIE CHAMBERS KETCHUM

WHEN WILL PAPA COME?

By a quiet cottage fireside
    She sits, a matron pale and fair;
Her eyes rest, with a troubled look,
    On her husband's vacant chair;
Her children—a lovely boy and girl—
    Are playing at her feet;
The wintry wind sighs mournfully,
    And the pattering rain and sleet
Upon the roof and window panes
    Their dreary tattoo beat.

"Mamma!" says the little girl,
    "When will papa come?
It seems to me such along, long time
    Since he left us at home.
He used to take me in his arms,
    And such pretty stories tell;
And then I'd sing those little songs
    Which he always loved so well;
But I've no one now to tell me tales—
    No one to hear my song!
Oh! when will papa come again?
    Say, mamma, will it be long?"
The mother shuddered as she heard
    The sound of the wind and rain.
And said: "My dear, when the war is o'er.
    Papa will come again."

She thought of the weary midnight march,
    As she gazed upon the hearth,
And of the bivouac, hungry and cold,
    Upon the frozen earth;
She thought of the bloody battle-field,
    The wounded and slain,
And she prayed to God to spare his life,
    And bring him home again.

"Mother," said the fair-haired boy,
    "Why don't my papa come?
He said he'd come back very soon
    When he went away from home.
We used to be so happy
    When he came home at night;
You never looked sad then, mamma,
    And your face was always bright.

He gave me such nice picture books,
    And, oh! so many toys!
And told me tales, as I sat on his knee,
    About good little boys.
I often think, my dear mamma,
    That he'd come back to me
If he only knew how very glad
    His little boy would be.
I wonder if papa is out
    In all this cold and rain!
What makes you cry, my mother dear?
    When will he come again?"

Thomas C. Hindman Jr. with his children.

She pressed her little one close to her heart,
    As if to still its pain,
While the rain rushed by with a sullen roar,
    And the pelting hail beat more and more
Against the window pane;
    And said, in a voice more sad than before,
"Hush, son, when the war is o'er,
    Papa will come again."

The night wind howls and the rain and sleet
    Sweep o'er the battle plain;
On the gory field so thickly strewn
    With the wounded and the slain.
A manly form lies stark and cold.
    His life-blood dyes the sod,
And with a prayer for his wife and babes,
    He gives his soul to God.

Ah, mother! clasp your little ones
    Still closer to our breast!
May God in tender mercy give
    Your troubled spirit rest;
For many a long and weary night,
    With an aching heart and brain,
Will you sit by that lonely fireside
    And wait and watch in vain;
For the winds may blow, and the wintry sleet,
    And the pattering rain may beat and bent
Against the window pane—
    But the husband and father dear
Will never come again.[190]
J. M. B.

THE SOUTHERN BATTLE FLAGS

Now, Southern men, take off your hats, and ho! ye, all the world,
Stand up and with uncovered heads, salute those flags unfurled!
Though faded much and tattered more, they once were banners bright,
As once were young those men whose hairs old age has rendered white.
And who so bravely followed them, in battle line arrayed,
In those discordant days of death when roared the cannonade.

All harmlessly for many a year those battle flags have lain
Upon the closet shelves of those who fought for them in vain.
The sore at first was hard to heal, as ever is the case
When fiercely meet in civil strife one nation and one race.
Yet, praised be God! 'tis ended now, and foreign foes shall dread
But all the more the Stars and Stripes for all the blood we've shed.

Yet why should not we Southern men who once, as Southern boys,
'Mid shot and shell and canister and battle's dreadful noise,
Followed a flag o'er many a field where, comrades, falling fast,
Gave for the cause they loved so well their best blood and their last,
Take off our hats at sight of it just one day in the year?
Think of the memories that well up and flow into that cheer!

In ragged clothes we marched with it the hot and dusty road,
And felt our haversacks grow light, our cartridge box a load.
And here and there, on wintry days, we saw the frozen sod
And trampled snow tinged with the blood of bleeding feet unshod;
Yet we were rich in high resolve, and though we oft lacked food,
We had what most a soldier needs—a flag and fortitude!
Oh! where is he, of North or South, who lives and bravely fought,
Who does not know how easily he finds himself o'erwrought
By all the memories of those days, so suddenly aroused
By his old flag, whichever be the cause that he espoused?

At Seven Pines we saw it borne amid the smoke and din,
While whistling bullets tore its folds and our full ranks grew thin;
At Gaines' Mill and at Frazier's Farm, and Malvern Hill it fell,
We saw it lifted up again and gave the "Rebel yell."
With Pickett's men at Gettysburg, it led the charge to death,
While bleeding heroes cheered it on with their last dying breath.

At Spottsylvania, Wilderness, and Chickamauga's field.
And twice a hundred more, foes had learned to it to yield.
At last it fell no more to rise—God's wisdom willed it so—
And few are left who fought with it, and they too soon must go;
Yet of the years still left to us we love one day in each
To see and cheer the flag we bore into the deadly breach.

You are the victors. Brave you were, you boys who wore the blue,
And Valor never yet denied a fallen foe his due.
The fight is o'er. Our wounds are healed. We clasp your hand again;
But while we hold it fast and fair, remember we're but men
Who cannot quite forget the flag for which our brave ones fell,
And so whene'er we see its folds, we feel our bosoms swell.

Then grudge us not, brave boys in blue, that once or so a year
We meet our comrades of lang syne and give the flag a cheer.
We have no cause for quarrel now, and never more shall face
Each other in intestine war, but rather would embrace,
And teach our children to defend the old Red, White and Blue—
The flag our common fathers loved, the only one they knew;
But give us credit for good faith, and it will all be well,
And ask us not to scorn the flag for which our brothers fell.

Do it dishonor? That battle flag? Look on it with disdain?
No: never while our pulses beat our honor will we stain;
Yet will we touch our elbows close to yours, if comes the need
That we for our united land be called upon to bleed.
And North and South as friends again shall be to each so true
That both can march to "Dixie's Land" and "Yankee Doodle," too;
But never ask that we shall be so false unto our dead
That we can turn our backs upon the flag for which they bled.[191]
FRANKLIN H. MACKEY

OUR VETERANS AT RICHMOND

They'll meet no more at Richmond—the men who fought with Lee,
Who met the marching legions of Sherman to the sea;
Who blazed the way with "Stonewall" and carved their glorious names
On the battlefields of Richmond, of "Richmond on the James."

They'll meet no more at Richmond; their brows are bowed and white.
And faint the campfires flicker from the valley of the night;
And "Farewell" echoes down the line, where flashed their crimsoned blades,
And the shadow's deepen, deepen round the boys of the brigades.

They'll meet no more at Richmond, where every battle clod,
In red memorial roses, sends messages to God;
Where brave and bright they faced the fight where Lee and Jackson led.
And left the dim vales glorious with the ashes of their dead.

They'll meet no more at Richmond; the long night's shadows fall;
O'er the dividing ramparts the phantom captains call,
And "Farewell" echoes down the line where flashed their warning blades—
A long farewell to Richmond from the boys of the brigades![192]

FRANK LEBBY STANTON

Reunion of Confederate veterans.

DAUGHTER OF THE CONFEDERACY

Proud? Yes, we are very proud to say
Our fathers wore Confederate gray,
   In that struggle for the right;
And we've united into a band
All over this sunny Southern land,
   For which they did nobly fight.

Since little children on papa's knee,
We've heard the praises of Robert Lee,
   And immortal is his name.
We have loved the cause our whole lives long,
We'll sing o'er and o'er the Dixie song,
   With never a pang of shame.

What is our mission, do you ask me?
'Tis to keep alive the memory
   Of the deeds so brave and bold,
When our men, in unequal strife,
Each nobly risked, for States' rights, his life,
   And the story must be told.

With flowers the rarest to be found,
We'll bedeck every lowly mound
   Of the fallen heroes brave;
And with gentle hands and words of cheer,
We'll smooth the paths of the soldiers here,
   As they wend toward the grave.

We'll perpetuate the rebel yell,
And all the South will the anthem swell
   With voices strong and loud;
For our soldier-boys, year after year,
Struggled on, knowing naught of fear,
   And we're proud of them—yes, proud![193]
Z. Z. T.

PRIVATE AT THE PLOW

His old blade is now a plowshare,
    And he makes as straight a row
As his bullets made their furrows
    Through the mad, invading foe.
Such men are not in places high,
    Nor on monumental stone;
But of grand and holy meaning
    They have made the word—Unknown![194]
IDA PORTER OCKENDEN

REBEL OR LOYALIST (TO A YANKEE)

I was a rebel, if you please,
    A reckless fighter to the last,
Nor do I fall upon my knees
    And beg forgiveness for the past.

A traitor! I a traitor? No!
    I was a patriot to the core;
The South was mine; I loved her so,
    I gave her all—I could do no more.

You scowl at me. And was it wrong
    To wear the gray my father wore?
Could I slink back, though young and strong,
    From foes before my mother's door?

My mother's kiss was hot with fight;
    My father's frenzy filled his son;
Through reeking days and sodden nights,
    My sister's courage urged me on.

And I, a missile steeped in hate,
    Hurled forward like a cannon ball
By the resistless hand of fate,
    Rushed wildly, madly through it all.

I stemmed the level flames of hell;
    O'er bayonet bars of death I broke;
I was so near when Cleburne fell,
    I heard the muffled bullet stroke!

But all in vain. With dull despair
    I saw the storm of conflict die;
Low lay the Southern banner fair,
    And yonder flag was waving high.

God! What a triumph had the foe!
    Laurel, and arch and trumpet-blare;
All round the earth their songs did go;
    Thundering through heaven their shouts did tear.

M mother, gray and bent with years,
    Hoarding love's withered aftermath,
Her sweet eyes burnt too dry for tears,
    Sat in the dust of Sherman's path.

My father, broken, helpless, poor,
    A gloomy, nerveless giant stood:
Too strong to cower and endure,
    Too weak to fight for masterhood.

M boyhood's home—a blackened heap
    Where lizards crawled and briars grew—
Had felt the fire of vengeance creep,
    The crashing round shot hurtle through.

I had no country; all was lost;
    I closed my eyes and longed to die,
While past me stalked the awful ghost
    Of mangled, murdered Liberty.

The scars upon my body burned;
    I felt a heel upon my throat;
A heel that ground, and, grinding, turned
    With each triumphant trumpet-note.

"Grind on," I cried; "nor doubt that I—
    If all your necks were one and low
As mine is now—delightedly,
    Would cut it by a single blow."

That was dark night; but day is here,
    The crowning victory is won;
Hark! how the sixty millions cheer,
    With freedom's flag across the sun.

Am I a traitor? Who are you
    That dare to breathe that word to me?
You never wore the Union blue;
    No wounds affirm your loyalty!

I do detest the sutler's clerk,
    Who skulked and dodged till peace had come.
Then found it more congenial work
    To beat the politician's drum.

I clasp the hand that made my scars,
    I cheer the flag my foeman bore;
I shout for joy to see the stars
    All on our common shield once more.

I do not cringe before you now,
    Or lay my face upon the ground;

I am a man, of men a peer,
    And not a cowering, cudgeled hound.

Remembering those dead boys in gray,
    With thoughts too deep and fine for words,
I lift this cup of love to-day
    And drink what only love affords.

Soldiers in blue, a health to you!
    Long life and vigor oft renewed!
While on your hearts, like honey-dew,
    Falls our great country's gratitude.[195]
MAURICE THOMPSON

TO COMPANY B, TWELFTH VIRGINIA CAVALRY

Bugler, bugler, sound the rally,
Call our boys home to the valley
    Loveliest vale of the world.
Whose glades and streamlets oft were red,
When her young heroes fought and bled
    For the bonnie flag now furled.

Sound, for they're scattered far and wide;
Some make their home by ocean's tide;
    Some dwell on the Western moors;
A few in the dear old homes remain;
For many the "call" will sound in vain—
    They're at rest on heaven's bright shores.

From far and near we'll have them all—
From lowly cot, from lordly hall,
    Come back and "dress on the line!"
We'll listen to the war-time story;
Tears we'll give to those in glory—
    Those comrades of auld lang syne.

Then they were all youthful and gay;
Now they are aged, saddened, and gray.
    But their hearts are true as steel;
Still they burn with the high desire
That stirred alike both son and sire
    To die for the Southland's weal.

"Fighting" sergeant, you call the roll
Name every daring, dauntless soul
    Of gallant Company B.
Through winter's snow, through summer's sun
They marched and fought and battles won
    With Jackson, with Stuart and Lee.

Had the plumed knights of the olden days.
Who are sung in Scotch and English lays,
    A purer, nobler chivalry?
Nay, their courage reached no grander height,
Nor do they shine in a purer light,
    Than the knights of Company B.[196]
FANNIE J. G. TIMBERLAKE

THE BURIAL OF CAPTAIN WILLIAM LATANÉ

The combat raged not long, but ours the day;
    And through the hosts that compassed us around
Our little band rode proudly on its way,
    Leaving one gallant comrade, glory-crowned,
Unburied on the field he died to gain,
Single of all his men amid the hostile slain.

One moment on the battle's edge he stood,
    Hope's halo like a helmet round his hair;
The next beheld him dabbled in his blood,
    Prostrate in death, and yet in death how fair!
E'en thus he passed through the red gate of strife
From earthly crowns and palms to an immortal life.

A brother bore his body from the field,
    And gave it unto strangers' hands, that closed
The calm blue eyes, on earth forever sealed,
    And tenderly the slender limbs composed;
Strangers, yet sisters, who, with Mary's love,
Sat by the open tomb, and, weeping, looked above.

A little child strewed roses on his bier,
    Pale roses, not more stainless than his soul,
Nor yet more fragrant than his life sincere,
    That blossomed with good actions, brief, but whole.
The aged matron and the faithful slave
Approached with reverent feet the hero's lowly grave.

No man of God might read the burial rite
    Above the Rebel—thus declared the foe
That blanched before him in the deadly fight;
    But woman's voice, in accents soft and low,
Trembling with pity, touched with pathos, read
Over this hallowed dust the ritual for the dead:

William Latané.

"'Tis sown in weakness, it is raised in power;"
    Softly the promise floated on the air,
And the sweet breathings of the sunset hour
    Came back responsive to the mourner's prayer;
Gently they laid him underneath the sod,
And left him with his fame, his country, and his God.

Let us not weep for him, whose deeds endure;
    So young, so brave, so beautiful, he died

As he had wished to die—the past is sure!
    Whatever yet of sorrow may betide
Those who still linger by the stormy shore.
Change cannot touch him now, nor fortune harm him more.

And when Virginia, leaning on her spear—
    "*Victrix et Vidua*,"[197] the conflict done—
Shall raise her mailed hand to wipe the tear
    That starts as she recalls each martyred son,
No prouder memory her breast shall sway
Than thine, our early lost, lamented Latané.[198]
JOHN REUBEN THOMPSON

"The Burial of Latané," by William Dickinson Washington.

A SOLDIER IN GRAY

A soldier at Antietam, in frenzied battle fray,
With gory wounds was bleeding his boyish life away;
The ashen hue of pallor that gathered o'er his face
Betokened that the soldier had well-nigh run his race.
The glassy, shining luster of his bright and tearless eye
Revealed beyond all doubting the youth was bound to die.
Though death at him was staring, he hummed a roundelay
Of his "Old Kentucky Home," so far, so far away.

A comrade heard him singing, and that delirious tongue
Was like the swan's when dying, the sweetest he'd e'er sung.
He knew that measured cadence was but a sad refrain,
Which, when it ceased its toning, he ne'er would sing again.
So, kneeling down beside him, he opened his canteen;
He bathed his face with water till it was white and clean.
The handsome youth was dying—belonged to Company K,
From an "Old Kentucky Home," so far, so far away.

"Some messages you'll carry? Then thank you, comrade true,
And I have something other I'd like to send by you
To her whose lovely image, 'mid battle's bloody fight,
Or 'mid the peaceful quiet of bivouac for the night,
Was ever present with me, a solace and a cheer,
In time of deepest trouble it ever hovered near.
Then take, O take this picture—she gave it me one day
In her 'Old Kentucky Home,' so far, so far away.

"Then tell her how I prized it, and wore it near my heart.
It was her love-medallion, my gift its counterpart.
The sulphurous glare of battle I'll never witness more,
For soon I'll cross the river and seek the other shore;
That 'mid Antietam's thunder, please say to her for me,
'Twas on my country's altar, I made libation free,
Poured out my life willingly, and wore with pride the gray
For my 'Old Kentucky Home,' so far, so far away.

"These letters too I'll send to her, with blood-spots here and there.
Please tell her 'bout the comfort these bright effusions were;
As cheering, glad talismans I conned them o'er and o'er,
For I loved the writer truly, as I never loved before.
Tell her how I loved her, and in the arms of death
I breathed for her a blessing, e'en with my latest breath,
And in my invocation asked a token for display
In her 'Old Kentucky Home,' so far, so far away.

"And now, my comrade, listen: This watch you'll take with you.
Please give it to my brother, the younger of us two,
And tell him he must wear it—a brother's dying gift.
Who, oft amid the battle, the smoke of battle whiffed,
And when the charging legion raised loud their wild war-cry,
Although mortally wounded, was not afraid to die.
Tell him that I still proudly wear my suit of gray,
For my 'Old Kentucky Home,' so far, so far away.

"You'll please say, too, to brother, for parents growing old
Attention he must shower—no kindness must withhold.
His tender care of mother, her sorrow may assuage,
While grieving that so early I closed my pilgrimage.
My country's wrongs demanded my arm and then my life.
I answered her demanding, and joined the dreadful strife;
I left ancestral plenty, and donned a suit of gray,
For my 'Old Kentucky Home,' so far, so far away.

"O would that I could wander once more o'er hill and dell,
Which once in childhood gamb'lings I loved, and loved so well.
Alas! I'm wounded—dying, on field of carnage grim,
O'er which the morning sunlight is swiftly growing dim.
To home and love and kindred, a long and last good-bye,
For I, who am a soldier, am ready now to die.
I fought the fight, and lost it—a sergeant dressed in gray,
From an 'Old Kentucky Home,' so far, so far away."

His whisper grew more feeble, his eyes assumed a stare,
Then limp his limbs fell trembling aside his body there.
The brave, heroic soldier had fallen into sleep,
'Round which the holy angels will constant vigils keep.
Till reveille is sounded by Gabriel, loud and clear,
To call the sleeping soldier to "line up in the rear,"
And to eternal camping, march him who wore the gray
From an "Old Kentucky Home," so far, so far away.[199]
J. T. PATTERSON

VIRGINIA

Virginia! land of the gentle and brave,
    Our love is as wide as thy woe;
It deepens beside every grave
    Where the heart of a hero lies low.

Virginia! land of the bluest of skies,
    Our love glows the more mid thy gloom;
Our hearts by saddest of ties
    Cling closest to thee in thy doom.

Virginia! land where the desolate weep
    In sorrow too deep to console;
Thy tears are but streams making deep
    The ocean of love in thy soul.

Virginia! land where the victor flag waves,
    Where only our dead are the free;
Each link of the chain that enslaves
    Shall bind us but closer to thee.

Virginia! land where the sign of the cross
    Its shadow of sorrow hath shed;
We measure thy love by thy loss,
    Thy loss by the graves of our dead.[200]
N. N. P.

Hot Springs Resort, Virginia.

THE OLD SOUTH

I love her hills, I love her dales,
Her towering peaks and sunny vales:
I love her best for struggles won
By fearless sires and gallant sons.

I love her laws, her history great,
Her manners, customs, and men of state;
But better still—her strength and might—
In battling for the cause of right.

I love her, too, for suffering much
From vandal hordes while at their worst;
I loved her then in sore distress,
But doubly so while in duress.

O mighty land! of natal birth,
I love your soil—your greater worth—
In struggling up from sore defeat
To industrial arts and humanizing peace.

Well may we love the old land yet,
That gave us men we can't forget—
Like Washington, our nation's guide,
And Robert Lee, the Southron's pride.[201]
ALEXANDER HELPER

VIRGE MOOSE

Here he is in a wreck of gray
With the brazen belt of the "C.S.A."
Men, do you know him? Far away,
Where battle blackened the face of day,
And the rapid rivers in crimson fled,
And God's white roses were reeked in red,
His strength he gave and his blood he shed—
Followed fearless where Stonewall led,
Or galloped wild in the wake of Lee,
In the dashing, mad artillery—
Shelled the ranks of the enemy
For the South that was and the South to be!
Or bore his musket with wounded hands
O'er icy rivers and burning sands,
Leveled straight at the hostile bands
That sped like death through the ravaged lands!
Men! do you know him? Grim and gray,
He speaks to you from the far away!

There he stands on the prison sod—
A statue carved by the hand of God;
And the deaths he dared and the paths he trod
Plead for him in a voice that seems
Wild and sad with the battle-dreams,
And memory's river backward streams
With its strange unrest and crimson gleams!
There he stands like a hero—see!
He bore his rags and his wound for ye!
He bore the flag of the warring South
With red-scarred hands to the cannon's mouth—
By heaven! I see, as I did that day,
His red wounds gleam through the rags of gray!

Men of the South! Your heroes stand
Statue-like in the new-born land!
Will ye pass them by? Will your lips condemn?
The wounds on their brave breasts plead for them!
Shall the South that they gave their blood to save
Give them only a nameless grave?
Nay! for the men who faced the fray
Are hers in trust till the judgment-day!
And God himself, in the far, sweet lands,
Will ask their blood of their country's hands!

Soldier! You in the wreck of gray,

With the brazen belt of the "C.S.A.,"
Take my love and my tears to-day!
Take them—all that I have to give.
But by God's grace, while my heart shall live,
It still shall keep in its faithful way
The camp-fires lit for the men in gray—
Aye! till the trump sounds far away,
And the silver bugles of heaven play,
And the roll is called at the judgment-day.[202]
FRANK LEBBY STANTON

A CONFEDERATE MONUMENT

A gleaming cross, on broken staff
    The stars and bars reclining;
A gallant sword, broken in half,
    Fond vines the base entwining.

Thus o'er the mold, in outlines bold,
    Hath some poetic master
Written in stone, in solemn tone,
    A story of disaster.

And scattered round in many a mound,
    Where sacred dust is sleeping;
While stony guard, all battle-scarred,
    His silent watch is keeping.

Here sleep the dead whose lives ran red,
    And Southern fields made gory;
With gallant stride they clasped the bride
    Whose nuptial veil is glory.

O may they rest among the blest
    In yonder fields Elysian,
Where, hand in hand with foeman band,
    They sanction might's decision![203]
M. A. CASSIDY

OUR VETERANS

They are passing from our midst,
    Crossing o'er the river,
Underneath the trees to rest
    In the shade forever.

O they were a gallant band,
    Boys who wore the gray!
When the storm of battle raged,
    Who so brave as they?

Who so true to face the worst
    When the strife was o'er,
And the flag they loved so well
    Furled for evermore?

Brothers all in heart are we
    Who once wore the gray;
When a gray-haired veteran dies—
    "One of us," we say.

And our ranks are thinning fast—
    Vacant places meet us
When we gather where of old
    Comrades used to greet us.

As the brave and noble die,
    Dies the veteran gray;
Comrades from the other side
    Beckon us away.

Soldiers of the Southern hosts—
    Men who knew no fear,
Leaders in the Southern cause
    Call us—we are here![204]
UNKNOWN

Confederate veterans.

THE CONFEDERACY

Born in a day, full-grown, our Nation stood,
    The pearly light of heaven was on her face;
Life's early joy was coursing in her blood;
    A thing she was of beauty and of grace.

She stood, a stranger on the great broad earth,
    No voice of sympathy was heard to greet
The glory-beaming morning of her birth,
    Or hail the coming of the unsoiled feet.

She stood, derided by her passing foes;
    Her heart beat calmly 'neath their look of scorn;
Their rage in blackening billows round her rose—
    Her brow, meanwhile, as radiant as the morn.

Their poisonous coils about her limbs are cast,
    She shakes them off in pure and holy ire,
As quietly as Paul, in ages past,
    Shook off the serpent in the crackling fire.

She bends not to her foes, nor to the world,
    She bears a heart for glory, or for gloom;
But with her starry cross, her flag unfurled,
    She kneels amid the sweet magnolia bloom.

She kneels to Thee, O God, she claims her birth,
    She lifts to Thee her young and trusting eye,
She asks of Thee her place upon the earth—
    For it is Thine to give or to deny.

Oh, let Thine eye but recognize her right!
    Oh, let Thy voice but justify her claim!
Like grasshoppers are nations in Thy sight,
    And all their power is but an empty name.

Then listen, Father, listen to her prayer!
    Her robes are dripping with her children's blood;
Her foes around "like bulls of Bashan stare,"
    They fain would sweep her off, "as with a flood."

The anguish wraps her close around, like death,
    Her children lie in heaps about her slain;
Before the world she bravely holds her breath,
    Nor gives one utterance to a note of pain.

But 'tis not like Thee to forget the oppressed,
    Thou feel'st within her heart the stifled moan—
Thou Christ! Thou Lamb of God! oh, give her rest!
    For Thou hast called her!—is she not Thine own?[205]

JANE T. H. CROSS

THOSE WHO CANNOT RALLY

I have sounded "boots and saddles," I have blown the "reveille,"
But they come not from the valleys nor the mountains nor the sea.
How we loved them in young manhood, when in pride they went away!
How we wept, yet how we gloried in the boys who wore the gray!

I have sounded "boots and saddles," yet how hollow, ghostly, drear,
Went the sound adown the sad winds! few there are now who can hear;
For the years on years have faded, orphan children gray have grown,
Since the father spilled his lifeblood on the battlefield alone.

I have sounded "boots and saddles" both on morn and eve, and then
Many proudly round me rallied in their strength to strike like men.
Straight they rode toward their foemen, rode like men to battle clash,
And above them in the sunlight might be seen the saber's flash.

Brave they were; and O how glorious was the cause they died to save!
Shall the bugler try to call them from a doubly-honored grave?
Shall we try to move the blood spots? Never! never! let them stay;
For they prove how true the men were who once wore the hallowed
    gray.

Let them rest—they did their duty; did their duty like men true;
For they freely shed their lifeblood—that was all that they could do;
And they left for us their glory, which they earned on many a day
When the red blood flowed so freely from the men who wore the gray.

I will sound now "boots and saddles," for there's still a remnant here;
Doubly loved and doubly honored, they, too, fought for this cause dear.
Old they are, but still the hot blood flows as wild as on the day
They with saber and with rifle made the world all love the gray.[206]
DR. J. B. STINSON

THE GREAT CONFEDERATE REUNION AT RICHMOND

O you should have been at Richmond, my dear fellow!
    Yes, you should have been at Richmond and have seen
The scarred and rusty veterans, sere and yellow,
    Going on as if they only were eighteen,
    And you should have seen their smiles with tears between.

And you should have seen their bearded, happy faces
    As they came across old comrades in the street,
And you should have seen their greetings and embraces—
    How they looked each other o'er from head to feet,
    Then went hunting, with hooked arms, the nearest seat.

And you should have seen that grandest of processions,
    Heard the bands a playing "Dixie" and "Lang Syne;"
Heard the shouting of the crowds, and the expressions
    From the women as they waved their kerchiefs fine
    To the men who walked so proudly in the line.

And you should have seen the faces of the people,
    Of two hundred thousand people in the town.
Every porch, every window, every steeple—
    They were crowded with those faces looking down,
    And on not a single one was there a frown.

And the men who bore their hardships as a trifle
    In those cruel days that now are days of old;
Who had stanched their bleeding wounds, yet could not stifle
    The warm tears, that were never bought nor sold,
    Which adown their cheeks involuntary rolled.

No, you never should have missed it, my dear fellow;
    'Twas a jubilee to channel through your heart.
And flush it till its fibers all grew mellow
    With the memories of which you were a part.
    And as faithful at the end as at the start.

Never monarch of his scepter could be prouder,
    Never lover giving kisses to his bride,
Than old Richmond, with her plaudits, loud and louder,
    As she greeted those who came from far and wide—
    The old soldiers who had laid their swords aside.

Did you ever see a wild tornado tearing
    Through the forest, bending trees upon its way?

So our battle-flags were swayed with every cheering,
    With the never-ceasing cheering of that day,
    With the soul-impassioned cheering of the gray!

What a thrilling, fervid swelling of each bosom!
    What an animated, stimulated crowd!
What a frantic, wild, and raving paroxysm
    Rose, full-throated, as those tattered flags were bowed.
    All forgetting how each one was but a shroud!

And to whom belonged those voices there uprising?
    To what ancestry is traced the blood of these?
Were they Huns and Goths and Vandals exorcising
    The red demons of their tribes upon their knees
    While a southern sun was shining through the trees?

Were they of the hordes of those who had invaded
    And had spat upon our loved land in the past,
When old England thought her manhood not degraded
    By her Hessians that she blushed for at the last,
    Yet in later days our kinsmen brought so fast?

Brought from Europe when an anger did embroil us,
    Brought from Europe with their jargon—gave them guns,
Waved the stars and stripes, and told them to despoil us;
    Give them bounties for the killing of our sons;
    Give this hired herd of foreign myrmidons?

No: those heart o'erflowing thousands have descended
    From the fathers! 'Twas their blood was boiling o'er;
They were children of the men who had defended
    Their country, and—as their fathers were before—
    Sons of the soil that their faithful feet upbore.

Yes, Americans, full-blooded, all untainted,
    Loving country, loving home, and loving God;
Swinging censers to the memory of the sainted
    Sons of Liberty, when Freedom felt the rod.
    Ere she builded here her temple on their sod.

Siring men whom all history presages,
    When America shall need her men, will be
Her true patriots, her statesmen, and her sages,
    Taught of Washington and Jackson and by Lee,
    And inspired by their noble pedigree.

"Rebel yells?" Brothers of the North, when your fathers

  Stood with ours, as they battled for one cause.
So they shouted—hear the echo as it gathers
  In these voices—hear the echo, and then pause,
  For their spirits now are shouting this applause.[207]
FRANKLIN H. MACKEY

NASHVILLE'S INVITATION

Come, you hoary-headed "gray-backs," though with feeble, halting gait—
    Come and warm your age-iced blood at eternal mem'ry's fire,
Swap a lie and crack a joke with any olden-time messmate,
    Share our grub, and drain our canteens if a "nip" you should desire;
For the portals of our city open wide to let you pass,
    And the latchstrings of the houses dangle outside in the air;
While, upon the threshold smiling, matrons staid and rosy lass
    Stand with open arms, inviting you to halt and enter there.

Widows, mothers, sisters, daughters, cheer us with your presence rare,
    Let the unforgotten glories of the South's undying past
Temper grief, and for the moment smooth away the lines of care,
    Since for many you shall smile at this parade will be the last.
Shades of Jackson, Lee, and Johnston, Stuart, Forrest, Morgan, too,
    Come and mingle with our spirits, lead once more your dwindling hosts;
Let us feel again inspiring, magic force of hearts so true;
    Make of glories past conception something more than shiv'ring ghosts.

Chickamauga, Appomattox, roll your battle clouds away;
    Gettysburg and Lookout Mountain, halt before this history page;
Ribs of sunken *Alabama*, from your bed in Cherbourg's Bay,
    Wraiths of war, "eyes front," beholding greatest wonder of this age.
From the Southland's farthest corners come the men who wore the gray—
    Come to write again their story on the leaf of history.
Come to mingle precious mem'ries with the sorrows of to-day,
    And triumphant, though defeated, chant the magic name of "Lee."

Here's a welcome for you "blue-coats"—you who faced us in the field;
    Come, and in fraternal greetings bury passions of that strife.
Hearts and hands are open to you—don't refuse us: simply yield.
    Such impulses as this greeting give and feed a nation's life.
We will welcome you as warmly as we did in sixty-one;
    But, instead of whistling bullets and destruction-dealing shell,
We will spread the festal table underneath our Southern sun.
    Come and hear once more the music of that curdling "Rebel yell."

Come then, "Rebels," "Johnnies," "Gray-backs," "Yanks," and "Blue-coats," come along.
    Tears for noble dead and cheering for the heroes with us yet.
Hearty grips from former foemen, wealth of beauty, bursts of song—
    Yes, combined will make a picture that the coldest can't forget.

And the sun will shine the brighter, and the rose, in proud array,
    Will give forth a richer fragrance; while the violets in their dells
Joyous lift their lowly heads upon that memorable day
    When the Tennessean heavens ring once more with "Rebel yells."[208]
ALBERT SIDNEY MORTON

Pierre G. T. Beauregard.

HE'LL SEE IT WHEN HE WAKES

Amid the clouds of battle smoke
    The sun had died away,
And where the storm of battle broke
    A thousand warriors lay.
A band of friends upon the field
    Stood round a youthful form,
Who, when the war cloud's thunder pealed,
    Had perished in the storm,
Upon his forehead, on his hair,
    The coming moonlight breaks,
And each dear brother standing there
    A tender farewell takes.

But ere they laid him in his home
    There came a comrade near,
And gave a token that had come
    From her the dead held dear.
A moment's doubt upon them pressed,
    Then one the letter takes
And lays it low upon his breast—
    "He'll see it when he wakes."
O thou who dost in sorrow wait,
    Whose heart in anguish breaks,
Though thy dear message came too late,
    "He'll see it when he wakes."

No more amid the fiery storm
    Shall his strong arm be seen,
No more his young and manly form
    Tread Mississippi's green;
And e'en thy tender words of love—
    The words affection speaks—
Came all too late; but O thy love
    Will "see them when he wakes!"
No jars disturb his gentle rest,
    No noise his slumber breaks;
But thy words sleep upon his breast—
    "He'll see them when he wakes."[209]
FRANK LEE

TO A STATUE OF SAM DAVIS

Hero, could thy steadfast eyes,
From the scaffold to the skies
Looking toward eternity,
See the great futurity?
When thy lips refused to speak
Words thy judge from thee would take,
Did thy brow so broad and fair
Lower with no line of care?

Couldst thou in thy self-reliance,
Bidding all the laws defiance,
As one then in honor should,
Know the coming attitude
Of the world when thy fair name
Would be honored, known to fame,
When thy great deed would inspire
Countless minds to something higher?

Couldst thou guess in bronze and story
Ages would repeat thy glory
When the fate was realized
That thy deed immortalized?
No, brave soul; thy death more glorious
Was, that thou, victorious,
Shouldst in simple bravery
Live heroic in life's memory.[210]
GABRIELLE TOWNSEND STEWART

Sam Davis statue, Pulaski, TN. Photo L. Seabrook.

THE SONG "DIXIE" WILL NOT BE BANNED

I love it well, the dear old song
Once borne by the wind along
Over fields where bullets did rain,
Heard 'mid cheers and cries of pain—
    The martial strains of "Dixie."

I loved it in the hour of rest,
When victory flushed, or fear oppressed,
In contests fierce, when foemen fly,
Where heroes fall, for victory die—
    I hear the strains of "Dixie."

I think of one in war so great,
Of one whom history shall relate
His purpose pure—bravest of men!
I think of Lee, and once again
    I hear the band play "Dixie."

Though we forget the battle's glare,
We can't forget what cheered us there.
Though foemen won at fearful cost,
Although our country's cause is lost,
    Left to us still is "Dixie."

I know that in a brighter land,
When sings again the noble band
Who fought with such a purpose strong,
Encouraged by the dear old song,
    I'll hear the tune of "Dixie."[211]
MISS EMMA E. WHITNEY

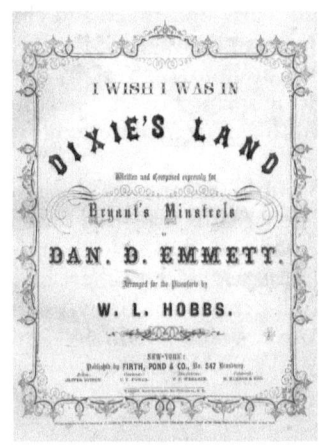

Sheet music.

DECKING SOUTHERN SOLDIERS' GRAVES

Beautiful feet! with maidenly tread,
Offerings bring to the gallant dead;
Footsteps light press the sacred sod,
Of souls untimely ascended to God.
Bring spring flowers, in fragrant perfume.
And offer sweet prayers for a merciful doom.

Beautiful hands! ye deck the graves
Above the dust of the Southern braves,
Here was extinguished their manly fire,
Rather than flinch from the Northman's ire.
Bring spring flowers! the laurel and rose,
And deck your defenders' place of repose.

Beautiful eyes! the tears ye shed,
Are brighter than diamonds to those who bled.
Spurned is the cause they fell to save,
But "little they'll reck," if ye love their grave.
Bring spring flowers! with tears and praise,
And chant o'er their tombs your grateful lays.

Beautiful lips! ye tremble now,
Memory wakens the sleeping one's vow;
Mute are the lips, and faded the forms,
That never knelt down, save to God and your charms.
Bring spring flowers! all dewy with morn,
And think how they loved you, whose graves ye adorn.

Beautiful hearts! of matron and maid,
Faithful were ye when apostles betrayed!
Here are your loved and cherished ones laid.
Peace to their ashes; the flowers ye strew
Are monuments worthy the faithful and true.
Bring spring flowers! perfume their sod,
With annual incense to glory and God.

Beautiful tribute at valor's shrine!
The wreaths that fond ones lovingly twine.
Let the whole world their ashes despise,
Those whom they cherished, with heart, hands, and eyes,
Will bring spring flowers, and bow the head,
And pray for the noble Confederate dead.[212]
A. W. SLAYBACK

GENERAL ARCHIBALD GRACIE OF ALABAMA

O sons of mighty stature,
    And souls that match the best,
When nations name their jewels,
    Let Alabama rest.

Gracie, of Alabama!
    'Twas on that dreadful day,
When hurtling hounds were fiercest
    With Petersburg at bay,

Gracie, of Alabama,
    Walked down the lines with Lee,
Marking, through mists of gunshot,
    The clouds of enemy:

Scanning the Anaconda
    At every scale and joint,
And halting, glasses leveled,
    At gaze on "Dead Man's Point."

Thrice Alabama's warning
    Fell on a heedless ear,
While the relentless lead-storm,
    Conveying, hurtled near;

'Till straight before his chieftain,
    Without a sound or sign,
He stood, a shield the grandest
    Against the Union line.

And then the glass was lowered,
    And voice that faltered not
Said in its measured cadence:
    "Why, Gracie, you'll be shot!"

And Alabama answered:
    "The South will pardon me
If the ball that goes through Gracie
    Comes short of Robert Lee."

Swept a swift flash of crimson
    Athwart the chieftain's cheek,
And the eyes whose glance was knighthood
    Spake as no king could speak.

And side by side with Gracie
   He turned from shot and flame;
Side by side with Gracie
   Up the grand aisle of fame.²¹³
FRANCIS ORRAY TICKNOR

THE RESCUE OF RYAN'S CONQUERED BANNER

He shared their every hardship, as he did their hopes and joys,
Inspiring faith and courage as he cheered those ragged boys.
Out soldier priest and poet stood unflinching at his post,
'Till the news of Lee's surrender told the story: "All is lost."

He could bare his breast to bayonet, be torn with shot and shell,
With victorious, tattered banner, he could bleed and die so well.
But when those dreadful words, "All lost," broke o'er him like a flood,
His very heart seemed weeping, and his tears all stained with blood.

How illy could he bear it all, so sudden was the blight,
But for the poet's genius, which filled his soul with light.
He sought in vain material his burning words to give
To future generations, and to hearts where he would live.

A crushed brown paper on the floor served then his purpose well,
For though it seemed a conquered cause, he must its story tell.
He wrote it out and fell asleep; next morn thought of it not,
New troubles filled the poet's heart, his poem was forgot.

The morning dawned: that broken priest, but soldier nevermore,
Was gone, but left, all blurred with tears, that paper on the floor.
A woman, loving well our cause, found, and its folds unfurled,
The "Conquered Banner," and it floats unconquered to the world.

At last he bivouacs in peace: no monument stands guard
To point us where the poet-priest sleeps sweetly 'neath the sod.
His glorious rhythmic poems rare a monument will stand;
He was its architect, and built both gracefully and grand.[214]
MRS. J. WILLIAM JONES

TRIBUTE TO THE FALLEN

Across the still blue air the summons broke,
    And all the world stood list'ning in alarm.
From out her startled sleep the South awoke
    And grasped her idle sword and bared her arm.
Along her hazy hills and tranquil skies
    There gathered now the sullen clouds of war;
On every side she saw her sons arise,
    And heard the foe's tumultuous tramp afar.
Her hour had come. She who in languorous breath
    From blue and balmy wave had lounged and smiled
Rushed, warrior-clad, and dared the dirk of death—
    The soldier's mother and the soldier's child.

Then came a day her sunlight ceased to smile—
    A day she saw her loved ones lying, all
Bleeding, upon her trodden pastures, while
    The great world read the story of her fall;
A day she yielded up her banners torn
    That on a happier breeze had waved and tossed;
A day they took the loyal arms she'd borne.
    And left her wretched mid her loved and lost.

Her loved and lost! From blue Nevada's towers
    To warm Atlanta's soft and slumbrous wave,
Scattered, she saw them, like her own fair flowers,
    Lying upon the land they'd died to save.

Ah! woe that day, when—vanquished, worn, and weak—
    She braved no more the storm of shot and shell!
Low, lost within her conqueror's joyous shriek,
    The wailing of her widowed rose and fell.

O conquered banner, furled and in the dust!
    Is all you wafted o'er forgotten now?
O sheathed sword, still cherished in your rust!
    Won ye no laurels for your bearer's brow?
Are trophies all that waken pride and praise?
    Full bravely fought those vanquished hands and well.
Have we no songs which laud their zeal to raise?
    Have we no great and glorious deeds to tell?
They tell us all was lost, and no applause
    Echoes to glory of so great a cost.
We gave our life and flower to the cause,
    We fed it with our heart-blood. Was it lost?

Lost? Never land can boast a prouder day
    Than that which saw our bonny flag unfurled,
When, brave and dauntless in his gold and gray,
    The Southern soldier burst upon the world—
Type of his own warm land, within whose frame
    Warrior of old and stainless knight did dwell,
Lift up thy head, O South! Where is our shame?
    Facing the foe he marched and forward facing fell.

Lost? Look along the ages bright with those
    Who peaceful olive bore or sword did wield.
Find we a nobler life than that whose close
    Was in a crimson tide on Shiloh's field?

Lost, when we think of him who, firm as stone,
    Stood with his tiny hand and kept his post?
Lost? Nay; the valor of a Lee has shone
    To make the field of Gettysburg our boast.

Aye, brother hands have clasped in pard'ning peace
    Above the mingled mounds, impartial strewn;
The sullen rolls of thunder slowly cease,
    The angry morning merges into noon.

Aye, well they turned him southward, he who stands
    The image of our valiant graved in stone—
The musket mold'ring in his passive hands,
    The wounds forgotten, and the graves o'ergrown.
Aye, let it be; we all are southward turned,
    Forgiving and forgiven; skies are calm.
But lo! our metal all the world has learned;
    We share the glory, though we yield the palm.

Then say not lost; great deeds can never die.
    We've won far more than that we sought to save.
Then say not lost so long as hearts can cry:
    "Lo! glory to the great, the valiant, and the brave!"[215]
MISS BELLE HOUSTON (a granddaughter of Sam Houston)

THE STRIFE IS O'ER

Hot from the thund'ring cannon's mouth
    Burst the noise of fire and hell,
And face to face from North and South
    Came noble men, who fought and fell,
At Manassas, Corinth, and Shiloh—
    Yes, on a hundred fields or more—
The brave in gray, the brave in blue,
    Lay dead and dying in their gore.

Each fought for his own precious cause,
    Each to his standard true;
Let them be praised, those gallant men—
    What if in gray or in the blue?
One cause was lost; the other won.
    United now, they stand to-day
A common brotherhood of men—
    The grand old blue, the noble gray.

The storm of conflict now is o'er,
    The queen of battle lies at rest;
Her thund'ring voice disturbs no more.
    And in her mouth the song-birds nest.
All strife is o'er—no North, no South.
    We hail the flag, our emblem grand.
Wave it on high, to teach our youth
    The peace and power of its command.

Then let our hearts and souls rejoice,
    For heav'nly peace reigns over all.
God, guide us by thy tender voice,
    O guide us! lest we stray or fall.[216]
GEORGE B. GRIGGS

OUR GENERAL JOSEPH ORVILLE SHELBY

A star from out our firmament of adoration
    Went down too soon, its radiance at its height,
Amid the grand, resplendent honor of a nation
    Entrammeled, yet untarnished, in her sorrowing night.

Within the azure vault of heaven's own great painting
    Bright lights grow dim and fade from mortal eye;
While others fixed, each round its orbit never fainting,
    Till earth is merged into eternity.

Beleaguered rays still glint to lume the dark horizon
    That settles down upon his helpless sleep,
And scintillations oft will come and help to liven
    Around the fragment of his scattered sheep.

Too soon, ah! soon the dreaded death-cloud gathered o'er us.
    In vain we reach to touch his guiding wand.
In mem'ry see it point and always press before us
    To plant our flag-staff toward the motherland.

His eagle vision flashed athwart this vast dominion,
    And pierced the future as it rose and fell.
His hovering crest was ours. Poor, broken pinion
    Is folded up too soon! Farewell! farewell!

Joseph O. Shelby.

A life so woven in with war and peace together!
    The gallant trophies of exalted dreams
Will come to us of olden times in roughest weather,
    And clear some dangers from these sullen streams.

Though threat'ning onslaughts now menace with wild inflections
    And deep imbroglios rise from sea to sea,
His bulwark stands beside in hallowed recollection,
    And brings some transport back to you and me.

With woof and warp entangled came this great hiatus,
    The stoppage of the shuttle working strong in death;
On life's platform standing, while hopes and fears await us.
    But the rushing engine's throttled; we are left.

Distressed, dismayed, alas! and know not whither trending;
    The leader gone, the hapless flock astray;
Like splintered reeds aghast, in consternation bending,
    The wind-break taken, nor the storm at bay.

And here we stand, distraught with grief and desolation,
    The night upon us, and no star to see,
All tethered down by age, in need of consolation

That oped unstinted to his boundless lee.

Wherein the old ship riding safely, with topsail furled,
    I've heard the hailing of his seamen: "Come!
Leaking! sinking! foundered!" Back the welcome echo hurled:
    "Steady, soldiers! out of breakers! here's room!"

I've heard the wails of widows, orphans, wives—aye, strangers—
    Struggling, crowding, on that crippled starboard;
I've seen the friendly hand-shake dripping out of dangers—
    Beggar, courtier, friend, alike were harbored.

Upon this field, with watch-fires quenched nor colors flying,
    We've come to lay him by his own to sleep.
The hard-fought battle here, the val'rous heroes dying,
    A soldier's vigils by our troths we'll keep.

Our darling's slain in youth's bright manhood here to cherish,
    Though many years have passed in bitter grief;
With loving care each cycling season comes to nourish
    The trees, the flowers, and the rip'ning sheaf.

These luscious perfumes seem so freighted down with sadness
    To've caught the drifting of our thoughts to-day;
The cheery little songsters have suppressed their gladness,
    Their whistlings seem like music far away.

Till wave on wave may've reached to distant homesteads broken;
    Poor mothers, if their souls had arms, would be
To-day around us weeping, with a loving token
    More plaintive far than this weird minstrelsy.

Forget not, O, the widow! 'reft and broken-hearted,
    For sunny days can come to her no more.
The blighting traces of this aching wound have smarted
    Till life-blood trickles from the anguished sore.

Let vandal tongues deride and scoff our soul's lost treasure!
    The scum on swelling tides must come and go;
But dreams and joys, crushed hopes in retrospective measure,
    Grow stronger, purer, as they ebb and flow.

Somewhere in mystic future armies, friends, once plighted,
    Will rise together on those happier planes,
And there, in glorious judgment, wrongs will be righted,
    For God Almighty still supremely reigns.[217]
MRS. DR. T. J. HENRY

A COUNTRY MAIDEN'S "GENERAL" INVITATION

Come! leave the noisy Longstreet,
    And come to the Field with me;
Trip o'er the Heth with flying feet,
    And skip along the Lee.
Then Ewell find the flowers that be
    Along the Stonewall still,
And pluck the buds of flaming pea
    That grow on A. P. Hill.
Across the Rodes the Forrest boughs
    A stately Archer form,
Where sadly pipes the Early bird
    That never caught the worm.
Come hasten! for the Bee is gone,
    And Watie lies on the plains.
Come! braid a Garland e'er the leaves
    Fall in the blasting Rains.[218]
UNKNOWN (created to help children remember our heroes' names)

Stand Watie.

THE OLD CANTEEN

How the memories of the past
    Doth fill my thoughts to-night!
Once more I hear the bugle-call,
    Again we're in the fight;
Once more I hear the Yankee cheers,
    The Rebel yell between,
Again the sweetest draught e'er drank,
    I'm drinking from the old canteen.

The strains of "Bonnie Blue Flag"
    Are borne upon the breeze,
"Yankee Doodle" just o'er the hill
    Comes floating through the trees;
But sweet as is this music,
    Not sweeter 'tis I ween
Than the gurgling of the water
    When drinking from the old canteen

But ah how soon the present makes
    The past to fade away!
For now there is no Yankee blue,
    No more the Rebel gray;
For in peace and in harmony
    Together can be seen
Our brothers, "Fed" and "Confed,"
    Drinking from the same canteen.

Soon we'll all cross o'er the river
    And camp where love holds sway,
Where hand in hand together
    Shall march the blue and gray;
Where deeds of earthly valor
    Are kept forever green
By drinking the water of life
    That flows from God's canteen.[219]
W. H. HOWARD

TO DIXIE LAND

In Dixie land, O land of cotton!
With all my childish cares forgotten,
I dreamed of countries yet unknown,
Which fairies had in slumber shown,
Thou wert then in my mind dethroned,
    O Dixie!

But time has changed, O Dixie land!
And weakened much the youthful hand
That from thy borders pushed away
And sailed for ports where fortune lay
In all her dazzling, rich display,
    O Dixie!

I wist not then thy noble worth,
Nor held I dear the humble hearth
Where home and happiness were mine
And beaming faces welcome shine
To strangers who their way might find
    To Dixie.

'Tis strange how fate my face has turned
And led me back where I have yearned
To rest my weary, restless head
And with thy bounties to be fed.
O, many a prodigal tear I've shed,
    My Dixie![220]
PHIPPS ALEXANDER

THE BONNIE BLUE FLAG

You may have traveled over all the world,
And seen all the flags, flying and furled,
But of all you have seen or yet may see,
There is one old flag far dearer to me.

It is not England's I regard with admiration.
Ah, 'twas not such a great and prosperous nation;
Or the Emerald Isle, with its flag of green,
Though few prettier could be seen.

Norway and Sweden, surrounded by the sea;
No, neither of their flags is the one for me;
Belgium's is peculiar, and Denmark's still more.
But both far less pretty than the one I adore.

Not the yellow of the great and mighty Russia,
Nor the pretty white that sways over Prussia;
United States, Holland, Turkey, ah no!
And not the flag that floats over Mexico.

This beautiful flag of ours few foreigners ever saw;
It floated o'er the South in a time of strife and war;
It was raised over the housetops in the days of yore,
But that loved old flag will be raised no more.[221]

'Twas the Confederates who formed that little band
And joined the army with heart and hand,
With brave Jefferson Davis at their head:
And the colors of the flag were red, white, and red.[222]
MISS NINA M. WINDER

Sheet music.

SAM DAVIS

When the Lord calls up earth's heroes
    To stand before his face,
Oh, many a name unknown to fame
    Shall ring from that high place!
And out of a grave in the Southland,
    At the just God's call and beck,
Shall one man rise with fearless eyes
    And a rope about his neck.

For men have swung from gallows
    Whose souls were white as snow.
Not how they die nor where, but why,
    Is what God's records show.
And on that mighty ledger
    Is writ Sam Davis' name—
For honor's sake he would not make
    A compromise with shame.

The great world lay before him,
    For he was in his youth.
With love of life young hearts are rife,
    But better he loved truth.
He fought for his convictions,
    And when he stood at bay
He would not flinch or stir one inch
    From honor's narrow way.

They offered life and freedom
    If he would speak the word;
In silent pride he gazed aside
    As one who had not heard.
They argued, pleaded, threatened—
    It was but wasted breath,
"Let come what must. I keep my trust,"
    He said, and laughed at death.

He would not sell his manhood
    To purchase priceless hope:
Where kings drag down a name and crown
    He dignified a rope.
Ah, grave! where was your triumph?
    Ah, death! where was your sting?
He showed you how a man could bow,
    To doom and stay a king.

Ella W. Wilcox.

And God, who loves the loyal
    Because they are like him,
I doubt not yet that soul shall set
    Among his cherubim.
O Southland! bring your laurels;
    And add your wreath, O North!
Let glory claim the hero's name,
    And tell the world his worth.[223]
ELLA WHEELER WILCOX

Sam Davis Memorial Window, Richmond, Virginia.

CLEBURNE'S BANNER

Folded now is Cleburne's banner,
    Furled the flag that kissed the stars,
Gone the dreams that dropped like manna
    From its skies of bonny bars.
Nameless they who fell before it,
    Dust the hearts that died in vain,
Dead the hero-hands that bore it
    Through the blight of battle's rain.

Folded now is Cleburne's banner,
    Like the hands that held it high;
Set its stars—oh, never, never,
    Shall they light a Southern sky!
But 'tis sacred in the glory
    Of a splendor once its own;
And 'tis hallowed in its story,
    Though its pride be sheared and shorn.

Folded now is Cleburne's banner,
    But one day it gleamed along
When the war-drum's stern hosanna
    Echoed in a nation's song.
Shiloh saw it sweep from under
    Like a tempest in its wrath:
Chickamauga heard its thunder,
    Felt the lightning of its path.

Ringgold Gap, New Hope, and Dalton,
    Peachtree Creek—Atlanta, too—
Till it kissed the bloody Harpeth,
    Where it broke the ranks of blue
Till it kissed the bloody Harpeth,
    And its blue was turned to red.
When it floated from the breastworks
    Over gallant Cleburne—dead!

Patrick R. Cleburne.

Folded now is Cleburne's banner—
    But one day will right the wrong
When the war drum's stern hosanna
    Calls again for Freedom's song.
Then, O then, 'twill float in glory
    In a just and holy war,
And 'twill tell the same old story:
    Fearless, and without a flaw.[224]
JOHN TROTWOOD MOORE

HER LETTER CAME TOO LATE

Your letter, lady, came too late,
    For heaven has claimed its own—
Ah! sudden change from prison bars
    Unto the great white throne.
And yet, I think he would have stayed
    For one more day of pain
Could he have read those tardy words
    Which you have sent in vain.

Why did you wait, fair lady,
    Through so many a weary hour?
Had you other lovers with you
    In that silken daisy bower?
Did others bow before your charms
    And twine bright garlands there?
And yet, I ween, in all the throng
    His spirit had no peer.

I wish that you were by me now,
    As I draw the sheet aside,
To see how pure the look he wore
    A while before he died.
Yet the sorrow that you gave him
    Still has left its weary trace.
And a meek and saintly sadness
    Dwells upon that pallid face.

"Her love," he said. "could change for me
    The winter's cold to spring."
Ah! trust a fickle maiden's love?
    Thou art a bitter thing.
For when these valleys fair in May
    Once more with blooms shall wave
The Northern violets shall blow
    Above his humble grave.

Your dole of scanty words had been
    But one more pang to bear,
Though to the last he kissed with love
    This tress of your soft hair.
I did not put it where he said:
    For when the angels come
I would not have them find the sign
    Of falsehood in his tomb.

I've read your letters, and I know
    The wiles that you have wrought
To win that noble heart of his;
    And gained it—cruel thought!
What lavish wealth men sometimes give
    For a trifle light and small!
What manly forms are often held
    In folly's flimsy thrall!

You shall not pity him, for now
    He's past your hope and fear;
Although I wish that you could stand
    With me beside his bier.
Still, I forgive you. Heaven knows
    For mercy you'll have need!
Since God his awful judgment sends
    On each unworthy deed.

To-night the cold wind whistles by
    As I my vigils keep
Within the prison dead-house, where
    Few mourners come to weep.
A rude plank coffin holds him now;
    Yet death gives always grace;
And I had rather see him thus
    Than clasped in your embrace.

To-night your rooms are very gay
    With wit and wine and song,
And you are smiling just as if
    You never did a wrong;
Your hand so fair that none would think
    It penned these words of pain,
Your skin so white—would God your soul
    Were half so free of stain!

I'd rather be this dear, dear friend
    Than you in all your glee;
For you are held in grievous bonds,
    While he's forever free.
Whom serve we in this life we serve
    In that which is to come,
He chose his way; you, yours. Let God
    Pronounce the fitting doom![225]
CONFEDERATE COLONEL W. S. HAWKINS

IN DIXIE LAND

In Dixie land: Out of the dust of years—
    The vanished past—her lengthening shadow falls,
Seen dimly through a veiling mist of tears
    As the faint echo of her last song calls.
Plaintively sweet, in hearts that fondly claim
    To share the storied splendors of her name.

Fair Dixie land! I see thee as of yore,
    When the fierce passion of the sun's hot breath
Burned the white cloud-piled battlements that soar
    High in the west, into one splendid wreath
Of rose and gold and opal, ere the night,
    In filmy darkness, hid the world from sight.

Brave Dixie land! There was an age of gold
    When thou didst stand strong, in thy new-born might,
As a young giant, valiant and free and bold—
    Eager to battle for the cause of right;
Nor spot nor blemish on thy fair, bright shield,
    To win or die; thou didst not know to yield.

Dead Dixie land! The years' dark curtain falls
    And hides lost glories of a long ago—
And nodding plumes wave over somber palls.
    While sobbing requiems whisper, faint and low,
And the night deepens, and dumb voices tell
    The tale that was. Dead Dixie land—farewell![226]
WILL MCGANN

THE UNKNOWN DEAD

Beneath the ragged, straggling boughs
    Of three old storm-swept trees,
Unmarked by slab or marble urn,
    Six soldiers sleep at ease.
From clang or din or noise of strife
    Their souls find sweet release,
Beyond the fray and war of life
    A grand eternal peace.

It was not theirs to win renown
    To brighten history's pages,
To have their names go thundering down
    Through all the coming ages;
No shaft or monumental stone
    Is seen above the sod;
Their names, their lives are now unknown
    To all except their God.

No mother's tear will mark the place
    Where they in quiet sleep;
No sister, sweetheart, friend, or wife
    Their patient vigils keep.
No father's moans or brother's sighs
    Will stir their last long rest,
But who shall judge their sacrifice
    But Him who knoweth best?

And he alone the cause shall try;
    We only see a part;
For while man judges by the act,
    He judges by the heart.[227]
JAMES E. RATIGAN

Monument to the unknown Confederate dead.

THE SENTINEL & THE SCOUT

"Jesus, Lover of my soul,"
    Sang a sentinel one night,
As he walked his lonely beat
    In the pale moon's waning light.
"Jesus, Lover of my soul,
    Let me to thy bosom fly,"
Pleadingly he sang, and low,
    While he felt that death was nigh.

"Cover my defenseless head"—
    Softly oil the still night air—
"With the shadow of thy wing";
    Sang he thus his sad heart's prayer.
Trustingly he sang the words
    Thinking only God would hear;
But the night winds wafted them
    To a hidden foeman's ear.

Through the murky shades of night,
    There had crept a daring scout
To that lonely picket's stand;
    And with sure, unerring aim,
On his heart had drawn a bead,
    When, in suppliant tone, he heard,
"Cover my defenseless head."

Down his deadly rifle came;
    He, himself a man of prayer,
Could not take the life of one
    Trusting in his Saviour's care.
Softly, from his covert then
    In the shadows, he withdrew;
Leaving still that heart to beat,
    Which he knew was brave and true.

"Jesus, Lover of my soul,"
    In life's battle be thou nigh;
And, amid its gathering gloom,
    "Let me to thy bosom fly."
When thou shaft to judgment bring,
    "Cover my defenseless head
With the shadow of thy wing."[228]
E. L. BYERS

IN THE TRENCHES

We were gathered in the trenches,
    Where the hissing shot and shell,
Winging their curved aerial flight,
    Unheeded round us fell.
Hearts there were that knew no quailing,
    Men there were that knew not fear,
Weather-beaten, grizzled warriors
    Sullenly assembled here—
Grouped around our loved commander,
    For on us did he depend;
Not a man but was determined
    To stand by him to the end.

Ah! that end was fast approaching,
    Bitterly the truth we knew;
How we cursed that false jade, Fortune,
    That to us had proved untrue!
Soon would sound the sullen echoes,
    Called to life by war's last gun;
Soon we'd turn our faces homeward,
    Prideful, yet in cause unwon.
Ah! "Lee's Miserables" were fallen—
    Thinning, lessening day by day,
And our ranks, war-swept and riven,
    Mustered now but scant array.

Where the shot and shell fell fewest,
    On a blanket old and torn.
Lay a sun-bronzed youthful soldier,
    wounded, dying, wearied, worn.
And we gathered round to listen,
    Harkening to his last request,
For he knew that ere an hour
    He would be in realms of rest.
O'er his face a look of sadness,
    Like the shadow of a cloud,
Slowly stole, and there it settled,
    As he gazed up at the crowd.

"Comrades, friends," he slowly murmured.
    While a tear rolled down his cheek,
"Rain and shine we've stood together,
    Side by side for many a week.
Many a friend I leave behind me;
    Many a comrade, gone before,

Now perhaps awaits our coming,
    Mustered out, the battles o'er.
Time is now for words of parting,
    For I know that death is near;
But we've met him oft in battle.
    What have such as we to fear?

"Far away in South Carolina,
    On the banks of old Santee,
Lives my gentle, waiting mother.
    Ah! how happy would I be
Could I raise the darkened shadows
    That must now enshroud her life,
Now that here her son has fallen,
    Fallen in this deadly strife.
She will have no one to cheer her;
    One she hoped to see again
Now is dying in the trenches,
    And her hopes are spent in vain.

"She it was, when Sumter's cannon
    Boomed and echoed through the land,
Bade me go and fight for freedom,
    While she, with her trembling hand,
Helped to fit me for the conflict,
    Telling me to ne'er forget
Death is better than dishonor;
    And I felt that scant regret
At the parting, for all luring
    Came day-dreams of victories won,
As she, in her sacred sadness,
    Blessed her wild, impatient son.

"Some of you will go and tell her—
    Tell her that my latest breath
Left my body but to murmur
    Her dear name, and that in death;
As my eyes had lost their power.
    And my sight grew faint and dim,
Her sweet face was still before me,
    As my soul returned to Him.
Tell her not to grieve and mourn me,
    For we part but for a time,
And we soon shall be together
    In that fairer, happier clime.

"Comrades, friends, good-by—God bless you!"

And his breath came thick and fast.
As with choking voice he whispered,
   "Mother!" then he breathed his last.
There we stood with heads bent lowly;
   Some of us a parting tear
Dropped in sorrow for the comrade
   Who in death was lying here.
Then with touch all rude, but kindly,
   Laid him on his lowly bed,
And, returning to the conflict,
   For a time forgot the dead.[229]
HENRY CHAMBERS

HOOD'S TEXANS AT LITTLE ROUND TOP

O'er the dead and the dying they swept,
Midst the scream of the shot and the shell,
In the face of a merciless fire,
And by scores and by hundreds they fell;
How they fell by the score,
How they fell in their gore,
At Little Round Top.

How they stood at the brow of the hill,
With their faces set grim, as in death;
And as heroes they stood, so they fell,
In the face of the cannon's hot breath;
In the face of grim death,
And the cannon's hot breath,
At Little Round Top.

And the steep—it grew crimson and wet
With the blood of the boys in the gray,
It was war, to the knife, to the hilt,
When the Texans swept forward that day;
For the boys in the gray,
Were in battle array,
At Little Round Top.

Here's a cheer for the boys in the gray,
Here's a cheer for the Texans with Hood;
For they charged o'er the dying and dead,
And as heroes they died—so they stood
At Little Round Top.
So they stood years ago,
In the face of the foe,
At Little Round Top.[230]
JUDGE WILLIAM E. FOWLER

John B. Hood.

SAM DAVIS

The light of early manhood
    Was in his sparkling eye;
Within his veins the tide of life
    Was beating full and high.

The strongest law of nature
    Was pleading in his breast.
"Oh, life is sweet," it whispered;
    "What matters all the rest."

But from life's smiling face he turned
    At duty's stern decree,
To meet his fate unfaltering,
    On that grim gallows tree.

Oh, earth hath million pebbles
    Of coarsest common clay,
But here and there a diamond
    Sends forth its sparkling ray.

Memorial at Sam's grave, erected by his father.

Oh, spring hath many a common weed
    That April's banks disclose,
But only here and there we find
    A rare and perfect rose.

And myriads of our fallen race
    This earthly sphere have trod,
But few and far between there walks
    An image of our God.

O Southern winds, sigh softly,
    Above his earthly grave.
O mother earth, lie lightly
    O'er heart so true and brave.

But 'tis the empty casket
    Lies moldering here alone;
The jewel God is keeping,
    For heaven has claimed its own.[231]
ALICE GARNETT

A SOLDIER OF ROBERT E. LEE

'Twas a bright summer morn and the beautiful sun
    Shone out in splendor so grand,
And the sweet-scented violets were kissed by the dew,
    With a blessing by Heaven's kind hand.
On a steep mountain-side was a lone mound of clay,
    O'er this grave stood a great willow tree.
By some unsteady hand was a board rudely carved:
    "Rest Ye, Soldier of Robert E. Lee."

To my eyes came sad tears as I gazed on that mound,
    And my heart with sorrow was filled,
As my thought wandered back to the days long gone by,
    And dear voices once heard, but now stilled;
Lying in this lone grave on the side of the hill
    Rests a hero from all sorrow free:
But perhaps some poor mother awaits the return
    Of this soldier of Robert E. Lee.

Calmly sleeps this brave soldier on Virginia's dear shore,
    And sweet birds sadly chirp o'er his mound;
But no sound of the music will e'er reach his ear,
    Till God's trumpet sweet music will sound.
On the great judgment-day, when heaven's gates open wide,
    And God's children from earthly cares flee,
A welcome will sound from the sweet pearly gates
    For a soldier of Robert E. Lee.

For a cause he has given his true noble life,
    For the sunny South's honor he died;
And Virginia has claimed him—he now lies at rest
    In a grave on the green mountainside.
O dear martyred son in that grave on the hill,
    Virginia has oft wept for thee,
As she wept when bereft of her two bravest sons.
    George Washington and Robert E. Lee. [232]
UNKNOWN

CONFEDERATE SOLDIERS: A MEMORIAL

With laurel oft your brows have been entwined,
    In other days when victories you have gained,
And got applause from all the world combined
    For feats of arms, with cruelty unstained.

Now that your days of warfare here are o'er,
    With cypress we do deck your resting-place,
And with sweet strains our love in sadness pour
    To you our heroes, grandest of your race.[233]
MRS. DAISY HODGSON

AN OLD CONFED WHO MORGAN LED

Only an old Confed, sir, only an old Confed,
Who fought for the South, sir, with the band that Morgan led;
Who fought for home and honor, sir, on many a bloody field,
And only laid down his arms, sir, when the fate of the South was sealed.
Who fought for the right as he saw it, and fought with might and main,
'Neath scorching heat of summer's sun and winter's sleet and rain.
Yes, I've suffered, sir, from hunger on many a midnight ride,
But he could boast who suffered most while riding at Morgan's side.

Ah, a gallant band was Morgan's, each man as true as steel,
Men who fought like tigers, and their leader well might feel
As Morgan felt—that, hacked by his heroes grand,
He could drive a host of Yankees from his native Southern land.
But we got licked—perhaps it's for the best,
And many of Morgan's raiders have long since gone to rest;
Only a few years, Colonel, and when the last old vet is dead,
There'll be no tear on the silent bier of a broken-down Confed.[234]
TRACY KINGMAN ROCKWOOD

John H. Morgan.

WILMINGTON'S ROLL-CALL OF HONOR

Ah, yes! the war is over, and the past
Is the eternal past;
But memory bridges the yawning space.
By the light of her torch we stand face to face
Again with our "deathless dead."
One by one, they march along;
One by one, they join the throng
Of heroes bold, of martyrs true,
Their country called to arms, they flew
To join in the carnage dread.

Our good old town sent forth to the fray
As noble a band in their jackets of gray
As ever marched to the battle-field
Or fought for their flag or died on their shield
In ancient or modern time.
We come to-day to deck the graves
Of Wilmington's dauntless Southern braves,
To their sacred mounds sweet flowers of spring.
A mournful tribute now we bring—
An offering of love sublime.

Reverse your arms and muffle the drum,
Lower your flag, and silently come,
Patiently wait while we con them o'er;
We've gathered their dust from mountain and shore.
Come hear the roll-call of fame:
First Col. Meares is borne from the field,
With Wooster and Moore cold on their shield—
The first instalment that Wilmington paid
On the great debt that principle made.
We buried them as they came.

The conflict deepens. Extinguished the light
In another home, for James A. Wright
Has crossed that narrow stream called Death;
And Wilmington stands with bated breath,
Counting the growing list so sad:
Lieut. Ed Meares, again a Wright,
Johnnie Van Bockerlin, in young manhood's mighty
Price and Davidson, Craige and McRee,
As part of the price of liberty,
Are among our "deathless dead."

The Shackelford brothers, Theo and Dan,

Are called to die for their native land.
And on Virginia's blood-stained soil
Lay down their lives to rest from toil,
But find with us a grave.
De Rossett and Cowan, from hospital ward,
We laid to rest in Oakdale's green sward;
Quince, Jacobs, Rothwell, and Moore,
With streaming eyes and hearts so sore,
We give each a soldier's grave.

Faster and faster the death-roll grows:
Pert and Walker are slain by their foes;
Reaves and Robinson, Kelly and Deems,
Sleep the sleep which knows no dreams—
And they are forever free!
Ravenscroft, Burr, Tennent, and Green,
Gallantly fighting when last they were seen;
Dodson and Martin, Lord and Lane,
Yield up their lives on battle-plain—
Another instalment for liberty.

Herring and Peck and another Lane
Join the host of Wilmington's slain;
McMillan, Respass, McGuire, and Barr,
Forever at rest from the clang of war,
So peacefully down on the plain.
The days wear on 'mid battle roar.
Giles has fallen, another Moore;
Two more of our boys in jackets of gray:
Majs. Robert and Henry McRae.
And yet grows the list of the slain.

Armstrong and Anderson, Johnson and Hill.
Prone on the ground so cold and still;
Gallant Matt Murphy, a stranger to fear,
Ready to lead or to bring up the rear—
These, too, for their country have died.
Montgomery, Farrow, Bannerman, too.
Rest from their toils where soft falls the dew.
Sneeden and Usher, Wallace and Gregg,
With Parsley, refuse not their life-blood to shed;
And now they sleep side by side.

Nearer and nearer the storm-clouds come;
They gather and settle just over our home
On Christmas, the birthday of Christ our King,
And our sad hearts refuse to sing.

Hosannas died on our tongues;
For, moment by moment, we heard the yell
Of booming cannon and bursting shell,
And knew that in Fisher's battlement wall
Full many a gallant form must fall;
And we had no heart for song.

O liberty! liberty! how great is thy price!
How vastly great the sacrifice
This beautiful city by the sea
Has paid, and still must pay, for thee
In tears and blood and heartache!
For still, on Bentonville's green plain,
The long, long list is growing again.
Rankin responds to his country's call,
And brave Zack Ellis, the last to fall—
And the list is forever complete.

These many years it has been our sad task
To honor our dead; and to-day we ask
That you deck their graves and shed a tear
In memory of our heroes dear,
Who died while they wore the gray.
They died for me, they died for you,
They died for principle just and true.
Angels watch over their sacred dust
Until the rising of the just.
When time shall pass away![235]
MARY F. SANDERS

CAROLINA, 1865

Pale, fainting from the battle-field,
Carolina leaned on dented shield;
Her broken sword and shivered spear
She laid aside to wipe a tear.
Sob-choked, I heard her feebly say:
"My sons! my sons! oh, where are they?"
The evening breeze, soft-whisp'ring, sighed:
"On freedom's battle-ground they died.
Fame's loudest trump shall proudly tell
How bravely fought, how nobly fell."
Loyal, true-hearted men were they,
They sought no portion in the fray;
But Sunny South they could not see
Bow down to Northern tyranny.[236]
WILLIAM J. CLARKE

TO THE MEMORY OF THE BRAVE

Who fears to speak of "sixty-one?"
    Who blushes at its fame?
When cowards sneer at deeds then done.
    Who hangs his head in shame?
He's all a knave or half a slave
    Who slights his record thus:
But a true man, like you, men,
    Will fill his glass with us.

We drink the memory of the brave,
    The faithful—not a few,
Some lie near Potomac's wave.
    Some sleep in "Oakdale," too;
Hundreds are gone, but still live on
    The names of those who died
All true men, like you, men.
    Remember them with pride.

Some 'neath the sod of distant states
    Their patient hearts have laid,
Where, with the stranger's heedless haste,
    Their unwatched graves were made.
But though their clay be far from us,
    Where friends may never come,
In true men, like you, men,
    Their spirit's still at home.

The dust of some is Southern earth;
    Among their own they rest,
For the same land that gave them birth
    Has caught them to her breast.
And we will pray that from their clay
    Full many a race may start
Of true men, like you, men,
    To act as brave a part.

They rose in dark and evil days
    To right their native land;
They kindled here a living blaze,
    That nothing could withstand.
Alas, that might should vanquish right!
    They fell, and passed away;
And true men, like you, men,
    Are far too few to-day.

Then here's their mem'ry! May it be
    For us a guiding-light
To cheer—though lost our liberty—
    And lead us in the right!
Through good and ill be patriots still,
    By each good impulse stirred.
And you, men, be true men,
    Like the dead of the gallant Third.[237]
UNKNOWN

AT REST

At rest among their own—
    Rest to be broken never—
Their folded flag for them outblown
    No more forever.

They did not think to come
    So silently, so late,
When, stepping to the sounding drum,
    They left the state.

They thought to see again
    The loved ones, kissed through tears;
Not in the trenches of the slain
    To lie for years.

But lips they kissed grew old.
    And eyes that wept grew blind,
And hearts that could not break lay cold,
    By grief enshrined.

And spirits veiled in woe,
    Looking toward life's west,
Were called in tenderness unto
    Eternal rest.

They came not: but they come—
    A vanquished, faithful few—
In silence: and are welcomed home
    In silence, too.

Their place of burial is
    Hallowed by woman's prayers.
A nobler epitaph than this
    Could not be theirs.[238]
JOHN H. BONER

THE CONFEDERATE DEAD

In pine-brake and on mountain battle-ground,
In river-drift and Mississippian swamp,
Each as he fell—their overt work undone,
Their country trodden down and desolate—
Rest until doomsday the Confederate dead.
Yet, in that bitter shipwreck and the crash
Of all which in the passionate resolve
Of patriotic zeal they staked and lost,
They were not servants profitless; their names
Glow on the roll which duty keeps for fame—
That golden roll with iron pen engraved.
Dipped in the heart-blood of the noble dead,
Weighed well with truthful balance, scrutinized
By eyes that love no guile and grovel not
In vulgar worship of a forced success.
They lived accepted in the chosen band
Of those who in short time encompassed deeds
Whose worth the span of rolling centuries
Preserves in undecaying memory—
Stout, working preachers to their fellow-men
Of single stern self-sacrifice.
Whose unwrit sermons shall be garnered up
In the dim cycles of the coming time
For the refreshment of sick human kind.[239]
HONONRABLE A. B. BERESFORD HOPE, M.P. (an Englishman)

Confederate cemetery.

TO AN OLD SABER

Motionless and sheathed, it hangs upon the ancestral wall,
No more to flash in sunlight or answer warlike call;
No more 'twill bid defiance to onward-moving foe.
Nor yet again with savage thrust will lay a chieftain low.

Yes; a relic of warlike days, it hangs a dreaming there
Of battle-shouts, of cannons' roar, of blood and savage glare;
But, its part in strife now ended, quiet is its meed,
And long will live in story the glory of each deed.[240]
R. B. DOW

MEETING OF THE PICKETS

The years creep swiftly by, Friend G.;
    We are on the same old spot,
Just where we met in sixty-three
    Mid shells and balls and shot.
Two armies slept beneath the stars,
    Two sentinels trudged their way
You wore a suit of blue that night,
    And I a coat of gray.

The place has greatly changed since then:
    No smoke bedims our sight;
No groans of pain come from the men,
    As after the first day's fight;
No clash of arms rings in our ears;
    No dead men round us lie.
You've changed your suit of blue, old friend;
    My jacket of gray's laid by.

Tall monuments are standing round
    Where brave men fought and died
On Chickamauga's battle-ground.
    They fell on every side,
Mid the booming of the guns
    And the shells which plowed their way
Through the bodies of the men in blue
    And the soldiers in the gray.

The snows of two and thirty years
    Have melted here in sorrow
On Chickamauga's stains and blur
    Of blood and strife and horror.
Where the aged and the young alike
    Were butchered in the fray.
Near the foot of Mission Ridge they fell,
    And died in blue and gray.

That night the throbbing stars shone down
    On the lonely picket's head.
On our dreary, dark, and gloomy round,
    And the faces of the dead;
On mangled forms and pallid lips,
    On life ebbing slowly away—
Pierced by balls and torn with shells
    Were the men in blue and gray.

And here, beneath the weathered leaves,
    Our friends and foes are laid;
They've crossed the river, their swords are sheathed,
    They are resting under the shade—
While we, at Chickamauga Park,
    Have met again to-day
To dedicate the untimely graves
    Of the dead in blue and gray.[241]
MRS. FRANK THOMPSON

THE BOYS IN GRAY

Now don't be crying, mother;
    You should be proud of Ben.
He looked, of all, the proudest
    Among a thousand men.
It set me straight to thinkin'
    How I too marched away
To join the noble army,
    Dressed in Confed'rate gray.

I somehow felt like fightin'
    When first our Ben marched out—
Right dress, front face, a standin'
    So tall and straight and stout.
But I cannot like the color
    Of the clothes he wore that day.
'Twould suit me whole lots better
    If they looked a little gray.

But he don't know the diff'rence,
    I s'pose he likes the blue;
Though as for me I can't forget
    I fought it four years through.
And though I am plumb willin'
    For Ben to have his way,
I just could fight lots better
    If my clothes were sort o' gray.

The flag's all right, I like it,
    It must not ever fall;
I sure would like to plant it
    On Morro Castle's wall,
And I know that I could do it,
    In the good old-fashioned way,
If I had a few old comrades,
    Dressed in Confed'rate gray.

They say its hot in Cuba,
    And when the boys get there
They'll shuck those hot blue fixin's,
    And canvas suits will wear.
I like that plan amazin',
    For when they march a day,
The dust and dirt will change 'em
    To the good old fightin' gray.

This is a great big country,
    And when it comes to blows
We'll keep the world from treading
    On Uncle Samuel's toes;
But if I should take a rifle,
    I've just got this to say:
I could handle her whole lots better
    If my clothes were sort o' gray.

It breaks my heart, old woman,
    To hear you sobbing so.
I lived through four years' fighting,
    Ben's coming back, I know.
But when he goes to lying
    (As he's almost sure to do)
About the gallant fighting.
    Of our volunteers in blue.

Why, then—why, then—confound him.
    I'll have a word to say,
And beat him with one bigger
    About the boys in gray.[242]
UNKNOWN

THE SWORD OF LEE

Forth from its scabbard, pure and bright,
    Flashed the sword of Lee!
Far in the front of the deadly fight,
High o'er the brave in the cause of right,
Its stainless sheen, like a beacon light,
    Led us to victory.

Out of its scabbard, where full long
    It slumbered peacefully.
Roused from its rest by the battle's song.
Shielding the feeble, smiting the strong,
Guarding the right, avenging the wrong.
    Gleamed the sword of Lee.

Forth from its scabbard, high in air
    Beneath Virginia's sky—
And they who saw it gleaming there,
And knew who bore it, knelt to swear
That where that sword led they would dare
    To follow and to die.

Out of its scabbard! Never hand
    Waved sword from stain as free;
Nor purer sword led braver band,
Nor braver bled for a brighter land,
Nor brighter land had a cause so grand.
    Nor cause a chief like Lee.

Forth from its scabbard! How we prayed
    That sword might victor be;
And when our triumph was delayed,
And many a heart grew sore afraid,
We still hoped on while gleamed the blade
    Of noble Robert Lee.

Forth from its scabbard all in vain
    Bright flashed the sword of Lee;
'Tis shrouded now in its sheath again,
It sleeps the sleep of our noble slain,
Defeated, yet without a stain.
    Proudly and peacefully.[243]

REVEREND ABRAM JOSEPH RYAN

WHEN THE ROLL IS CALLED UP YONDER

Soon our comrades, gone before us to the camp beyond the skies,
    Shall with us their tents, by glory guarded, share;
We will lie with them and slumber, watched by sleepless angel eyes,
    Till we're waked to answer roll call over there.

Chorus
When the roll is called up yonder,
When the roll is called up yonder,
When the roll is called up yonder,
When the roll is called up yonder we'll be there.

Not with shouts and hearts exulting, as in days forever gone,
    Rush we on to where the battle banners flare;
But with footsteps slow and weary, and in silence, one by one,
    When the signal sounds we'll gather over there.

Oh, my comrades! oh, my brothers! by the sacred days of yore,
    And the ashes of our heroes, let us swear,
That our bonds of love shall bind us soul to soul for evermore,
    And when roll is called up yonder we'll be there.[244]
CHARLES W. HUBNER

THE CONFEDERATE DEAD

Wreathe the graves with flowers,
    Let fair hands adorn the sod;
Beneath it all that's mortal lies,
    While the soul has winged to God.

Their battles fought, the cause was lost.
    The brave and noble sons here lie;
Let charity's mantle o'erspread them now,
    They rest in peace with God on high.

No bugle's sound will call them hence.
    Their work on earth was nobly done;
The truth let history's pages tell
    Of valor, chivalry, battles won.

No curfew tolled their parting time.
    No loved ones near to soothe their brow;
They gave their all, they gave their life.
    Their only hope a country's vow.

No winding sheet, no funeral dirge
    These noble Southern sons were given;
In hurried graves their bodies rest,
    Their souls are resting now in heaven.[245]
DR. W. E. BROWN

A BALLAD OF EMMA SANSOM

The courage of man is one thing, but that of a maid is more;
For blood is blood and death is death, and grim is the battle gore;
And the rose that blooms, though blistered by the sleet of an open sky,
Is fairer far than its sisters are who sleep in the hothouse nigh.

Word came up to Forrest that Streight was on a raid—
Two thousand booted bayonets were riding down the glade.
Eight thousand were before him—he was holding Dodge at bay—
But he turned on his heel, like the twist of a steel, and was off at the break of day.

Six hundred troopers had he, game as a Claiborne cock,
Tough as the oak root grappling with the gray Sand Mountain rock;
And they charged like young Comanches, by the flash of the Yankee gun,
And they fell at the ford and shot as they rode, and fought from sun to sun.

But Streight went whirling southward, with never a limp or lag.
His front was a charging huntsman, but his rear was a hounded stag.
And the gray troops followed after, their saddle blankets wet
With the bloody rack from their horses' back, and Streight not headed yet.

A fight to the death in the valley and a fight to the death on the hill,
But still Streight thundered southward, and Forrest followed still;
And the goaded hollows bellowed to the bay of the Rebel gun.
For Forrest was hot as a solid shot when its flight is just begun.

A running fight in the morning and a charging fight at noon,
Till spurs clung red and reeking around their bloody shoon.
The morning star paled on them, but the evening star rose red
As the ruddy tinge of the border fringe that purpled the path of dead.

A midnight fight on the mountain and a daybreak in the glen,
And when Streight stopped for water he had lost three hundred men;
But he gained the bridge at the river, and planted his batteries there;
And the halt of the gray was a hound at bay, and the blue a wolf in his lair.

And out from the bridge at the river a white-heat lightning came
Like the hungry tongues of a forest fire with the autumn woods aflame;
And the death smoke burst above them and the death heat blazed below,
But the men in gray cheered the smoke away and bared their breasts to the blow.

Should they storm the bridge at the river, through melting walls of fire,
And die in the brave endeavor to plant their standard higher?
Should they die at the bridge on the river or die where they stood in their track,
Like a through-speared boar with death at his door, but tossing the challenge back?

"To the ford! to the ford!" rang the bugle; "and flank the enemy out!"
And quick to the right the gray lines wheel, and answer with a shout.
But the river was mad and swollen—to left, to right, no ford;
And still the sting of the maddened thing at the bridge, and still the goad.

"To the ford! to the ford!" rang the bugle; "to the ford! Retreat or die!"
And still the flail of a bullet hail from out a mortar sky.
And they stood like a blue bull wounded in wallowing mud and mire,
And still the flash from a deadly lash, and still the barbs of fire.

Then out from a near-by cabin a mountain maiden came,
Her cheeks were banks of snowdrifts, but her eyes were skies of flame;
And she drew her sunbonnet closer as the bullets whispered low
(Lovers of lead, and one of them said: "I'll clip a curl as I go").

Straight through the blistering bullets she fled like a hunted doe,
While the hound guns down at the river bayed in her wake below;
And around their hot breath shifted, and behind, their pattering feet.
But still she fled through the thunder red and still through the lightning sleet.

And she stood at the General's stirrups, flushed as a mountain rose
When the sun looks down in the morning and the gray mist upward goes.
She stood at the General's stirrups, and this was all she said:
"I'll lead the way to the ford to-day. I'm a girl, but I'm not afraid."

How the gray troops thronged around her! And then the Rebel yell!
With that brave girl to lead them they would take the gates of hell.
And they tossed her behind the General; and again the echoes woke,
For she clung to him there with her floating hair as the wild vine clings to the oak.

Down through the bullets she led them, down through an unused road:
And, when the General dismounted to use his glass on the ford,
She spread her skirts before him—the troopers gave a cheer—
"Better get behind me, General, for the bullets will hit you here."

And then the balls came singing and ringing quick and hot,
But the gray troops gave them ball for ball and answered shot for shot.

"They have riddled your skirts," the General said; "I must take you out of this din."
"O, that's all right!" she answered light; "they are wounding my crinoline."

And then, in a blaze of beauty, her sunbonnet off she took;
Right in the front she waved it high, and at their lines it shook.
And the gallant bluecoats cheered her—ceased firing, to a man—
And the gray coats rode through the bloody ford, and again the race began.

Do you wonder they rode like Romans adown the winnowing wind,
With Mars himself in the saddle and Minerva up behind?
Was ever a foe confronted and captured by such means
Since days of old and warrior bold and the Maiden of Orleans?

The courage of man is one thing, but that of a maid is more;
For blood is blood and death is death, and grim is the battle gore;
And the rose that blooms, though blistered by the sleet of an open sky,
Is sweeter far than its sisters are who sleep in the hothouse nigh.[246]
JOHN TROTWOOD MOORE

Emma Sansom.

OUR PAST

As down the vista of long years
    I sadly cast my eye,
The past, with all its hopes and fears,
Its breaking hearts, its blinding tears,
    Comes sweeping slowly by.

I see the hostile ranks arrayed
    In our once peaceful land,
Fair happy homes in ruins laid,
A mournful desolation made
    By war's relentless hand.

I see the slain on every field
    Bathed in a crimson flood;
Gallant and brave, they could not yield;
Loyal and true, their faith they sealed
    With their most noble blood.

I see the fair old Southern life—
    That life of love and mirth—
Perish amid the bitter strife
And change, with which the air was rife,
    And vanish from the earth.

And now new ways on every side,
    And faces new I see;
Like useless seaweed flung aside,
Or drift cast up by ocean's tide,
    The old has come to be.

Yet hold the past life something worth,
    For it was good and fair;
It brightened up this dull old earth,
And gave some gallant heroes birth,
    Whose names we could not spare.[247]
NINA M. ROGERS

THE HOMESPUN DRESS

Yes, I am a Southern girl,
    I glory in the name.
And boast it with far greater pride
    Than glittering wealth or fame.
I envy not the Northern girl
    Her robes of beauty rare:
Though diamonds grace her snowy neck,
    And pearls bedeck her hair.

CHORUS
Hurrah! hurrah for the Sunny South so dear!
Three cheers for the homespun dress
That Southern ladies wear!

This homespun dress is plain, I know,
    My hat's quite common too;
But then it shows what Southern girls
    For Southern rights will do.
We've sent the bravest of our land
    To battle with the foe.
And we would lend a helping hand—
    We love the South, you know.

The Southern land's a glorious land,
    And hers a glorious cause:
Then here's three cheers for Southern rights,
    And for the Southern boys!
We've sent our sweethearts to the war,
    But, dear girls, never mind:
Your soldier love will not forget
    The girl he left behind.

A soldier boy is the lad for me,
    A brave heart I adore;
And when the Sunny South is free,
    And fighting is no more,
I'll choose me then a lover brave
    From out that gallant band;
The soldier lad I love the best
    Shall have my heart and hand.

And now, young men, a word to you:
    If you would win the fair,
Go to the field where honor calls
    And win your lady there.

Remember that our brightest smiles
    Are for the true and brave;
And that our tears fall for the one
    Who fills a soldier's grave.

CHORUS
Hurrah! hurrah for the Sunny South so dear!
Three cheers for the sword and plume
That Southern soldiers wear.[248]
CARRIE BELL SINCLAIR

APPEAL FOR A SOLDIER'S HOME

A battle-scarred old veteran,
    One who had worn the gray
And fought beneath the Southern flag
    With glory as his pay.
Now bent with age and worn by time,
    Stands waiting at the door
And asks his State for shelter—
    He's homeless, old, and poor.

Each scar upon his battered frame
    Will eloquently tell
How, answering his State's behest,
    He fought where foemen fell.
No straggler in the line was he,
    But, like the knight of old,
The crash of arms for sacred cause
    Was music to his soul.

When thunders of secession
    Were heard on every hand,
From the war clouds that had gathered
    Above our sunny land.
And roaring guns on Sumter
    The jarring sections woke,
Till peace at Appomattox
    Rolled back the battle smoke.

This veteran stood to duty
    Like the needle to the pole,
And went wherever duty led
    Through hardships never told.
He comes now with a shambling step,
    Of health, of all, bereft,
And asks the State to help him
    O'er the few short years that are left.

But the men who make the laws
    And crowd our halls of state
Have failed to offer him a home,
    And so he'll have to wait
Until some kindly hand
    shall lead him from the storm,
That break above his hoary head
    And racks his tired form.

The State is poor, they tell us;
    Ah, she must poor indeed,
To see such heroes suffer
    And not supply their need.
Hard is the fate of the infirm and poor,
    Sad to be thus denied.
But short the passage to the friendly tomb,
    Where the burden is laid aside.

Old veteran you must stand aside,
    You're thirty years too late:
With a pittance for a pension,
    We leave you to your fate.
Yet history, in coming years,
    These truthful words shall say:
God never chastened braver men
    Than those who wore the gray.

On Chickamauga's bloody field,
    At Malvern Hill, as well,
In fact upon a hundred fields,
    These heroes fought and fell.
Full many sleep in unmarked graves,
    And will till judgment day.
But God, the giver of all good,
Will not o'erlook the gray.[249]
LUTHER MANSHIP

Confederate veterans' home, Maryland.

GOD SPEED THE BRIGHT & GLORIOUS DAY

We fought in battle long and well
    Where rolls the Cumberland in pride,
And from the hills of Dover Swell
    Our cannon poured an iron tide.

We fought with men as proud and brave
    As any in our own brave line,
And I have sent to the dark grave
    Many a comelier form than mine.

God rest them in their narrow home!
    No battle can their slumber mar
As calm they sleep from manhood's home
    And childhood haunts afar.

My comrades fell on every hand,
    Pierced through pulsing heart and brain,
Where all our guns now idle stand,
    Which we can never man again.

Green grow the sweet wild flowers
    Which their lone graves will strew
When come the balm and sunny hours,
    And May shall bring the morning dew.

We fought for freedom from a chain
    No Anglo-Saxon soul would wear,
Yet alas! we fought in vain,
    And yet the galling links we bear.

We pine in this cold prison hall,
    Beneath the scorpion's lash of wrong,
While the dark days of bondage crawl
    Like wounded snakes along.

    God speed the bright and glorious day,
    Where demon war and strife shall cease,
    And man forbeareth man to slay![250]
OWEN GLASS

IN MEMORY OF JUDGE FARRAR

Now, call the roll. Are they all here?
Hark to their answers swift and clear;
No music like their voices dear,
Responding with their old-time cheer.

No answer here? The Judge asleep?
Ah no! 'Tis but his jest to keep
A silence so profoundly deep
That in our hearts dark shadows creep.

Call out his name! call once again,
And hear how quick he'll answer then.
He's never yet been absent when
We called the roll of Pickett's men.

No answer yet? What do you say?
He's missing from the camp to-day?
He never wanders far astray;
He'll answer now without delay.

What message comes along the line
To dim the morning's bright sunshine.
And with our gladsome roses twine
The sadness of the cypress vine?

That he will answer nevermore
To roll call, as in days of yore.
His brave, strong soul has gone before,
To wait for us at heaven's door.

'Tis grand upon the field to fall
Right up against the flaming wall
Mid deadly showers of leaden ball,
Where battle smoke makes funeral pall.

A glorious death the soldier craves,
Where his loved flag above him waves,
Amid the host of fallen braves
Who march through blood to honored graves.

But greater far, when battle's o'er,
And peace has stilled the cannon's roar,
To take up tangled threads once more
And life's bright golden web restore;

To hide the grief beneath the jest;
To make of mirth a welcome guest;
In calm and storm to do life's best.
And in God's care leave all the rest;

Then with a smile to pass away
To heaven's bright eternal day.
And leave with us a golden ray
Of love to light our hearts for aye.

Upon his grave, O New Year snows,
Lie lightly where the wild wind blows,
While in our hearts in beauty glows
Sweet memory's unfading rose.[251]
MRS. LASALLE CORBELL PICKETT

THE CONFEDERATE CABINET

The famed Confederate Cabinet! of what was it composed?
On Toombs and Hunter, gifted both, the State trust first reposed;
While Benjamin, the versatile, its lustrous record closed.

With Treasury Portfolio two names are proudly joined;
And Memminger, with Trenholm true, their noble mission find
In guiding well the finances of their embattled kind.

Attorneys-General four had we to guard the Justice arm,
Whereof were Benjamin and Bragg, the first to shield from harm;
In Watts's and Davis' keeping, then, our interests warm.

The post of War was ably manned, and Walker's brilliant lead
Was matched by that of Benjamin and Randolph, as we read;
While Seddon, Smith, and Breckinridge most worthily succeed.[252]
CHARLES EDGEWORTH JONES

Confederate President Jefferson Davis and his cabinet.

THE BIVOUAC OF THE DEAD

The muffled drum's sad roll has beat
    The soldier's last tattoo:
No more on life's parade shall meet
    The brave and daring few.
On Fame's eternal camping ground
    Their silent tents are spread,
And Glory guards with solemn round
    The bivouac of the dead.

No rumor of the foe's advance
    Now swells upon the wind:
No troubled thought at midnight haunts
    Of loved ones left behind:
No vision of the morrow's strife
    The warrior's dream alarms;
No braying horn nor screaming fife
    At dawn shall call to arms.

Their shivered swords are red with rust,
    Their plumed heads are bowed;
Their haughty banner, trailed in dust,
    Is now their martial shroud;
And plenteous funeral tears have washed
    The red stains from each brow.
And their proud forms in battle gashed
    Are free from anguish now.

The neighing steed, the flashing blade,
    The trumpet's stirring blast,
The charge, the dreadful cannonade,
    The din and shout are past;
No war's wild note, nor glory's peal,
    Shall thrill with fierce delight
Those breasts that nevermore shall feel
    The rapture of the fight.

Like the dread Northern hurricane
    That sweeps his broad plateau,
Flushed with the triumph yet to gain,
    Came down the serried foe.
Our Heroes felt the shock, and leapt
    To meet them on the plain;
And long the pitying sky hath wept
    Above our gallant slain.

Sons of our consecrated ground.
    Ye must not slumber there.
Where stranger steps and tongues resound
    Along the heedless air.
Your own proud land's heroic soil
    Shall be your fitter grave,
She claims from war his richest spoil—
    The ashes of her brave.

So 'neath their parent turf they rest,
    Far from the gory field.
Borne to a Spartan mother's breast
    On many a bloody shield.
The sunshine of their native sky
    Smiles sadly on them here,
And kindred hearts and eyes watch by
    The heroes' sepulcher.

Rest on, embalmed and sainted dead!
    Dear as the blood you gave.
No impious footsteps here shall tread
    The herbage of your grave:
Nor shall your glory be forgot
    While Fame her record keeps,
Or Honor points the hallowed spot
    Where Valor proudly sleeps.

Yon marble minstrel's voiceful stone
    In deathless song shall tell,
When many a vanished age hath flown,
    The story how ye fell:
Nor wreck nor change, nor winter's blight,
    Nor time's remorseless doom
Shall dim one ray of holy light
    That gilds your glorious tomb.[253]
THEODORE O'HARA

TO THE SONS & DAUGHTERS OF VETERANS

O'er thirty years have passed away
    Since our Confederate war.
O time of sorrow, wretched day.
    That Lee's surrender saw!

And well the men, and women too.
    Who lived and suffered then
Remember how the brave and true
    Fought to the bitter end.

They honor and revere the names
    Of those who bled and died,
And for each one who still remains
    Their portals open wide.

But time will soon have gathered all
    Who figured in that scene.
On whom, then, will the duty fall
    To keep their memory green?

'Tis yours, O sons, and daughters, too,
    To lift the ensigns high
To those brave souls who, though but few,
    'Gainst odds so great did try.

And though the end they did not gain,
    Their manhood was not lost:
The principle is still the same,
    And worth all that it cost.

Then see to it you don't forget
    That which you've heard them tell
Of glorious deeds—you owe that debt
    To those who bravely fell.

Nor let the flippant tongue of youth
    Speak slightingly of such
Because they failed, as if, forsooth,
    That did their glory smirch.

As long as gallant men still live
    Their country's hest to do,
To patriots pure they still will give
    All praise, and reverence too.

And think ye what a heritage
    Of honor, if not fame,
Is yours to write on history's page
    And with affection frame.
ELIZABETH REES LEGARE

WAR HYMN

Our Father, while we pray,
In all we do and say,
    Direct this hour.
May we, with one accord,
Here fill our hearts, dear Lord,
With thoughts from thine own Word,
    And feel their power.

Like children come we now,
To praise and humbly bow
    Before thy throne.
Thy love in us instill:
Open our minds until
We love thy holy will
    More than our own.

Send now, in mercy mild,
Strength, that each suffering child
    May bear its pain.
Let him thus learn of thee
Each lesson patiently,
Till thou dost set him free
    In health again.

Pardon what we have done
To wound thy bruised Son,
    Restore thy peace.
Guard us from harm to-day.
Walk with us all the way,
Till from this earthly clay
    We find release.[255]

JEANNETTE ROBINSON MURPHY

THE OLD COAT OF GRAY

It lies there alone; it is rusted and faded,
    With a patch on the elbow, a hole in the side;
But we think of the brave boy who wore it, and ever
    Look on it with pleasure and touch it with pride.
A history clings to it; over and over
    We see a proud youth hurried on to the fray.
With his frame like the oak's and his eye like the eagle's,
    How gallant he rode in the ranks of "The Gray."

It is rough, it is worn, it is tattered in places,
    But I love it the more for the story it bears—
A story of courage in struggle with sorrows,
    And a breast that bore bravely its burden of cares.
It is ragged and rusty, but once it was shining
    In the silkiest sheen when he wore it away,
And his face was as bright as the smile of the morning
    When he sprang to his place in the ranks of "The Gray."

There's a rip in the sleeve and the collar is tarnished,
    The buttons all gone with their glitter and gold.
'Tis a thing of the past, and we reverently lay it
    Away with the treasures and relics of old.
As the gifts of love, solemn, sweet, and unspoken,
    And cherished as leaves from a long-vanished day,
We will keep the old coat for the sake of the loved one
    Who rode in the van in the ranks of "The Gray."

Shot through with a bullet right here in the shoulder,
    And down there the pocket is splintered and soiled;
Ah! more—see the lining is stained and discolored!
    Yes, blood drops the texture have stiffened and spoiled
It came when he rode at the head of the column,
    Charging down in the battle one deadliest day,
When squadrons of foemen were broken asunder
    And victory rode with the ranks of "The Gray."

Its memory is sweetest and sorrow commingled:
    To me it is precious—more precious than gold;
In the rent and the shot hole a volume is written,
    In the stains of the lining is agony told.
That was long years ago, when in life's sunny morning
    He rode with his comrades down into the fray,
And the old coat he wore and the good sword he wielded
    Were all that came back from the ranks of "The Gray."

And it lies here alone, I will reverence it ever—
    The patch in the elbow, the hole in the side
For a gallanter heart never breathed than the loved one
    Who wore it with honor and soldierly pride.
Let me brush off the dust from its tatter and tarnish,
    Let me fold it up closely and lay it away—
It is all that remains of the loved and the lost one
    Who fought for the right in the ranks of "The Gray."[256]
UNKNOWN

AT STONEWALL JACKSON'S TOMB

All, here is Valor's sepulcher!
    The god of war lies buried here.
    The matchless skill of his career
Makes former foe now worshiper!
Truth's champions in this concur:
    He was a dauntless cavalier
    Of martial genius, and no peer
In feats of war and might to stir!
He made weak nerves as strong as steel,
    And faint hearts followed where he led.
He filled his army with a zeal
    That never died till he was dead!
But when he fell all Dixie reeled.
And when he died her doom was sealed![257]
BURTON T. DOYLE

Stonewall Jackson.

INVITATION TO THE VETERANS

Come! gather round the dear old flag as in the days of yore,
Veterans, don your coats of gray, let's talk our battles o'er.
Let's stand together, side by side, and sing with might and main
The dear old songs we loved so well that cheered our hard campaign.

Come! See again old Sumter; she stands as strong and brave
As when above her battlements our dear old flag did wave.
Though wind and wave and cannon roar have vied to make her falter
Serene she stands and guards us like the Fortress of Gibraltar.

Come! Gather, dear old comrades; the years go by so fast
The reunions soon will be a memory of the past.
Each year our ranks grow smaller, our hearts oft throb with pain,
That so many ne'er will answer to the roll call here again.

When last we gathered, comrades, "Our Daughter" stood to greet
Each old Confederate soldier, with smile both true and sweet.
Now she has joined the number who have only gone before
And with comrades waits to greet us where partings are no more.

Come, rally round the dear old flag! To her our hearts are true,
Although the stars and stripes now wave, our boys now wear the blue.
Come! Bring the poor old tattered flags, and on Memorial Day
Unfurl them o'er the sacred spot where sleep our men in gray.[258]
NELLIE DICKINSON PERRY

FOR JUST A GLIMPSE OF SOUTHLAND

The city is most splendid with its throng and blaze of light
Ushered into glist'ning beauty by the winged hours of night;
But my heart turns to the Southland, its flowers and skies of blue,
And it almost breaks with longing for just a glimpse of you!

You may talk to me of Broadway, its theaters so grand,
And the opera with its singers, the finest in the land,
What to me these lights and music, these sights both great and new,
If my eyes are always aching for just a glimpse of you?

So I brush away the tear-drops that will start into my eyes,
And I shut from out my mem'ry our laughing Southern skies.
For it makes the work the harder to thus the old times rue—
But there steals in still the longing for just a glimpse of you![259]
GERTRUDE ELOISE BEALER

THE YANK & THE REB

White fingers were strewing memorial flowers where the fallen
    Confederates lay,
The boys who had fought 'neath the stars and the bars in their ragged old
    suits of gray,
And I laid a white rose on a grave at my side, a token tender and true
To the courage of those who had fought as my foes, as I was wearing the
    blue.

Near by stood a veteran, grizzled and bent, who held in his trembling
    hand
A tattered old flag that in many a fight had led his Confederate band,
And I saw the tears start to his dim, misty eyes as he gazed on that
    banner there,
And folded it round the bullet-scarred staff with a sad and reverent air.

Then one who had worn not the blue nor the gray, standing there by the
    graves of the dead,
With a cold, sneering smile on his lips the while, in a tone of mockery
    said:
"Just see that crippled old Johnny there, with his worn-out shred of a
    flag.
Wiping the tears from his watery eyes at the sight of the old rebel rag.

"The flag of a cause that he knew was unjust and of ignominious birth,
That represented no tangible thing in the heavens or on the green earth:
A flag"—"Hold a moment, my friend," I said, "while I ask you a question
    or two:
Pray, where were you then, in the sixties, when the Gray was fighting
    the Blue?

"Not following where that old banner led, or you would acknowledge,
    I ween,
That it represented a courage as great as the world has ever seen:
Nor bravely facing those legions in gray, or you would certainly know
That none but a coward would cast a slur on a gallant but fallen foe.

"I stood on the line in many a fight, and heard the wild Rebel yell,
And saw those ragged old legions charge through storms of shot and
    shell;
And my heart said then, and repeats it now, as every true heart must,
That never an army fought like that for a cause they deemed unjust.

"I thought they were wrong, and I think so still, for I am a Yank, you see:
But through triumph and rout I had never a doubt they were thinking the
    same of me:

For no hypocrite host could ever boast of soldiers who fought so well,
Of those who would face with an equal grace the battle's raging hell;

"And I yield no jot of my loyal pride, or of love for the flag of the free,
When I bow my head o'er the graves of the dead who fell in the ranks of Lee,
And I claim the right of a soldier, who did his best for the Union flag,
To honor the vet whose eyes grow wet at the sight of that battle-torn rag.

"For 'tis proof to me of a loyal soul, that will never desert a fight.
But will bravely defend to the bitter end the cause he deems the right;
And I know that henceforth he will prove more true to the Union stripes and stars,
Because he will not dishonor now the fallen stars and bars.

"And whenever within our time, my friend, a foreign foeman comes,
And a call to arms, with the rude alarms of the bugles and the drums,
Then you, once more, as you did before, safe at your home may stay,
While your country's foes will be thrashed by those who wore both the blue and the gray."[260]
LUCIUS PERRY HILLS (a Yankee soldier)

REUNION HYMN

The sound of battle dies along our broken line,
    The roaring of our guns is stilled for evermore.
God of our fathers, aid us with thy power divine;
    Be thou our Captain, as thou wast in days of yore.

I hear the trampling of the great Confederate host,
    The marching of the lion hearts who fought with Lee.
Teach us, God, the cause we fought for is not lost;
    Instruct our hearts to know the things we cannot see.

From out the darkness and the shadow and the cloud,
    Amid our agony and suffering and pain,
Speak thou, Jehovah, from thy mighty throne, aloud;
    Teach us our fathers' blood has not been shed in vain.

The nation that they wrought for is vanished from the earth:
    The freedom that they fought for was not won;
But the glory of our hopes shall know another birth.
    That shall lift our hearts to heaven as the rising of the sun.

In the coming of the morning, in the breaking of the day;
    In the building of the puissant mighty people now to be;
The shedding of our fathers' blood the nation shall repay,
    And in the nation's halls their sons shall make the nation free.

Steel thou O God, our arm, and make it strong and true
    To guide our banded Union to its destined goal,
Till the bloody sweat and bitter sorrow that we knew
    Shall melt in human love and make thy people whole.[261]

ST. JULIEN GRIMK

THE CONFEDERATE FLAG

Ah, dear old flag, how you carry me back
    To the roll of the drum and the bugle's blast,
To the martial tread of the men in gray,
    To the brave, bright days of the dear, dead past.

And like a mirage in eastern skies
    The longed-for scenes flash into view,
And I see once more the long gray line,
    As Dixie's troops march strong and true.

I see far off on the distant plain,
    Where white tents gleam 'neath the setting sun.
The Southern Cross float on the breeze,
    And the soldiers thrill at the echoing gun.

Far off to the right in a wooded dale
    "The wilderness" fight is raging still,
And the stars and bars, as they rise and float,
    With hope and courage the soldiers fill.

And rank and file, as they fire and load,
    Look to that flag as their guiding star.
While the wounded warrior, who carried it once,
    Cheers as he sees it flashing afar.

In storm and siege and battle's roar
    This flag has floated fair,
And many a hero gave his life
    To uphold its proud career.

And many a woman has prayed and wept,
    As she stitched and stitched with love
Red bars and white together,
    And stars in the blue above.

And many a wife and mother
    Has charged her heart's delight
To guard the flag from danger
    Throughout the deadly fight.

And many a noble Southern lad
    Has died in the foremost van.
Charging for home and honor,
    The Confederate flag in his hand.

Ah! well, but the storm has swept us,
    Ah! well, but the day is past—
Still, out through the rifts in the storm clouds
    Gleam colors that glow and last.

And rolling adown through the ages.
    Wherever brave deeds are told,
The Southern Cross above the clouds
    Will float till the world grows cold.[262]
SUSANNA BRYAN

Sheet music.

LEAVE US OUR DEAD

Leave us our dead! for they alone are ours;
    "They died for us!" And so we claim one day
To scatter on their graves our woodland flowers,
    In memory of a country passed away.
Touch not our closing wounds with salve of gold,
    Else would they bleed afresh, recalling youth.
If we are "rebels" yet, our dead we hold
    As blessed of God! We cannot barter truth.

You called them "traitors"—they who calmly rest
    Beneath our cypress hung with mosses gray,
As tired children on their mother's breast
    Await the dawning of the perfect day.
If they were "traitors" so are we, forsooth,
    And flattery cannot soothe our fearful guilt away.
If it be treason to defend the State
    And hold the faith our fathers held of old—
If this be treason, we have borne the weight
    Of Northern taunts and obloquy. Insult us not with gold!

Restore the dead! Then can we stoop to hear
    The charmer's voice, so subtle and so sweet;
Bring back the brave, the true, the ever-dear,
    Who gave up life in sacrifice complete;
Or blame us not if to our tear-dimmed eyes
    Your stripes seem dyed in reddest Southern blood,
While the fixed stars in marshaled order wise
    Shine on us from the conquered banner's rood—
As on our heroes' graves we blossoms lay
    Sweet as the memories of long ago
Not for the purpose of a grand display,
    But just because we loved and prized them so![263]
JUDITH GRAY

THE SWORD OF THE SOUTH

How thy polished blade leaped
    From its warlike sheath!
Like a simoon it swept
    From mountain and heath;
And the slogan's shrill cry
    From hamlet and glen
Pierced the echoing sky
    And rallied thy men.

Drawn forth for right,
    Thou scabbardless blade,
Though conquered by might,
    By nations betrayed,
Thy cause in liberty's name
    Shall live when ages are old,
And thy illustrious fame
    Will glitter in letters of gold.

Sword of the Southland, no more
    Shall victory leap
From thy blade; the eagles that bore
    Thee no more shall keep
Step. Each broken shield
    Pillows each hero's head;
Their lips are sealed
    With the seal of the dead.

No more shall thy legions in gray,
    With shout of exultant thrill,
Sweep onward in battle array—
    Resistless, defiant—until
Victory rang from each stroke,
    And the mad battle fell
Where the lines grimly broke
    Midst the carnage of hell.

Rest, O sword, in thy sheath,
    Rest! but never shall rust
Tarnish thy wreath,
    Nor memory's dust
Lie thick on thy blade;
    But fame's immortelles
Shall bloom in Mnemosyne's glade,
    Where deathless eternity dwells.

On liberty's altar
    This sword shall be laid.
Let no history falter.
    'Twas the knightliest blade
Ere drawn by a knightly race—
    Drawn in liberty's name.
No time can deface
    From the chaplet of fame
        Its renown.

Let minstrel bard weave
    For the heroes to-day
Some paean; let him retrieve
    From the years now gray
The prowess, that knew not defeat,
    Of the ranks that went down—
That ne'er knew retreat—
    Sing of their daring renown.

Farewell, thou glittering blade!
    Hang from dear memory's wall.
The part you so nobly played
    Shall surely and truly enthrall
With history's unvarnished page
    Brave truth; and, forsooth,
The year's pilgrimage
    Will be the bright Mecca of youth.[264]
JUNIUS L. HEMPSTED

THE MEN OF MOSBY'S COMMAND

Patriot sons of patriot mothers,
Banded in one band as brothers,
One task only of all others
    Calls us here to meet again!—
Calls us 'neath the blue of heaven,
Here to praise and honor seven
    Heroes, martyrs: Mosby's men.
Lit by memory's sunset tender,
See, their names shine out in splendor,
Each our Southland's staunch defender.
    Minstrel's song and poet's pen,
Sing, write, and tell their story,
They who passed through death to glory—
    Heroes, martyrs: Mosby's men.

Rise, O shaft, and tell the story
Of our comrades! It was glory,
    And not death, that claimed its own.
While with tears our eyes grow dimmer,
We behold their dear names glimmer
    On thy consecrated stone.
Rise while prayers and music, blending.
Greet thee as some soul ascending
Where life's smiles and tears have ending
    Close beside the shining throne.
Rise! the cry goes up again—
Love's last gift for Mosby's men.[265]
UNKNOWN

John S. Mosby (center) and his men.

THE OLD FLAG

Furl the old flag gently, comrades,
    Put it by with loving care;
It will flutter no more, comrades,
    O'er the land we love so dear!
Cherished in its gory splendor,
    Hallowed every woven thread:
Mid the music low and tender
    Bury it among the dead.
Lay it down beside the valiant,
    O'er whose heads it once did wave;
Touch it gently, for 'tis holy,
    Mutely yield it to the grave!

Furl it, fold it, O my comrades;
    For the last time touch it, then
Wrap it round the bleeding, broken
    Hearts of valiant Southern men!
Though it never won the glory
    It aspired to in the strife,
It is covered with the gory
    Drops of Southern soldiers' life!
It is steeped within the ocean
    Of the briny tears which flood
The eyes of soldiers' wives, and mingle
    With the dying soldiers' blood!

Furl the dear, defeated banner,
    Shield it e'er from scenes of woe,
For the hand that once upheld it
    Now is lying cold and low!
Touch it softly—aye, and sadly.
    For 'tis dead, my comrades, dead;
Heroes bore it bravely, madly,
    Who no more this earth shall tread.
Then furl it, comrades—valiant soldiers—
    Mutely, meekly, for 'tis best;
With the Southern heroes, calmly,
    Let that flag forever rest![266]
CHARLES HANFORD JR.

DEATHLESS FAME

They call to the Southrons from the North:
  "Come, take your dead away,
    Or we'll plow the sod
    And break the clod
  That covers the rebel clay."

The loyal hands that carried the flag,
  The men who wore the blue,
    On whatever earth
    They had their birth,
  They are counted good and true.

They raise for their own the sodded graves,
  And range them row by row;
    And the billowy grounds
    Lift up in mounds—
  The furrows of death and woe.

And thus with proud acclaim is filled
  The cemetery wide,
    While high o'er the graves
    Splendidly waves
  The banner for which they died.

Our dead died, too, for the dear, loved land
  Whose soil hath given them birth,
    And where'er they fell
    It served them well—
  A handful of mother earth.

No pious hands have lifted the dust
  Of men who nobly died;
    But they sleep a sleep
    As sweet and deep
  As if urned in marble pride.

A voice by the ear of faith is heard:
  "My people keep your trust;
    Behold with your eyes
    Beyond the skies
  That your heroes are not dust."

Their home is with those who fought for truth,
  For God, for fatherland:
    With the blest they dwell,

   And not where swell
  These battle-scarred mounds of sand.

They live on the lips of seraphim,
  And on the tongues of men;
    In the unheeded grave.
    Or 'neath the wave,
  Their glory will bloom again.

Then, tender mother, weep not thy boy,
  Though no stone record his name;
    In brave hearts he'll dwell
    When minstrels tell
  His story of deathless fame.[267]
CONFEDERATE COLONEL WILLIAM PRESTON JOHNSTON

Confederate war heroes.

PRAYER FOR SUBMISSION IN A YANKEE PRISON

Almighty God, Eternal Sire and King!
    Ruler supreme, who all things did create;
Whose everlasting praise the angels sing;
    Whose thought is mercy, and whose word is fate.

Trembling before thy awful throne I kneel,
    Beseeching mercy at thy gracious hand;
Praying that in compassion thou wilt heal
    The bleeding wounds of this most suffering land.

We know our sins are manifold, O God!
    And that thy auger 'gainst us is but right;
For we have wandered widely from thy Word,
    And things committed wrongful in thy sight.

But thou, O God, art powerful to save!
    Full of love and full of mercy art thou;
Else had I not the courage thus to brave
    Thy righteous wrath, and at thy feet to bow.

O'er all our land where late the genial air
    Struck rustling music from the waving grain;
Now the sad earth lies stark and bare.
    And groans beneath the burden of our slain.

O'er all our hearths where late the genial fires
    Beamed bright on scenes of innocent delight,
Now little children vainly call their sires,
    And fly their burning homes with sad affright.

But as thou leddest thy chosen people forth
    From Egypt's sullen wrath, King of kings,
So smite the armies of the cruel North,
    And bear us to our hopes on eagles' wings.

But if thy wisdom still defer the day—
    The wished-for day when freedom shall be won—
Grant us the humility to say:
    "Not human will, but thine, O God, be done"[268]
CONFEDERATE CAPTAIN JOEL P. WALKER

THE UNKNOWN DEAD

The rain is plashing on my sill,
But all the winds of heaven are still;
And so it falls with that dull sound
Which thrills us in the churchyard ground
When the first spadeful drops like lead
Upon the coffin of the dead.
Beyond my streaming window pane
I cannot see the neighboring vane;
Yet from its old familiar tower
The bell comes, muffled, through the shower.
What strange and unsuspected link
Of feeling touched has made me think—
While with a vacant soul and eye
I watch that gray and stony sky—
Of nameless graves on battle plains,
Washed by a single winter's rains,
Where—some beneath Virginian hills,
And some by green Atlantic rills.
And some by the waters of the West—
A myriad unknown heroes rest?
Ah! not the chiefs who, dying, see
Their flags in front of victory,
Or at their life blood's noble cost
Pay for a battle nobly lost,
Claim from their monumental beds
The bitterest tears a nation sheds.
Beneath yon lonely mound—the spot
By all save some fond few forgot—
Lie the true martyrs of the fight
Which strikes for freedom and the right.
Of them, their patriot zeal and pride,
The lofty faith that with them died.
No grateful page shall further tell
Than that so many bravely fell;
And we can only dimly guess
What worlds of all this world's distress,
What utter woe, despair, and dearth,
Their fate has brought to many a hearth.
Just such a sky as this should weep
Above them always as they sleep.
Yet, haply, at this very hour
Their graves are like a lover's bower,
And Nature's self, with eyes unwet,
Oblivious of the crimson debt
To which she owes her April grace,
Laughs gayly o'er their burial place.[269]
HENRY TIMROD

IN MEMORIAM—THE RAID, THE CHARGE, AT REST

(To Confederate Major-General J. E. B. Stuart)

Forward's the watchword to-night, my men. New spurs are to be won,
For a blow must be struck with a will and with might ere the morrow's rising sun—
A blow for Virginia's heroes famed on history's honored page,
Who left to worthy scions here a princely heritage.
A blow for Virginia's hearthstones, round which her daughters sit
With hearts of love and hands of toil to fill the soldier's kit.
A blow for our fallen comrades, for liberty and right.
I'll lead, and who'd be near me must be foremost in the fight,
For 'twill be no long-drawn combat, with rifle range between.
But breast to breast and blow for blow with saber swift and keen.
Then on, my lads! No song to-night; no saber's noisy clank—
For a fettered tread must our squadrons lead to the invaders' watchful flank.

The Southron knight kept well his word when his bugle rang from afar.
And his troop charged down to the welcomed fray with a shout and wild huzza.
Like the storm down an Alpine gorge, with its blasting, blighting breath,
Leaving wild waste behind it and heaping the spoils of death.
At its head, with flashing falchion, rode a cavalier—to life—
A man of mirth for a merry mood, but a foe to be feared in strife.
When the beacon blaze of his watchful eye swept o'er the opposing field,
And the menace flashed from his lifted steel bade the foe to die or yield;
When a stubborn will and a fierce resolve the unstained gauntlet threw
To the countless host of the Northern brave from the peerless Southern few.
For he charged in the van of his cavaliers—this "Rupert of sable plume"—
And who measured his blade with "The Pearl of the Gray" but courted a soldier's doom,
Where the stroke of his trusty saber fell with the force of the vernal flood.
As the eagle swoops from his eyrie down when his young ones cry for food.

'Tis an envied thrill the statesman feels as he bends o'er the enraptured throng.
On the impetuous tide of his eloquence to his purpose borne along;
'Tis a cherished pride the mariner boasts as he curbs mad old ocean's sport
And pages his fame on each homestead hearth as his bark safely rides to port.

But give me the sense that courses his frame and wraps every nerve chord with fire
As the patriot leaps to his country's call in the glow of a sacred ire;
As he gauges each thrust of his trusty steel by the depth of his country's wrong;
Yields, drop by drop, a patriot's blood his country's foes among;
Reclaims with each blow from his lusty arm every footstep his childhood trod,
And offers his life for the land of his birth as a saint yields his soul to God.
So he brooked not to follow, who was born to lead, this Cavalier bold at their head,
Nor danger deterred nor death dismayed, where the still voice bade him tread;
For his soul's rich pride was the State's true weal, and his duty performed and well.
As he lived, so he died. As he fought, so he fell: at the front, freedom's faithful sentinel.

Now is hushed the neigh of his martial steed, and his bugle call is still;
Nor his guidon floats in the battle's van on the crest of each blood-bought hill;
And his saber rests by its master's side in the vale of peace and rest.
Where the arms to his own so tried and true lie folded across his breast.
But list! whilst a comrade stoops to drop a tear o'er his hero's grave.
Where the sweet white rose of his firstborn sleeps by the side of the parent brave.
From fair Richmond's spires steal the church bell chimes as they tell down the twilight air
Of Virginia's homes, now redeemed from the dust, and of rose wreaths clustering there;
While as long as Virginia's name shall last and her soil be trod by the free
Sire to son shall tell how bold Stuart fell and shall treasure his memory.[270]
DR. CHARLES BOWER

THE SOUTHLAND

There the slow rivers glide down to the sea,
There the wind quivers the vine and the tree;

There the bird voices give life to the air,
All earth rejoices, and nature is fair.

There the shy springtime first stops on her way,
Careless what King Time or winter may say.

There every flower gives home to a bee;
There every hour is happy and free.

Hearts there are truthful and friendship is dear,
Growing more youthful with love every year.

Honor a boast is, o'er all and before;
Kindness stands hostess at each Southern door.

Breezes are blowing o'er valley and hill;
Blossoms are snowing in memory still.

Northland is home, though, and there must I be;
Whene'er I roam, though, the Southland for me.[271]
JAMES G. BURNETT

THE FELLOWS THAT TRAMPED IT WITH LEE

While over the Southland the voices
    Of speakers and poets let fall
The accents of praise for the chieftain
    So richly deserving it all.
I think it would please the great captain,
    If he could look down here and see
That some one remembers his heroes,
    The fellows that tramped it with Lee.

How oft in his tent at the midnight
    He plotted the brilliant campaign!
How oft, ere the daylight was dawning,
    They followed in sleet and in rain!
How oft they rushed into battle,
    Their hearts in a tumult of glee!
The steady, the ready old fellows,
    The fellows that tramped it with Lee.

Tho' mighty the brain in its scheming,
    The feet at its bidding must run;
And vic'tries on paper are proven
    By privates that level the gun.
So, great as the captain we honor
    (And great may his fame ever be!)
'Tis shared by the shaggy old heroes,
    The fellows that tramped it with Lee.

'Tis easy in shock of the battle
    To pass out of life with a smile,
A hero secure of his laurels:
    But to sweat with the rank and the file.
And afterwards live and be patient,
    Still struggling, appeareth to me
Yet nobler: and such be the fellows,
    The fellows that tramped it with Lee.

They followed their dauntless commander,
    Him who to the warrior's art
United the lore of the scholar
    And the patriot's temperate heart;
And yet in their zealous devotion
    These men were as great as he—
These grizzled, grim, veteran soldiers,
    These fellows that tramped it with Lee.

The frosts of the winter are whitening
    The locks that the bullets once kissed;
And soon they will meet with a foeman
    The stoutest can never resist
To us they'll bequeath inspiration
    When at length, mustered out, they are free
To cross o'er the River of Silence
    And tramp it again there with Lee.

And so if the general is conscious
    Of things that are done here below,
He'd be glad if the speakers and poets
    Some sprigs of their laurel bestow.
On such as did win him his glory,
    And back him from mountains to sea—
On them, both the dead and the living,
    The fellows that tramped it with Lee.[272]

WILLIAM T. DUMAS

Robert E. Lee.

DEATH OF GENERAL BENJAMIN HARDIN HELM

Nigh Chickamauga's turbid stream
("River of Death" in the Indian's dream)
He fell without a sigh or groan
When the South's bright star of victory shone.

He led his brave Kentuckians forth
To meet the invader from the North.
And ere in death he closed his eye
He heard his proud men's triumph cry.

His saber flashed in the golden sun
Like the blade of Attila, the royal Hun.
And hired Hessians fled away
And hid from his might in the glory fray.

So blameless was the hero's life,
Who fell in the ensanguined strife.
The nation's great heart throbbed in pain
When she saw his cold form 'mid the slain.

He has gone to a long and dreamless rest
On a dark couch in the green earth's breast.
And woman will oft to his shrine repair
And twine her tribute garlands there.

Children, in future and better years,
Will read of his fall with silent tears:
While men, strong men, will heave a sigh
That one like him should bleed and die.

To him we bid a long farewell,
Whom death now binds in a silent spell.
And hope that in the eternal realm
Jehovah smiles on the patriot Helm.[273]
VIRGINIA HUTCHEN

Benjamin H. Helm.

THE GLORIOUS GHOST OF LEE

When all those famous old Confeds
    Have gone to take their rest,
What can we, their sons, do then
    But bravely stand and do our best?

'Tis true we cannot fight their battles o'er
    Or die for the Southland's sake;
But shall we then sit idly down
    And be content a coward's part to take?

Shall we let them be traitors called,
    Their names suffer disgrace and shame?
No! Rise we will, and keep alive
    Their sacred patriot flame!

No history shall for its own gain
    Degrade them to the dust.
For while their sons and daughters stand
    Their shining deeds will never rust.

Their names are now put down
    On the immortal roll of fame,
And as long as history is just
    Will remain there without a stain.

But on the shores of that other land
    Are they not: O may it not be,
That they are there, in serried ranks, being marshaled,
    By the glorious ghost of Lee.[274]
CARROLL GIBSON WALTER

A RIDE WITH STUART

Booted and spurred and mounted,
    Away at the bugle call;
And now for a ride by Stuart's side,
    To conquer, or fighting fall.

In the cold gray dawn of the morning,
    Ere the flush of the coming sun,
We ride with the dash of an arrow's flash
    To the spot where the pass is won.

And we hold it, too, 'til the shadowy forms
    Of the men who are dressed in gray,
Like sonic phantom host on a cloud-wrapped coast
    Sweep grimly into the fray.

And then once more to saddle
    And away with the hurricane's speed
To strike the flank of the foeman's rank
    Till it bends like a broken reed.

Afar in the thick of the battle,
    Half hid by the smoke and the gloom,
Strikes a knight full brave 'neath the beckoning wave
    Of Stuart's snow-white plume.

Hurrah! The field is ours!
    The routed foemen flee!
And we follow the lead of the charging steed
    Of the flower of Southern chivalry.[275]
CLIFFORD MCKINNEY TAYLOR

THE OLD JACKET OF GRAY

See this old jacket, faded and torn!
In Morgan's raid it was proudly worn—
    This very old jacket of gray.
It was one of many that covered then
The breasts of true-hearted Southern men,
All thrilled with the hope that filled them when
    John Morgan was leading the way.

This haversack, see! it hung of yore—
Bearing of hardtack a meager store
    Across the old jacket of gray.
Though tired and ragged and hungry too,
What cared we, with victory full in view?
We feared not defeat, for well we knew
    John Morgan was leading the way.

From Lee to the humblest soldier who
His sword for the honor of Dixie drew,
    All wore just such jackets of gray.
Though the cause we love is a "lost cause," still
It lives in hearts that will ever thrill
At sight of the gray, though no more will
    John Morgan be leading the way.

He led the way up fair glory's height
With the patriot heroes, who waged a fight
    In their tattered jackets of gray
That will live for aye on the roll of fame
And carved on time's rock brave Dixie's name
To fill Southern hearts with the patriot's flame
    Of Morgan while leading the way.

There are many here who fought and bled,
By love for freedom and honor led,
    In just such old jackets of gray;
And many whose hearts enshrine with pride
Loved ones who fell in the battle tide
With Dixie's name on their lips, and died
    While Morgan was leading the way.

O heroes of Dixie, one and all—
The living and dead—on you I call.
    Who wore the old jackets of gray!
On the living to teach by tongue and pen;
On the dead, by those who loved them then,

Our youth to glory in the men
    Who, like Morgan, once led the way.

To glory in Lee and old Stonewall,
In the Johnstons, Hampton, Stuart, and all
    Who wore the dear jackets of gray;
In the privates who joined the hero band
From Maryland to the Lone Star's strand.
In the stars and bars of Dixie's land,
    And in Davis, who led the way.[276]
ANNIE BARNWELL MORTON

THE RECOMPENSE

We never give, but, giving, get again;
    There is no burden that we may not bear;
Our sweetest love is always sweetest pain;
    And yet the recompense, the recompense is there.

Who weeps, yet worships some sweet, silent star,
    E'en through his tears shall catch uplifting light.
We grow to what our aspirations are—
    Look up, O soul, and be a star to-night.

Who pours his soul out to some flower rare
    On scaleless cliff, above a sailless sea,
Shall drink its perfume, if he linger there.
    Until his very soul that flower shall be.

Who bares his head where God's star altars rise,
    Yet strives to probe with prayer their mystery.
E'en with the act claims kindred with the skies—
    We are the wish of all we will to be.

Who loves his love through death and riftless ruth,
    Yet ne'er shall clasp and kiss her in his leal.
Shall wedded be in spirit and in truth—
    We are the deed of all we think and feel.

We never give, but, giving, get again;
    There is no burden that we may not bear;
Our sweetest love is always sweetest pain;
    And yet the recompense, the recompense is there.[277]

JOHN TROTWOOD MOORE

OLD TIME CONFEDERATES

We are a band of brothers,
    And comrades kind and true,
We've fought in many battles
    'Gainst those who wore the blue.

CHORUS
    We are old-time Confederates,
    We are old-time Confederates,
    We are old-time Confederates,
    And that's good enough for me.

Our ties are more than brothers
    To those who wore the gray;
That tie will last forever,
    Till time shall pass away.

Then in shades beyond the river
    Our souls will there unite.
In songs of joy forever,
    In worlds of heavenly light.

When Venus gleams her tinted rays,
    To light a world afar,
There's not a glint of light so clear
    As gleams from Forrest's star.[278]
G. I. GOODWIN

A REQUIEM

And all the orbs that deck the sky,
    Shine brighter, as the drum,
With muffled tones and litter tells,
    "Another soldier's come."

The living heroes o'er the earth,
    Will point to crowns above,
Circling the brows of warriors,
    Who died for country's love.

A Lee, a Jackson, Johnston, Bragg,
    Await at heaven's door.
To hear the "taps" of coming years,
    And welcome thousands more.

O heroes of life's valiant age,
    With patriot visions bright.
There's none so brave as he who fails—
    Or dies—for freedom's right.[279]
JOHN W. FAXON

John W. Faxon.

THE LAST WORDS OF STONEWALL JACKSON

Brilliant, complete, but O how brief
Were the chivalrous deeds of the world's great chief!
But crowded within that little span
Were records of glory scarce known to man.

Two continents watched with wonder and awe
As he sprang, full-armed, from the god of war;
That quiet Professor, unknown to the world,
This offspring of thunder was suddenly hurled.

Into the arena, with God as his guide,
He fearlessly charged the great odds he defied;
And victory followed that old coat of gray
Till furrowed by bullets that ill-fated day.

On Sunday he heard that the end was so near,
When calmly he said, without tremor or fear:
"I have always wanted to die on this day."
So the way of his Father was Stonewall's way.

With feverish brain he's a soldier still—
Crisp orders he sends to A. P. Hill.
The fire of battle burns in his eyes—
A warrior grand, though he lowly lies.

The soldier grows weary, the camp is in sight.
His countenance beams with celestial light.
"Let us cross over"—into heaven he sees—
"The river and rest 'neath the shade of the trees."[280]
MRS. J. WILLIAM JONES

TO OUR SACRED CONFEDERATE DEAD

Go, scatter the flowers, one by one!
What are their names, and where are they from?
We know not, we care not—dead and unknown,
Without name or date to carve on the stone.

'Tis full enough for our hearts to know
They bravely faced and fought the foe;
Enough on each marble slab to say:
"A brother soldier who wore the gray."

They fought for a cause some say is "lost;"
But we, whose hearts fully know the cost.
Know that for us the cause hath shed
A glory and honor which hallows our dead.

On the living hath fallen their mantles of trust;
Immortal they reign, while we honor their dust.
'Tis a history now; 'twas a poem then,
All fraught with the glorious deeds of men.

Women and children sang the proud song
Which echoed our battle lines along
And floated on breezes from shore to shore—
Such grand achievements ne'er won before.

We honored and loved our soldiers then,
And crowned with laurel the bravest of men.
A history now, with unsullied page,
Hath been handed down to the present age;

And the deeds of the "boys who wore the gray"
Gives to our Southland a grandeur to-day—
Our hearts wildly throbbing with love and with pride,
As, shoulder to shoulder, we stand side by side.[281]
MRS. N. STEELE MOORE

THE SWORD OF CLEBURNE

The good right hand that wielded it
 Is moldering in dust,
But comrades have not yielded it
 To idle, useless rust,
For they remember well that day,
 And treasured ever be
The sword he wore who fell that day
 At Franklin, Tennessee.

Three times he turned the battle rout
 And waved that brand on high.
While loudly rang his battle shout
 And flashed his fiery eye;
And then that fourth and fated ride,
 His banner floating free,
And there, where glory waited, died,
 At Franklin, Tennessee.

The cause he loved in drear defeat
 As death itself went down,
But never did he fear to meet
 Its foes, and his renown
Shalt live with those that stood with him,
 And fame shall tell how he
Led those who shed their blood with him
 At Franklin, Tennessee.

Brave Erin's blood flowed in his veins,
 And his escutcheon bright
Bore none save honor's sinless stains,
 And never truer knight
Left home and country far behind
 And crossed the distant sea,
And left a name incarnadined,
 At Franklin, Tennessee.[282]
MONTGOMERY M. FOLSOM

SOUTHERN WOMEN—A TRIBUTE

To Southern women all praise is due
    For courage strong and fearless zeal;
Whose daring spirit and love so true
    The Northern arms were made to feel.

Time in its flight, how many years
    Have fled beyond recall,
And in our hearts there is no strife,
    For peace heads one and all.

No class of women so brave e'er lived,
    Sending their sons to war,
No poverty can e'er disgrace,
    No shadow devotion mar.

Thrown to the breeze so fearlessly,
    Flap of the Bonnie Blue,
No braver men yet faced a foe,
    No hearts more pure and true.

Their homes were made a sacrifice,
    And jewels that women prize
To buy our guns at any price
    To flash in foemen's eyes.

All things of value followed fast,
    All, all, they gave to shield
Their homes and honored patriarchs
    From wanton sword and steel.

What they endured is traced in gold
    Across a cloudless sky,
The honor of our women true
    In records now on high.

And when that roll on high is called,
    And justice claims its worth,
In foremost ranks will peerless stand
    The women of the South.[283]
NAME ILLEGIBLE

THE BOY HERO OF THE WAR

And lo! thy matchless boy, O Tennessee!
With pinioned arms beneath the gallows tree.
Looked forth, unmoved, into the wintry skies,
The nut-brown ringlets falling o'er his eyes;
He, by kind gaolers, had been oft implored:
"Speak but one word! To freedom be restored!"
The lifted signal, "Hold," the messenger cried;
And, springing up, stood by the hero's side.
"My boy! This bitter cup must pass you by!
Too brave, too noble, and too young to die!
Your mother, father, sisters—when they learn—
Even now, perhaps, they wait your long return.
Speak but one word—the real culprit's name!
'Tis he should bear this penalty and shame.
Live for your mother! Think a moment how"—
"Not with the brand of fraud upon my brow!
I and the 'culprit,' true, might both go free;
The broken pledge would haunt not him, but me.
How light soever what promise man may make,
Should be kept sacred for his honor's sake!
My mother!"
(And choking back the sob, but half concealed,
His head drooped low! At last must nature yield?)
"My mother!" flashed again the tear-dimmed eyes,
"At her dear knees she taught me how to die!
Her loving heart would be too sorely pained
If to her lips were pressed her boy's with falsehood stained."
"My brave, brave boy," the pleader spoke again;
"A boy in years, but worth a thousand men,
Like him for whom, the coward, traitor, knave,
You'd lay your own brave, young life down to save.
Speak out! Life is so sweet! Be free once more!"
"I never knew how sweet life was before!
Still—words are useless, General, but forgive—
You're kind; yet if I had a thousand lives to live,
I'd give them all ere I could face the shame,
And wear, for one hour, a base, dishonored name."
The die was cast! Our tears were idle tears,
For him, who gave one day and gained a thousand years!
Centuries on centuries shall go circling by,
But still he is not dead! Sam Davis cannot die![284]
UNKNOWN

TO THE ONLY CONFEDERATE MONUMENT IN GETTYSBURG

Your top should be reaching the sky,
    Proclaiming what you represent:
How true men and patriots can die,
    O silent and lone monument.

You speak of the soldiers in gray,
    Whose pluck, though their numbers were few,
In triumph so oft won the day.
    And wrested the palm from the blue.

The fame of their deeds shall abide
    In the hearts of our people who dwell
In the land at whose mandate they died,
    "The storm-cradled nation that fell."

But gone are the heroes in gray;
    They sleep by the heroes in blue;
And discord no longer holds sway
    O'er our Union cemented anew.

As a heart-broken mother who weeps,
    When they lay her sweet darling to rest,
Long after comes back where it sleeps
    And kneeling there whispers, "'Tis best!"

So the South, after sorrowful years
    Views the ground where her proud banner fell,
And, looking to heaven through tears,
    She trustingly whispers: "'Tis well."[285]

MRS. W. M. ROBBINS

TRUEST, BRAVEST, & BEST

Go, call the men who fought
    In '61 to '65,
And have them stand in ranks, when brought,
    As soldiers still alive!

I mean the Southern band
    Who stood for Southern rights,
Defenders of their native land
    In many bloody fights.

The great commanders place
    In long-extended line,
Distinguished men, in form and grace—
    They stir this heart of mine!

Subalterns, too, a host
    Well worthy of renown.
And common men, who, at their post,
    Could die without a frown.

Then call the women, too.
    The best the world has seen:
Matron and maid, and sweetheart who
    Entranced some heart as queen.

To all thus placed in line
    Proclaim a vote be cast
For one whose valor did outshine,
    In conflict now o'erpast.

Returns would show, I ween,
    One name would lead the rest:
Sam Davis, hanged heav'n and earth between,
    Was truest, bravest, best.[286]

J. H. BRUNNER

ABRAM JOSEPH RYAN, THE POET PRIEST

He furled his last banner, and, folded to rest.
Now peacefully sleeps in the land he loved best;
He loved our sweet Southland 'mid sorrow and gloom,
He wreathed her fair forehead with beauty and bloom.

A friend to his country, a patriot he;
No Southerner ever more faithful could be,
And gratitude claims for his memory now
A wreath of immortelles to circle his brow.

Sweet nature had stamped him a poet by birth,
With an ear attuned to the music of earth:
This genius begotten of sorrow and pain,
A wail or a dirge, a mournful refrain.

A fragrance exhaled from crushed roses that lie
With their pitiful faces turned up to the sky;
Or a strain of wild music burdened with pain,
When heart strings are trembling and bursting in twain.

A weary soul treading life's pathway alone.
With never a heart to respond to its own;
But so long as earth's sorrows must sadden our days
Shall the memory of Ryan be circled with bays.[287]
MRS. MARY WARE

Abram J. Ryan.

THE "BATTERED SCARECROWS"

"Talk of pluck!" pursued the sailor,
Set at euchre on his elbow,
"I was on the wharf at Charleston,
Just ashore from off the runner.

"It was gray and dirty weather,
And I heard a drum go rolling,
Rub-a-dubbing in the distance,
Awful dourlike and defiant.

"In and out among the cotton,
Mud, and chains, and stores, and anchors,
Tramped a squad of battered scarecrows—
Poor old Dixie's bottom dollar.

"Some had shoes, but all had rifles
Them that wasn't bald was beardless;
And the drum was rolling 'Dixie.'
And they stepped to it like men, sir

"Rags and tatters, belts and bayonets,
On they swung, the drum a rolling,
Mum and sour. It looked like fighting,
And they meant it, too, by thunder!"[288]
WILLIAM ERNEST HENLEY (an Englishman)

A CONFEDERATE SPY

A moment gazed those war-worn men;
    Stern faces lit then on the air;
Echoing: from mountain height and glen,
    Sudden there rose a last, long cheer!

Rough hand dashed blinding tears aside;
    Then reverently, with drooping head,
Slowly each went with heavy stride
    As from the presence of the dead.

A thousand years will come, and then
The theme will be of noble men;
    The heroes of the earth
    By deeds, not of birth;
    And about the home's sacred hearth
Where'er are gathered children,
Where'er are loyal men
Who will have known what 'tis to be
Freemen of a country free.
To our Great War's written pages
(Which will brighten with the ages)
    Those loyal sires and sons will turn
For the deeds and the names
That then and there were fame's
    Immortaled in historic urn.

Of the mighty spirits of this age,
Of the loyal names on that page,
    One's, and the saddest story
    Ever writ in glory
There will green, as the fragrant bay
    Rooted by the river's side,
    Watched by the river's tide;
A youth that one of manly mold,
    Whose stout heart, tongue, nor pen
    To the living ears of men
Will scarce its virtues quite unfold.
    And who and what was he
    That he should immortal be?
    That in the urn of fame
    Should burn a lamp his name?
A soldier boy who wore the gray;
    Nor on this stars nor bars
    Slight were battle scars,
Tho' oft he stood in battle array

He boasted not a stately tree:
Humbly born of, and 'mong the free
Of the commonwealth of Tennessee.
    A martyr! nameless here,
    His name is written there
On the rocks—those eternal spires
Where burn the incense fires
    (Made brighter by his blood)
    Ascending up to God.
From the rising to the setting sun,
    These ignitions heights,
    Burning incense lights,
Shed splendor 'bout that martyred one—
    That immortal name
    Of Confederate fame:
That true and tried Confederate spy
Who chose, 'tween life and death, to die
    Rather than he'd betray
    A comrade in the gray.

Life to the hero's heart is sweet,
Loves and hopes in his bosom beat,
    And death to him hath dread
Where'er met, in whatever way,
But most, that terror, grim, shadowy,
    The living's cheeks make pallid,
Is when the doomed stands all alone,
    And life's fond hopes in pall
    Come trooping to the call
Of death, and cold, and mute as stone
    Stand shriveled, blanching, all alone,
Then and there, of earth's mortals, few
Can summon to that last review,
    Life's highest noblest aim
    The soul's inspiring name
Which cannot die; and like a god,
Enshrined above this earthly sod,
Say unto Death: "Thou hath not bribe
To which, for life, I would subscribe.
    Now, and where now I stand
    Let the heavy hand,
    Unto him who gave it,
    My soul He shall receive it,
Untarnished by disloyalty
    To Him, God, or to man."
    But such of earth there be,
    And such of earth was he,

Who went down to death that day
    And up to heaven's van;
And he, but a soldier of the Gray,
    Condemned and doomed to die
    For loyal Confederate spy.[289]

"TEXAS"

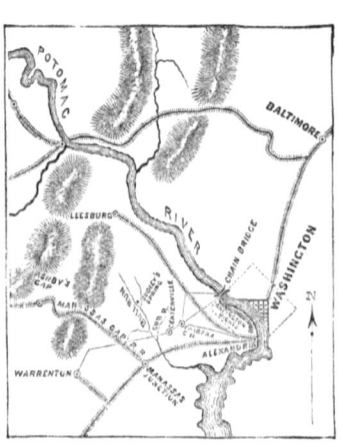

TO THE CONFEDERATE SURVIVORS OF THE WAR

Faintly ring's out a bugle horn.
    And fainter still its echoes die.
Breaking the soft, sweet hush of morn
    With mimic war's wild minstrelsy.

And memories of the long ago
    Come thronging, as its notes I hear,
When all the future seemed aglow
    With radiancy of promise fair.

Adown the coming years did beat
    The pulse of hope, life seemed so bright
That little recked we of defeat,
    Nor dreamed such days should close in night.

Freedom had gathered thirteen stars,
    Soft blue from out the sky she rent,
Caught from the rainbow crimson bars,
    That with the stars and blue were blent.

Into a banner shall we live
    On history's page in song and story,
By heroes wreathed with immortelles,
    A people's pride, a nation's glory,

She gave this standard to our trust,
    And bade us to the conflict go
Never to trail it in the dust,
    Or yield one fair star to the foe.

For four long years we kept at bay,
    'Gainst desperate odds, their countless host;
We fought and starved for many a day,
    Nor dreamed our cause could e'er be lost.

But as the years went slowly by,
    Our sun adown the west had crept;
The flower of Southern chivalry
    On blood-stained fields by thousands slept.

Disease and want had worn away
    Our shattered ranks, until at last
Night's darkness fell athwart a day
    When hope of victory was past

On Appomattox's fatal plain
    Faded from out our flag the stars,
The blue crept back to heaven again,
    The rainbow claimed its blood-stained bars.

Ragged, hungry, weary men!
    Brave veterans of a hundred fields,
You rallied for the last time then,
    And wrote defeat upon your shields.

O, who can forget that hour
    In the long lapse of coming years?
Men though we were we had no power
    To stay our sobs and bitter tears.

At length 'twas o'er, and as we turned,
    Stilled by a deep and voiceless pain,
Suddenly aloft there burned
    A glory we ne'er would see again.

From splintered staff was floating far
    Tattered and battle-stained and riven,
A banner whereon each radiant star
    Shone as though from the vault of heaven.

A moment gazed those war worn men;
    Stern faces lit then on the air;
Echoing from mountain height and glen,
    Sudden there rose a last, long cheer!

Rough hands dashed blinding tears aside;
    Then reverently, with drooping head,
Slowly each went with heavy stride
    As from the presence of the dead.[290]
ANNA ALEXANDER CAMERON

IN MEMORIAM

From the shadow land of memory
    Scenes long past return again;
Phantoms thronging weird around me
    Waken slumbering thoughts of pain.
Once again, mid din of battle,
    Can I hear the bugle's call;
See the marshaled forces forming,
    For our homes to stand or fall;
While amid the dreadful carnage,
    And above the cannon's mouth,
Waves the banner of our daring
    Spartan soldiers of the South.

But though valiantly they bore it
    Over many a glorious field,
Till, when foiled at last by numbers,
    Sadly they were forced to yield,
Still their valiant deeds will ever
    Sound along the Hall of Fame,
And the ages will remember
    All they did in Freedom's name;
And our banner, wreathed in glory,
    Tattered, furled though it may be,
Thrill each Southern heart with memories
    Of our struggle to be free.

Can we e'er forget the heroes,
    Who with dauntless heart and brave
Swore that flag should float forever
    O'er their freedom or their grave?
No! we'll seek our richest treasure
    In the memory of the dead,
And with pride we'll tell the story,
    How for rights of men they bled.
And with springtime's fairest flowers
    We will weave a chaplet now,
Laurel crown with cypress mingled
    Place above each hero's brow.[291]
SALLIE JONES

THE ROAD TO IMMORTALITY
(To the Army Without a Gun)

Hail! brave vet'rans, ensign's tattered,
    Panoplied no more for war;
Heroes scarred and maimed and battered,
    Bowed with age and weight of care;
Year by year your roll's decreasing,
Silenced lips, and heart beats ceasing.

Gleams of battle clear and frigid
    Flit before the soldier's mind;
Where death, stalking stark and rigid,
    Seemed to "leave all hope behind."
Iron hailstorms, bayonets flashing;
Troops now rushing, sabers clashing.

How these "comrades," mingling, blending,
    Speak of deeds of bloody strife,
Tell of shrapnel, case shot rending,
    As they hurled the breath from life;
Bombshells bursting, rockets flying,
Carnage heaping, brothers dying.

Yet, in saddest, darkest moments,
    Whilst the death knell sounded forth,
Ties were formed which trouble foments,
    Pledging friends who'd proved their worth.
Whilst the drums kept solemn tapping
To the soil's pure lifeblood lapping.

Cleanse from Southern soil the blood spots,
    Stained by angered brothers' arms;
Veil them 'neath the rarest flow'r plots—
    Peace's emblems, Memory's charms
Monoliths will tell the story,
Manhood's valor, country's glory.

Forrest brave, unflinching, daring—
    Gave his State his meed of fame;
Still the painful truth is glaring:
    No memorial bears his name.
Name so worthy, fame deserving;
Firm and faithful, never swerving.

Breasts for Southern woman baring,
    Bore the brunt of four long years;

She, for heroes' graves now caring.
    Keeps them green with grateful tears—
Tears of sorrow, flowers of beauty,
Sacred proofs of "well done" duty.

Rear to sisters, wives, and mothers
    Shaft of marble pure and tall;
On it trace those deeds for brothers,
    Living vet'rans now recall.
Years may glide; time cannot sever
Humane acts—they live forever.

Lovely woman took upon her
    Noble hands a duty fair;
Gave to you the "Cross of Honor"—
    There's another "cross" to bear:
Cross of Jesus, crown of glory!
Capture both, ye vet'rans hoary.

When the last sad "taps" are sounded,
    When the "Rebel shout" is stayed,
Heaven's the happy camp unbounded,
    Where God's orders are obeyed,
Where the Prince of Peace benignly
Lulls to rest the soul divinely.[292]
JOHN W. FAXON

FORREST

It was out of the South that the lion heart came,
From the ranks of the Gray like the flashing of flame,
A juggler with fortune, a master with fame—
The rugged heart born to command.

And he rode by the star of an unconquered will,
And he struck with the might of an undaunted skill;
Unschooled, but as firm as the granite-flanked hill—
As true and as tried as steel.

Though the Gray were outnumbered, he counted no odd,
But fought like a demon and struck like a god.
Disclaiming defeat on the blood-curdled sod,
As he pledged to the South that he loved.

'Twas saddle and spur, or on foot in the field,
Unguided by tactics that knew how to yield;
Stripped of all, save his honor, but rich in that shield,
Full armored by nature's own hand.

As the rush of the storm he swept on the foe:
It was "Come!" to his legions—he never said "Go!"
With sinews unbending, how could the world know
That he rallied a starving host?

For the wondering ranks of the foe were like clay
To these men of flint in the molten day;
And the hell-hounds of war howled afar for their prey,
When the arm of a Forrest led.

Was he devil or angel? Life stirred when he spoke,
And the current of courage, if slumbering, woke
At the yell of the leader, for never was broke
The record men wondering read.

With a hundred he charged like a thousand men,
And the hoofbeats of one seemed the tattooed ten.
What bar were burned bridges or flooded fords when
The wizard of battle was there?

But his pity could bend to a fallen foe,
The mailed hand soothed a brother's woe;
He had time to be human, for tears to flow—
For the heart of the man to thrill.

Then "On!" as though never a halt befell,
With a swinging blade and the rebel yell.
Through the song of the bullets and the plowshares of hell—
The hero, half iron, half soul!

Swing, rustless blade in the strong left hand—
Ride, soul of a god, through the dauntless band—
Through the low, green mounds of the breadth of the land—
Wherever your legions dwell!

Swing, rebel blade, through the halls of fame,
Where courage and justice have left your name;
By the torches of glory your deeds shall flame
With the reckoning of Time![293]
VIRGINIA FRAZER BOYLE

Nathan B. Forrest.

CONFEDERATE CEMETERY, SPRINGFIELD, MISSOURI

Sleep on, brave heroes of a deathless past;
    How sacred is this spot!
Although no granite shaft yet marks the place,
    Ye shall not be forgot!
Like germ of flower deep hidden away
    Within the heart of earth,
The marble waits the touch of sculptor hand,
    To speak it into birth.

The grass has been kept green above your heads
    Through all the tardy years,
While loving hearts have garlanded your graves
    And watered them with tears;
Soft winds have sighed a lonely requiem,
    The bended skies have wept;
Since the brave charge on that long summer day
    Heroes, uncrowned, have slept.

Some day the granite base and marble shaft
    In grandeur here will rise.
To tell how fought Missouri's gallant sons
    Beneath their native skies.
O stars, ye silent sentinels, shine on!
    And dews of heaven descend:
While sunlight gleams, where warriors bravely fell,
    Home altars to defend.

It matters not, though stately marble spire
    Should never here arise;
Their deeds will live in every patriot heart;
    True valor never dies.
Sleep on, brave heroes of a deathless past,
    Than that in which defeated valor,
There is no holier ground rests,
    And patriots lie uncrowned.[294]
UNKNOWN

CROSS OF HONOR

Here, Veterans, we give a cross to you—
    Not a cross that is hard to bear—
But a cross for your bravery, tried and true,
    A badge you are proud to wear.

The years have been long and hard and drear
    To many that meet here to-day,
And we Daughters are adding a bit of cheer
    To your loyal hearts ere you pass away.

Your ranks grow thin as the years go down,
    And your battles are almost won,
And this cross of bronze will turn to a crown
    When the Master shall say, "Well done."

The four grand years that you fought so well
    Have been followed by grief and strife;
But you aimed so true, each shot would tell,
    And you've mastered the battle of life.

What if at San Juan our veterans won,
    Has the gray turned any more blue?
And what if they fought for a Union gun,
    Has the heart grown any less true?

No, comrades, the same old men to-day
    Are as loyal in heart and hand
As they ever were, and their heartstrings play
    When the band starts "Dixie Land."

And now we have brought this cross to you,
    That is bronzed with our love and faith,
And we pin it there on your breast so true,
    As an emblem of honored worth.

And we pledge our word that the Daughters all
    Will never let fade your name,
And when you have answered the reveille call
    We will still keep alive your fame.[295]
UNKNOWN

TRIBUTE POEM TO MAJOR PHILIP H. FALL

At Sabine Pass, in sixty-three,
In a little mud fort near by the sea,
Stood a noble band of high degree,
    And with them brave Dick Dowling.

Of the Davis Guards there doth remain
But few who bear the honored name;
But the dead live on in the Temple of Fame,
    With their leader, brave Dick Dowling.

To those still left our hearts beat true,
And Houston's sons now call to you
To join them and once more renew
    The memory of Dick Dowling.

Come, though many years have rolled,
Your locks are gray, you're growing old.
Come, with your great heroic souls,
    To honor brave Dick Dowling.

Remember that September day
You held that Yankee fleet at bay!
Just forty-one men, all wearing the gray,
    Led on by brave Dick Dowling.

Just forty-one men, with the Texas yell;
But they scattered those Yankee ships pell-mell.
O, but they fought right nobly and well!
    Those heroes with brave Dick Dowling.

They were sons of Erin, and never were found
Grander knights of "The Table Round,"
And their names through ages shall resound
    With their leader, brave Dick Dowling.

"Wave, Texas, all thy banners wave!"
And with bright laurels crown the grave
Of him, the bravest of the brave,
    Immortal young Dick Dowling.[296]
MRS. ELLEN R. CROOM

THE OLD SWORD ON THE WALL

    Where the warm spring sunlight, streaming
    Through the window, sets it gleaming
With a softened silver sparkle in the dim and dusky hall,
    With its tassel torn and tattered,
    And its blade deep-bruised and battered,
Like a veteran, scarred and weary, hangs the old sword on the wall.

    None can tell its stirring story,
    None can sing its deeds of glory,
None can say which cause it struck for, or from what limp hand it fell.
    On the battlefield they found it,
    Where the dead lay thick around it,
Friend and foe—a gory tangle—tossed and torn by shot and shell.

    Who, I wonder, was its wearer,
    Was its stricken soldier bearer?
Was he some proud Southern stripling, tall and straight and brave and true?
    Dusky locks and lashes had he?
    Or was he some Northern laddie,
Fresh and fair, with cheeks of roses, and with eyes and coat of blue?

    From New England's fields of daisies,
    Or from Dixie's bowered mazes,
Rode he proudly forth to conflict? What, I wonder, was his name?
    Did some sister, wife, or mother
    Mourn a husband, son, or brother?
Did some sweetheart look with longing for a love who never came?

    Fruitless question! Fate forever
    Keeps its secret, answering never.
But the grim old blade shall blossom on this mild Memorial Day;
    I will wreathe its hilt with roses
    For the soldier who reposes
Somewhere 'neath the Southern grasses in his garb of blue or gray.

    May the flowers be fair above him.
    May the bright buds bend and love him,
May his sleep be deep and dreamless till the last great bugle call;
    And may North and South be nearer
    To each other's heart, and dearer,
For the memory of their heroes and the old swords on the wall![297]
JOE LINCOLN

SOMETIME

Sometime, when all life's lessons have been learned,
    And sun and stars for evermore have set,
The things which our weak judgments here have spurned,
    The things o'er which we grieved with lashes wet,
Will flash before us 'mid our darkest night,
    As stars shine out in deepest tints of blue,
And we shall see how all God's plans were right,
    And what most seemed reproof was love most true.

And we shall see how, while we fret and sigh,
    God's plans go on as best for you and me;
How, when we called, he heeded not our cry,
    Because his wisdom to the end could see;
And e'en as prudent parents disallow
    Too much of sweets to craving babyhood,
So God, perhaps, is keeping from us now
    Life's sweetest things because it seemeth good.

And you shall shortly know that lengthened breath
    Is not the sweetest gift God sends his friend;
But that, sometime, the sable pall of death
    Conceals the fairest boon his love can send.
If we could push ajar the gates of life,
    And all God's workings see,
We could interpret all this doubt and strife,
    And for each mystery find there a key.

But not to-day! So be content, poor heart;
    God's plans, like lilies, pure and white, unfold;
We must not tear the close-shut leaves apart;
    Time will reveal their calyxes of gold!
And if through patient toil we reach the land
    Where tired feet, with sandals loosed, may rest,
Where we may clearly know and understand,
    I think that we shall say: "God knew the best."[298]
UNKNOWN

WOOING IN THE SIXTIES

When the scarlet lips of summer
    Touched the roses as they grew,
When the katydids were telling
    What poor Katy didn't do,
Came the languid month of August,
    Moving waist deep in the corn,
Filled the cup of morning-glories
    With the dews of sunny morn.
        Wooing, wooing, till October,
            In a pretty cap and gown,
        To the doors of sad November
            Spread her russet carpets down.

When the sun had left the berries,
    And had turned the peach's cheek
From its green leaf to be bitten,
    Then my love began to speak,
And call me ladies of the books
    That we had read together,
And kept me fanning blushes down
    Throughout the balmy weather.
        Thus he wooed me till October,
            In her petticoats so bright
        Tracked with little golden slippers,
            Here and there a path of light.

He named me Walhelm's true Lenore
    Nina, proud and strong and sweet;
From Goethe's winsome girls of song
    To Zschokke's Marguerite.
He called me all things sweet he knew.
    Inanimate or human;
But I was proudest when he said:
    "O, little Southern woman."
        Wooing, wooing, till October
            Spread her russet carpets down;
        When he wore a Dixie jacket
            And I wore a homespun gown.

Once I heard him humming softly,
    In low measured bits of tune:
"Ah! I have sighed to rest me!"
    Then a silver-fingered moon
Looked that way and threw my image
    Penciled lightly on his breast,

As a shadow of the substance
    Where his sighs would find a rest.
        Wooing, wooing, till October,
            In a hazy mantle bright,
        Here and there through fading forest
           Trailed a shining thread of light.

It was under sweet gum shadows
    Leaning on a knotted vine,
Just beyond a woodchuck's hammer
    Tapped a hollow-hearted pine
Then again when lilies panted,
    And the fireflies darted low;
When the sweet magnolia blossoms
    Swing their incense to and fro,
        Wooing, wooing, till October
            Spread her russet carpets down;
        When he wore a Dixie jacket,
            And I wore a homespun gown.

Ah, we saw the cloud fleet sailing
    With white pennons idly free,
Westward ho! to silver islands
    Drifting in a rosy sea;
Heard the whistling birds of forest
    Rouse September from her nap;
Watched the cunning, bright-eyed squirrels
    Dropping chestnuts in her lap.
        Wooing, wooing, till October,
            In a petticoat so bright,
        Tracked with little golden slippers
            Here and there a ray of light.

'Twas an honest Southron's wooing,
    Like a simple tale of old,
And I gave my simple answer
    In a broken bit of gold.
I was queen, and my possessions
    Were the roses on my breast,
And the goldenrods were twisted
    O'er my forehead for a crest.
        Wooing, wooing, till October,
            In a petticoat so bright
        Here and there with dainty slippers
            Tracked a shining path of light.

Morning-glories found me blushing

In the shine of autumn sun;
And the young moon of November
　　　Told the stars that I was won;
Then the lovely Indian summer,
　　　Shaking down her yellow hair,
Veiled her face and died in beauty,
　　　But the world seemed wondrous fair.
　　　　　Thus he won me, when October
　　　　　　　Laid her shining scepter down,
　　　　　While he wore an old gray jacket,
　　　　　　　And I wore a homespun gown.

Then he called me "Little Pauper."
　　　And I answered "Prison Bird!"
Though I could not laugh for weeping
　　　At the meaning of each word.
Ah! the good God makes the poorest
　　　With his holy presence bright,
And that old Confederate jacket
　　　Is a treasure in my sight.
　　　　　Wooing, wooing till October
　　　　　　　Spread her russet carpets down;
　　　　　When he wore a Dixie jacket,
　　　　　　　And I wore a homespun gown.[299]

INA M. PORTER

HOME, SWEET HOME

Out of the shadows of sadness
Into the sunshine of gladness,
   Into the light of the blest;
Out of a land very dreary,
Out of the world very weary,
   Into the rapture of rest.

Out of to-day's sin and sorrow
Into a blissful to-morrow,
   Into a day without gloom;
Out of a land filled with sighing,
Land of the dead and the dying,
   Into a land without tomb.

Out of the world of the wailing,
Thronged with the anguished and ailing.
   Out of the world of the sad
Into the world that rejoices—
World of bright visions and voices—
   Into the world of the glad.

Out of a land in whose bowers
Perish and fade all the flowers,
   Out of the land of decay
Into the Eden where fairest
Of flowerets, and sweetest and rarest,
   Never shall wither away.

Out of a life ever mournful,
Out of a land very lornful,
   Where in bleak exile we roam,
Into a joy land above us,
Where there's a Saviour to love us—
   Into our "Home, Sweet Home."

O how sweet to feel, when closing
   Here on earth our weary eyes,
We shall see those who wait for us
   On the hills of Paradise;
To know that, when at last our feet
   Shall touch that unknown strand,
We shall find the reassuring clasp
   Of some dear outstretched hand.[300]

UNKNOWN

THE RED, WHITE, & RED

On the banks of the Potomac, an army so grand
Had gathered to subjugate Dixie's fair land.
They said we had split their great union in two
And changed their old colors from red, white, and blue.

CHORUS
Hurrah, hurrah, for a nation who said
They would all die defending the red, white, and red.

On the plains of Manassas the Yankees we met;
We gave them a threshing they ne'er can forget,
When they started for Richmond, but back they all flew,
With their old union's banner all twisted in two.

If you want to hear Greeley in Yankeedom rare,
Just glance through the Mason and Slidell affair.
It's when that they got them they thought that would do,
But now they curse England and her red, white, and blue.

We had a nice little fight on the tenth of last June,
Magruder at Bethel whipped old Picayune,[301]
It commenced in the morning and lasted it's said,
And victory waved o'er the red, white, and red.

They ne'er shall subjugate us, and that you shall see,
Whilst we have Bragg, Beauregard, Johnston, and Lee,
Magruder, McCullouch, and others who said
They would all die defending the red, white, and red.

The dearest, the happiest spot upon earth
Is Dixie, sweet Dixie, the land of my birth.
I love, I adore her, and I've always said
That we'll all die defending the red, white, and red.

Hurrah, hurrah for a nation who said,
They would fight for Jeff Davis and the red, white, and red.[302]
UNKNOWN

THE CONFEDERATE CROSS OF HONOR

As even a tiny shell recalls
    The presence of the sea,
So, gazing on this cross of bronze,
    The past recurs to me.

I see the stars and bars unfurled,
    And like a meteor rise,
To flash across a startled world,
    A wonder in the skies.

I see that gathering of the hosts
    As like a flood they come;
I hear the shrieking of the fife,
    The growling of the drum.

I see the tattered flag afloat
    Above the flaming line—
Its ragged folds, to dying eyes,
    A token and a sign.

I see the charging hosts advance;
    I see the slow retreat;
I hear the shouts of victory,
    The curses of defeat.

I see the grass of many fields
    With crimson lifeblood wet;
I see the dauntless eyes ablaze
    Above the bayonet.

I hear the crashing of the shells
    Mid Chickamauga's pines;
I hear the shrill, defiant yells
    Ring down the waiting lines.

I hear the voices of the dead,
    Of comrades tried and true;
I see the smiling lips of men
    Who died for me and you.

And all the varied scenes of war
    Upon my vision rise—
I hear the widow's piteous wail,
    I hear the orphan's cries.

I see the stars and bars repulsed,
    Unstained, in Glory's hand,
And Peace again her wings unfold
    Above a stricken land.

All this and more this magic cross
    Recalls to heart and brain;
Beneath its mystic influence
    The dead past lives again.

And friends who take a parting look
    When I am laid to rest
Will see, beside the cross of Christ,
    This cross upon my breast.[303]
HARRY LYNDEN FLASH

SCATTER SWEET FLOWERS O'ER THE DEAD

O lovingly scatter sweet flowers o'er the dead,
Weave chaplets to cover each dear soldier's head,
And think, as you linger in tenderness near,
Of the green, mossy hillocks to loved ones so dear,
Where patriots are sleeping in meadow and vale,
And breathe their dear names to the flower-scented gale.

They rest on the fields where their glory was won,
Where comrades had laid them, their life's battle done.
Affection's fond eye on their tombs mossy cover
Ne'er traced the dear name of a friend or a lover;
But the wild flowers of spring, in their fragrance and bloom,
Weave a mantle to cover the dead hero's tomb
And the soft Southern breeze chants a requiem of love,
While the "sentinel stars" keep their watch from above.

O softly and mournfully tread round their graves,
And crown with devotion our dear fallen braves.
Where danger was thickest they valiantly stood,
And gave for their country their pure, priceless blood.
But better by far as a patriot to fall
Than recreant to live, shirking duty's stern call.
Honored martyrs of freedom, we bow at thy shrine,
And pay the sweet tributes our hands now entwine;
Yet frail, votive chaplets but feebly portray
Our unfading love for the soldiers in gray.[304]
SALLIE JONES

SOUTHERN MAIDEN'S LAMENT FOR HER COUNTRY

Mute, mute are the harp strings—all music is hushed;
Our heart-sighs, our longings, our hopes are all crushed!
(The bird from its nestlings torn flutt'ring away
Lives but to die prisoned—the forester's prey.)
O West native land! O dear Southland mine!
How long for thy freedom in vain shall I pine?

Where, where are thy proud sons, so lordly in might?
They're mown down and fallen in blood-curdling fight:
Thy cities are ruin, thy valleys lie waste,
Their sunny enchantment the foe hath erased.
O Fatherland sweet! O Fatherland mine!
When, when will the Lord cry, "Revenge, it is mine?"

The clank of the fetter falls fearful and loud
From the arm of thy chained sons—so brave and so proud!
The day draggeth long—long, longer the night—
Captivity withers the South with its blight.
O Fatherland dear! O dear Southland mine!
Our stricken hearts pray: May sweet peace yet be thine![305]
UNKNOWN

A MOTHER'S SORROW

I know the sun shines, and the lilacs are bloomin,
    And the summer sends kisses to beautiful May;
O to see the rich treasures the spring is bestowing,
    And think my boy Willie enlisted to-day!

It seems but a day since at twilight, low humming,
    I rocked him to sleep with his cheek upon mine,
While Robby, the four-year-old, watched for the coming
    Of father adown the street's indistinct line.

It is many a year since my Harry departed
    To come back no more in the twilight or dawn;
And Robby grew weary of watching, and started
    Alone on the journey his father had gone.

It is many a year, and this afternoon, sitting
    At Robby's old window, I heard the band play,
And suddenly ceased dreaming over my knitting
    To recollect Willie was twenty to-day;

And that, standing beside him this soft Mayday morning,
    The sun making gold of each lock that I stroke,
I saw in his sweet eye and lips a faint warning,
    And choked down the tears when he eagerly spoke.

"Dear mother, you know how these Northmen are crowing;
    They will trample the rights of the South in the dust.
The boys are all fire, and they wish I were going"—
    He stopped, but his eyes said: "O, say if I must."

I smiled on my boy, though my heart it seemed breaking;
    My eyes filled with tears as I turned them away;
I answered him: "Willie, 'tis well you are waking
    Go do as your father would bid you to-day."

I sit on the window and see the flags flying,
    And dreamily list to the roll of the drum.
And smother the pain in my heart that is lying,
    And bid all the fears in my bosom be dumb.

And if he should fall, his young life has been given
    For freedom's sweet sake; and for me, I will pray
Once more, with my Harry and Robby in heaven,
    To meet the dear boy that enlisted to-day. [306]
UNKNOWN (note found on the body of one of Lee's young soldiers)

MAJOR GENERAL PATRICK RONAYNE CLEBURNE

All hail to Cleburne, patriot true,
From whom sprang exploits, not a few,
That would adorn a poet's page
Or fill with pride historian sage.

His dashing deeds will still inspire
The land he loved; his noble fire
Will thrill the heroes whom he led
Until he was, alas! struck dead.

And when at lethal Franklin fight
God sheathed fore'er his steel so bright,
Then fell a chief in memory blessed
As "Stonewall" Jackson of the West.[307]
CHARLES EDGEWORTH JONES

RABBI BEN-HISSAR

Rabbi Ben-Hissar rode one day
Beyond the city gates. His way

Lay toward a spot where his own hand
Had buried deep within the sand;

A treasure vast of gems and gold
He dared not trust to man to hold.

But, riding in the failing light,
A pallid figure met his sight—

An awful shape. He knew full well
'Twas the great angel Azrael.

The dreadful presence froze his breath:
He waited tremblingly for death.

"Fear not!" the angel said, "I bear
A message, Rabbi Ben-Hissar.

One thing the Lord has asked of thee,
To prove thy love and loyalty.

Therefore now I am come to bring
Thy rarest jewel to thy King."

Rabbi Ben-Hissar bowed his head.
"All that I have is his," he said.

The angel vanished. All that day
He rode upon his lonely way.

Wondering much what precious stone
God would have chosen for his own.

But when he reached the spot he found
No other hand had touched the ground.

Rabbi Ben-Hissar looked and sighed,
"It was a dream!" he sadly cried.

"I thought that God would deign to take
Of my poor store for his dear sake.

But 'twas a dream! My brightest gem
Would have no luster meet for him!"

Slowly he turned and took his way
Back to the vale where the city lay.

The path was long, but when he came
Unto the street which bore his name

He saw his house stand dark and drear;
No voice of welcome, none of cheer.

Entering, he saw what the Lord had done;
Lo! death had stricken his only son!

Clay he lay, in the darkened hall,
On the stolid bier, with the funeral pall.

The pale death angel Azrael
Had chosen a jewel that pleased him well.

Rabbi Ben-Hissar bent his head;
"I thank thee, Lord," was all he said.[308]
POST WHEELER

MEMORIAL ODE

When this time with us shall be no more and final taps shall sound,
    And the Death's last cruel battle shall be fought;
When the good of all the armies shall tent on yonder camping ground,
    When the roll is called up yonder, let's be there.

CHORUS
When the roll is called up yonder,
When the roll is called up yonder,
When the roll is called up yonder,
When the roll is called up yonder, let's be there.

On that mistless, lonely morning when the saved of Christ shall rise,
    In the Father's many-mansioned home to share;
Where our Lee and Jackson call to us their homes beyond the skies,
    When the roll is called up yonder, let's be there.

Let us labor while it's called to-day, or ere the shining sun
    Sets forever on the wicked and the fair;
When life's fitful dream is over and the new life is begun,
    When the roll is called up yonder, let's be there.

Steady, comrades, for the scythe of time is cutting fast and true;
    Would that vision dim and whitened locks were rare;
Tho' your forms are bending low, there's youth up yonder yet for you,
    When the roll is called up yonder, let's be there.

If all's not well with thee, my comrades, for thy entrance at the gate,
    Haste thy calling and election to prepare;
You will find that precious peace, sweet peace,
    When the roll is called up yonder, let's be there.[309]
DR. J. B. STINSON

SOUTHERN SENTIMENT

The North may think that the South will yield,
    And seek for a place in the Union again;
But never will Southrons abandon the field
    And place themselves under tyrannical reign.

Sooner by far would we yield to the grave,
    Than form an alliance with so hated a foe;
To join the "old Union" would be to enslave
    Ourselves, our children, in want and in woe!

What! sons of the South! submit to be ruled
    By the minions of Abraham Lincoln, the fool?
Our fair ones insulted—our wealth all controlled
    By Yankees, [uneducated] free negroes, and every such tool!

Heaven forbid it! and arm us with might,
    To drive back our foes, and grind them to dust!
In every conflict may we put them to flight,
    Aided by thee, thou God of the just!

Our bosoms we'll bare to the glorious strife,
    And our oath is recorded on high,
To prevail in the cause is dearer than life,
    Or crushed in its ruins to die!

The battle is not to the strong we know,
    But to the just, the true, and the brave—
With faith in our God, right onward we'll go,
    Our country, our loved ones, to save.[570]
REVEREND A. M. BOX

JUSTICE IS OUR PANOPLY

We're free from Yankee despots,
    We've left the foul mud-sills,
Declared for e'er our freedom—
    We'll keep it spite of ills.

Bring forth your scum and rowdies,
    Thieves, vagabonds, and all;
March down your Seventh Regiment,
    Battalions great and small.

We'll meet you in Virginia,
    A Southern battle-field,
Where Southern men will never
    To Yankee foemen yield.

Equip your Lincoln cavalry,
    Your negro light-brigade,
Your hodmen, bootblacks, tinkers,
    And scum of every grade.

Pretended love for negroes
    Incites you to the strife;
Well, come each Yankee white man,
    And take a negro wife.

You'd make fit black companions,
    Black heart joined to black skin;
Such unions would be glorious—
    They'd make the Devil grin.

Our freedom is our panoply—
    Come on, you base black-guards,
We'll snuff you like wax-candles,
    Led by our Beauregards.

P. G. T. B. is not alone,
    Men like him with him fight;
God's providence is o'er us,
    He will protect the right.[311]
UNKNOWN

WAR SONG

Huzza! huzza! let's raise the battle-cry,
    And whip the Yankees from our land,
Or with them fall and die.
    Rush on our Southron columns,
    And make the brigands feel
        That all the booty they will get,
Will be our Southron steel.
        Huzza! huzza! let's raise our banner high,
        And nobly drive the Yankees out,
        Or with them fall and die.

Rush on the columns—let every Southron brave
    Nobly charge the accursed foe,
Or find a soldier's grave.
    With bowie and with pike,
We'll rally to the field,
    And bravely to the last we'll strike,
Resolved we'll never yield.
        Huzza! huzza! let's raise our banner high,
        And nobly drive the Yankees out,
        Or with them fall and die.

We are fighting for our mothers, our sisters, and our wives;
    For these, and our country's rights,
We'll sacrifice our lives.
    Then, trusting still to Heaven,
We'll charge the invading host,
    Till liberty and independence
Shall be the nation's boast.
        Huzza! huzza! let's raise our banner high,
        And nobly drive the Yankees out,
        Or with them fall and die.

Then on with our columns—slay the vandal foe—
    Beat them from our sunny soil,
And lay their colors low.
    To the great God of nations
Our sacred cause confide,
    For we are fighting for our liberty,
And He is on our side.
        Huzza! huzza! let's raise our banner high,
        And nobly drive the Yankees out,
        Or with them fall and die.[312]
J. H. WOODCOCK

A NEW RED, WHITE, & BLUE

Missouri is the pride of the nation,
The hope of the brave and the free;
The Confederacy will furnish the rations,
But the fighting is trusted to thee;
For, brave boys, your soil has been noted,
And your flag has been trusted to you;
For freedom you have not yet voted,
But you fight for the Red, White, and Blue.

The Stars shall shine bright in the heaven,
But the Stripes should be trailed in the dust,
For they are no longer the sign of the haven
Of the brave, of the free, or the just;
The Bars now in triumph shall wave
O'er the land of the faithful and true;
O'er the home of the Southern brave
Shall float the new Red, White, and Blue.[313]
JEFF THOMPSON

SOUTHRONS

You can never win them back—
    Never! never!
Though they perish on the track
    Of your endeavor;
Though their corpses strew the earth,
That smiled upon their birth,
And blood pollutes each hearthstone
    Forever!

They have risen to a man,
    Stern and fearless;
Of your curses and your ban
    They are careless.
Every hand is on its knife,
Every gun is primed for strife,
Every palm contains a life,
    High and peerless!

You have no such blood as theirs
    For the shedding:
In the veins of cavaliers
    Was its heading:
You have no such stately men
In your "abolition den,"
To march through foe and fen,
    Nothing dreading!

They may fall before the fire
    Of your legions,
Paid with gold for murderous hire—
    Bought allegiance;
But for every drop you shed,
You shall have a mound of dead,
So that vultures may be fed
    In our regions!

But the battle to the strong
    Is not given,
When the Judge of Right and Wrong
    Sits in heaven;
And the God of David still
Guides the pebble with His will;
There are giants yet to kill—
    Wrongs unshriven![314]
CATHERINE ANNE WARFIELD

CHIVALROUS C.S.A.

I'll sing you a song of the South's sunny clime,
    Chivalrous C.S.A.!
Which went to house-keeping once on a time;
    Bully for C.S.A.!
Like heroes and princes they lived for awhile,
    Chivalrous C.S.A.!
And routed the Hessians in most gallant style;
    Bully for C.S.A.!

    CHORUS
    Chivalrous, chivalrous people are they!
    Chivalrous, chivalrous people are they!
    In C.S.A.! In C.S.A.!
    Aye, in chivalrous C.S.A.!

They have a bold leader—Jeff Davis his name—
    Chivalrous C.S.A.!
Good generals and soldiers, all anxious for fame;
    Bully for C.S.A.!
At Manassas they met the North in its pride,
    Chivalrous C.S.A.!
But they easily put McDowell aside;
    Bully for C.S.A.!

    CHORUS
    Chivalrous, chivalrous people are they!
    Chivalrous, chivalrous people are they!
    In C.S.A.! In C.S.A.!
    Aye, in chivalrous C.S.A.!

Ministers to England and France, it appears,
    Have gone from the C.S.A.!
Who've given the North many fleas in its ears;
    Bully for C.S.A.!
Reminders are being to Washington sent,
    By the chivalrous C.S.A.!
That'll force Uncle Abe full soon to repent;
    Bully for C.S.A.!

    CHORUS
    Chivalrous, chivalrous people are they!
    Chivalrous, chivalrous people are they!
    In C.S.A.! In C.S.A.!
    Aye, in chivalrous C.S.A.!

Oh, they have the finest of musical ears,
    Chivalrous C.S.A.!
Yankee Doodle's too vulgar for them, it appears;
    Bully for C.S.A.!
The North may sing it and whistle it still,
    Miserable C.S.A.!
Three cheers for the South!—now, boys, with a will!
    And groans for the U.S.A.!

    CHORUS
    Chivalrous, chivalrous people are they!
    Chivalrous, chivalrous people are they!
    In C.S.A.! In C.S.A.!
    Aye, in chivalrous C.S.A.![315]
UNKNOWN

THE SOLDIER'S HEART

The trumpet calls, and I must go
To meet the vile, invading foe;
But listen, dearest, ere we part—
Thou hast, thou hast the soldier's heart!

It could not be so true to thee
Were it not true to liberty;
Far rather fill a soldier's grave
Than live a dastard and a slave!

Thine eyes shall light dark danger's path,
The gloomy camp, the foeman's wrath;
Above the battle's fiery storm,
I shall behold thy beauteous form!

With thoughts of thee, for thy dear sake,
Redoubled efforts I will make;
And strike with an avenging hand
For lady-love and native land!

Then fare thee well, the trumpet's sound
Commands me to the battle ground;
But listen, dearest, ere we part—
Thou hast, thou hast the soldier's heart.[316]
F. P. BEAUFORT

MY WIFE & CHILD

The tattoo beats, the lights are gone,
    The camp around in slumber lies;
The night with solemn pace moves on,
    And sad, uneasy thoughts arise.
I think of thee, oh, dearest one!
    Whose love my early life has blest;
Of thee and him, our baby son,
    Who slumbers on thy gentle breast.

God of the tender, hover near
    To her whose watchful eye is wet;
The mother, wife—the doubly dear—
    And cheer her drooping spirits yet.
Now, while she kneels before thy throne,
    Oh, teach her, Ruler of the Skies!
No tear is wept to thee unknown,
    No hair is lost, no sparrow dies.

That thou canst stay the ruthless hand
    Of dark disease, and soothe its pain;
That only by thy stern command
    The battle's lost, the soldier's slain.
By day, by night—in joy or woe—
    By fear oppressed, or hopes beguiled,
From every danger, every foe,
    Oh, God! protect my wife and child![317]
CONFEDERATE GENERAL HENRY ROOTES JACKSON

THOUGHTS SUGGESTED BY A PICTURE

The sun had set in all his glory
    O'er a field of ice and snow,
O'er a field stained red and gory
    With the life-blood of the foe.

There on a drift of snow transplanted
    Was the banner of the brave,
Pointing upward, ever upward,
    Like the cause it could not save.

The snow- white field bright red was dyed
    With the life-blood of their country's pride,
Men who had shown themselves so brave
    Now passed to glory and the grave.

Three cheers for the glorious ensign,
    And three for the cause divine,
And three for Lee's brave soldier boys
    Who fought but all in vain.

And that banner pointing upward,
    Ever upward to the sky,
Borne by an angel's small white hand
    Shall be token of our Southern land,
And shall keep afresh the memory
    Of that glorious land of Lee.[318]
J. C. TAYLOR

WOMAN'S WAR MISSION

Fold away all your bright-tinted dresses,
    Turn the key on your jewels to-day,
And the wealth of your tendril-like tresses
    Braid back, in a serious way:
No more delicate gloves, no more laces,
    No more trifling in boudoir and bower;
But come with your souls in your faces—
    To meet the stern needs of the hour!

Look around! By the torchlight unsteady,
    The dead and the dying seem one.
What! paling and trembling already,
    Before your dear mission's begun?
These wounds are more precious than ghastly;
    Fame presses her lips to each scar,
As she chants of a glory which vastly
    Transcends all the horrors of war.

Pause here by this bedside—how mellow
    The light showers down on that brow!
Such a brave, brawny visage!—Poor fellow!
    Some homestead is missing him now.
Some wife shades her eyes in the clearing,
    Some mother sits moaning, distressed,—
While the loved one lies faint, but unfearing,
    With the enemy's ball in his breast.

Here's another: a lad—a mere stripling—
    Picked up from the field, almost dead;
With the blood through his sunny hair rippling
    From a horrible gash in the head.
They say he was first in the action,
    Gay-hearted, quick-handed, and witty;
He fought till he fell with exhaustion,
    At the gates of our fair Southern city.

Fought and fell 'neath the guns of that city,
    With a spirit transcending his years;
Lift him up in your large-hearted pity,
    And touch his pale lips with your tears.
Touch him gently—most sacred the duty
    Of dressing that poor shattered hand!
God spare him to rise in his beauty,
    And battle once more for the land!

Who groaned? What a passionate murmur—
    "In thy mercy, O God, let me die!"
Ha! surgeon, your hand must be firmer,
    That grape-shot has shattered his thigh.
Fling the light on those poor furrowed features,
    Gray-haired and unknown—bless the brother!
O God! that one of thy creatures
    Should e'er work such woe on another!

Wipe the sweat from his brow with your kerchief;
    Let the stain tattered collar go wide,
See! he stretches out blindly to search if
    The surgeon still stands at his side.
"My son's over yonder! he's wounded—
    Oh! this ball that has broken my thigh!"
And again he burst out, all a-tremble,—
    "In thy mercy, O God! let me die!"

Pass on! It is useless to linger
    While others are claiming your care;
There is need of your delicate finger,
    For your womanly sympathy, there!
There are sick ones athirst for caressing—
    There are dying ones raving for home—
There are wounds to be bound with a blessing—
    And shrouds to make ready for some.

They have gathered about you the harvest
    Of death, in its ghastliest view;
The nearest as well as the farthest
    Is here with the traitor and true!
And crowned with your beautiful patience,
    Made sunny with love at the heart,
You must balsam the wounds of a nation,
    Nor falter, nor shrink from your part!

Up and down through the wards, where the fever
    Stalks noisome, and gaunt and impure,
You must go with your steadfast endeavor
    To comfort, to counsel, to cure!
I grant that the task's superhuman,
    But strength will be given to you
To do for these dear ones what woman
    Alone in her pity can do.

And the lips of the mothers will bless you
    As angels sweet visaged and pale!

And the little ones run to caress you,
    While the wives and the sisters cry "Hail!"
But e'en if you drop down unheeded,
    What matter? God's ways are the best;
You've poured out your life where 'twas needed,
    And He will take care of the rest.[319]
UNKNOWN

HARP OF THE SOUTH, AWAKE!

Harp of the South, awake!
   From every golden wire,
Let the voice of thy power go forth,
   Like the rush of a prairie fire;
With the rush and the rhythm of a power
   That dares a freeman's grave,
Rather than live to wear
   The chains of a truckling slave.

Harp of the South, awake!
   Thy sons are aroused at last,
And their legions are gathering now,
   To the sound of the trumpet blast;
To the scream of the piercing fife,
   And the beat of the rolling drum,
From mountain, and hill, and plain,
   And field, and town, they come.

Harp of the South, awake!
   Their banners are on the breeze;
Tell the world how vain the thought
   To subdue such men as these,
With hero hearts that beat,
   To the throbs of the spirit-flame,
Which will kindle their battle-fires
   In freedom's holy name.

Harp of the South, awake!
   But not to sing of love,
In shady forest-bower,
   Or fragrant orange grove;
Oh, no, but thy song must be
   The wrath of the battle crash,
Inscribed on the cloud of war,
   With the pen of its lightning flash.

Harp of the South, awake!
   And strike the strains once more,
Which nerved thy heroes' hearts
   In the glorious days of yore;
Which gave a giant's strength
   To the arm of Marion,
Of Sumter, Morgan, Lee,
   And your own great Washington.

Harp of the South, awake!
    Your freedom's angel calls,
In the laugh of the rippling rills,
    And the roar of the waterfalls.
See how she bends to hear,
    As she walks the valleys through,
And along the mountain tops,
    In robes of gold and blue.

Harp of the South, awake!
    The proud, the full-soul'd South—
With the, dusk of her flashing eyes,
    And the lure of her rosy mouth—
With love, or pride, or wrath,
    Thrilling her noble form,
As she smiles like a summer sky,
    Or frowns like a summer storm!

Harp of the South, awake!
    Though the soldier's beaming tear
May fall on thy trembling strings,
    As he breathes his farewell prayer;
Yet, tell him how to die
    On the bloody battle-field,
Rather than to her foes
    The gallant South should yield.[320]
J. M. KILGOUR

"Away down South in Dixie..."

O'ER THE TOMB

The prints of feet are worn away,
    No more the mourners come;
The voice of wail is mute to-day
    As his whose life is dumb.

The world is bright with other bloom;
    Shall the sweet summer shed
Its living radiance o'er the tomb
    That shrouds the doubly dead?

Unknown! Beneath our Father's face
    The starlit hillocks lie;
Another rosebud! lest His grace
    Forget us when we die.[321]
UNKNOWN

CLOUDS IN THE WEST

Hark! on the wind that whistles from the West
    A manly shout for instant succor comes,
From men who fight, outnumbered, breast to breast,
    With rage-indented drums;

Who dare for child, wife, country, stream and strand,
    Though but a fraction to the swarming foe,
There, at the flooded gateways of the land,
    To stem a torrent's flow.

To arms! brave sons of each embattled State,
    Whose queenly standard is a Southern star:
Who would be free must ride the lists of Fate
    On Freedom's victor-car!

Forsake the field, the shop, the mart, the hum
    Of craven traffic, for the mustering clan:
The dead themselves are pledged that you shall come
    And prove yourself a man.

Blow, summoning trumpets, a compulsive stave
    Through all the bounds from Beersheba to Dan;
Come out! come out! who scorns to be a slave,
    Or claims to be a man!

Hark! on the breezes whistling from the West
    A manly shout for instant succor comes,
From men who fight, outnumbered, breast to breast,
    With rage-indented drums;

Who charge and cheer amid the murderous din,
    Where still your battle-flags unbended wave,
Dying for what your fathers died to win,
    And you must fight to save.[322]

JUDGE AUGUSTUS JULIAN REQUIER

THE SOLDIER BOY

I give my soldier boy a blade,
    In fair Damascus fashioned well;
Who first the glittering falchion swayed,
    Who first beneath its fury fell,
I know not: but I hope to know
    That for no mean or hireling trade,
To guard no feeling, base or low,
    I give my soldier boy a blade.

Cool, calm, and clear the lucid flood
    In which its tempering work was done;
As calm, as cool, as clear of mood
    Be thou whene'er it sees the sun;
For country's claim, at honor's call,
    For outraged friend, insulted maid,
At mercy's voice to bid it fall,
    I give my soldier boy a blade.

The eye which marked its peerless edge,
    The hand that weighed its balanced poise,
Anvil and pincers, forge and wedge,
    Are gone with all their flame and noise;
And still the gleaming sword remains.
    So when in dust I low am laid,
Remember by these heartfelt strains
    I give my soldier boy a blade.[323]
UNKNOWN

ROLL-CALL

"Corporal Green!" the Orderly cried;
    "Here!" was the answer, loud and clear,
    From the lips of the soldier who stood near,—
And "Here!" was the word the next replied.

"Cyrus Drew!"—then a silence fell:
    This time no answer followed the call;
    Only his rear-man had seen him fall:
Killed or wounded—he could not tell.

There they stood in the failing light,
    These men of battle, with grave, dark looks,
    As plain to be read as open books,
While slowly gathered the shades of night.

The fern on the hill-sides was splashed with blood,
    And down in the corn where the poppies grew
    Were redder stains than the poppies knew
And crimson-dyed was the river's flood.

For the foe had crossed from the other side
    That day, in the face of a murderous fire
    That swept them down in its terrible ire,
And their life-blood went to color the tide.

"Herbert Kline!" At the call there came
    Two stalwart soldiers into the line,
    Bearing between them this Herbert Kline,
Wounded and bleeding, to answer his name.

"Ezra Kerr!"—and a voice answered, "Here!"
    "Hiram Kerr!"—but no man replied.
    They were brothers, these two; the sad winds sighed,
And a shudder crept through the cornfield near.

"Ephraim Deane!"—then a soldier spoke:
    "Deane carried our regiment's colors," he said;
    "Where our ensign was shot I left him dead,
Just after the enemy wavered and broke.

"Close to the road-side his body lies;
    I paused a moment and gave him a drink;
    He murmured his mother's name, I think,
And Death came with it, and closed his eyes."

'Twas a victory; yes, but it cost us dear,—
    For that company's roll, when called at night,
    Of a hundred men who went into the fight,
Numbered but twenty that answered "Here!"[324]
N. G. SHEPHERD

Edmund W. Rucker.

THE VIRGINIANS OF THE VALLEY

The knightliest of the knightly race,
    Who, since the days of old,
Have kept the lamp of chivalry
    Alight in hearts of gold;
The kindliest of the kindly band,
    Who, rarely hunting ease,
Yet rode with Spotswood round the land,
    And Raleigh round the seas;

Who climbed the blue Virginian hills,
    Against embattled foes,
And planted there in valleys fair
    The lily and the rose;
Whose fragrance lives in many lands,
    Whose beauty stars the earth,
And lights the hearts of many homes
    In loveliness and worth.

We thought they slept—the sons who kept
    The names of noble sires,
And slumbered while the darkness crept
    Around the vigil fires.
But still the Golden Horseshoe knights
    Their old dominion keep,
Whose foes have found enchanted ground,
    But not a knight asleep.[325]
FRANCIS ORRAY TICKNOR

THE BIVOUAC IN THE SNOW

Halt!—the march is over,
    Day is almost done;
Loose the cumbrous knapsack,
    Drop the heavy gun.
Chilled and wet and weary,
    Wander to and fro,
Seeking wood to kindle
    Fires amidst the snow.

Round the bright blaze gather,
    Heed not sleet nor cold;
Ye are Spartan soldiers,
    Stout and brave and bold.
Never Xerxian army
    Yet subdued a foe
Who but asked a blanket
    On a bed of snow.

Shivering, 'midst the darkness,
    Christian men are found,
There devoutly kneeling
    On the frozen ground—
Pleading for their country,
    In its hour of woe—
For its soldiers marching
    Shoeless through the snow.

Lost in heavy slumbers,
    Free from toil and strife,
Dreaming of their dear ones—
    Home, and child, and wife,
Tentless they are lying,
    While the fires burn low—
Lying in their blankets,
    'Midst December's snow.[326]

MARGARET JUNKIN PRESTON

STONEWALL JACKSON'S WAY

Come, stack arms, men! Pile on the rails,
    Stir up the camp-fire bright;
No growling if the canteen fails,
    We'll make a roaring night.
Here Shenandoah brawls along,
There burly Blue Ridge echoes strong,
To swell the Brigade's rousing song
    Of "Stonewall Jackson's way."

We see him now—the queer slouched hat
    Cocked o'er his eye askew;
The shrewd, dry smile; the speech so pat,
    So calm, so blunt, so true.
The "Blue-Light Elder" knows 'em well;
Says he, "That's Banks—he's fond of shell;
Lord save his soul! we'll give him—"; well!
    That's "Stonewall Jackson's way."

Silence! ground arms! kneel all! caps off!
    Old Massa's goin' to pray.
Strangle the fool that dares to scoff!
    Attention! it's his way.
Appealing from his native sod,
In forma pauperis[327] to God:
"Lay bare Thine arm; stretch forth Thy rod!
    Amen!" That's "Stonewall's way."

He's in the saddle now. Fall in!
    Steady! the whole brigade!
Hill's at the ford, cut off; we'll win
    His way out, ball and blade!
What matter if our shoes are worn?
What matter if our feet are torn?
"Quick step! we're with him before morn!"
    That's "Stonewall Jackson's way."

The sun's bright lances rout the mists
    Of morning, and, by George!
Here's Longstreet, struggling in the lists,
    Hemmed in an ugly gorge.
Pope and his Dutchmen, whipped before;
"Bay'nets and grape!" hear Stonewall roar;
"Charge, Stuart! Pay off Ashby's score!"
    In "Stonewall Jackson's way."

Ah! Maiden, wait and watch and yearn
    For news of Stonewall's band!
Ah! Widow, read, with eyes that burn,
    That ring upon thy hand.
Ah! Wife, sew on, pray on, hope on;
Thy life shall not be all forlorn;
The foe had better ne'er been born
    That gets in "Stonewall's way."[328]
DR. J. W. PALMER

Little Sorrel, Jackson's warhorse.

THE CONFEDERATE FLAG

No more o'er human hearts to wave,
    Its tattered folds forever furled:
We laid it in an honored grave,
    And left its memories to the world.

The agony of long, long years,
    May, in a moment, be compressed,
And with a grief too deep for tears,
    A heart may be oppressed.

Oh! there are those who die too late
    For faith in God, and Right, and Truth,—
The cold mechanic grasp of Fate
    Hath crushed the roses of their youth.

More blessed are the dead who fell
    Beneath it in unfaltering trust,
Than we, who loved it passing well,
    Yet lived to see it trail in dust.

It hath no future which endears,
    And this farewell shall be our last:
Embalm it in a nation's tears,
    And consecrate it to the past!

To moldering hands that to it clung,
    And flaunted it in hostile faces,
To pulseless arms that round it flung,
    The terror of their last embraces—

To our dead heroes—to the hearts
    That thrill no more to love or glory,
To those who acted well their parts,
    Who died in youth and live in glory—

With tears forever be it told,
    Until oblivion covers all:
Until the heavens themselves wear old,
    And totter slowly to their fall.[329]
UNKNOWN

LEE TO THE REAR

Dawn of a pleasant morning in May
Broke through the Wilderness cool and gray;
While perched in the tallest tree-tops, the birds
Were carolling Mendelssohn's "Songs Without Words."

Far from the haunts of men remote,
The brook brawled on with a liquid note;
And Nature, all tranquil and lovely, wore
The smile of the spring, as in Eden of yore.

Little by little as daylight increased,
And deepened the roseate flush in the East—
Little by little did morning reveal
Two long glittering lines of steel;

Where two hundred thousand bayonets gleam,
Tipped with the light of the earliest beam,
And the faces are sullen and grim to see
In the hostile armies of Grant and Lee.

All of a sudden, ere rose the sun,
Pealed on the silence the opening gun—
A little white puff of smoke there came,
And anon the valley was wreathed in flame.

Down on the left of the Rebel lines,
Where a breastwork stands in a copse of pines,
Before the Rebels their ranks can form,
The Yankees have carried the place by storm.

Stars and Stripes on the salient wave,
Where many a hero has found a grave,
And the gallant Confederates strive in vain
The ground they have drenched with their blood, to regain.

Yet louder the thunder of battle roared—
Yet a deadlier fire on the columns poured;
Slaughter infernal rode with Despair,
Furies twain, through the murky air.

Not far off, in the saddle there sat
A gray-bearded man in a black slouched hat;
Not much moved by the fire was he,
Calm and resolute Robert Lee.

Quick and watchful he kept his eye
On the bold Rebel brigades close by,—
Reserves that were standing (and dying) at ease,
While the tempest of wrath toppled over the trees.

For still with their loud, deep, bull-dog bay,
The Yankee batteries blazed away,
And with every murderous second that sped
A dozen brave fellows, alas! fell dead.

The grand old graybeard rode to the space
Where Death and his victims stood face to face,
And silently waved his old slouched hat—
A world of meaning there was in that!

"Follow me! Steady! We'll save the day!"
This was what he seemed to say;
And to the light of his glorious eye
The bold brigades thus made reply:

"We'll go forward, but you must go back"—
And they moved not an inch in the perilous track:
"Go to the rear, and we'll send them to hell!"
And the sound of the battle was lost in their yell.

Turning his bridle, Robert Lee
Rode to the rear. Like waves of the sea,
Bursting the dikes in their overflow,
Madly his veterans dashed on the foe.

And backward in terror that foe was driven,
Their banners rent and their columns riven,
Wherever the tide of battle rolled
Over the Wilderness, wood and wold.

Sunset out of a crimson sky
Streamed o'er a field of ruddier dye,
And the brook ran on with a purple stain,
From the blood of ten thousand foemen slain.

Seasons have passed since that day and year—
Again o'er its pebbles the brook runs clear,
And the field in a richer green is drest
Where the dead of a terrible conflict rest.

Hushed is the roll of the Rebel drum,
The sabres are sheathed, and the cannon are dumb;

And Fate, with his pitiless hand, has furled
The flag that once challenged the gaze of the world;

But the fame of the Wilderness fight abides;
And down into history grandly rides,
Calm and unmoved as in battle he sat,
The gray-bearded man in the black slouched hat.[330]
JOHN REUBEN THOMPSON

Lee monument.

THE C.S.S. *ALABAMA*

She has gone to the bottom! the wrath of the tide
    Now breaks in vain insolence o'er her;
No more the rough seas like a queen shall she ride,
    While the foe flies in terror before her!

Now captive or exiled, or silent in death,
    The forms that so bravely did man her;
Her deck is untrod, and the gale's stirring breath
    Flouts no more the red cross of her banner!

She is down 'neath the waters, but still her bright name
    Is in death, as in life, ever glorious,
And a sceptre all barren the conqueror must claim,
    Though he boasts the proud title "Victorious."

Her country's lone champion, she shunned not the fight,
    Though unequal in strength, bold and fearless;
And proved in her fate, though not matchless in might,
    In daring at least she was peerless.

No trophy hung high in the foe's hated hall
    Shall speak of her final disaster,
Nor tell of the danger that could not appall,
    Nor the spirit that nothing could master!

The death-shot has sped—she has grimly gone down,
    But left her destroyer no token,
And the mythical wand of her mystic renown,
    Though the waters o'erwhelm, is unbroken.

For lo! ere she settles beneath the dark wave
    On her enemies' cheeks spreads a pallor,
As another deck summons the swords of the brave
    To gild a new name with their valor.

Her phantom will yet haunt the wild roaring breeze,
    Causing foemen to start and to shudder,
While their commerce still steals like a thief o'er the seas,
    And trembles from bowsprit to rudder.

The spirit that shed on the wave's gleaming crest
    The light of a legend romantic
Shall live while a sail flutters over the breast
    Of thy far-bounding billows, Atlantic!

And as long as one swift keel the strong surges stems,
    Or "poor Jack" loves his song and his story,
Shall shine in tradition the valor of Semmes
    And the brave ship that bore him to glory![331]
MAURICE BELL

GENERAL WORSELY TO GENERAL LEE

The grave old bard, who never dies,
    Receive him in our native tongue;
I send thee, but with weeping eyes,
    The story that he sung.

Thy Troy has fallen; thy dear land
    Is marred beneath the spoiler's heel;
I cannot trust my trembling hand
    To write the grief I feel.

Oh, home of tears! But let her bear
    This blazon to the end of time:
No nation rose so white and fair,
    None fell so pure of crime.

The widow's moan, the orphan's wail,
    Are around thee; but in truth be strong.
Eternal right, though all things fail,
    Can never he made wrong.

An angel's heart, an angel's mouth
    (Not Homer's), could alone for me
Hymn forth the great Confederate South;
    Virginia first—then Lee.[332]
PHILIP STANHOPE WORSLEY (an Englishman)

CHARLESTON

Calm as that second summer which precedes
    The first fall of the snow,
In the broad sunlight of heroic deeds,
    The City bides the foe.

As yet, behind their ramparts stern and proud,
    Her bolted thunders sleep—
Dark Sumter, like a battlemented cloud,
    Looms o'er the solemn deep.

No Calpe frowns from lofty cliff or scar
    To guard the holy strand;
But Moultrie holds in leash her dogs of war
    Above the level sand.

And down the dunes a thousand guns lie couched,
    Unseen, beside the flood—
Like tigers in some Orient jungle crouched
    That wait and watch for blood.

Meanwhile, through streets still echoing with trade,
    Walk grave and thoughtful men,
Whose hands may one day wield the patriot's blade
    As lightly as the pen.

And maidens, with such eyes as would grow dim
    Over a bleeding hound,
Seem each one to have caught the strength of him
    Whose sword she sadly bound.

Thus girt without and garrisoned at home,
    Day patient following day,
Old Charleston looks from roof, and spire, and dome,
    Across her tranquil bay.

Ships, through a hundred foes, from Saxon lands
    And spicy Indian ports,
Bring Saxon steel and iron to her hands,
    And Summer to her courts.

But still, along yon dim Atlantic line,
    The only hostile smoke
Creeps like a harmless mist above the brine,
    From some frail, floating oak.

Shall the Spring dawn, and she still clad in smiles,
    And with an unscathed brow,
Rest in the strong arms of her palm-crowned isles,
    As fair and free as now?

We know not; in the temple of the Fates
    God has inscribed her doom;
And, all untroubled in her faith, she waits,
    The triumph or the tomb.[333]
HENRY TIMROD

Henry Timrod.

READING THE LIST

"Is there any news of the war?" she said.
"Only a list of the wounded and dead,"
    Was the man's reply,
      Without lifting his eye
        To the face if the woman standing by.
"'Tis the very thing I want," she said;
"Read me a list of the wounded and dead."

He read the list—'twas a sad array
Of the wounded and killed in the fatal fray.
    In the very midst, was a pause to tell
    Of a gallant youth who fought so well
That his comrades asked: "Who is he, pray?"
"The only son of the Widow Gray,"
      Was the proud reply
      Of his Captain nigh . . . .
What ails the woman standing near?
Her face has the ashen hue of fear!

"Well, well, read on; is he wounded? Quick!
O God! but my heart is sorrow-sick!
    Is he wounded?" "No; he fell, they say,
    Killed outright on that fatal day!"
    But see, the woman has swooned away!

Sadly she opened her eyes to the light;
Slowly recalled the events of the fight;
Faintly she murmured: "Killed outright!
    It has cost me the life of my only son;
    But the battle is fought, and the victory won;
    The will of the Lord, let it be done!"

God pity the cheerless Widow Gray,
And send from the halls of eternal day
The light of His peace to illumine her way.[334]
UNKNOWN

THE MEN

In the dusk of the forest shade
    A sallow and dusty group reclined;
Gallops a horseman up the glade—
    "Where will I your leader find?
Tidings I bring from the morning's scout—
    I've borne them o'er mound and moor and fen."
"Well, sir, stay not hereabout,
    Here are only a few of 'the men.'

"Here no collar has bar or star,
    No rich lacing adorns the sleeve;
Further on our officers are,
    Let them your report receive.
Higher up on the hill up there,
    Overlooking this shady glen,
There are their quarters—don't stop here,
    We are only some of 'the men.'

"Yet stay, courier, if you bear
    Tidings that a fight is near;
Tell them we're ready, and that where
    They wish us to be we'll soon appear;
Tell them only to let us know
    Where to form our ranks and when;
And we'll teach the vaunting foe
    That they've met with some of 'the men.'

"We're the men, though our clothes are worn—
    We're the men, though we wear no lace—
We're the men, who the foe have torn,
    And scattered their ranks in dire disgrace—
We're the men who have triumphed before—
    We're the men who will triumph again;
For the dust and the smoke and the cannon's roar,
    And the clashing bayonets— 'we're the men.'

"Ye who sneer at the battle-scars,
    Of garments faded and soiled and bare,
Yet who have for the 'stars and bars'
    Praise and homage and dainty fare;
Mock the wearers and pass them on,
    Refuse them kindly word—and then
Know if your freedom is ever won
    By human agents—these are the men!"[335]
MAURICE BELL

THE UNIFORM OF GRAY

The Briton boasts his coat of red,
    With lace and spangles decked;
In garb of green the French are seen,
    With gaudy colors flecked;
The Yankees strut in dingy blue,
    And epaulets display;
Our Southern girls more proudly view
    The uniform of gray.

That dress is worn by gallant hearts
    Who every foe defy,
Who stalwart stand, with battle-brand,
    To conquer or to die!
They fight for freedom, hope and home,
    And honor's voice obey,
And proudly wear where'er they roam
    The uniform of gray.

What though 'tis stained with crimson hues,
    And dim with dust and smoke,
By bullets torn, and rent and shorn
    By many a hostile stroke;
The march, the camp, the bivouac,
    The onset and the fray
But only serve more dear to make
    The uniform of gray.

When wild war's tiger-strife is past,
    And liberty restored;
When independence reigns at last,
    By valor's arm secured;
The South will stand, erect and grand,
    And loftiest honors pay
To those who bore her flag, and wore
    The uniform of gray.

And woman's love, man's best reward,
    Shall cluster round their path,
And soothe and cheer the volunteer
    Who dared the foeman's wrath.
Bright wreaths she'll bring, and roses fling
    Around his triumph-way,
And long in song thy fame prolong
    Old uniform of gray.[336]
EVAN ELBERT

THE BAREFOOTED BOYS

By the sword of St. Michael
    The old dragon through;
By David his sling
    And the giant he slew;
Let us write us a rhyme,
    As a record to tell
How the South on a time
    Stormed the ramparts of Hell
        With her barefooted boys!

Had the South in her border
    A hero to spare,
Or a heart at her altar,
    Lo! its life's blood was there!
And the black battle-grime
    Might never disguise
The smile of the South
    On the lips and the eyes
        Of her barefooted boys!

There's a grandeur in fight,
    And a terror the while,
But none like the light
    Of that terrible smile—
The smile of the South,
When the storm-cloud unrolls
The lightning that loosens
    The wrath in the souls
        Of her barefooted boys!

It withered the foe
Like the red light that runs
Through the dead forest leaves,
And he fled from his guns!
Grew the smile to a laugh,
Rose the laugh to a yell,
As the iron-clad hoofs
    Clattered back into Hell
        From our barefooted boys![337]
FRANCIS ORRAY TICKNOR

Francis O. Ticknor.

DIRGE FOR ASHBY

Heard ye that thrilling word—
    Accent of dread—
Fall, like a thunderbolt,
    Bowing each head?
Over the battle dun,
Over each booming gun—
Ashby, our bravest one!
    Ashby is dead!

Saw ye the veterans—
    Hearts that had known
Never a quail of fear,
    Never a groan—
Sob, though the fight they win,
Tears their stern eyes within—
Ashby, our Paladin,[338]
    Ashby is dead!

Dash, dash the tear away—
    Crush down the pain!
Dulce et decus,[339] be
    Fittest refrain!
Why should the dreary pall,
Bound him, be flung at all?
Did not our hero fall
    Gallantly slain!

Catch the last words of cheer,
    Dropt from his tongue;
Over the battle's din,
    Let them be rung!
"Follow me! Follow me!"
Soldier, oh! could there be
Pæan or dirge for thee,
    Loftier sung?

Bold as the lion's heart—
    Dauntlessly brave—
Knightly as knightliest
    Bayard might crave;
Sweet, with all Sydney's grace,
Tender as Hampden's face,
Who now shall fill the space,
    Void by his grave?

'Tis not one broken heart,
    Wild with dismay—
Crazed in her agony,
    Weeps o'er his clay!
Ah! from a thousand eyes,
Flow the pure tears that rise—
Widowed Virginia lies
    Stricken to-day!

Yet, charge as gallantly,
    Ye, whom he led!
Jackson, the victor, still
    Leads, at your head!
Heroes! be battle done
Bravelier, every one
Nerved by the thought alone—
    Ashby is dead![340]
MARGARET JUNKIN PRESTON

MISSING

In the cool sweet hush of a wooded nook,
    Where the May buds sprinkle the green old sward,
And the winds, and the birds and the limpid brook,
    Murmur their dreams with a drowsy sound,
Who lies so still in the plushy moss,
    With his pale cheek pressed on a breezy pillow,
Couched where the light and the shadows cross,
    Thro' the nickering fringe of the willow?
        Who lies, alas!
    So still, so chill in the whispering grass?

A soldier, clad in the zouave dress,
    A bright-haired man, with his lips apart,
One hand thrown up o'er his frank, dead face,
    And the other clutching his pulseless heart,
Lies there in the shadow, cool and dim;
    His musket swept by a trailing bough,
With a careless grace in his quiet limbs,
    And a wound on his manly brow;
        A wound, alas!
Whence the warm blood dripped on the quiet grass.

The violets peer from their dusky beds,
    With a tearful dew in their great pure eyes;
The lilies quiver their shining heads,
    Their pale lips full of sad surprise;
And the lizard darts thro' the glistening fern,
    And the squirrel rustics the branches hoary,
Strange birds fly out with a cry, to bathe
    Their wings in the sunset glory;
        While the shadows pass
    O'er the quiet face and the dewy grass.

God pity the bride who waits at home,
    With her lily cheeks and her violet eyes,
Dreaming the sweet old dream of love,
    While her lover is walking in Paradise;
God strengthen her heart as the days go by,
    And the long dreary nights of her vigil follow.
No bird, no moon, nor a whispering wind,
    May breathe the tale of the hollow;
        Alas! Alas!
    The secret is safe with the woodland grass.[341]
UNKNOWN (written shortly after the Battle of Seven Pines)

I'M GWINE BACK TO DIXIE

I'm gwine back to Dixie, no more I'se gwine to wander,
My heart's turned back to Dixie, I can't stay here no longer.
I miss de ole plantation, my home and my relation,
My heart's turned back to Dixie, and I must go.

CHORUS
I'm gwine back to Dixie, I'm gwine back to Dixie,
I'm gwine where de orange blossoms grow,
For I hear de children callin', I see sad tears a fallin',
My heart's turned back to Dixie, and I must go.

I've hoed in fields of cotton, I've worked upon de ribber,
I used to think if I got off I'd go back dare no nebber;
But time has changed de ole man, his head is bending low,
His heart's turned back to Dixie, and he must go.

CHORUS
I'm gwine back to Dixie, I'm gwine back to Dixie,
I'm gwine where de orange blossoms grow,
For I hear de children callin', I see sad tears a fallin',
My heart's turned back to Dixie, and I must go.

I'm travelin' back to Dixie, my step is slow and feeble,
I pray de Lord to help me, and lead me from all evil;
And should my strength forsake me, den kind friends come and take me,
My heart's turned back to Dixie, and I must go.

CHORUS
I'm gwine back to Dixie, I'm gwine back to Dixie,
I'm gwine where de orange blossoms grow,
For I hear de children callin', I see sad tears a fallin',
My heart's turned back to Dixie, and I must go.[342]
CHARLES A. WHITE

THE OATH OF FREEDOM

Born free, thus we resolve to live:
    By Heaven, we will be free!
By all the stars which burn on high—
By the green earth—the mighty sea—
By God's unshaken majesty,
    We will be free or die!
        Then let the drums all roll!
            Let all the trumpets blow!
                Mind, heart, and soul,
            We spurn control
        Attempted by a foe!

Born free, thus we resolve to live:
    By Heaven, we will be free!
And, vainly now the Northmen try
To beat us down—in arms we stand
To strike for this our native land!
    We will be free or die!
        Then let the drums all roll!

Born free, we thus resolve to live:
    By Heaven, we will be free!
Our wives and children look on high,
Pray God to smile upon the right!
And bid us in the deadly fight
    As freemen live or die!
        Then let the drums all roll!

Born free, thus we resolve to live:
    By Heaven, we will be free!
And ere we cease this battle-cry,
Be all our blood, our kindred's spilt,
On bayonet or sabre hilt!
    We will be free or die!
        Then let the drums all roll!

Born free, thus we resolve to live:
    By Heaven, we will be free!
Defiant let the banners fly,
Shake out their glories to the air,
And, kneeling, brothers, let us swear
    We will be free or die!
        Then let the drums all roll!

Born free, thus we resolve to live:

By Heaven, we will be free!
And to this oath the dead reply—
Our valiant fathers' sacred ghosts—
These with us, and the God of hosts,
    We will be free or die!
        Then let the drums all roll!³⁴³
JAMES BARRON HOPE

UNDER ONE BLANKET

The sun went down in flame and smoke,
    The cold night passed without alarms,
And when the bitter morning broke
    Our men stood to their arms.

But not a foe in front was found
    After the long and stubborn fight.
The enemy had left the ground
    Where we had lain that night.

In hollows where the sun was lost
    Unthawed still lay the shining snow,
And on the rugged ground the frost
    In slender spears did grow.

Close to us, where our final rush
    Was made at closing in of day,
We saw, amid an awful hush,
    The rigid shapes of clay:

Things, which but yesterday had life,
    And answered to the trumpet's call,
Remained as victims of the strife,
    Clods of the Valley all!

Then, the grim detail marched away
    A grave from the hard soil to wrench
Wherein should sleep the Blue and Gray
    All in a ghastly trench!

A thicket of young pines arose,
    Midway upon that frosty ground;
A shelter from the winds and snows,
    And by its edge I found

Two stiffened forms, where they had died,
    As sculptured marble white and cold,
Lying together side by side
    Beneath one blanket's fold.

My heart already touched and sad
    The blanket down I gently drew
And saw a sturdy form, well clad
    From head to heel in Blue.

Beside him, gaunt from a many a fast,
    A pale and boyish "rebel" lay,
Free of all pangs of life, at last,
    In tattered suit of Gray.

There side by side those soldiers slept
    Each for the cause that he thought good,
And bowing down my head I wept
    Through human brotherhood.

Oh, sirs! it was a piteous thing
    To see how they had vainly tried
With strips of shirts, and bits of string
    To stay life's ebbing tide!

The story told itself aright;
    (Print scarce were plainer to the eye)
How they together in the night
    Had laid them down to die.

The story told itself, I say,
    How smitten by their wounds and cold
They'd nestled close, the Blue and Gray,
    Beneath one blanket's fold.

All their poor surgery could do
    They did to stop their wounds so deep,
Until at last the Gray and Blue
    Like comrades fell asleep.

We dug for them a generous grave,
    Under that somber thicket's lee,
And there we laid the sleeping brave
    To wait God's reveille.

That grave by many a tear was graced
    From ragged heroes ranged around
As in one blanket they were placed
    In consecrated ground.

Aye! consecrated, without flaw,
    Because upon that bloody sod,
My soul uplifted stood and saw
    Where Christ had lately trod![344]
JAMES BARRON HOPE

JOHN PELHAM

Just as the spring came laughing through the strife,
    With all its gorgeous cheer,
In the bright April of historic life
    Fell the great cannoneer.

The wondrous lulling of a hero's breath
    His bleeding country weeps;
Hushed, in the alabaster arms of Death,
    Our young Marcellus sleeps.

Nobler and grander than the child of Rome,
    Curbing his chariot steeds,
The knightly scion of a Southern home
    Dazzled the land with deeds.

Gentlest and bravest in the battle-brunt—
    The Champion of the Truth—
He bore his banner to the very front
    Of our immortal youth.

A clang of sabers mid Virginian snow,
    The fiery pang of shells,—
And there's a wail of immemorial woe
    In Alabama dells:

The pennon droops, that led the sacred band
    Along the crimson field;
The meteor blade sinks from the nerveless hand,
    Over the spotless shield.

We gazed and gazed upon that beauteous face,
    While, round the lips and eyes,
Couched in their marble slumber, flashed the grace
    Of a divine surprise.

O mother of a blessed soul on high,
    Thy tears may soon be shed!
Think of thy boy, with princes of the sky,
    Among the Southern dead.

How must he smile on this dull world beneath,
    Fevered with swift renown,—
He, with the martyr's amaranthine wreath,
    Twining the victor's crown![345]

JAMES RYDER RANDALL

SUMTER IN RUINS

Ye batter down the lion's den,
    But yet the lordly beast goes free;
And ye shall hear his roar again,
From mountain height, from lowland glen,
From sandy shore and reedy fen—
Where'er a band of freeborn men
    Rears sacred shrines to liberty.

The serpent scales the eagle's nest,
    And yet the royal bird, in air,
Triumphant wins the mountain's crest,
And sworn for strife, yet takes his rest,
And plumes, to calm, his ruffled breast,
Till, like a storm-bolt from the west,
    He strikes the invader in his lair.

What's loss of den, or nest, or home,
    If, like the lion, free to go;—
If, like the eagle, wing'd to roam,
We span the rock and breast the foam,
Still watchful for the hour of doom,
When, with the knell of thunder-boom,
    We bound upon the serpent foe!

Oh! noble sons of lion heart!
    Oh! gallant hearts of eagle wing!
What though your batter'd bulwarks part,
Your nest be spoiled by reptile art—
Your souls, on wings of hate, shall start
For vengeance, and with lightning-dart,
    Rend the foul serpent ere he sting!

Your battered den, your shattered nest,
    Was but the lion's crouching-place;—
It heard his roar, and bore his crest,
His, or the eagle's place of rest;—
But not the soul in either breast!
This arms the twain, by freedom bless'd,
    To save and to avenge their race![346]
WILLIAM GILMORE SIMMS

William G. Simms.

THE TWO ARMIES

Two armies stand enrolled beneath
The banner with the starry wreath:
One, facing battle, blight, and blast,
Through twice a hundred fields has passed;
Its deeds against a ruffian foe,
Stream, valley, hill, and mountain know,
Till every wind that sweeps the land
Goes, glory-laden, from the strand.

The other, with a narrower scope,
Yet led by not less grand a hope,
Hath won, perhaps, as proud a place,
And wears its fame with meeker grace.
Wives march beneath its glittering sign,
Fond mothers swell the lovely line:
And many a sweetheart hides her blush
In the young patriot's generous flush.

No breeze of battle ever fanned
The colors of that tender band;
Its office is beside the bed,
Where throbs some sick or wounded head.
It does not court the soldier's tomb,
But plies the needle and the loom;
And, by a thousand peaceful deeds,
Supplies a struggling nation's needs.

Nor is that army's gentle might
Unfelt amid the deadly fight;
It nerves the son's, the husband's hand,
It points the lover's fearless brand;
It thrills the languid, warms the cold,
Gives even new courage to the bold;
And sometimes lifts the veriest clod
To its own lofty trust in God.

When Heaven shall blow the trump of peace,
And bid this weary warfare cease,
Their several missions nobly done,
The triumph grasped, and freedom won,
Both armies, from their toils at rest,
Alike may claim the victor's crest,
But each shall see its dearest prize
Gleam softly from the other's eyes.[347]
HENRY TIMROD

SENTINEL SONGS

When falls the soldier brave,
    Dead at the feet of wrong,
The poet sings and guards his grave
    With sentinels of song.

Songs, march! he gives command,
    Keep faithful watch and true;
The living and dead of the conquered land
    Have now no guards save you.

Gray ballads, mark ye well!
    Thrice holy is your trust!
Go! halt by the fields where warriors fell;
    Rest arms! and guard their dust.

List, songs! your watch is long,
    The soldiers' guard was brief;
Whilst right is right, and wrong is wrong,
    Ye may not seek relief.

Go! wearing the gray of grief!
    Go! watch o'er the dead in gray!
Go! guard the private and guard the chief,
    And sentinel their clay!

And the songs, in stately rhyme,
    And with softly-sounding tread,
Go forth to watch for a time, a time,
    Where sleep the deathless dead.

And the songs, like funeral dirge,
    In music soft and low,
Sing round the graves whilst hot tears surge
    From hearts that are homes of woe.

What though no sculptured shaft
    Immortalize each brave!
What though no monument, epitaphed,
    Be built above each grave!

When marble wears away
    And monuments are dust,
The songs that guard our soldiers' clay
    Will still fulfill their trust.

With lifted head and steady tread,
    Like stars that guard the skies,
Go watch each bed, where rest the dead,
    Brave songs, with sleepless eyes.[348]

REVEREND ABRAM JOSEPH RYAN (written after the U.S. government refused the South permission to build a Confederate monument)

GATHERING SONG

Come, brothers! rally for the right!
    The bravest of the brave
Sends forth her ringing battle-cry
    Beside the Atlantic wave!
She leads the way in honor's path;
    Come, brothers, near and far,
Come rally 'round the Bonnie Blue Flag
    That bears a single star!

We've borne the Yankee trickery,
    The Yankee gibe and sneer,
Till Yankee insolence and pride
    Know neither shame nor fear;
But ready now with shot and steel
    Their brazen front to mar,
We hoist aloft the Bonnie Blue Flag
    That bears a single star!

Now Georgia marches to the front,
    And close beside her come
Her sisters by the Mexique Sea,
    With pealing trump and drum;
Till, answering back from hill and glen
    The rallying cry afar,
A Nation hoists the Bonnie Blue Flag
    That bears a single Star!

By every stone in Charleston Bay,
    By each beleaguered town,
We swear to rest not, night nor day,
    But hunt the tyrants down!
Till, bathed in valor's holy blood
    The gazing world afar
Shall greet with shouts the Bonnie Blue Flag
    That bears the cross and star![349]
ANNIE CHAMBERS KETCHUM

LITTLE GIFFEN OF TENNESSEE

Out of the focal and foremost fire,
Out of the hospital walls as dire;
Smitten of grapeshot and gangrene
(Eighteenth battle and he sixteen!),
Specter, such as you seldom see,
"Little Giffen," of Tennessee!

"Take him, and welcome!" the surgeons said;
"Little the doctor can help the dead."
So we took him, and brought him where
The balm was sweet in the summer air;
And we laid him down on a wholesome bed—
Utter Lazarus from heel to head!

And we watched the war with bated breath,
Skeleton boy against skeleton death.
Months of torture, how many such?
Weary weeks of the stick and crutch;
And still a glint of the steel-blue eye
Told of a spirit that wouldn't die.

And didn't, nay, more! in death's despite
The crippled skeleton "learned to write."
"Dear mother," at first, of course; and then
"Dear captain," inquiring about the men.
Captain's answer: "Of eighty and five,
Giffen and I are left alive."

Word of gloom from the war one day;
Johnston pressed at the front, they say.
Little Giffen was up and away;
A tear, his first, as he bade good-bye,
Dimmed the glint of his steel-blue eye.
"I'll write, if spared." There was news of the fight,
But none of Giffen. He did not write.

I sometimes fancy that, were I king
Of the princely Knights of the Golden Ring,
With the song of the minstrel in mine ear,
And the tender legend that trembles here,
I'd give the best on his bended knee,
The whitest soul of my chivalry,
For "Little Giffen," of Tennessee.[350]
FRANCIS ORRAY TICKNOR

WE CONQUER OR DIE

The war drum is beating, prepare for the fight,
The stern bigot Northman exults in his might,
Gird on your bright weapons, your foemen are nigh;
Let this be our watchword, "We conquer or die!"

The trumpet is sounding from mountain to shore,
Your swords and your lances must slumber no more,
Fling forth to the sunlight your banner on high,
Inscribed with the watchword, "We conquer or die!"

March to the battlefield, there do or dare,
With shoulder to shoulder, all danger to share,
And let your proud watchword ring up to the sky,
Till the blue arch re-echoes "We conquer or die!"

Press forward undaunted, nor think of retreat,
The enemy's host on the threshold to meet;
Strike firm till the foeman before you shall fly,
Appalled by the watchword, "We conquer or die!"

Go forth in the pathway our forefathers trod;
We, too, light for freedom—our Captain is God;
Their blood in our veins, with their honor we vie,
Theirs, too, was the watchword, "We conquer or die!"

We strike for the South—mountain, valley and plain—
For the South we will conquer again and again;
Her day of salvation and triumph is nigh,
Ours, then, be the watchword, "We conquer or die!"[351]
JAMES PIERPONT

ON THE DEATH OF GEN. LEONIDAS POLK

A flash from the edge of a hostile trench,
    A puff of smoke, a roar
Who's echo shall roll from Kennesaw's hill
    To the farthermost Christian shore—
Proclaim to the world that the warrior-priest
    Will battle for right no more!

And that, for a cause which is sanctified
    By the blood of martyrs unknown—
A cause for which they give their lives,
    And for which he gave his own—
He kneels, a meek embassador,
    At the foot of the Father's throne.

And up to the courts of another world,
    That angels alone have trod,
He lives, away from the din and strife
    Of this blood-be-sprinkled sod—
Crowned with the amaranthine wreath
    That is worn by the blest of God![352]
HARRY LYNDEN FLASH

Leonidas Polk.

SONNET

Rise from your gory ashes stern and pale,
Ye martyred thousands! and with dreadful ire,
A voice of doom, a front of gloomy fire,
Rebuke those faithless souls, whose querulous wail
Disturbs your sacred sleep!—"The withering hail
Of battle, hunger, pestilence, despair,
Whatever of mortal anguish man may bear,
We bore unmurmuring I strengthened by the mail
Of a most holy purpose!—then we died!—
Vex not our rest by cries of selfish pain,
But to the noblest measure of your powers
Endure the appointed trial! Griefs defied,
But launch their threatening thunderbolts in vain,
And angry storms pass by in gentlest showers!"[353]
PAUL HAMILTON HAYNE

STONEWALL JACKSON

In vict'ry's loving arms the hero fell,
Admired and honored by his fiercest foes.
The trump of fame sounds forth his glorious name
To every land where valor is esteemed.[354]
DRUMMOND WELLBURN

General Jackson, age 33.

THE COUNTERSIGN

Alas! the weary hours pass slow,
    The night is very dark and still;
And in the marshes far below
    I hear the bearded whippoorwill;
I scarce can see a yard ahead,
    My ears are strained to catch each sound;
I hear the leaves about me shed,
    And the spring's bubbling through the ground.

Along the beaten path I pace,
    Where white rags mar my sentry's track;
In formless shrubs I seem to trace
    The foeman's form with bending back,
I think I see him crouching low:
    I stop and list—I stoop and peer,
Until the neighboring hillocks row
    To groups of soldiers far and near.

With ready piece I wait and watch,
    Until my eyes, familiar grown,
Detect each harmless earthern notch,
    And turn guerrillas into stone;
And then, amid the lonely gloom,
    Beneath the tall old chestnut trees,
My silent marches I resume,
    And think of other times than these.

Sweet visions through the silent night!
    The deep bay-windows fringed with vine,
The room within, in softened light,
    The tender milk-white hand in mine;
The timid pressure, and the pause
    That often overcame our speech—
That time when by mysterious laws
    We each felt all in all to each.

And then that bitter, bitter day,
    When came the final hour to part;
When, clad in soldier's honest gray,
    I pressed her weeping to my heart;
Too proud of me to bid me stay,
    Too fond of me to let me go,—
I had to tear myself away,
    And left her, stolid in my woe.

So rose the dream—so passed the night
    When, distant in the darksome glen,
Approaching up the sombre height
    I heard the solid march of men;
Till over stubble, over sward,
    And fields where lay the golden sheaf,
I saw the lantern of the guard
    Advancing with the night relief.

"Halt! Who goes there ?" My challenge cry,
    It rings along the watchful line;
"Relief!" I hear a voice reply;
    "Advance, and give the countersign!"
With bayonet at the charge I wait—
    The corporal gives the mystic spell;
With arms aport I charge my mate,
    Then onward pass, and all is well.

But in the tent that night awake,
    I ask, if in the fray I fall,
Can I the mystic answer make
    When the angelic sentries call?
And pray that Heaven may so ordain,
    Where'er I go, what fate be mine,
Whether in pleasure or in pain,
    I still may have the countersign.[355]
ANONYMOUS CONFEDERATE SOLDIER

HIGH TIDE AT GETTYSBURG

A cloud possessed the hollow field.
The gathering battle's smoky shield;
    Athwart the gloom the lightning flashed,
    And through the cloud some horsemen dashed,
And from the heights the thunder pealed.

Then, at the brief command of Lee,
Moved out that matchless infantry,
    With Pickett leading grandly down,
    To rush against the roaring crown
Of those dread heights of destiny.

Far heard above the angry guns,
A cry across the tumult runs;
    The voice that rang through Shiloh's woods,
    And Chickamauga's solitudes:
The fierce South cheering on her sons.

Ah, how the withering tempest blew
Against the front of Pettigrew!
    A khamsin wind that scorched and singed,
    Like that infernal flame that fringed
The British squares at Waterloo!

A thousand fell where Kemper led;
A thousand died where Garnett bled;
    In blinding flame and strangling smoke,
    The remnant through the batteries broke,
And crossed the works with Armistead.

"Once more in Glory's van with me!"
Virginia cries to Tennessee:
    "We two together, come what may,
    Shall stand upon those works to-day!"
The reddest day in history

Brave Tennessee! Reckless the way.
Virginia heard her comrade say:
    "Close round this rent and riddled rag!"
    What time she set her battle flag
Amid the guns of Doubleday.

But who shall break the guards that wait
Before the awful face of fate?
    The tattered standards of the South

Were shrivelled at the cannon's mouth,
And all her hopes were desolate.

In vain the Tennessean set
His breast against the bayonet;
    In vain Virginia charged and raged,
    A tigress in her wrath uncaged,
'Till all the hill was red and wet!

Above the bayonets mixed and crossed
Men saw a gray, gigantic ghost
    Receding through the battle cloud.
    And heard across the tempest loud
The death-cry of a nation lost!

The brave went down! Without disgrace
They leaped to ruin's red embrace;
    They only heard fame's thunder wake,
    And saw the dazzling sunburst break
In smiles on glory's bloody face!

They fell who lifted up a hand,
And bade the sun in heaven to stand;
    They smote and fell who set the bars
    Against the progress of the stars,
And stayed the march of Motherland!

They stood who saw the future come
On through the fight's delirium;
    They smote and stood who held the hope
    Of nations on that slippery slope,
Amid the cheers of Christendom!

God lives! He forged the iron will,
That clutched and held that trembling hill!
    God lives and reigns! He built and lent
    The height's for freedom's battlement,
Where floats her flag in triumph still!

Fold up the banner's! Smelt the guns!
Love rules. Her gentler purpose runs.
    A mighty mother turns in tears
    The pages of her battle years,
Lamenting all her fallen sons![356]
WILL H. THOMPSON

CALL ALL! CALL ALL!

Whoop! the Doodles have broken loose,
Roaring round like the very deuce!
Lice of Egypt, a hungry pack,—
After 'em, boys, and drive 'em back.

Bull-dog, terrier, cur, and fice,
Back to the beggarly land of ice;
Worry 'em, bite 'em, scratch and tear
Everybody and everywhere.

Old Kentucky is caved from under,
Tennessee is split asunder,
Alabama awaits attack,
And Georgia bristles up her back.

Old John Brown is dead and gone!
Still his spirit is marching on,—
Lantern-jawed, and legs, my boys,
Long as an ape's from Illinois!

Want a weapon? Gather a brick,
Club or cudgel, or stone or stick;
Anything with a blade or butt,
Anything that can cleave or cut.

Anything heavy, or hard, or keen!
Any sort of slaying machine!
Anything with a willing mind,
And the steady arm of a man behind.

Want a weapon? Why, capture one!
Every Doodle has got a gun,
Belt, and bayonet, bright and new;
Kill a Doodle, and capture two!

Shoulder to shoulder, son and sire!
All, call all! to the feast of fire!
Mother and maiden, and child and slave,
A common triumph or a single grave.[357]
UNKNOWN

GENERAL ALBERT SIDNEY JOHNSTON

In thickest fight triumphantly he fell,
    While into victory's arms he led us on;
A death so glorious our grief should quell:
    We mourn him, yet his battle-crown is won.

No slanderous tongue can vex his spirit now,
    No bitter taunts can stain his blood-bought fame;
Immortal honor rests upon his brow,
    And noble memories cluster round his name.

For hearts shall thrill and eyes grow dim with tears,
    To read the story of his touching fate;
How in his death the gallant soldier wears
    The crown that came for earthly life too late.

Ye people! guard his memory—sacred keep
    The garlands green above is hero-grave;
Yet weep, for praise can never wake his sleep,
    To tell him he is shrined among the brave![358]
MARY JERVEY

Albert S. Johnston.

FAREWELL TO JOHNSON'S ISLAND

Hoarse sounding billows of the white cupped lake,
That 'gainst the barriers of our hated prison break,
Farewell! Farewell! thou giant inland sea:
Thou, too, subservest the modes of tyranny—
Girding this Isle, washing its lonely shore
With moaning echoes of thy melancholy roar.
Farewell thou lake! Farewell thou inhospitable land!
Thou hast the curses of this patriot band.—
All, save the spot, the holy sacred bed,
Where rest in peace our Southern warriors dead.[359]
UNKNOWN

FORT WAGNER

Glory unto the gallant boys who stood
    At Wagner, and, unflinching, sought the van;
Dealing fierce blows, and shedding precious blood,
    For homes as precious, and dear rights of man!
They've won the meed, and they shall have the glory;—
    Song, with melodious memories, shall repeat
The legend, which shall grow to themes for story,
    Told through long ages, and forever sweet!

High honor to our youth—our sons and brothers,
    Georgians and Carolinians, where they stand!
They will not shame their birthrights, or their mothers,
    But keep, through storm, the bulwarks of the land!
They feel that they must conquer! Not to do it,
    Were worse than death—perdition! Should they fail,
The innocent races yet unborn shall rue it,
    The whole world feel the wound, and nations wail!

No! They must conquer in the breach or perish!
    Assured, in the last consciousness of breath,
That love shall deck their graves, and memory cherish
    Their deeds, with honors that shall sweeten death!
They shall have trophies in long future hours,
    And loving recollections, which shall be
Green as the summer leaves, and fresh as flowers,
    That, through all seasons, bloom eternally!

Their memories shall be monuments, to rise
    Next those of mightiest martyrs of the past;
Beacons, when angry tempests sweep the skies,
    And feeble souls bend crouching to the blast!
A shrine for thee, young Cheves, well devoted,
    Most worthy of a great, illustrious sire;—
A niche for thee, young Haskell, nobly noted,
    When skies and seas around thee shook with fire!

And others as well chronicled shall be!
    What though they fell with unrecorded name—
They live among the archives of the free,
    With proudest title to undying fame!
The unchisell'd marble under which they sleep,
    Shall tell of heroes, fearless still of fate;
Not asking if their memories shall keep,
    But if they nobly served, and saved, the State!

For thee, young Fortress Wagner—thou shalt wear
    Green laurels, worthy of the names that now,
Thy sister forts of Moultrie, Sumter, bear!
    See that thou lift'st, for aye, as proud a brow!
And thou shalt be, to future generations,
    A trophied monument; whither men shall come
In homage; and report to distant nations,
    A shrine, which foes shall never make a tomb![360]
WILLIAM GILMORE SIMMS

TO MY SOLDIER BROTHER

When softly gathering shades of ev'n
    Creep o'er the prairies broad and green,
And countless stars bespangle heav'n,
    And fringe the clouds with silv'ry sheen,
My fondest sigh to thee is giv'n,
My lonely wand'ring soldier-boy;
    And thoughts of thee
    Steal over me
Like ev'ning shades, my soldier boy.

My brother, though thou'rt far away,
    And dangers hurtle round thy path,
And battle lightnings o'er thee play,
    And thunders peal in awful wrath,
Think, whilst thou'rt in the hot affray,
Thy sister prays for thee, my boy.
    If fondest prayer
    Can shield thee there,
Sweet angels guard my soldier boy.

Thy proud young heart is beating high
    To clash of arms and cannons' roar;
That firm set lip and flashing eye
    Tell how thy heart is brimming o'er.
Be free and live, be free or die!
Be that thy motto now, my boy;
    And though thy name's
    Unknown to fame's
'Tis graven on my heart, my boy.[361]
SALLIE E. BALLARD

THE SOUTHRON MOTHER'S CHARGE

You go, my son, to the battle-field,
    To repel the invading foe;
Mid its fiercest conflicts never yield
    Till death shall lay you low.

Our God, who smiles upon the Right
    And frowns upon the Wrong,
Will nerve you for our holy fight,
    And make your courage strong.

Our cause is just, for it we pray
    At morning, noon, and night,
Upon our banners we inscribe,
    God, Liberty, and Right.

I love you as I love my life,
    You are my only son;
Your country calls, go forth and fight
    Till Freedom's cause is won.

It may be that you fall in death,
    Contending for your home,
Yet your aged mother will not be
    Forsaken though alone.

A thousand generous hearts there are
    Throughout this sunny land,
Whose ample fortunes will be spent
    With an unsparing hand.

Now go, my son, a mother's prayers
    Will ever follow thee;
And in the thickest of the fight
    Strike home for liberty!

On every hill, in every glen,
    We'll fight till we are free;
We'll fight till every limpid brook
    Runs crimson to the sea.

No truce we know, till every foe
    Shall leave our hallowed sod,
And we regain that heaven-born boon,
    "Freedom to worship God."[362]
THOMAS B. HOOD

THE SOUTHERN PLEIADES

When first our Southern flag arose,
    Beside the heaving sea,
It bore upon its silken folds
    A green Palmetto tree.
All honor to that banner brave,
    It roused the blood of yore,
And nerved the arm of Southern men
    For valiant deeds once more.

When storm clouds darkened o'er our sky,
    That star, the first of seven,
Shone out amid the mist and gloom,
    To light our country's heaven.
The glorious seven! long may their flag
    Wave proudly on the breeze;
Long may they burn on fame's broad sky—
    The Southern Pleiades![363]
LAURA LORRIMER

First National Confederate Flag
with seven stars.

THE STARS & BARS

Fling wide the dauntless banner
    To every Southern breeze,
Baptized in flame, with Sumter's name—
A patriot and a hero's fame—
    From Moultrie to the seas!
That it may cleave the morning sun
    And, streaming, sweep the night,
The emblem of a battle won
    With Yankee ships in sight.

Come, hucksters, from your markets,
    Come, bigots, from your caves,
Come, venal spies, with brazen lies
Bewildering your deluded eyes,
    That we may dig your graves;
Come, creatures of a sordid clown [Lincoln]
    And driveling traitor's breath,
A single blast shall blow you down
    Upon the fields of Death.

The very flag you carry
    Caught its reflected grace,
In fierce alarms, from Southern arms,
When foemen threatened all your farms,
    And never saw your face;
Ho! braggarts of New England's shore,
    Back to your hills and delve
The soil whose craven sons foreswore
    The flag in eighteen-twelve!

We wreathed around the roses
    It wears before the world,
And made it bright with storied light,
In every scene of bloody fight
    Where it has been unfurled;
And think ye, now, the dastard hands
    That never yet could hold
Its staff, shall wave it o'er our lands,
    To glut the greed of gold?

No! by the truth of Heaven
    And its eternal Sun,
By every sire whose altar fire
Burns on to beckon and inspire,
    It never shall be done;

Before that day the kites shall wheel
    Hail-thick on Northern heights,
And there our bared, aggressive steel
    Shall countersign our rights!

Then spread the flaming banner
    O'er mountain, lake, and plain,
Before its bars, degraded Mars
Has kissed the dust with all his stars,
    And will be struck again;
For could its triumph now be stayed
    By Hell's prevailing gates,
A sceptred Union would be made
    The grave of sovereign States.[364]
JUDGE AUGUSTUS JULIAN REQUIER

First National Confederate Flag with 13 stars.

THE MARCH

Tramp, tramp, tramp, tramp!
    Go the Southern braves to battle,
How they shine, each gleaming line!
    Flashing sabers! how they rattle!
Every lip is now compressed,
    Every heart now yearns for glory,
Every eye with patriot fire
    Burns for battle fierce and gory!

Tramp, tramp, tramp, tramp!
    Death is in each hidden saber,
Reaper of the fields of Time,
    Look ye for a giant's labor!
How sublime! when patriots feel
    All the strength of self-reliance,
Marching on to meet the foe,
    With a stern and grim defiance!

See how proudly floats our flag!
    White! our cause is pure and grand, man!
Red! a living flood shall flow
    From every foe now in the land, man!
Blue! aye, heaven's stars are there!
    Sparkling in their azure beauty!
Tramp, tramp, tramp, tramp!
    Go the messengers of duty![365]
JOHN W. OVERALL

THE SOUTH IN ARMS

Oh! see ye not the sight sublime,
Unequaled in all previous time,
Presented in this Southern clime,
    The home of chivalry?

A warlike race of freemen stand,
With martial front and sword in hand,
Defenders of their native land,—
    The sons of Liberty.

Unawed by numbers, they defy
The tyrant North, nor will they fly,
Resolved to conquer or to die,
    And win a glorious name.

Sprung from renowned heroic sires,
Inflamed with patriotic fires,
Their bosoms burn with fierce desires,
    They thirst for victory.

'Tis not the love of bloody strife,
The horrid sacrifice of life,
But thoughts of mother, sister, wife,
    That stir their manly hearts.

A sense of honor bids them go,
To meet a hireling, ruthless foe,
And deal in wrath the deadly blow
    Which vengeance loud demands.

In freedom's sacred cause they fight,
For Independence, Justice, Right,
And to resist a desperate might.
And by Manassas' glorious name,
And by Missouri's fields of fame,
We hear them swear, with one acclaim,
We'll triumph or we'll die![366]
REVEREND J. H. MARTIN

MELT THE BELLS

Melt the bells, melt the bells,
Still the tinkling on the plain,
And transmute the evening chimes
Into war's resounding rhymes,
That the invaders may be slain
    By the bells.

Melt the bells, melt the bells,
That for years have called to prayer,
And, instead, the cannon's roar
Shall resound the valleys o'er,
That the foe may catch despair
    From the bells.

Melt the bells, melt the bells,
Though it cost a tear to part
With the music they have made,
Where the friends we love are laid,
With pale cheek and silent heart,
    'Neath the bells.

Melt the bells, melt the bells,
Into cannon, vast and grim,
And the foe shall feel the ire
From the heaving lungs of fire,
And we'll put our trust in Him,
    And the bells.

Melt the bells, melt the bells,
And when foes no more attack,
And the lightning cloud of war
Shall roll thunderless and far,
We will melt the cannon back
    Into bells.

Melt the bells, melt the bells,
And they'll peal a sweeter chime,
And remind of all the brave
Who have sunk to glory's grave,
And will sleep through coming time
    'Neath the bells.[367]
F. Y. ROCKETT

GLORIOUS MEMORIES OF THE OLD SOUTH

Gather the sacred dust
    Of the warriors tried and true,
Who bore the flag of our nation's trust,
And fell in a cause, though lost, still just,
    And died for me and you.

And the dead thus meet the dead,
    While the living o'er them weep;
And the men whom Lee and Stonewall led,
And the hearts that once together bled,
    Together still shall sleep.

Oh, the sweet South! the sunny, sunny South!
    Land of true feeling, land forever mine!
I drink the kisses of her rosy mouth,
    And my heart swells as with a draught of wine;
She brings me blessings of maternal love;
    I have her smile, which hallows all my toil;
Her voice persuades, her generous smiles approve.
    She sings me from the sky and from the soil.
Oh! by her lovely pines that wave and sigh,
    Oh! by her myriad flowers, that bloom and fade,
By all the thousand beauties of her sky,
    And the sweet solace of her forest shade,
    She's mine—she's ever mine!

Oh! by her virtues of the cherished past—
    By all her hopes of what the future brings—
I glory that my lot with her is cast,
    And my soul flushes and exulting sings:
    She's mine—she's ever mine![368]
UNKNOWN

OUR SOUTHERN WOMEN

The maid who binds the warrior's sash
And, smiling, all her pain dissembles
The while beneath the drooping lash,
One starry tear-drop hangs and trembles;
Though Heaven alone records the tear,
And fame shall never know her story,
Her heart has shed a drop as dear
As ever dewed the field of glory.

The wife who girds the husband's sword,
'Mid little ones that weep and wonder,
And bravely speaks the parting word,
Although her heart be rent asunder;
Doomed nightly, in her dreams, to hear
The bolts of war around him rattle,
Has shed as sacred blood as e'er,
Was poured upon the plain of battle.

The mother, who conceals her grief
While to her breast her son she presses,
Then speaks a few brave words and brief,
Kissing the patriot's brow she blesses;
With no one but a secret God
To know the pain that weighs upon her,
Sheds holy blood as e'er the sod
Received on Freedom's field of honor.[369]
UNKNOWN

Varina Anne Davis.

ONLY A PRIVATE

Only a private—and who will care
    When I may pass away,
Or how, or why I perish, or where
    I mix with the common clay?
They will fill my empty place again
    With another as bold and brave;
And they'll blot me out ere the autumn rain
    Has freshened my nameless grave.

Only a private—it matters not
    That I did in duty well,
That all through a score of battles I fought,
    And then, like a soldier, fell.
The country I died for never will heed
    My unrequited claim;
And History cannot record the deed,
    For she never has heard my name.

Only a private—and yet I know
    When I heard the rallying-call
I was one of the very first to go,
    And . . . I'm one of the many who fall:
But as here I lie, it is sweet to feel
    That my honor's without a stain,—
That I only fought for my country's weal,
    And not for glory or gain.

Only a private—yet He who reads
    Through the guises of the heart,
Looks not at the splendor of the deeds,
    But the way we do our part;
And when He shall take us by the hand,
    And our small service own,
There'll a glorious band of privates stand
    As victors around the throne![370]

MARGARET JUNKIN PRESTON

THE GRAVE OF A SOUTHERN SOLDIER

A gentleman was passing by
    An old farmyard one time—
'Twas on a verdant mountain high
    In Georgia's sunny clime.

While strolling thus, absorbed in thought,
    He saw a faithful slave
Standing near a marble slab
    Which marked his master's grave.

The old man saw him drawing near,
    And made a graceful bow.
"My dear old friend, why stand'st thou here?
    Thy heart is sad, I trow."

He lifted up his hoary head,
    A tear coursed down his face.
"O gent'man, sah, ain't yo' dun hea'
    De his'try ob dis place?

'Twuz on dis spot, long time ago,
    One pleasant summah day,
De Yankees shot po' Massa Joe,
    En dis am whar he lay.

Yo' see Mars Joe wuz comin' home
    To see his maw and paw,
'Cause he be'n fightin' fo' de Souf
    Since fust de 'gin de wah.

Wile he wuz wa'kin' lazy like,
    His face towa'ds de ground,
He thought he heared de bushes crack,
    En' tu'nin, looked aroun'.

Law bless ma soul! w'at he see den
    Among dem cedah trees
Wuz 'nough to meek de blood ob e'en
    De bravest sojer freeze.

De Yankees swaumed all th'ough de woods,
    Like bees aroun' de hive;
W'ere e'er you'd look a sojer stood—
    De place wuz jes alive.

Po' massa dun fell in a trap,
    But 'twasn' none his fault;
He did'n' see no Yankees dere
    Till some one called out: 'Halt!'

'Good mawnin', gents!' Mars Joe den say,
    Wile passin' by de ranks.
Den he tu'ned en' run'd away—
    Close 'hind 'im run'd de Yanks.

Da run'd en' yelled en' shot at him,
    But he did'n' min' none dat.
De bullets went all th'ough his coat,
    En' one tuck off his hat.

He run'd right straight on pas' his dooh—
    He knew to stop meant deaf—
But jes' ez he got neah de woods
    He fell, all out'er breaf.

Quick ez a thought da had 'im bound,
    En led 'im pas' his dooh.
He looked so sorry at his home
    He neber saw no mo'.

Den come his pooh ole feeble maw
    To beg fo' his release;
But dey jes' tole 'er he mus' die,
    His noble life mus' cease.

Pooh massa hear, den tu'ned en' say:
    'Den, men, ef I mus' die,
Release me from dese cruel bonds,
    En' please mah hands untie.

Yo' all well knows de Southe'n men
    Will fight yo', one en' all.
Gih me a swo'd, no murder's noose;
    Wile fightin' let me fall.'

Dey only laugh en shake dey heads.
    'No, Reb, yo' knell am rung.
Yo' hab yo' choice: will yo' be shot?
    Or maybe yo'll be hung?'

'No sahs; ef I'm to lose ma life,
    I choose a sojer's deaf.

Long lib de Souf! I'll always cry,
    E'en wid mah dyin' breaf.'

Dey led 'im to dat big ole tree.
    Po' massa called me dere.
'Good-bye, ole Sam; gib lub to maw.
    I place 'er in yo' care.'

Jes' den de cap'n called out, 'Load!'
    Den, 'Aim!' en 'Fire!' he cried.
An awful bang—de smoke clar'd off,
    En' dar's w'ere massa died."

He pointed to the little grave
    Beneath the sad old oak.
"It wuzn't long 'fo' missus died;
    Her po' ole heart wuz broke."

The man was silent for awhile;
    He seemed absorbed in thought.
His mind went back to scenes of war,
    Of battles he had fought.

"I feel much touched," at length he said,
    "And all you say is true.
O God forgive me for that sin,
    I led those boys in blue."[371]
UNKNOWN

SPRING IN WAR-TIME

Spring, with that nameless pathos in the air
Which dwells with all things fair,
Spring, with her golden suns and silver rain,
Is with us once again.

Out in the lonely woods the jasmine burns
Its fragrant lamps, and turns
Into a royal court with green festoons
The banks of dark lagoons.

In the deep heart of every forest tree
The blood is all aglee,
And there's a look about the leafless bowers
As if they dreamed of flowers.

Yet still on every side appears the hand
Of Winter in the land,
Save where the maple reddens on the lawn,
Flushed by the season's dawn;

Or where, like those strange semblances we find
That age to childhood bind,
The elm puts on, as if in Nature's scorn,
The brown of Autumn corn.

As yet the turf is dark, although you know
That, not a span below,
A thousand germs are groping through the gloom,
And soon will burst their tomb.

Already, here and there, on frailest stems
Appear some azure gems,
Small as might deck, upon a gala day,
The forehead of a fay.

In gardens you may see, amid the dearth,
The crocus breaking earth;
And near the snowdrop's tender white and green,
The violet in its screen.

But many gleams and shadows needs must pass
Along the budding grass,
And weeks go by, before the enamored South
Shall kiss the rose's mouth.

Still there's a sense of blossoms yet unborn
In the sweet airs of morn;
One almost looks to see the very street
Grow purple at his feet.

At times a fragrant breeze comes floating by,
And brings, you know not why,
A feeling as when eager crowds await
Before a palace gate.

Some wondrous pageant; and you scarce would start,
If from a beech's heart
A blue-eyed Dryad, stepping forth, should say—
"Behold me! I am May!"

Ah, who would couple thoughts of war and crime
With such a blessed time!
Who in the west-wind's aromatic breath
Could hear the call of Death!

Yet not more surely shall the Spring awake
The voice of wood and brake,
Than she shall rouse, for all her tranquil charms
A million men to arms.

There shall be deeper hues upon her plains
Than all her sunlight rains,
And every gladdening influence around
Can summon from the ground.

Oh! standing on this desecrated mould,
Methinks that I behold,
Lifting her bloody daisies up to God,
Spring, kneeling on the sod,

And calling with the voice of all her rills
Upon the ancient hills
To fall and crush the tyrants and the slaves
Who turn her meads to graves.[372]
HENRY TIMROD

OUR MARTYRS

I am sitting lone and weary
　　On the hearth of my darkened room,
And the low wind's *miserere*
　　Makes sadder the midnight gloom;
There's a terror that's nameless nigh me—
　　There's a phantom spell in the air,
And methinks that the dead glide by me,
　　And the breath of the grave's in my hair!

'Tis a vision of ghastly faces,
　　All pallid, and worn with pain,
Where the splendor of manhood's graces
　　Give place to a gory stain;
In a wild and weird procession
　　They sweep by my startled eyes,
And stern with their fate's fruition,
　　Seem melting in blood-red skies.

Have they come from the shores supernal,
　　Have they passed from the spirit's goal,
'Neath the veil of the life eternal,
　　To dawn on my shrinking soul?
Have they turned from the choiring angels,
　　Aghast at the woe and dearth
That war, with his dark evangels,
　　Hath wrought in the loved of earth?

Vain dream! 'mid the far-off mountains
　　They lie, where the dew-mists weep,
And the murmur of mournful fountains
　　Breaks over their painful sleep;
On the breast of the lonely meadows,
　　Safe, safe from the despot's will,
They rest in the star-lit shadows,
　　And their brows are white and still!

Alas! for the martyred heroes
　　Cut down at their golden prime,
In a strife with the brutal Neroes,
　　Who blacken the path of Time!
For them is the voice of wailing,
　　And the sweet blush-rose departs
From the cheeks of the maidens, paling
　　O'er the wreck of their broken hearts!

And alas! for the vanished glory
    Of a thousand household spells!
And alas I for the tearful story
    Of the spirit's fond farewells!
By the flood, on the field, in the forest,
    Our bravest have yielded breath,
But the shafts that have smitten sorest,
    Were launched by a viewless death!

Oh, Thou, that hast charms of healing,
    Descend on a widowed land,
And bind o'er the wounds of feeling
    The balms of Thy mystic hand!
Till the hearts that lament and languish,
    Renewed by the touch divine,
From the depths of a mortal anguish
    May rise to the calm of Thine![373]
PAUL HAMILTON HAYNE

Paul H. Hayne.

CONFEDERATE MONUMENT INSCRIPTION
(Columbia, SC)

To South Carolina's Dead 1861 of the 1865, Confederate Army.
Erected by the women of South Carolina.
This monument perpetuates the memory of those who,
True to the instincts of their birth,
Faithful to the teaching of their fathers,
Constant in their love for the State,
Died in the performance of their duty;
Who have glorified a fallen cause by the simple manhood of their lives.
The patient endurance of suffering, and the heroism of death;
And who, in the dark hours of imprisonment,
And the hopelessness of the hospital,
In the short, sharp agony of the field,
Found support and consolation in the belief
That at home they would not be forgotten.
Let the stranger, who may in future times, read this inscription,
Recognize that these were men whom power could not corrupt,
Whom death could not terrify,
Whom defeat could not dishonor.
And let their virtue plead for just judgment
Of the cause in which they perished;
Let the South Carolinian of another generation remember
That the State taught them how to live and how to die,
And that from her broken fortunes she has preserved for her children
The priceless treasures of their memories;
Teaching all who may claim the same birthright,
That truth, courage, and patriotism endureth forever.[374]
UNKNOWN

Confederate monument, Fayetteville, TN.
Photo L. Seabrook.

CAROLINA

The despot treads thy sacred sands,
Thy pines give shelter to his hands,
Thy sons stand by with idle hands,
  Carolina!
He breathes at ease thy airs of balm,
He scorns the lances of thy palm;
Oh, who shall break thy craven calm,
  Carolina!
Thy ancient fame is growing dim,
A spot is on thy garment's rim;
Give to the winds thy battle-hymn,
  Carolina!

Call on thy children of the hill,
Wake swamp and river, coast and rill,
Rouse all thy strength and all thy skill,
  Carolina!
Cite wealth and science, trade and art,
Touch with thy fire the cautious mart,
And pour thee through the people's heart,
  Carolina!
Till even the coward spurns his fears,
And all thy fields and fens and meres
Shall bristle like thy palm with spears,
  Carolina!

Hold up the glories of thy dead;
Say how thy elder children bled,
And point to Eutaw's battle-bed,
  Carolina!
Tell how the patriot's soul was tried,
And what his dauntless breast defied;
How Rutledge ruled and Laurens died,
  Carolina!
Cry! till thy summons, heard at last,
Shall fall like Marion's bugle-blast
Re-echoed from the haunted Past,
  Carolina!

I hear a murmur as of waves
That grope their way through sunless caves,
Like bodies struggling in their graves,
  Carolina !
And now it deepens; slow and grand
It swells, as, rolling to the land

An ocean broke upon thy strand,
          Carolina !
Shout! let it reach the startled Huns,
And roar with all thy festal guns;
It is the answer of thy sons,
          Carolina!

They will not wait to hear the call;
From Sachem's Head to Sumter's wall
Resounds the voice of hut and hall,
          Carolina!
No! thou hast not a stain, they say,
Or none save what the battle-day
Shall wash in seas of blood away,
          Carolina!
Thy skirts indeed the foe may part,
Thy robe be pierced with sword and dart,
They shall not touch thy noble heart,
          Carolina!

Ere thou shalt own the tyrant's thrall
Ten times ten thousand men must fall;
Thy corpse may hearken to his call,
          Carolina!
When, by thy bier, in mournful throngs
The women chant thy mortal wrongs,
'Twill be their own funereal songs,
          Carolina!
From thy dead breast by ruffians trod
No helpless child shall look to God;
All shall be safe beneath thy sod,
          Carolina!

Girt with such wills to do and bear,
Assured in right, and mailed in prayer,
Thou wilt not bow thee to despair,
          Carolina!
Throw thy bold banner to the breeze!
Front with thy ranks the threatening seas
Like thine own proud armorial trees,
          Carolina !
Fling down thy gauntlet to the Huns,
And roar the challenge from thy guns;
Then leave the future to thy sons,
          Carolina![375]
HENRY TIMROD

COERCION: A POEM FOR THEN & NOW

Who talks of coercion? who dares to deny
    A resolute people the right to be free?
Let him blot out forever one star from the sky,
    Or curb with his fetter the wave of the sea!

Who prates of coercion? Can love be restored
    To bosoms where only resentment may dwell?
Can peace upon earth be proclaimed by the sword,
    Or good-will among men be established by shell?

Shame! shame!—that the statesman and trickster, forsooth,
    Should have for a crisis no other recourse,
Beneath the fair day-spring of light and of truth,
    Than the old *brutum fulmen*[376] of tyranny—force!

From the holes where fraud, falsehood, and hate slink away—
    From the crypt in which error lies buried in chains—
This foul apparition stalks forth to the day,
    And would ravage the land which his presence profanes.

Could you conquer us, men of the North—could you bring
    Desolation and death on our homes as a flood—
Can you hope the pure lily, affection, will spring
    From ashes all reeking and sodden with blood?

Could you brand us as villains and serfs, know ye not
    What fierce, sullen hatred lurks under the scar?
How loyal to Hapsburg is Venice, I wot!
    How dearly the Pole loves his father, the Czar!

But 'twere well to remember this land of the sun
    Is a *nutrix leonum*,[377] and suckles a race
Strong-armed, lion-hearted, and banded as one,
    Who brook not oppression and know not disgrace.

And well may the schemers in office beware
    The swift retribution that waits upon crime,
When the lion, Resistance, shall leap from his lair,
    With a fury that renders his vengeance sublime.

Once, men of the North, we were brothers, and still,
    Though brothers no more, we would gladly be friends;
Nor join in a conflict accursed, that must fill
    With ruin the country on which it descends.

But, if smitten with blindness, and mad with the rage
    The gods gave to all whom they wished to destroy,
You would act a new Iliad, to darken the age
    With horrors beyond what is told us of Troy—

If, deaf as the adder itself to the cries,
    When wisdom, humanity, justice implore,
You would have our proud eagle to feed on the eyes
    Of those who have taught him so grandly to soar—

If there be to your malice no limit imposed,
    And you purpose hereafter to rule with the rod
The men upon whom you already have closed
    Our goodly domain and the temples of God:

To the breeze then your banner dishonored unfold,
    And, at once, let the tocsin be sounded afar;
We greet you, as greeted the Swiss, Charles the Bold—
    With a farewell to peace and a welcome to war!

For the courage that clings to our soil, ever bright,
    Shall catch inspiration from turf and from tide;
Our sons unappalled shall go forth to the fight,
    With the smile of the fair, the pure kiss of the bride;

And the bugle its echoes shall send through the past,
    In the trenches of Yorktown to waken the slain;
While the sod of King's Mountain shall heave at the blast,
    And give up its heroes to glory again.[378]

JOHN REUBEN THOMPSON

HEROES OF THE SOUTH

    Four deadly years we fought,
Ringed by a girdle of unfaltering fire
That coiled and hissed in lessening circles nigher.
    Blood dyed the Southern wave;
From ocean border to calm inland river,
There was no pause, no peace, no respite ever.
    Blood of our bravest brave
Drenched in a scarlet rain the western lea,
Swelled the hoarse waters of the Tennessee,
Incarnadined the gulfs, the lakes, the rills,
    And from a hundred hills
Steamed in a mist of slaughter to the skies,
Shutting all hope of heaven from mortal eyes.
The Beaufort blooms were wither'd on the stem;
    The fair Gulf City in a single night
    Lost her imperial diadem;
And wheresoe'er men's troubled vision roamed
They viewed *might* towering o'er the humbled crest of *right!*
    But for a time, but for a time, O God!
The innate forces of our knightly blood
Rallied, and by the mount, the fen, the flood,
    Upraised the tottering standards of our race.
O grand Virginia! though thy glittering glaive
Lies sullied, shattered in a ruthless grave,
    How it flashed once!
    They dug their trenches deep
(The implacable foe), they ranged their lines of wrath;
But watchful ever on the imminent path
    Thy steel-clad genius stood;
North, South, East, West,—they strove to pierce thy shield:
    Thou wouldst not yield!
Until—unconquered, yea, unconquered still
Nature's weakened forces answered not thy will,
And gored with wound on wound,
Thy fainting limbs and forehead sought the ground;
And with thee, the young nation fell, a pall
Solemn and rayless, covering one and all!

God's ways are marvellous; here we stand to-day
Discrown'd, and shorn in wildest disarray,
The mock of earth! yet never shone the sun
On sterner deeds, or nobler victories won.
Not in the field alone; ah, come with me
To the dim bivouac by the winter's sea;
Mark the fair sons of courtly mothers crouch

O'er flickering fires; but gallant still, and gay
As on some bright parade. Or mark the couch
   In reeking hospitals, whereon is laid
The latest scion of a line perchance
Whose veins were royal. Close your blurred romance,
Blurred by the dropping of a maudlin tear,
And watch the manhood here;
    That firm but delicate countenance,
Distorted sometimes by an awful pang,
Borne in meek patience. When the trumpets rang
"To horse!" but yester-morn, that ardent boy
Sprung to his charger, thrilled with hope and joy
To the very finger-tips; and now he lies,
The shadows deepening in those falcon eyes,
   But calm and undismayed
As if the Death that chills him, brow and breast,
Were some fond bride who whispered, "Let us rest!"

Enough! 'tis over! the last gleam of hope
Hath melted from our mournful horoscope—
   Of all, of all bereft;
   Only to us are left
Our buried heroes and their matchless deeds.
These cannot pass; they hold the vital seeds
Which in some far, untracked, unvisioned hour
May burst to vivid bud and glorious flower.
   Meanwhile, upon the nation's broken heart
Her martyrs sleep. Oh, dearer far to her
Than if each son, a wreathed conqueror,
   Rode in triumphant state
   The loftiest crest of fate;
Oh, dearer far, because outcast and low,
She yearns above them in her awful woe.[379]
PAUL HAMILTON HAYNE

GONE FORWARD

Yes, "Let the tent be struck": victorious morning
    Through every crevice flashes in a day
Magnificent beyond all earth's adorning:
      The night is over; wherefore should he stay?
    And wherefore should our voices choke to say,
      "The General [Lee] has gone forward"?

Life's foughten field not once beheld surrender;
    But with superb endurance, present, past,
Our pure commander, lofty, simple, tender,
    Through good, through ill, held his high purpose fast,
      Wearing his armor spotless,—till at last
        Death gave the final "Forward!"

All hearts grew sudden palsied: Yet what said he
    Thus summoned?—"Let the tent be struck!"—For when
Did call of duty fail to find him ready
    Nobly to do his work in sight of men,
    For God's and for his country's sake—and then
      To watch, wait, or go forward?

We will not weep,— we dare not! Such a story
    As his large life writes on the century's years,
Should crowd our bosoms with a flush of glory,
    That manhood's type, supremest that appears
    To-day, he shows the ages. Nay, no tears
      Because he has gone forward!

Gone forward?—whither? Where the marshalled legions,
    Christ's well-worn soldiers, from their conflicts cease,—
Where Faith's true Red-Cross Knights repose in regions
    Thick-studded with the calm, white tents of peace,—
    Thither, right joyful to accept release,
      The General has gone forward![380]

MARGARET JUNKIN PRESTON

ADDRESS OF THE WOMEN TO SOUTHERN TROOPS

Southern men, unsheathe the sword,
Inland and along the board;
Backward drive the Northern horde—
    Rush to Victory!

Let your banners kiss the sky,
Be "The Right" your battle cry!
Be the God of Battles nigh—
    Crown you in the fight!

Pressing back the tears that start,
We behold your hosts depart,
Saying, with heroic heart,
    Clothe your arms with might!

Lower the proud oppressor's crest!
Or, if he should prove the best,
Dead, not dishonored, rest
    On the field of blood!

We—may God so give us grace!—
Sons will rear, to take your place;
Strong the foemen's steel to face—
    Strong in heart and hand!

Death your serried ranks may sweep,
Proud shall be the tears we weep—
Sacredly our hearts shall keep
    Memory of your deeds!

Though our land be left forlorn,
Spirit of the Southron-born
Northern rage shall laugh to scorn—
    Northern hosts defy.

He that last is doomed to die
Shall, with his expiring sigh,
Send aloft the battle-cry,
    "God defend the Right!"[381]
JANE T. H. CROSS

THE CAVALIERS OF DIXIE

Ye Cavaliers of Dixie!
Who guard the Southern shores,
Whose standards brave the battle storm
Which o'er our border roars;
Your glorious sabers draw once more,
And charge the Northern foe;
And reap their columns deep,
Where the raging tempests blow,
And the iron hail in floods descends,
And the bloody torrents flow.

Ye Cavaliers of Dixie!
Though dark the tempest lower,
What arms will wear the tyrants chains,
What dastard heart will cower?
Bright o'er the night a sign shall rise
To lead to victory!
And your swords reap their hordes,
Where the battle tempests blow;
Where the iron hail in floods descends,
And the bloody torrents flow.

The South! she needs no ramparts,
No lofty towers to shield;
Your bosoms are her bulwarks strong,
Breastworks that never yield!
The thunders of your battle blades
Shall sweep the servile foe;
While their gore stains the shore,
Where the battle tempests blow;
Where the iron hail in floods descends,
And the bloody torrents flow.

The battle-flag of Dixie!
With crimson field shall flame,
Her azure cross and silver stars
Shall light her sons to fame!
When peace with olive-branch returns,
That flag's white folds shall glow
Still bright on every height,
When storm has ceased to blow,
And the battle tempests roar no more;
Nor the bloody torrents flow.

Oh! battle-flag of Dixie!

Long, long, triumphant wave!
Where'er the storms of battle roar,
Or victory crowns the brave!
The Cavaliers of Dixie!
In woman's song shall glow
The fame of your name,
When the storm has ceased to blow,
When the battle tempests rage no more
Nor the bloody torrents flow.[382]
BENJAMIN F. PORTER

Confederate veterans, 1901.

SOUTHERN MARSEILLAISE

Ye men of Southern hearts and feeling,
    Arm, Arm! your struggling country calls—
Hear ye the guns now loudly pealing,
    From Sumter's high embattled walls!
Shall a fanatic horde in power
    Send forth a base and hireling band,
    To desolate our happy land,
And make our Southern freemen cower.
        To arms, to arms! each one,
        The sword unsheathe, raise the gun,
        Then on, rush on, ye brave and free,
        To death or victory.

Now clouds of war begin to gather,
    And black and murky is our sky—
Shall we submit—no, never, never!
    Let death or freedom be our cry—
In Heaven's justice firm relying,
    We'll nobly struggle to be free,
    And bravely gain our liberty,
Or die, our Northern foes defying.
        To arms, to arms! each one,
        The sword unsheathe, raise the gun,
        Then on, rush on, ye brave and free,
        To death or victory.

The peaceful homes of Texas burning,
    And Harper's Ferry's blood-stained soil,
Proclaim how strong their hearts are yearning
    For murder, pillage, crime, and spoil.
Shall we our feelings longer smother,
    And bear with patience yet our wrongs,
    Their jeers, their crimes, their taunts and thongs,
And greet them still as friend and brother?
        To arms, to arms! each one,
        The sword unsheathe, raise the gun,
        Then on, rush on, ye brave and free,
        To death or victory.

Their tyranny we'll bear no longer,
    But burst asunder every tie,
Although in numbers they are stronger,
    We will be free, or we will die!
Too long the South has wept, bewailing
    That falsehood's dagger Yankees wield,

But freedom is our sword and shield,
And all their arts are unavailing.
    To arms, to arms! each one,
    The sword unsheathe, raise the gun,
    Then on, rush on, ye brave and free,
    To death or victory.[383]
"BEAUREGARD SONGSTER"

Confederate war heroes.

FROM THE SOUTH TO THE NORTH

There is no union when the hearts
    That once were bound together
Have felt the stroke that coldly parts
    All kindly ties forever.
Then oh! your cruel hands draw back,
    And let us be divided
In peace, since it is proved we lack
    The grace to live united.

We cannot bear your scorn and pride,
    Your malice and your taunting,
That have for years our patience tried—
    Your hypocritic canting.
We will not bow our necks beneath
    The yoke that you decree us,
We will be free, though only death
    Should have the power to free us!

Oh, Southern sons are bold to dare,
    And Southern hearts courageous.
Nor meekly will they longer bear
    Oppression so outrageous.
And you shall feel our honest wrath,
    If hearts so cold can feel;
Shall meet us in your Southern path
    And prove our Southern steel.

We ask no favor at your hand,
    No gifts and no affection;
But only peace upon our land,
    And none of your protection.
We ask you now, henceforth, to know
    We are a separate nation;
And be assured we'll fully show
    We scorn your "proclamation."[384]

We were not first to break the peace,
    That blessed our happy land;
We loved the quiet, calm, and ease,
    Too well to raise a hand,
Till fierce oppression stronger grew,
    And bitter were your sneers—
Then to our land we must be true,
    Or show a coward's fears!

We loved our banner while it waved
    An emblem of our Union,
The fiercest danger we had braved
    To guard that sweet communion.
But when it proved that "stripes" alone
    Were for our sunny South,
And all the "stars" in triumph shone
    Above the chilly North—

Then, not till then, our voices rose
    In one tumultuous wave—
We will the tyranny oppose,
    Or find a bloody grave!
Another flag shall lead our hosts
    To battle on the plain,
The "rebels" will defy your boasts,
    And prove your sneering vain!

There is no danger we could fear—
    No hardship or privation—
To free the land we hold so dear,
    From tyrannous dictation.
Blockade her ports—her seas shall swell
    Beneath your ships of war,
And every breeze in anger tell
    Your tyranny afar.

Her wealth may fail—her commerce droop
    With every foreign nation;
But mark you, if her pride shall stoop,
    Or her determination!
The products of her fields will be
    For food and raiment too—
From mountain cliff to rolling sea
    Her children will be true.

Her banner may not always wave
    On victory's fickle breath,
The young, chivalrous, and the brave,
    May feel the hand of death.
But, when her gallant sons have died,
    Her daughters will remain—
Nor crushed will be the Southern pride,
    Till they too, all are slain.[385]
C. L. S.

THE CONFEDERATE FLAG

Flag of the South! Flag of the free!
   Thy stars shall cheer each eye,
Thy folds a sacred banner be,
   To all beneath our sky;
From where the blue Ohio flows,
   Far to the sea-gulf's stream,
Borne by each gentle breath that blows,
   Thy hues shall flush and gleam.

Flag of the South! Flag of the free!
   Type of a new estate,
Thy folds shall wave o'er land and sea,
   And heart and home elate;
At thy approach shall tyrants quail
   And despots, trembling, flee;
Nor wrong thy sway of right assail—
   Nought mar thy liberty.

Flag of the South! Flag of the free!
   Bright symbol of a land
Wrung from the grasp of tyranny,
   Ere fettered heart and hand;
Freedom fixed in thy firm embrace,
   A home for age shall find,
Linking the high hopes of our race
   With the grand march of mind.

Flag of the South! Flag of the free!
   The one to which we clung
In years agone, hath ceased to be
   The pride on which we hung;
Long trampled in the dust, that flag
   Hath lost the charm it bore;
No longer vale, and glen, and crag,
   Swell with its praise of yore.

Flag of the South! Flag of the free!
   Type of the Land of Flowers;
Thy stars shall light our victory
   O'er all contending powers;
Where law and order still shall reign,
   Thou shall a signal be
To man, that he may still attain
   The boon of Liberty![386]

J. R. BARRICK

PATRIOTISM

The holy fire that nerved the Greek
    To make his stand at Marathon,
Until the last red foeman's shriek
    Proclaimed that Freedom's fight was won,
Still lives unquenched—unquenchable!
    Through every age its fires will burn—
Lives in the hermit's lonely cell,
    And springs from every storied urn!

The hearthstone embers hold the spark
    Where fell Oppression's foot hath trod;
Through Superstition's shadow dark
    It flashes to the living God!
From Moscow's ashes spring the Russ;
    In Warsaw Poland lives again;
Schamyl, on frosty Caucasus,
    Strikes Liberty's electric chain!

Tell's freedom-beacon lights the Swiss;
    Vainly the invader ever strives;
He finds "Sic Semper Tyrannis"
    In San Jacinto's bowie-knives!
Than these—than all—a holier fire
    Now burns thy soul, Virginia's son!
Strike then for wife, babe, gray-haired sire;
    Strike for the grave of Washington!

The Northern rabble aims for greed;
    The hireling parson goads the train—
In that foul crop from bigot seed,
    Old "Praise God Barebones" howls again!
We welcome them to "Southern lands"—
    We welcome them to "Southern slaves"—
We welcome them "with bloody hands
    To hospitable Southern graves!"[387]
UNKNOWN

THE CONFEDERATE FLAG

Bright banner of freedom, with pride I unfold thee;
Fair flag of my country, with love I behold thee,
Gleaming above us, in freshness and youth,
Emblem of liberty—symbol of truth;
For this flag of my country in triumph shall wave
O'er the Southerner's home and the Southerner's grave.

All bright are the stars that are beaming upon us,
And bold are the bars that are gleaming above us;
The one shall increase in their number and light,
The other grow bolder in power and might;
For this flag of my country in triumph shall wave
O'er the Southerner's home and the Southerner's grave.

Those bars of bright red show our firm resolution
To die, if need be, shielding thee from pollution;
For man in this hour must give all he holds dear,
And woman her prayers and her words of high cheer,
If they wish this fair banner in triumph to wave
O'er the Southerner's home and the Southerner's grave.

To the great God of battles we look with reliance;
On our fierce Northern foe with contempt and defiance;
For the South shall smile on in her fragrance and bloom
When the North is fast sinking in silence and gloom;
For the flag of our country in triumph must wave
O'er the Southerner's home and the Southerner's grave.[388]
MRS. C. D. ELDER

THE SOUTH

The bright rose of beauty, unnurtured by art,
And purity's lily doth thrive in thy heart,
While honor hath crowned thee with glory's bright ray,
And Flora hath decked thee with flowers of May.
Oh, beautiful South! cherished home of my birth,
Thou fairest, thou loveliest land of the earth!
My heart, like the ivy, still clings unto thee,
Oh, beautiful, beautiful land of the free!
      Chorus—The South! the South! my own beautiful South!
      Land of chivalry! home of liberty!
      Fondly I love thee, dear land of the South!
      Dear land of the South! dear land of the South!

Dear liberty, virtue, and truth, most sublime,
The flowers that bloom in that sun-smiling clime,
And these the base tyrant would crush to the earth,
And mangle and bruise on the soil of their birth.
All crimson thy land, with the life-glowing flood,
And dabble his hands in thy heart's reeking blood!
But oh! by the God of the righteous and free,
Bright region! it never! no, never! shall be.

Like swarms of foul demons, his minions come down,
And their war-rusted weapons insultingly frown,
To fright thy fair fields with their bloody alarms,
And rob thee, dear land, of all of thy charms.
But thy free spirit still rides on the swift gale,
Like the eagle that sweeps o'er the mountain and dale;
And thy sons, they rush forth with the courage of men,
To fight, and to bleed, and to conquer again.

The tyrant, with shackles, would manacle thee—
Would strangle thy spirit, dear land of the free,
Would trample the banner of right in the dust,
And yoke thee with iron, proud queen of the just!
But the hearts of thy sons, unappalled by a fear,
As their swords leap up fiercely and flame in the air,
Now swear that it never! no! never! shall be,
Bright queen of the lovely! sweet home of the free!
      Chorus—The South! the South! my own beautiful South!
      Land of chivalry! home of liberty!
      Fondly I love thee, dear land of the South!
      Dear land of the South! dear land of the South![389]

CHARLIE WILDWOOD

OLD BETSY

Come, with the rifle so long in your keeping,
    Clean the old gun up and hurry it forth;
Better to die while "Old Betsy" is speaking
    Than live with arms folded the slave of the North.

Hear ye the yelp of the North-wolf resounding,
    Scenting the blood of the warm-hearted South;
Quick! or his villainous feet will be bounding
    Where the gore of our maidens may drip from his mouth.

Oft in the wildwood "Old Bess" has relieved you,
    When the fierce bear was cut down in his track—
If at that moment she never deceived you,
    Trust her to-day with this ravenous pack.

Then come, with the rifle so long in your keeping,
    Clean the old girl up and hurry her forth;
Better to die while "Old Betsy" is speaking
    Than live with arms folded the slave of the North.[390]
JOHN KILLUM

NO SURRENDER

Ever constant, ever true,
　　Let the word be, No Surrender.
Boldly dare and greatly do!
They shall bring us safely through,
　　No Surrender; No Surrender.
And though Fortune's smiles be few,
Hope is always springing new,
Still inspiring me and you,
　　With a magic No Surrender.

Nail the colors to the mast,
　　Shouting gladly, No Surrender;
Troubles near are all but past,
Serve them as you did the last.
　　No Surrender, No Surrender;
Though the skies be overcast,
And upon the sleety blast
Disappointment gathers fast,
　　Beat them off with No Surrender!

Constant and courageous still,
　　Mind, the word is, No Surrender;
Battle, though it be up hill,
Stagger not at seeming ill,
　　No Surrender, No Surrender.
Hope, and thus your hope fulfill;
There's a way where there's a will,
And the way all cares to kill
　　Is to give them No Surrender.[391]
N. P. W.

THE DYING SOLDIER

Gather round him where he's lying,
    Hush your footsteps, whisper low,
For a soldier here is dying,
    In the sunset's radiant glow.

Beating, beating, slowly beating,
    Runs the life-blood through his frame;
Swift the soldier's breath is fleeting,
    And he calls his mother's name:

"Mother, mother, come and kiss me,
    Ere my spirit fades away,
For I know you oft will miss me,
    When you watch the sinking day.

"Brother, sister, nearer, nearer!
    Place, oh, place your hands in mine,
You whose love than life was dearer,
    Let your arms around me twine.

"Father, see the sun is fading
    From the hill-tops of the west,
And the valley night is shading—
    Farewell, loved ones, I'm at rest."

Dying, dying! yes, he's dying!
    Close the eyelids, let him rest;
No more sorrow, no more sighing,
    E'er again shall heave his breast.

Sleeping, sleeping, calmly sleeping,
    In the church-yard cold and drear,
And the wintry winds are heaping
    O'er him leaflets brown and sear.

And he's resting, where forever
    Clang of trumpet, roll of drum,
Roar of cannon, never, never,
    Never more to him shall come.[392]
JAMES A. MECKLIN

VOICES OF THE FOUNDING FATHERS

(Or What the Spirits of the Fathers of the First Revolution Say to Their Sons now Engaged in the Second)

We are watching that land where Liberty woke—
Like beams of the morning through darkness it broke—
Then up from the mountain the bold eagle sprung,
And wide to the breeze his broad pinions flung.
    Rise! rise! ye sons of the South and be free!

The mighty have fallen, yet death can not chill,
Those noble emotions the soul ever thrill;
The grave hath no confines the spirit to hold,
While back to its kindred it flies to unfold
    Truth! Truth! safeguard of the South and the free.

Shall Washington rest, while a wail of discord
Reminds him the North is forgetting the Lord?
Will hero and statesman—the country's bright light—
Look down without pity from yonder far height,
    On this Land of Hope, for the brave and the free?

That same noble spirit now watches above,
With thousands of others, to guide and guard you with love;
For here, true, earnest, and brave men are found,
With hearts uncorrupted, to their native land bound.
    Awake! awake! O ye sons of the South, and be free!

Down with the hireling that seeks now to rend
The homes which your ancestors fought to defend;
Rekindle the beacon ere the last spark is fled,
And light up the camp-fires round Liberty's bed!
    Ye sons of the sunny South, strike to be free!

Fear not the Northern despot, or his feeble frown,
Who seeks, through his minions, the South to put down;
Look to your God, from whence comes all power,
And seek His aid and protection in each darkened hour.
    Strike again and again, O ye sons of the free!

Carolina's sons to this platform have come—
Protection to Liberty, to fireside, and home—
Their watch-word to-day, as their Fathers' of old,
Truth, Justice, and Freedom, before Northern gold.
    Ye are the sons of the Fathers who bled to be free!

Then loud ring the anvil, the hammer, and bell;
The South her new anthem, say what does it tell?
Cotton, Grain, and Sugar, have proved threefold cord—
Columbia, the envied, the blest of the Lord!
    Sun of the sunny land, shine still o'er the free!

On heaven's fair arches, see graven the names
Of patriot and soldier, who drained life's pure veins;
Then down with the Northern despot, let him hide his head,
Who by heartless oppression would sever one thread
    Of this Southern Confederacy, the hope of the free!

Once again at the altar, brothers, gather and kneel;
Our pledge, the South—one family, in woe or in weal;
One God and one Country—in peace or in war;
The South, Free, United, and Truth the pole-star
    Of this sunny land, which for ye must be free![393]
HENRY LOMAS

Thomas Jefferson.

HEART-VICTORIES

There's not a stately hall,
    There's not a cottage fair,
That proudly stands on Southern soil,
    Or softly nestles there,
But in its peaceful walls,
    With wealth or comfort blest,
A stormy battle fierce hath raged
    In gentle woman's breast.

There Love, the true, the brave,
    The beautiful, the strong,
Wrestles with Duty, gaunt and stern,
    Wrestles and struggles long;
He falls—no more again
    His giant foe to meet;
Bleeding at every opening vein,
    Love falls at Duty's feet.

Oh! daughter of the South!
    No victor's crown be thine;
Not thine, upon the tented field,
    In martial pomp to shine;
But, with unfaltering trust
    In Him who rules on high,
To deck thy loved ones for the fray,
    And send them forth to die.

With wildly throbbing heart—
    With faint and trembling breath—
The maiden speeds her lover on,
    To victory or death;
Forth from caressing arms,
    The mother sends her son,
And bids him nobly battle on,
    Till the last field is won.

While she, the tried, the true,
    The loving wife of years,
Chokes down the rising agony,
    Drives back the starting tears:
"I yield thee up," she cries,
    "In the country's cause to fight;
Strike for our own, our children's home,
    And God defend the right."

Oh! daughter of the South,
    When our fair land is free,
When peace her lovely mantle throws
    Softly o'er land and sea,
History shall tell, how thou
    Hast nobly borne thy part,
And won the proudest triumphs yet—
    The victories of the heart.[394]

A CONFEDERATE SOLDIER'S WIFE

GOD SAVE THE SOUTH

God bless our Southern land!
Guard our beloved land!
    God save the South!
Make us victorious,
Happy and glorious;
Spread Thy shield over us;
    God save the South!

God of our sires, arise!
Scatter our enemies,
    Who mock Thy truth;
Confound their politics,
Frustrate their knavish tricks:
In Thee our faith we fix;
    God save the South!

In the fierce battle-hour,
With Thine almighty power,
    Assist our youth;
May they, with victory crowned,
Joining our choral round,
With heart and voice resound,
    "God save the South!"[395]
REUBEN NASON

Confederate monument, Baltimore, Maryland.

THE BOY-SOLDIER

He is acting o'er the battle,
    With his cap and feather gay,
Singing out his soldier prattle,
    In a mockish, manly way—
With the boldest, bravest footstep,
    Treading firmly up and down,
And his banner waving softly
    O'er his boyish locks of brown.

And I sit beside him sewing,
    With a busy heart and hand,
For the gallant soldiers going
    To the far-off battle-land;
And I gaze upon my jewel,
    In his baby-spirit bold,
My little blue-eyed soldier,
    Just a second summer old.

Still a deep, deep well of feeling,
    In my mother's heart is stirred,
And the tears come softly stealing
    At each imitative word.

There's a struggle in my bosom,
    For I love my darling boy—
He's the gladness of my spirit,
    He's the sunlight of my joy!
Yet I think upon my country,
    And my spirit groweth bold,
Oh! I wish my blue-eyed soldier
    Were but twenty summers old!

I would speed him to the battle,
    I would arm him for the fight,
I would give him to his country,
    For his country's wrong and right!
I would nerve his hand with blessing,
    From the "God of Battles" won;
With His helmet and His armor,
    I would cover o'er my son.

Oh! I know there'd be a struggle,
    For I love my darling boy;
He's the gladness of my spirit,
    He's the sunlight of my joy!

Yet in thinking of my country,
    Oh! my spirit groweth bold;
And I wish my blue-eyed soldier
    Were but twenty summers old.[396]
A LADY OF SAVANNAH

CONFEDERATE LAND

States of the South! Confederate land!
    Our foe has come—the hour is nigh;
His bale-fires rise on every hand—
    Rise as one man, to do or die!
From mountain, vale, and prairie wide,
    From forest vast, and field, and glen,
And crowded city, pour thy tide,
    Oh! fervid South! of patriot men.
        Up! old and young; the weak, be strong!
        Rise for the right—hurl back the wrong,
        And foot to foot, and hand to hand,
        Strike for our own Confederate land!

Make every house, and rock, and tree,
    And hill, your forts; and fen and flood
Yield not! our soil shall rather be
    One waste of flame, one sea of blood!
Fear not their steel, but fear their gold—
    Not Yankee force, but Yankee fraud;
Trust not the race—as false as cold—
    Whose very prayers are lies to God.
        Up! old and young; the weak, be strong!
        Rise for the right—hurl back the wrong,
        And foot to foot, and hand to hand,
        Strike for our own Confederate land!

Armed, or unarmed, stand fearless forth,
    Sons of the South! stand, wife and maid!
Against the foul insidious North,
    Our babes shall wield the battle-blade!
On! though perennial be the strife,
    For honor dear, for hearth-stone fire;
Give blow for blow! take life for life!
    "Strike! till the last armed foe expire!"
        Up! old and young; the weak, be strong!
        Rise for the right—hurl back the wrong,
        And foot to foot, and hand to hand,
        Strike for our own Confederate land![397]

H. H. STRAWBRIDGE

A CHRISTMAS OF LONG AGO

I am thinking to-night in sadness
    Of a Christmas of long ago,
When the air was filled with gladness,
    And the earth was wrapped in snow;
When the stars like diamonds glistened
    And the night was crisp and cold,
As I eagerly watched and listened
    For the Santa Claus of old.

    The forest was robbed of its treasures,
        The house was a mass of green,
    And I reveled in Christmas pleasures,
        At the dawn of Aurora's sheen;
    Some talked of the Savior's mission,
        But I of my pretty toys;
    Some knelt in devout petition—
        I romped and played with the boys.

We went to the pond for skating,
    To the stable to take a ride,
And we found new joys awaiting,
    To whatever spot we hied;
But the climax of my story
    Was that evening's fireworks show!
Went out in a blaze of glory—
    That Christmas of long ago!

    But in sadness I think of that Christmas,
        For many then happy and gay
    Have gone to the realm of silence
        And sleep in their beds of clay;
    The hands that filled kindly my stockings,
        I shall grasp in this world no more,
    But when at Heaven's portals I'm knocking
        They'll open the beautiful door.

They will lead me in tenderness clinging,
    And place me before the throne,
Where the choirs angelic are singing
    And the heavenly gifts are strown,
And there in the realm of glory,
    With my loved ones at my side,
I'll repeat the old Bethlehem story
    And join in that Christmas tide.[398]
MORTON BRYAN WHARTON

THE GUERILLAS

Awake! and to horse my brothers,
    For the dawn is glimmering gray,
And hark! in the crackling brushwood,
    There are feet that tread this way.

"Who cometh?" "A friend." "What tidings?"
    "O God! I sicken to tell,
For the earth seems earth no longer,
    And its sights are the sights of hell.

"There's rapine and fire and slaughter,
    From the mountain down to the shore,
There's blood on the trampled harvest,
    And blood on the homestead floor.

"From the far-off conquered cities,
    Comes the voice of a stifled wail,
And the shrieks and moans of the homeless
    Ring like the dirge of a gale.

"I have seen from the smoking village,
    Our mothers and daughters fly,
I've seen where the little children,
    Sank down in the furrows to die.

"On the banks of the battle-stained river,
    I stood as the moonlight shone,
And it glared on the face of my brother,
    As the sad wave swept him on.

"Where my home was glad, are ashes,
    And horror and shame had been there,
For I found on the fallen lintel,
    This tress of my wife's torn hair.

"They are turning the slave upon us,
    And with more than the fiend's worst art.
Have uncovered the fires of the savage,
    That slept in his untaught heart.

"The ties to our hearts that bound him,
    They have rent with curses away,
And madden him in their madness
    To be almost as brutal as they.

"With halter and torch and Bible,
    And hymns to the sound of the drum,
They preach the gospel of murder,
    And pray for lust's kingdom to come.

"To saddle! my brothers! to saddle!
    Look up to the rising sun,
And ask of the God who shines there,
    Whether deeds like these shall be done.

"Whither the vandal cometh,
    Press home to his heart with your steel,
And where'er at his bosom ye cannot,
    Like the serpent, go strike at his heel.

"Through thicket and wood go hunt him,
    Creep up to his camp-fire side,
And let ten of his corpses blacken,
    Where one of our brothers hath died.

"In his fainting footsore marches,
    In his flight from the stricken fray,
In the snare of the lonely ambush,
    The debts that we owe him, pay.

"In God's hands alone is vengeance,
    But he strikes with the hands of men,
And his blight would wither our manhood,
    If we smote not the smiter again.

"By the graves where our fathers slumber,
    By the shrines where our mothers prayed,
By our homes and hopes of freedom,
    Let every man swear by his blade.—

"That he will not sheathe nor stay it,
    Till from point to hilt it glow,
With the flush of Almighty justice,
    In the blood of the cruel foe."

They swore; and the answering sunlight
    Leapt from their lifted swords,
And the hate in their hearts made echo,
    To the wrath of their burning words.[399]
SEVERN TEACKLE WALLIS

A CRY TO ARMS

Ho! woodsmen of the mountain-side!
    Ho! dwellers in the vales!
Ho! ye who by the chafing tide
    Have roughened in the gales!
Leave barn and byre, leave kin and cot,
    Lay by the bloodless spade;
Let desk, and case, and counter rot,
    And burn your books of trade.

The despot roves your fairest lands;
    And till he flies or fears,
Your fields must grow but armed bands,
    Your sheaves be sheaves of spears!
Give up to mildew and to rust
    The useless tools of gain;
And feed your country's sacred dust
    With floods of crimson rain!

Come, with the weapons at your call—
    With musket, pike, or knife;
He wields the deadliest blade of all
    Who lightest holds his life.
The arm that drives its unbought blows
    With all a patriot's scorn,
Might brain a tyrant with a rose,
    Or stab him with a thorn.

Does any falter? let him turn
    To some brave maiden's eyes,
And catch the holy fires that burn
    In those sublunar skies.
Oh! could you like your women feel,
    And in their spirit march,
A day might see your lines of steel
    Beneath the victor's arch.

What hope, O God! would not grow warm
    When thoughts like these give cheer?
The lily calmly braves the storm,
    And shall the palm-tree fear?
No! rather let its branches court
    The rack that sweeps the plain;
And from the lily's regal port
    Learn how to breast the strain!

Ho! woodsmen of the mountain-side!
    Ho! dwellers in the vales!
Ho! ye who by the roaring tide
    Have roughened in the gales!
Come! flocking gayly to the fight
    From forest, hill, and lake;
We battle for our country's right,
    And for the lily's sake![400]
HENRY TIMROD

THE TOURNAMENT

Lists all white and blue in the skies;
    And the people hurried amain
To the Tournament under the ladies' eyes
    Where jousted Heart and Brain.

Blow, herald, blow! There entered Heart,
    A youth in crimson and gold.
Blow, herald, blow! Brain stood apart,
    Steel-armored, glittering, cold.

Heart's palfrey caracoled gayly round,
    Heart tra-li-raed merrily;
But Brain sat still, with never a sound—
    Full cynical-calm was he.

Heart's helmet-crest bore favors three
    From his lady's white hand caught;
Brain's casque was bare as Fact—not he
    Or favor gave or sought.

Blow, herald, blow! Heart shot a glance
    To catch his lady's eye;
But Brain looked straight a-front, his lance
    To aim more faithfully.

They charged, they struck; both fell, both bled;
    Brain rose again, ungloved;
Heart fainting smiled, and softly said,
    "My love to my Beloved!"

Heart and Brain! no more be twain,
    Throb and think, one flesh again!
Lo! they weep, they turn, they run,
    Lo! they kiss: Love, thou art one![401]
SIDNEY LANIER

THE INVOCATION

God bless the land of flowers,
And turn its winter hours
    To bright summer time!
Be the brave soldier's friend,
And from dangers defend,
When Northern balls descend
    On the Southern line!

Father, we implore Thee,
Let Thy people go free
    From their foes once more!
And they will bend the knee,
And Thine the praise shall be,
On sunny land and sea,
    As in days of yore!

Lord, bid the carnage cease,
Let the banner of peace
    Again be unfurled!
Two nations make from one,
And when the work is done,
Over both reign alone—
    Saviour of the world![402]
B. W. W.

The End

APPENDICES

Why the South fought . . .

APPENDIX A

SINCE I WROTE THESE SONG LYRICS IN 2006, THEY ARE OBVIOUSLY NOT VICTORIAN. HOWEVER, THEY ARE CONFEDERATE AND ARE SET IN THE VICTORIAN PERIOD (IN THIS CASE, IN THE LATE 1800S). THUS, I HAVE INCLUDED THIS POEM HERE AS MY PERSONAL CONTRIBUTION TO THE GENRE. "SOMEONE'S DARLIN'" WAS A VICTORIAN TERM FOR A DECEASED SOLDIER, OFTEN UNKNOWN.

SOMEONE'S DARLIN'

It was a cool grey morning in Autumn,
    Time to restock winter supplies;
Rode my horse down the trail toward Richmond,
    Under dark and unhappy skies.

I followed White Oak Creek into Sandston,
    Across the Henrico County line;
There lay a Civil War cemetery
    To the Battle of Seven Pines.

CHORUS
I cast my eyes up and down the endless rows
    At the names on the faded white stones—
    These young men died on that Virginia field alone.
And I thought of those they left behind,
The anger, the grief, and despair,
    Because that's someone's darlin' buried there.

Took my hat off and stood there in silence,
    And I prayed for America's sons;
My heart was filled with pride and with sorrow,
    As I mourned the sweet fallen ones.

Didn't recognize any names there,
    So I climbed my horse to go on my way;
When I glanced at one last lonely headstone,
    And there I saw my grandfather's name.

CHORUS
I cast my eyes up and down the endless rows
    At the names on the faded white stones—
    These young men died on that Virginia field alone.
And I thought of those they left behind,
The anger, the grief, and despair,
    Because that's someone's darlin' buried there.
    Because that's someone's darlin' lyin' there.
    That's someone's darlin' buried there.[403]
LOCHLAINN SEABROOK (BMI-Nashville, Copyright © 2006)

APPENDIX B

THOUGH THIS VICTORIAN POEM WAS FIRST PUBLISHED IN 1838, AND IS THUS FROM THE ANTEBELLUM PERIOD (NOT A WAR POEM), I HAVE INCLUDED IT HERE NOT ONLY FOR ITS UNERRING FORESHADOWING OF LINCOLN'S WAR, BUT FOR ITS ALLURING AND ENERGETIC PRO-SOUTH SENTIMENT—AND ALSO BECAUSE IT PERFECTLY ARTICULATES ONE OF THE MANY REASONS THE SOUTHERN PEOPLE TOOK UP ARMS AGAINST THE YANKEE INVADERS.

LAND OF THE SOUTH

Land of the South!—imperial land!—
    How proud thy mountains rise!
How sweet thy scenes on every hand!
    How fair thy covering skies!
But not for this—oh, not for these—
    I love thy fields to roam;
Thou hast a dearer spell to me,—
    Thou art my native home!

Thy rivers roll their liquid wealth,
    Unequaled to the sea;
Thy hills and valleys bloom with health,
    And green with verdure be!
But not for thy proud ocean streams,
    Not for thy azure dome,
Sweet, sunny South, I cling to thee,—
    Thou art my native home!

I've stood beneath Italia's clime,
    Beloved of tale and song,
On Helvyn's[404] hills, proud and sublime,
    Where nature's wonders throng;
By Tempe's classic sunlit streams,
    Where Gods, of old, did roam,—
But ne'er have found so fair a land
    As thou, my native home!

And thou hast prouder glories, too,
    Than nature ever gave;
Peace sheds o'er thee her genial dew,
    And Freedom's pinions wave;
Fair Science flings her pearls around,
    Religion lifts her dome,—
These, these endear thee to my heart,
    My own, loved native home!

And "Heaven's best gift to man" is thine
    God bless thy rosy girls!
Like sylvan flowers they sweetly shine,
    Their hearts are pure as pearls!
And grace and goodness circle them,
    Where'er their footsteps roam;
How can I then, whilst loving them,
    Not love my native home?

Land of the South!—imperial land!—
    Then here's a health to thee:
Long as thy mountain barriers stand,
    May'st thou be blest and free!
May dark dissension's banner ne'er
    Wave o'er thy fertile loam!
But should it come, there's one will die
    To save his native home![405]
ALEXANDER BEAUFORT MEEK

APPENDIX C

MIRABEAU B. LAMAR, A U.S. GENERAL FROM GEORGIA, WAS BORN IN 1798 AND DIED IN 1859, TWO YEARS BEFORE THE START OF LINCOLN'S WAR. LIKE MOST OTHER SOUTHERNERS, HOWEVER, HE BELIEVED THAT A MAJOR CONFLICT WITH THE LIBERAL NORTH WAS IMMINENT, A PROPHETIC FEELING WHICH INSPIRED THE FOLLOWING POEM. SINCE THIS POEM WAS WRITTEN BEFORE 1857 (THE YEAR IT WAS PUBLISHED), IT CANNOT BE STRICTLY CONSIDERED A "CIVIL WAR" POEM. IT IS, IN FACT, AN ANTEBELLUM PRO-SOUTH WORK. NONETHELESS, I INCLUDE IT BECAUSE IT PROVIDES FURTHER EVIDENCE OF THE EMOTIONAL MOOD IN THE SOUTH PRIOR TO 1861.

ARM FOR THE SOUTHERN LAND

Arm for the Southern Land,
    All fear of death disdaining;
Low lay the tyrant band,
    Our sacred rights profaning!
Each hero draws in Freedom's cause,
    And meets the foe with bravery;
The servile race, and Tory base,
    May safety seek in slavery.
Chains for the dastard knave—
    Recreant limbs should wear them;
But blessings on the brave
    Whose valor will not bear them!

Stand by your injured State,
    And let no feuds divide you;
On tyrants pour your hate,
    And common vengeance guide you.
Our foes should feel proud freemen's steel,
    For freemen's rights contending;
Where'er they die, there let them lie,
    To dust in scorn descending.
Thus may each traitor fall
    Who dare as foe invade us;
Eternal fame to all
    Who shall in battle aid us!

Proud land! shall she invoke
    Another's hand to right her?
No! her own avenging stroke
    Shall backward roll the smiter.
Ye tyrant band, with ropes of sand
    Go bind the rushing river;
More weak and vain your cursed chain,
    While God is freedom's giver.
Then welcome to the day
    We meet the proud oppressor,
For God will be our stay,
    Our right hand and redresser.[406]
U.S. GENERAL MIRABEAU BUONAPARTE LAMAR

NOTES

1. Woods, p. 47.
2. On Lincoln's socialistic, Marxist, and communist thoughts, ideas, and tendencies, see e.g., McCarty, passim; Browder, passim; Benson and Kennedy, passim.
3. See J. W. Jones, TDMV, pp. 144, 200-201, 273.
4. See Seabrook, TAHSR, passim. See also, Pollard, LC, p. 178; J. H. Franklin, pp. 101, 111, 130, 149; Nicolay and Hay, ALCW, Vol. 1, p. 627.
5. BISG (the "Book Industry Study Group"), for example—a Left-wing organization which describes itself as "the leading book trade association for standardized best practices, research and information, and events"—gives its BISAC ("Book Industry Standards and Communications") listing for works on the War for Southern Independence under the heading "Civil War Period, 1850-1877." Nearly all books published in the U.S.A. today are under the categorizational control of this progressive group located in New York City.
6. See e.g., Seabrook, TQJD, pp. 30, 38, 76.
7. See e.g., J. Davis, RFCG, Vol. 1, pp. 55, 422; Vol. 2, pp. 4, 161, 454, 610. Besides using the term "Civil War" himself, President Davis cites numerous other individuals who use it as well.
8. See e.g., *Confederate Veteran*, March 1912, Vol. 20, No. 3, p. 122.
9. Minutes of the Eighth Annual Meeting, July 1898, p. 87.
10. The Republican Party of Lincoln was founded in 1854 by Liberals, socialists, and anti-American radicals in general, and as such has no relationship to the Republican Party of today. For more on this topic, see Seabrook, LW, passim.
11. For more on this topic, see Seabrook, ALWALJDWAC, passim.
12. Simms, pp. v-vi.
13. Ellinger, p. 17. My emphasis. Note: Ellinger was born in Baltimore, MD, in the late Victorian period.
14. Newcomer, Andrews, and Hall, p. 815.
15. F. Moore, SABOTSP, pp. 109-110.
16. Confederate Veteran, March 1901, Vol. 9, No. 3, p. 138. Note: The original title was "Dedication to the Confederate Government."
17. Confederate Veteran, May 1901, Vol. 9, No. 5, p. 213.
18. Simms, pp. 180-181. Note: Tucker (1828-1863), a lieutenant-colonel in the Confederate army, is variously known as St. George Tucker, Henry St. George Tucker, and St. George Henry Tucker. He is not to be confused with the many other famous men named "St. George Tucker" who preceded him. Tucker is said to be the son of Congressman Henry St. George Tucker (1780-1848), and the grandson of Judge St. George Tucker (1752-1827).
19. F. Moore, SABOTSP, pp. 164-166.
20. Simms, pp. 156-158.
21. Confederate Veteran, January 1893, Vol. 1, No. 1, p. 3.
22. Confederate Veteran, February 1899, Vol. 7, No. 2, p. 86.
23. Confederate Veteran, January 1893, Vol. 1, No. 1, p. 32.
24. Manley, pp. 390-392.
25. Confederate Veteran, August 1895, Vol. 3, No. 8, p. 238.

26. Kent, pp. 68-70. The author of this poem is usually credited to a woman, Ethel Lynn Beers, or Ethelinda (Elliott) Beers. However, internal evidence proves that it was written by a male; a Confederate soldier, in fact; one named Thaddeus Oliver of Twiggs County, GA.
27. Banks, pp. 188-189.
28. De Leon, pp. 27-28.
29. Eggleston, pp. 212-213.
30. Bronson, pp. 497-498.
31. Manley, pp. 324, 326.
32. Confederate Veteran, February 1893, Vol. 1, No. 2, p. 40.
33. Confederate Veteran, April 1893, Vol. 1, No. 4, p. 111.
34. F. Moore, SABOTSP, pp. 226-227.
35. Confederate Veteran, January 1895, Vol. 3, No. 1, p. 21.
36. A reference to "The Star Spangled Banner," written by Mrs. Blunt's ancestor Francis Scott Key.
37. A reference to the U.S. Flag.
38. A reference to the C.S. Flag.
39. A reference to Scotland's St. Andrew's Cross, which forms the Christian "x" on the C.S. flags.
40. F. Moore, pp. SABOTSP, pp. 292-294.
41. Simms, pp. 430-432. Written shortly after the Seven Days Battle, near Richmond.
42. Browne, pp. 119-120. Original note: Manassas, August 30, 1862.
43. Browne, pp. 122-124. Original note: Lee's first invasion of Maryland, September, 1862.
44. F. Moore, SABOTSP, pp. 149-151.
45. Browne, pp. 140-142. Original note: On the appointment of General Joseph E. Johnston to the command of the Confederate armies in the West, November, 1862.
46. *Agen* is an obsolete spelling of "again."
47. Browne, pp. 146-147. Original note: In the Army of Northern Virginia.
48. F. Moore, SABOTSP, pp. 111-114.
49. Confederate Veteran, October 1894, Vol. 2, No. 10, p. 316.
50. Kent, pp. 72-73.
51. Confederate Veteran, September 1898, Vol. 6, No. 9, p. 415.
52. Fort Moultrie.
53. Simms, pp. 319-322.
54. Confederate Veteran, January 1901, Vol. 9, No. 1, p. 40. Note: This 1863 poem, anti-North and pro-South in tone, was written by Yanks for Yanks.
55. Browne, pp. 167-168.
56. Fulton, pp. 247-248.
57. F. Moore, SABOTSP, pp. 201-204.
58. Confederate Veteran, May 1893, Vol. 1, No. 5, p. 133.
59. Confederate Veteran, February 1894, Vol. 2, No. 2, p. 46.
60. Confederate Veteran, September 1894, Vol. 2, No. 9, p. 260. Note: I do not have the exact year this poem was composed, but it would have been in 1864 or 1865, after General Duke's release from a Yankee prison in Ohio.
61. Simms, p. 437.
62. Browne, pp. 209-211.
63. Manley, pp. 393-394.
64. Confederate Veteran, March 1895, Vol. 3, No. 3, p.74.

65. Confederate Veteran, July 1898, Vol. 6, No. 7, p. 308. The exact year this poem was written is unknown; only that it was written "during the Civil War."
66. Confederate Veteran, April 1899, Vol. 7, No. 4, p. 166.
67. F. Moore, APAIOTW, p. 32.
68. Browne, pp. 305-308. Original note: Written while Jefferson Davis was a prisoner in Fortress Monroe where he was confined far two years after the downfall of the Confederacy.
69. The Ashley River, located in Berkeley County, South Carolina.
70. Browne, pp. 272-273.
71. Confederate Veteran, March 1893, Vol. 1, No. 3, p. 77.
72. Confederate Veteran, July 1894, Vol. 2, No. 7, cover.
73. Manley, pp. 388-389.
74. Confederate Veteran, September 1894, Vol. 2, No. 9, p. 267.
75. Confederate Veteran, October 1894, Vol. 2, No. 10, p. 293.
76. C. H. Page, p. 611.
77. Confederate Veteran, January 1896, Vol. 4, No. 1, p. 1.
78. Confederate Veteran, February 1897, Vol. 5, No. 2, p. 65.
79. Confederate Veteran, August 1897, Vol. 4, No. 8, p. 437. I could not more strongly disagree with the sentiment expressed in Father Ryan's poem. It is, in fact, demonstrably false. The Confederate Flag, a symbol of American conservatism (Americanism), was not "conquered" in 1865, and the principles for which it stood are still very much alive today in the hearts and minds of all conservatives. For more on this topic, see Seabrook, LW, passim.
80. Confederate Veteran, November 1894, Vol. 2, No. 11, p. 333. This uplifting poem was written in response to Father Abram J. Ryan's pessimistic poem "The Conquered Banner."
81. Augustin, pp. 61-62.
82. F. Moore, APAIOTW, p. 11.
83. Confederate Veteran, September 1900, Vol. 8, No. 9, p. 415.
84. In the Victorian period the word "gay" meant "good-natured" or "happy-go-lucky."
85. Confederate Veteran, May 1893, Vol. 1, No. 5, p. 150.
86. Confederate Veteran, July 1898, Vol. 6, No. 7, p. 317. Note: This poem was written during the early days of "Reconstruction," when the state of Virginia was under martial law.
87. Simms, pp. 383-385. This poem appear to have been written around 1867.
88. Manly, pp. 319-321. This poem appear to have been written around 1867.
89. Kent, p. 48. Original note: Sung on the occasion of decorating the graves of the Confederate Dead at Magnolia Cemetery, Charleston, South Carolina, 1867.
90. Confederate Veteran, October 1896, Vol. 4, No. 10, pp. 356-357.
91. Simms, pp. 389-391.
92. After she was scuttled the U.S.S. *Merrimac* was rebuilt by the Confederacy as the C.S.S. *Virginia*.
93. Simms, pp. 391-393. Notes: "Buchanan" was commander of the *Merrimac*; "Hutter" was a midshipman on the *Patrick Henry*.
94. F. Moore, SABOTSP, pp. 302-304. Original note: [The lines in the fourth section] . . . were suggested by the following, published in [the Yankee publication] *Frank Leslie's Illustrated Newspaper*: "We know a great deal about war now; but, dear readers, the Southern women know more. Blood has not dripped on our door-sills yet; shells have not burst above our homesteads. Let us pray they never may."
95. Simms, pp. 410-411.
96. Simms, pp. 436-437.
97. Simms, pp. 441-442.

98. Usually spelled Israfîl, this is an Arabic name for the Jewish archangel Raphael.
99. Simms, pp. 452-454.
100. Confederate Veteran, May 1895, Vol. 1, No. 5, p. 135.
101. Confederate Veteran, February 1901, Vol. 9, No. 2, pp. 84-85.
102. Confederate Veteran, February 1896, Vol. 4, No. 2, p. 64. The occasion for this poem was a moment when, during the War, General Lee fell asleep from exhaustion on the side of a road.
103. Confederate Veteran, May 1899, Vol. 7, No. 5, p. 234.
104. Confederate Veteran, April 1901, Vol. 9, No. 4, p. 187. Original note accompanying poem: "Written, at time of President Cleveland's revocation of his famous order to restore to the Southern people their battle flags."
105. Manley, p. 372. Note: This is an excerpt from a larger work written for the laying of the cornerstone of the Lee Monument at Richmond, VA, 1887.
106. Confederate Veteran, May 1893, Vol. 1, No. 5, p. 147.
107. Confederate Veteran, February 1893, Vol. 1, No. 2, p. 33.
108. Confederate Veteran, February 1893, Vol. 1, No. 2, p. 40.
109. Confederate Veteran, February 1893, Vol. 1, No. 2, p. 53.
110. Confederate Veteran, March 1893, Vol. 1, No. 3, p. 83.
111. Confederate Veteran, June 1893, Vol. 1, No. 6, p. 175.
112. Confederate Veteran, June 1893, Vol. 1, No. 6, p. 175. Note: In 1889, the year of his death, Jefferson Davis was temporarily buried in New Orleans, Louisiana. In 1893 his remains were taken to Richmond, Virginia, and re-interred in Hollywood Cemetery.
113. Confederate Veteran, June 1893, Vol. 1, No. 6, p. 175.
114. Confederate General George Pierce Doles.
115. Confederate Veteran, July 1893, Vol. 1, No. 7, p. 198.
116. Confederate Veteran, July 1893, Vol. 1, No. 7, p. 207.
117. Confederate Veteran, July 1893, Vol. 1, No. 7, p. 208.
118. Confederate Veteran, July 1893, Vol. 1, No. 7, p. 209.
119. Confederate Veteran, July 1893, Vol. 1, No. 7, p. 209.
120. Confederate Veteran, July 1893, Vol. 1, No. 7, p. 213.
121. Confederate Veteran, August 1893, Vol. 1, No. 8, p. 236.
122. Confederate Veteran, August 1893, Vol. 1, No. 8, p. 237.
123. Confederate Veteran, August 1893, Vol. 1, No. 8, p. 248.
124. Simms, pp. 22-24.
125. Confederate Veteran, September 1893, Vol. 1, No. 9, p. 277.
126. Confederate Veteran, September 1893, Vol. 1, No. 9, p. 277.
127. Confederate Veteran, October 1893, Vol. 1, No. 10, p. 296.
128. Confederate Veteran, October 1893, Vol. 1, No. 10, p. 303.
129. Confederate Veteran, December 1893, Vol. 1, No. 12, p. 373.
130. Confederate Veteran, February 1894, Vol. 2, No. 2, p. 46.
131. Confederate Veteran, March 1894, Vol. 2, No. 3, p. 65.
132. Confederate Veteran, April 1894, Vol. 2, No. 4, p. 109. This poem was read on Confederate Memorial Day in 1894.
133. Confederate Veteran, April 1894, Vol. 2, No. 4, p. 114.
134. Confederate Veteran, April 1894, Vol. 2, No. 4, p. 119.
135. Confederate Veteran, May 1894, Vol. 2, No. 5, p. 143.
136. Confederate Veteran, June 1894, Vol. 2, No. 6, p. 178.
137. Confederate Veteran, June 1894, Vol. 2, No. 6, p. 180.

138. Confederate Veteran, August 1894, Vol. 2, No. 8, p. 245.
139. Confederate Veteran, September 1894, Vol. 2, No. 9, p. 273.
140. Confederate Veteran, September 1894, Vol. 2, No. 9, p. 274.
141. Confederate Veteran, September 1894, Vol. 2, No. 9, p. 275.
142. Confederate Veteran, September 1894, Vol. 2, No. 9, p. 273.
143. Confederate Veteran, September 1894, Vol. 2, No. 9, p. 278.
144. Confederate Veteran, September 1894, Vol. 2, No. 9, p. 280.
145. Confederate Veteran, September 1894, Vol. 2, No. 9, p. 283.
146. Simms, pp. 130-131.
147. Confederate Veteran, October 1894, Vol. 2, No. 10, p. 308.
148. Confederate Veteran, December 1894, Vol. 2, No. 12, p. 354.
149. Confederate Veteran, December 1894, Vol. 2, No. 12, p. 375.
150. Confederate Veteran, March 1895, Vol. 3, No. 3, p. 74.
151. Watson, pp. 186-187.
152. Confederate Veteran, June 1895, Vol. 3, No. 6, p. 184.
153. Confederate Veteran, July 1895, Vol. 3, No. 7, p. 210.
154. Confederate Veteran, July 1895, Vol. 3, No. 7, p. 222. Note: The author may possibly be William Hodges.
155. Confederate Veteran, August 1895, Vol. 3, No. 8, p. 228.
156. Confederate Veteran, August 1895, Vol. 3, No. 8, p. 232.
157. Confederate Veteran, August 1895, Vol. 3, No. 8, p. 239. Note: The author may possibly be Mrs. Lee C. Harby.
158. Confederate Veteran, August 1895, Vol. 3, No. 8, p. 245.
159. Confederate Veteran, August 1895, Vol. 3, No. 8, pp. 247-248.
160. Confederate Veteran, August 1895, Vol. 3, No. 8, p. 248.
161. Confederate Veteran, October 1895, Vol. 3, No. 10, p. 303. Note accompanying the poem: "On the dedication of the monument to the Confederate dead at Oakwood Cemetery, Chicago, by the First Regiment Infantry, I.N.G., Decoration Day, August 25, 1895."
162. Confederate Veteran, November 1895, Vol. 3, No. 11, p. 342.
163. Confederate Veteran, December 1895, Vol. 3, No. 12, p. 378.
164. Confederate Veteran, December 1895, Vol. 3, No. 12, p. 382.
165. Confederate Veteran, December 1895, Vol. 3, No. 12, p. 385.
166. Original note: Captain Thomas Pelot, C.S.N., killed at the capture of the *Water Witch*.
167. Simms, pp. 457-458.
168. Confederate Veteran, December 1895, Vol. 3, No. 12, p. 386.
169. Confederate Veteran, January 1896, Vol. 4, No. 1, p. 2.
170. Confederate Veteran, February 1896, Vol. 4, No. 2, p. 43. Note: The Battle of Franklin (II), Tennessee, was fought on November 30, 1864. For more on this conflict, see Seabrook, EOTBOF, passim.
171. Confederate Veteran, February 1896, Vol. 4, No. 2, p. 63.
172. T. N. Page, TNSSAPOTNP, Vol. 10, pp. 256-257. Note: Page may or may not have considered this a war poem. It is highly applicable, however, and so I have included it.
173. Confederate Veteran, February 1896, Vol. 4, No. 2, p. 63.
174. Confederate Veteran, April 1896, Vol. 4, No. 4, p. 115.
175. Confederate Veteran, April 1896, Vol. 4, No. 4, p. 120.
176. Confederate Veteran, April 1896, Vol. 4, No. 4, p. 141.
177. Confederate Veteran, May 1896, Vol. 4, No. 5, p. 165.
178. Confederate Veteran, June 1896, Vol. 4, No. 6, p. 195.

179. Confederate Veteran, July 1896, Vol. 4, No. 7, p. 209.
180. Confederate Veteran, July 1896, Vol. 4, No. 7, p. 234.
181. Confederate Veteran, August 1896, Vol. 4, No. 8, p. 272.
182. Confederate Veteran, August 1896, Vol. 4, No. 8, p. 282.
183. Confederate Veteran, September 1896, Vol. 4, No. 9, p. 294.
184. Confederate Veteran, September 1896, Vol. 4, No. 9, p. 297.
185. "One heart, one way."
186. "Adds grace to ancestry."
187. "By courage, not craft."
188. "The Lord will provide."
189. Simms, pp. 89-91.
190. Confederate Veteran, September 1896, Vol. 4, No. 9, p. 311.
191. Confederate Veteran, September 1896, Vol. 4, No. 9, p. 313. Note accompanying the poem: "This is a reply to those Grand Army men [Yanks] who objected to the cheering of these flags by the Confederate Veterans at the Richmond Reunion, July, 1896."
192. Confederate Veteran, September 1896, Vol. 4, No. 9, p. 318.
193. Confederate Veteran, November 1896, Vol. 4, No. 11, p. 361.
194. Confederate Veteran, November 1896, Vol. 4, No. 11, p. 386.
195. Confederate Veteran, December 1896, Vol. 4, No. 12, p. 430.
196. Confederate Veteran, March 1897, Vol. 5, No. 3, p. 122.
197. Literally, "victress (a victorious woman) and widow."
198. Browne, pp. 114-116.
199. Confederate Veteran, March 1897, Vol. 5, No. 3, p. 126.
200. Confederate Veteran, March 1897, Vol. 5, No. 3, p. 135.
201. Confederate Veteran, April 1897, Vol. 5, No. 4, p. 159.
202. Confederate Veteran, April 1897, Vol. 5, No. 4, p. 163.
203. Confederate Veteran, April 1897, Vol. 5, No. 4, p. 176.
204. Confederate Veteran, April 1897, Vol. 5, No. 4, p. 185.
205. Simms, pp. 128-129.
206. Confederate Veteran, May 1897, Vol. 5, No. 5, p. 206.
207. Confederate Veteran, May 1897, Vol. 5, No. 5, p. 221.
208. Confederate Veteran, May 1897, Vol. 5, No. 5, pp. 222-223.
209. Confederate Veteran, June 1897, Vol. 5, No. 6, p. 245.
210. Confederate Veteran, June 1897, Vol. 5, No. 6, p. 307.
211. Confederate Veteran, June 1897, Vol. 5, No. 6, p. 308.
212. Confederate Veteran, July 1897, Vol. 5, No. 7, p. 390.
213. Confederate Veteran, August 1897, Vol. 5, No. 8, p. 432.
214. Confederate Veteran, August 1897, Vol. 5, No. 8, p. 437. Note: I have shortened the title. The original title was: "How Father Ryan's Conquered Banner Was Rescued From Oblivion."
215. Confederate Veteran, October 1897, Vol. 5, No. 10, p. 513.
216. Confederate Veteran, October 1897, Vol. 5, No. 10, p. 518.
217. Confederate Veteran, October 1897, Vol. 5, No. 10, p. 522.
218. Confederate Veteran, October 1897, Vol. 5, No. 10, p. 522. Note: Some of the surnames in the original of this poem were misspelled or were unidentifiable. I have made corrections where necessary. LS.
219. Confederate Veteran, October 1897, Vol. 5, No. 10, p. 523.
220. Confederate Veteran, October 1897, Vol. 5, No. 10, p. 528.

221. Actually, the Bonnie Blue Flag is still displayed by patriots and South-lovers all across the U.S.
222. Confederate Veteran, November 1897, Vol. 5, No. 11, p. 547.
223. Confederate Veteran, November 1897, Vol. 5, No. 11, p. 557.
224. Confederate Veteran, November 1897, Vol. 5, No. 11, p. 569.
225. Confederate Veteran, November 1897, Vol. 5, No. 11, p. 577. The following note accompanies the original poem: "Col. W. S. Hawkins, of the Confederate army, and a prisoner of war at Camp Chase in 1864, wrote this well-known poem. A near friend and fellow prisoner was engaged to be married to a young lady in the South, who proved faithless to him, and had written him a letter which arrived soon after his death. The letter was opened and answered by Col. Hawkins in these lines." This poem was controversial, even in the late 1800s, because it was thought to be "unjust to Southern women in general."
226. Confederate Veteran, November 1897, Vol. 5, No. 11, p. 579.
227. Confederate Veteran, November 1897, Vol. 5, No. 11, p. 582.
228. Confederate Veteran, November 1897, Vol. 5, No. 11, p. 586. This poem is based on an actual occurrence.
229. Confederate Veteran, November 1897, Vol. 5, No. 11, p. 587.
230. Confederate Veteran, December 1897, Vol. 5, No. 12, p. 633.
231. Confederate Veteran, December 1897, Vol. 5, No. 12, p. 634.
232. Confederate Veteran, February 1898, Vol. 6, No. 2, p. 69.
233. Confederate Veteran, February 1898, Vol. 6, No. 2, p. 74.
234. Confederate Veteran, February 1898, Vol. 6, No. 2, p. 91.
235. Confederate Veteran, May 1898, Vol. 6, No. 5, pp. 225-226.
236. Confederate Veteran, June 1898, Vol. 6, No. 6, p. 264.
237. Confederate Veteran, June 1898, Vol. 6, No. 6, p. 265.
238. Confederate Veteran, June 1898, Vol. 6, No. 6, p. 265.
239. Confederate Veteran, July 1898, Vol. 6, No. 7, p. 310.
240. Confederate Veteran, July 1898, Vol. 6, No. 7, p. 319.
241. Confederate Veteran, July 1898, Vol. 6, No. 7, p. 319.
242. Confederate Veteran, August 1898, Vol. 6, No. 8, pp. 360-361.
243. Kent, pp. 64-65.
244. Confederate Veteran, August 1898, Vol. 6, No. 8, p. 377. Note: These are the lyrics to a popular Victorian Southern song.
245. Confederate Veteran, August 1898, Vol. 6, No. 8, p. 385.
246. Confederate Veteran, October 1898, Vol. 6, No. 10, pp. 488-489.
247. Confederate Veteran, January 1899, Vol. 7, No. 1, p. 39.
248. Confederate Veteran, February 1899, Vol. 7, No. 2, p. 86. These lyrics were designed to be sung to the popular Southern tune "The Bonnie Blue Flag."
249. Confederate Veteran, February 1899, Vol. 7, No. 2, p. 88.
250. Confederate Veteran, March 1899, Vol. 7, No. 3, p. 114. Note: As there was no title attached to this poem, I created one. L.S.
251. Confederate Veteran, March 1899, Vol. 7, No. 3, p. 115.
252. Confederate Veteran, April 1899, Vol. 7, No. 4, p. 166.
253. Fulton, pp. 205-208.
254. Confederate Veteran, May 1899, Vol. 7, No. 5, p. 208.
255. Confederate Veteran, May 1899, Vol. 7, No. 5, p. 211.
256. Confederate Veteran, May 1899, Vol. 7, No. 5, p. 217.
257. Confederate Veteran, May 1899, Vol. 7, No. 5, p. 223.

258. Confederate Veteran, May 1899, Vol. 7, No. 5, p. 233.
259. Confederate Veteran, July 1899, Vol. 7, No. 7, p. 295.
260. Confederate Veteran, August 1899, Vol. 7, No. 8, p. 353.
261. Confederate Veteran, September 1899, Vol. 7, No. 9, p. 421.
262. Confederate Veteran, September 1899, Vol. 7, No. 9, p. 423.
263. Confederate Veteran, October 1899, Vol. 7, No. 10, p. 441.
264. Confederate Veteran, October 1899, Vol. 7, No. 10, p. 472.
265. Confederate Veteran, November 1899, Vol. 7, No. 11, p. 512.
266. Confederate Veteran, January 1900, Vol. 8, No. 1, p. 42.
267. Confederate Veteran, February 1900, Vol. 8, No. 2, p. 61. Note: As there was no title attached to this poem, I created one. L.S.
268. Confederate Veteran, February 1900, Vol. 8, No. 2, p. 64.
269. Simms, pp. 251-252.
270. Confederate Veteran, March 1900, Vol. 8, No. 3, p. 125.
271. Confederate Veteran, March 1900, Vol. 8, No. 3, p. 135.
272. Confederate Veteran, April 1900, Vol. 8, No. 4, p. 182.
273. Confederate Veteran, April 1900, Vol. 8, No. 4, p. 184.
274. Confederate Veteran, May 1900, Vol. 8, No. 5, p. 242.
275. Confederate Veteran, May 1900, Vol. 8, No. 5, p. 243.
276. Confederate Veteran, June 1900, Vol. 8, No. 6, p. 275.
277. Confederate Veteran, June 1900, Vol. 8, No. 6, p. 291.
278. Confederate Veteran, July 1900, Vol. 8, No. 7, p. 298.
279. Confederate Veteran, July 1900, Vol. 8, No. 7, p. 298.
280. Confederate Veteran, July 1900, Vol. 8, No. 7, p. 309.
281. Confederate Veteran, August 1900, Vol. 8, No. 8, p. 368.
282. Confederate Veteran, August 1900, Vol. 8, No. 8, p. 379.
283. Confederate Veteran, October 1900, Vol. 8, No. 10, p. 454.
284. Confederate Veteran, December 1900, Vol. 8, No. 12, p. 517.
285. Confederate Veteran, January 1901, Vol. 9, No. 1, p. 19.
286. Confederate Veteran, January 1901, Vol. 9, No. 1, p. 23.
287. Confederate Veteran, January 1901, Vol. 9, No. 1, p. 40.
288. Confederate Veteran, March 1901, Vol. 9, No. 3, p. 136.
289. Confederate Veteran, March 1901, Vol. 9, No. 3, p. 137.
290. Confederate Veteran, March 1901, Vol. 9, No. 3, p. 141.
291. Confederate Veteran, April 1901, Vol. 9, No. 4, p. 186.
292. Confederate Veteran, May 1901, Vol. 9, No. 5, p. 225.
293. Confederate Veteran, June 1901, Vol. 9, No. 6, p. 251.
294. Confederate Veteran, July 1901, Vol. 9, No. 7, p. 293.
295. Confederate Veteran, August 1901, Vol. 9, No. 8, p. 341.
296. Confederate Veteran, September 1901, Vol. 9, No. 9, p. 400.
297. Confederate Veteran, September 1901, Vol. 9, No. 9, p. 404.
298. Confederate Veteran, September 1901, Vol. 9, No. 9, p. 406.
299. Confederate Veteran, September 1901, Vol. 9, No. 9, p. 407.
300. Confederate Veteran, September 1901, Vol. 9, No. 9, p. 424.
301. "Old Picayune," a nickname for detested Union General Benjamin F. Butler.
302. Confederate Veteran, October 1901, Vol. 9, No. 10, p. 468.
303. Confederate Veteran, October 1901, Vol. 9, No. 10, p. 474.
304. Confederate Veteran, October 1901, Vol. 9, No. 10, p. 476.

305. Confederate Veteran, November 1901, Vol. 9, No. 11, p. 492.
306. Confederate Veteran, November 1901, Vol. 9, No. 11, p. 516.
307. Confederate Veteran, November 1901, Vol. 9, No. 11, p. 521.
308. Confederate Veteran, December 1901, Vol. 9, No. 12, p. 567.
309. Confederate Veteran, December 1901, Vol. 9, No. 12, p. 567.
310. F. Moore, SABOTSP, pp. 78-79.
311. F. Moore, SABOTSP, pp. 81-82.
312. F. Moore, SABOTSP, pp. 151-153.
313. F. Moore, SABOTSP, pp. 153-154.
314. F. Moore, SABOTSP, pp. 156-157.
315. F. Moore, SABOTSP, pp. 96-98.
316. F. Moore, SABOTSP, pp. 108-109.
317. F. Moore, SABOTSP, pp. 114-115.
318. Confederate Veteran, April 1893, Vol. 1, No. 4, p. 110.
319. Eggleston, pp. 156-159.
320. F. Moore, SABOTSP, pp. 17-19.
321. Fulton, p. 299.
322. Browne, pp. 139-140.
323. Fulton, pp. 270-271.
324. Eggleston, pp. 261-262.
325. Orgain, pp. 135-136.
326. Browne, p. 143.
327. "In the manner of a pauper."
328. Browne, pp. 89-91.
329. Fulton, pp. 272-273.
330. Carman, pp. 401-404.
331. Browne, pp. 224-225. Original note: [The C.S.S. *Alabama* was] sunk in the harbor of Cherbourg, France, by the United States Steamer *Kearsarge*, June 19, 1864.
332. Confederate Veteran, March 1894, Vol. 2, No. 3, p. 87.
333. Bronson, pp. 490-491.
334. Browne, pp. 197-198.
335. Eggleston, pp. 243-244.
336. F. Moore, SABOTSP, pp. 27-28.
337. Ticknor, pp. 151-152.
338. One of the warriors of Charlemagne's court. There were 12, the typical mystical number found in all religions and myths, who, in this case, were known as the Twelve Peers. For more on the sacrality of the number 12, see Seabrook, SBD, passim. For more on the number 12 and its role in religious mythology, see Seabrook, CBC, passim.
339. "Sweet (is) the honor."
340. Simms, pp. 433-436.
341. Confederate Veteran, August 1895, Vol. 3, No. 8, p. 237.
342. Confederate Veteran, April 1894, Vol. 2, No. 4, p. 104.
343. Eggleston, pp. 197-199.
344. Newcomer, Andrews, and Hall, pp. 820-821.
345. Fulton, pp. 243-244.
346. Simms, pp. 325-327.
347. Simms, pp. 164-166.
348. Confederate Veteran, April 1894, Vol. 2, No. 4, p. 108.

349. Eggleston, pp. 189-190.
350. Confederate Veteran, November 1894, Vol. 2, No. 11, p. 323.
351. F. Moore, SABOTSP, pp. 29-30.
352. Confederate Veteran, May 1895, Vol. 3, No. 5, p. 139.
353. Simms, p. 217.
354. Confederate Veteran, May 1895, Vol. 3, No. 5, p. 140.
355. Browne, pp. 71-73.
356. Confederate Veteran, May 1895, Vol. 3, No. 5, p. 140.
357. F. Moore, SABOTSP, pp. 31-33.
358. Browne, p. 79.
359. Confederate Veteran, August 1895, Vol. 3, No. 8, p. 252. Note accompanying the poem: "Penciled by an unknown hand upon a wall of one of the prison buildings of Johnson's Island."
360. Simms, pp. 323-325.
361. F. Moore, SABOTSP, pp. 44-45.
362. F. Moore, SABOTSP, pp. 139-140.
363. F. Moore, SABOTSP, p. 142.
364. F. Moore, SABOTSP, pp. 143-145.
365. F. Moore, SABOTSP, pp. 145-146.
366. F. Moore, SABOTSP, pp. 45-46.
367. F. Moore, SABOTSP, pp. 47-48. Original note: These lines were written when Confederate General Beauregard appealed to the people of the South to contribute their bells, that they might be melted into cannon.
368. Confederate Veteran, January 1896, Vol. 4, No. 1, p. 5.
369. Confederate Veteran, October 1896, Vol. 4, No. 10, p. 342.
370. Browne, pp. 69-70.
371. Confederate Veteran, August 1897, Vol. 4, No. 8, p. 438.
372. Browne, pp. 93-95.
373. Simms, pp. 277-279.
374. Confederate Veteran, February 1901, Vol. 9, No. 2, p. 78.
375. Orgain, pp. 182-185.
376. Literally, a "meaningless thunderbolt." Figuratively, an "empty threat."
377. Literally, "nurse (lion) cubs." Figuratively, one who "raises lion-hearted young."
378. Simms, pp. 46-48.
379. Browne, pp. 319-321. Original note: From an "Ode on the Valor and Sufferings of Confederate Soldiers."
380. Kent, pp. 43-44. Original note: Among the broken sentences uttered by General Lee on his death bed (1870) was this: "Let the tent be struck, the General has gone forward."
381. F. Moore, SABOTSP, pp. 160-162.
382. F. Moore, SABOTSP, pp. 162-164.
383. F. Moore, SABOTSP, pp. 170-171.
384. Southerners were not against Lincoln's Emancipation Proclamation because it was meant to "free the slaves" (which it failed to do anyway). After all, the American abolition movement got its start in the South. Their dislike for it was due to the fact that it was illegal (unconstitutional), and also because it was nothing more than a transparent spiteful edict intended to hurt the South socially, economically, and psychologically. As I have pointed out in my other books, Victorian Liberals, like today's Liberals, had no real love for blacks. Authentic American history shows that the Left has always cynically viewed blacks as political

tools; another weapon in their ongoing effort to destroy conservatism and permanently take over Washington. For more on this topic see Seabrook, EYWTAASIW, passim.
385. F. Moore, SABOTSP, pp. 175-179.
386. F. Moore, SABOTSP, pp. 192-193.
387. F. Moore, SABOTSP, pp. 294-295.
388. F. Moore, SABOTSP, pp. 222-223.
389. F. Moore, SABOTSP, pp. 223-225.
390. F. Moore, SABOTSP, pp. 233-234.
391. F. Moore, SABOTSP, pp. 234-235.
392. F. Moore, SABOTSP, pp. 239-241.
393. F. Moore, SABOTSP, pp. 253-256. Note: The title is mine, created to replace the descriptive but overly long original title (which I have placed in parentheses below it).
394. F. Moore, SABOTSP, pp. 256-258.
395. F. Moore, SABOTSP, pp. 268-269.
396. F. Moore, SABOTSP, pp. 284-286.
397. F. Moore, SABOTSP, pp. 298-299.
398. Wharton, pp. 133-135.
399. Eggleston, pp. 245-248.
400. Eggleston, pp. 181-183.
401. Browne, pp. 328-329.
402. F. Moore, SABOTSP, pp. 306-307.
403. I composed the music for these lyrics as well. If you are an artist, band, film producer, etc., and are interested in this song, please contact my publisher, Sea Raven Press.
404. Original note: Helvyn, poetical name for Switzerland.
405. Kent, pp. 23-25.
406. F. Moore, SABOTSP, pp. 235-237.

"More precious than the wealth of empires."

BIBLIOGRAPHY

And Suggested Reading

Adams, James Eli. *A History of Victorian Literature*. Chichester, UK: John Wiley and Sons, 2009.
Alderman, Edwin Anderson, Joel Chandler Harris, and Charles William Kent (eds.). *Library of Southern Literature*. 17 vols. New Orleans, LA: Martin and Hoyt Co., 1909.
Anonymous ("a Confederate"). *The Grayjackets: And How They Lived, Fought, and Died for Dixie (With Incidents and Sketches of Life in the Confederacy)*. Richmond, VA: Jones Brothers and Co., 1867.
Armstrong, Isobel. *Victorian Poetry: Poetry, Poetics and Politics*. London, UK: Routledge, 2002.
Arnold, Sarah Louise, and Charles Benajah Gilbert. *Stepping Stones to Literature*. New York, NY: Silver, Burdett and Co., 1904.
Augustin, John. *War Flowers: Reminiscences of Four Years' Campaigning*. New Orleans, LA: self-published, 1865.
Bailey, Elmer James. *Religious Thought in the Greater American Poets*. Boston, MA: Pilgrim Press, 1922.
Banks, Louis Albert. *Immortal Songs of Camp and Field: The Story of Their Inspiration Together With Striking Anecdotes of Their History*. Cleveland, OH: Burrows Brothers Co., 1898.
Bates, Katharine Lee (ed.). *America the Beautiful and Other Poems*. New York, NY: Thomas Y. Crowell and Co., 1911.
Beeton, Samuel Orchart, and William Michael Rossetti (eds.). *Encyclopedia of English and American Poetry: From Cædmon and King Alfred's Boethius to Browning and Tennyson*. 2 vols. London, UK: Ward, Lock and Tyler, 1873.
Benson, Al, Jr., and Walter Donald Kennedy. *Lincoln's Marxists*. Gretna, LA: Pelican, 2011.
Bevis, Matthew (ed.). *The Oxford Handbook of Victorian Poetry*. Oxford, UK: Oxford University Press, 2013.
Birch, Dinah. *The Oxford Companion to English Literature*. Oxford, UK: Oxford University Press, 2009.
Blair, Kirstie. *Victorian Poetry and the Culture of the Heart*. Oxford, UK: Oxford University Press, 2006.
Boyd, James P. *Parties, Problems, and Leaders of 1896: An Impartial Presentation of Living National Questions*. Chicago, IL: Publishers' Union, 1896.
Boyle, George. *The English and American Poets and Dramatists of the Victorian Age; With Biographical Notices*. Frankfort, Germany: Adolphus Gestewitz, 1886.
Boynton, Percy Holmes (ed.). *American Poetry*. New York, NY: Charles Scribner's Sons, 1921.

Bristow, Joseph (ed.). *The Cambridge Companion to Victorian Poetry.* Cambridge, UK: Cambridge University Press, 2000.

Brock, Sallie A. (ed.). *The Southern Amaranth: A Carefully Selected Collection of Poems Growing Out Of and In Reference to the Late War.* New York, NY: George S. Wilcox, 1869.

Bronson, Walter C. *American Poems (1625-1892).* 1912. Chicago, IL: University of Chicago Press, 1922 ed.

Browder, Earl. *Lincoln and the Communists.* New York, NY: Workers Library Publishers, Inc., 1936.

Browne, Francis Fisher (ed.). *Bugle-Echoes: A Collection of the Poetry of the Civil War, Northern and Southern.* New York, NY: Frederick A. Stokes and Brother, 1886.

Bryan, William Jennings. *The First Battle: A Story of the Campaign of 1896.* Chicago, IL: W. B. Conkey Co., 1896.

Bryant, William Cullen (ed.). *A Library of Poetry and Song: Being Choice Selections From the Best Poets.* New York, NY: J. B. Ford, 1874.

Burns, James MacGregor. *The Vineyard of Liberty.* New York, NY: Alfred A. Knopf, 1982.

Callaway, Morgan (ed.). *Select Poems of Sidney Lanier.* New York, NY: Charles Scribner's Sons, 1895.

Carhart, Margaret Sprague (ed.). *Selections From American Poetry.* New York, NY: Macmillan, 1922.

Carman, Bliss (ed.). *The World's Best Poetry.* 10 vols. New York, NY: University Society, 1904.

Chapman, Edwin O. (ed.). *A Thousand and One Gems of English and American Poetry: From Chaucer to Tennyson.* New York, NY: Thomas Y. Crowell and Co., 1884.

Christian, George Llewellyn. *Abraham Lincoln: An Address Delivered Before R. E. Lee Camp, No. 1 Confederate Veterans at Richmond, VA, October 29, 1909.* Richmond, VA: L. H. Jenkins, 1909.

———. *A Capitol Disaster: A Chapter of Reconstruction in Virginia.* Richmond, VA: self-published, 1915.

———. *Confederate Memories and Experiences.* Richmond, VA: self-published, 1915.

Clark, John Scott. *A Study of English and American Poets: A Laboratory Method.* New York, NY: Charles Scribner's Sons, 1907.

Collins, John Churton. *Studies in Poetry and Criticism.* London, UK: George Bell and Sons, 1905.

Collins, Thomas J., and Vivienne J. Rundle (eds.). *The Broadview Anthology of Victorian Poetry and Poetic Theory.* 2000. Peterborough, Canada: Broadview Press, 2005 ed.

Confederate Veteran (Sumner A. Cunningham, ed.). 40 vols. Nashville, TN: Confederate Veteran, 1893-1932.

Coppée, Henry. *A Gallery of Famous English and American Poets.* Philadelphia, PA: J. M. Stoddart and Co., 1873.

Crandall, Charles Henry (ed.). *Representative Sonnets by American Poets.* Boston, MA: Houghton, Mifflin and Co., 1891.

Cronin, Richard, Alison Chapman, and Antony H. Harrison (eds.). *A Companion to Victorian Poetry.* Hoboken, NJ: Wiley-Blackwell, 2007.

Cunningham, Valentine (ed.). *The Victorians: An Anthology of Poetry and Poetics.* Hoboken, NJ: Wiley-Blackwell, 2000.
Davis, Jefferson. *The Rise and Fall of the Confederate Government.* 2 vols. New York, NY: D. Appleton and Co., 1881.
De Leon, Thomas Cooper (ed). *South Songs: From the Lays of Later Days.* New York, NY: Blelock and Co., 1866.
Driver, Paul. *Victorian Poetry.* Harmondsworth, UK: Penguin Books, 1996.
Duff, Mountstuart E. Grant (ed.). *An Anthology of Victorian Poetry.* New York, NY: E. P. Dutton and Co., 1902.
Edmunds, Albert Joseph. *English and American Poems.* Philadelphia, PA: self-published, 1888.
Eggleston, George Cary (ed.). *American War Ballads and Lyrics: A Collection of the Songs and Ballads of the Colonial Wars, the Revolution, the War of 1812-1815, the War With Mexico and the Civil War.* 2 vols in one. New York, NY: G. P. Putnam's Sons, 1889.
Ellinger, Esther Parker. *The Southern War Poetry of the Civil War.* Philadelphia, PA: Hershey Press, 1918.
Franklin, John Hope. *Reconstruction After the Civil War.* Chicago, IL: University of Chicago Press, 1961.
Fulton, Maurice Garland (ed.). *Southern Life in Southern Literature: Selections of Representative Prose and Poetry.* Boston, MA: Ginn and Co., 1917.
Gibbons, Reginald (ed.). *The Poet's Work: 29 Masters of 20th Century Poetry on the Origins and Practice of Their Art.* Boston, MA: Houghton Mifflin Co., 1979.
Gilman, Arthur. *Poets' Homes: Pen and Pencil Sketches of American Poets and Their Homes.* Boston, MA: D. Lothrop and Co., 1879.
Granger, Edith (ed.). *An Index to Poetry and Recitations: Being a Practical Reference Manual for the Librarian, Teacher, Bookseller, Elocutionist, etc.* Chicago, IL: A. C. McClurg and Co., 1904.
Greene, Roland (ed.). *The Princeton Encyclopedia of Poetry and Poetics.* Princeton, NJ: Princeton University Press, 2012.
Guthrie, Anna Lorraine. *Early American Literature: A Study Outline.* White Plains, NY: H. W. Wilson Co., 1916.
Howard, John Raymond (ed.). *One Hundred Best American Poems.* New York, NY: Thomas Y. Crowell and Co., 1905.
——. (ed.) *Poems of Heroism in American Life.* New York, NY: Thomas Y. Crowell and Co., 1922.
Hows, John William Stanhope (ed.). *Golden Leaves From the American Poets.* New York, NY: Bunce and Huntington, 1864.
Hughes, Linda K. *The Cambridge Introduction to Victorian Poetry.* Cambridge, UK: Cambridge University Press, 2010.
Johnstone, Huger William. *Truth of War Conspiracy, 1861.* Idylwild, GA: H. W. Johnstone, 1921.
Jones, John William. *The Davis Memorial Volume; Or Our Dead President, Jefferson Davis and the World's Tribute to His Memory.* Richmond, VA: B. F. Johnson, 1889.
Kent, Charles William (ed.). *Southern Poems.* Boston, MA: Houghton Mifflin Co., 1913.

Knowles, Frederic Lawrence (ed.). *Poems of American Patriotism, 1776-1898.* Boston, MA: L. C. Page and Co., 1898.
Lanier, Henry W. (ed.). *Selections From Sidney Lanier: Prose and Verse.* New York, NY: Charles Scribner's Sons, 1916.
Lanier, Mary Day (ed.). *Poems of Sidney Lanier.* 1884. New York, NY: Charles Scribner's Sons, 1912 ed.
Larcom, Lucy. *Landscape in American Poetry.* New York, NY: D. Appleton and Co., 1879.
Leighton, Angela, and Margaret Reynolds. *Victorian Women Poets: An Anthology.* Hoboken, NJ: Wiley-Blackwell, 1999.
Linton, William James (ed.). *Poetry of America: Selections From one Hundred American Poets, From 1776 to 1876.* London, UK: George Bell and Sons, 1878.
Low, Charles Rathbone. *Soldiers in the Victorian Age.* 2 vols. London, UK: Chapman and Hall, 1880.
Lumm, Emma Griffith. *The International Speaker: Containing the Best and Noblest Readings and Orations That Have Been Presented During the Last One Hundred Years.* Chicago, IL: International Publishing Co., 1903.
Magliocca, Gerard N. *The Tragedy of William Jennings Bryan: Constitutional Law and the Politics of Backlash.* New Haven, CT: Yale University Press, 2011.
Manly, Louise. *Southern Literature, From 1579-1895: A Comprehensive Review, With Copious Extracts and Criticisms.* Richmond, VA: B. F. Johnson Publishing Co., 1895.
McCarty, Burke (ed.). *Little Sermons in Socialism by Abraham Lincoln.* Chicago, IL: The Chicago Daily Socialist, 1910.
McCaskey, John Piersol (ed.). *Favorite Songs and Hymns for School and Home.* New York, NY: Harper and Brothers, 1899.
——. (ed.) *Treasury of Favorite Song In Three Volumes: Songs and Hymns of the Millions of Yesterday, Today and To-morrow.* Lancaster, PA: self-published, 1916.
McPherson, James M. *Abraham Lincoln and the Second American Revolution.* New York, NY: Oxford University Press, 1991.
Meriwether, Elizabeth Avery (pseudonym, "George Edmonds"). *Facts and Falsehoods Concerning the War on the South, 1861-1865.* Memphis, TN: A. R. Taylor and Co., 1904.
Mims, Edwin. *Sidney Lanier.* Boston, MA: Houghton, Mifflin and Co., 1905.
Minutes of the Eighth Annual Meeting and Reunion of the United Confederate Veterans, Atlanta, GA, July 20-23, 1898. New Orleans, LA: United Confederate Veterans, 1907.
Minutes of the Ninth Annual Meeting and Reunion of the United Confederate Veterans, Charleston, SC, May 10-13, 1899. New Orleans, LA: United Confederate Veterans, 1907.
Minutes of the Twelfth Annual Meeting and Reunion of the United Confederate Veterans, Dallas, TX, April 22-25, 1902. New Orleans, LA: United Confederate Veterans, 1907.
Moore, Frank (ed.). *The Civil War in Song and Story, 1860-1865.* New York, NY: Peter Fenelon Collier, 1865.
——. *Anecdotes, Poetry and Incidents of the War: North and South, 1860-1865.* New York, NY: self-published, 1866.

———. (ed.) *Songs and Ballads of the Southern People, 1861-1865.* New York, NY: D. Appleton and Co., 1886.
Moran, Maureen. *Victorian Literature and Culture.* London, UK: Contiuum International, 2006.
Muzzey, David Saville. *The United States of America: Vol. 1, To the Civil War.* Boston, MA: Ginn and Co., 1922.
———. *The American Adventure: Vol. 2, From the Civil War.* 1924. New York, NY: Harper and Brothers, 1927 ed.
Newcomer, Alphonso Gerald, Alice Ebba Andrews, and Howard Judson Hall (eds.). *Three Centuries of American Poetry and Prose.* Chicago, IL: Scott, Foresman and Co., 1917.
Nicolay, John G., and John Hay (eds.). *Abraham Lincoln: A History.* 10 vols. New York, NY: The Century Co., 1890.
———. *Complete Works of Abraham Lincoln.* 12 vols. 1894. New York, NY: Francis D. Tandy Co., 1905 ed.
———. *Abraham Lincoln: Complete Works.* 12 vols. 1894. New York, NY: The Century Co., 1907 ed.
O'Gorman, Francis (ed.). *Victorian Poetry: An Annotated Anthology.* Oxford, UK: Blackwell Publishing, 2004.
ORA (full title: *The War of the Rebellion: A Compilation of the Official Records of the Union and Confederate Armies*). 70 vols. Washington, DC: Government Printing Office, 1880.
Orgain, Kate Alma. *Southern Authors in Poetry and Prose.* New York, NY: Neale Publishing Co., 1908.
ORN (full title: *Official Records of the Union and Confederate Navies in the War of the Rebellion*). 30 vols. Washington, DC: Government Printing Office, 1894.
Page, Curtis Hidden (ed.). *The Chief American Poets: Selected Poems by Bryant, Poe, Emerson, Longfellow, Whittier, Holmes, Lowell, Whitman and Lanier.* Boston, MA: Houghton Mifflin and Co., 1905.
Page, Thomas Nelson. *Two Little Confederates.* New York, NY: Charles Scribner's Sons, 1888.
———. *The Novels, Stories, Sketches and Poems of Thomas Nelson Page.* 15 vols. 1903. New York, NY: Charles Scribner's Sons, 1908 ed.
———. *Red Rock: A Chronicle of Reconstruction.* New York, NY: Charles Scribner's Sons, 1904.
Peet, Louis Harman. *Who's the Author? A Guide to the Authorship of Novels, Stories, Speeches, Songs and General Writings of American Literature.* New York, NY: Thomas Y. Crowell and Co., 1901.
Philpott, William Bledsoe (ed.). *The Sponsor Souvenir Album and History of the United Confederate Veterans' Reunion, 1895.* Houston, TX: Sponsor Souvenir Co., 1895.
Piatt, John James (ed.). *The Union of American Poetry and Art: A Choice Collection of Poems by American Poets.* Cincinnati, OH: W. E. Dibble and Co., 1882.
Pollard, Edward Alfred. *The Lost Cause.* New York, NY: E. B. Treat and Co., 1867.
Polley, Joseph Benjamin. *A Soldier's Letters to Charming Nellie.* New York, NY: Neale Publishing Co., 1908.

Reilly, Catherine W. *Mid-Victorian Poetry 1860-1879.* London, UK: Mansell, 2000.
Richards, Edwin Bradley (ed.). *Representative American Poetry.* New York, NY: Charles E. Merrill Co., 1919.
Richardson, Charles Francis. *American Literature, 1607-1885: American Poetry and Fiction.* 2 vols. New York, NY: G. P. Putnam's Sons, 1894.
Ridley, Bromfield Lewis. *Battles and Sketches of the Army of Tennessee.* Mexico, MO: Missouri Printing and Publishing, 1906.
Riede, David G. *Allegories of One's Own Mind: Melancholy in Victorian Poetry.* Columbus, OH: Ohio State University Press, 2005.
Rittenhouse, Jessie Belle (ed.). *The Little Book of American Poets, 1787-1900.* Boston, MA: Houghton Mifflin Co., 1915.
Rogers, William P. *The Three Secession Movements in the United States: Samuel J. Tilden, the Democratic Candidate for Presidency; the Advisor, Aider and Abettor of the Great Secession Movement of 1860; and One of the Authors of the Infamous Resolution of 1864; His Claims as a Statesman and Reformer Considered.* Boston, MA: John Wilson and Son, 1876.
Ross, John Dawson (ed.). *Scottish Poets in America, With Biographical and Critical Notices.* New York, NY: Pagan and Ross, 1889.
Rossetti, William Michael (ed.). *American Poems.* London, UK: E. Moxon, Son, and Co., 1873.
Rove, Karl. *The Triumph of William McKinley: Why the Election of 1896 Still Matters.* New York, NY: Simon and Schuster, 2015.
Rutherford, Mildred Lewis. *The South in History and Literature: A Hand-Book of Southern Authors, From the Settlement of Jamestown, 1607, to Living Writers.* Athens, GA: self-published, 1906.
——. *Truths of History: A Fair, Unbiased, Impartial, Unprejudiced and Conscientious Study of History.* Athens, GA: self-published, 1920.
Sargent, Epes (ed.). *Harper's Cyclopedia of British and American Poetry.* New York, NY: Harper and Brothers, 1881.
Saunders, Frederick (ed.). *A Festival of Art, Poetry, and Song: Selections From the Greatest Poets of the English Language.* St. Louis, MO: Scammell and Co., 1880.
Scott, Patrick Greig. *Victorian Poetry, 1830-1870: An Anthology.* Harlow, UK: Longman, 1971.
Seabrook, Lochlainn. *Carnton Plantation Ghost Stories: True Tales of the Unexplained from Tennessee's Most Haunted Civil War House!* 2005. Franklin, TN, 2016 ed.
——. *Nathan Bedford Forrest: Southern Hero, American Patriot.* 2007. Franklin, TN, 2010 ed.
——. *Abraham Lincoln: The Southern View.* 2007. Franklin, TN: Sea Raven Press, 2013 ed.
——. *The McGavocks of Carnton Plantation: A Southern History - Celebrating One of Dixie's Most Noble Confederate Families and Their Tennessee Home.* 2008. Franklin, TN, 2011ed.
——. *A Rebel Born: A Defense of Nathan Bedford Forrest.* 2010. Franklin, TN: Sea Raven Press, 2011 ed.
——. *A Rebel Born: The Screenplay* (for the film). 2011. Franklin, TN: Sea Raven Press.

——. *Everything You Were Taught About the Civil War is Wrong, Ask a Southerner!* 2010. Franklin, TN: Sea Raven Press, revised 2014 ed.
——. *The Quotable Jefferson Davis: Selections From the Writings and Speeches of the Confederacy's First President.* Franklin, TN: Sea Raven Press, 2011.
——. *The Quotable Robert E. Lee: Selections From the Writings and Speeches of the South's Most Beloved Civil War General.* Franklin, TN: Sea Raven Press, 2011 Sesquicentennial Civil War Edition.
——. *Lincolnology: The Real Abraham Lincoln Revealed In His Own Words.* Franklin, TN: Sea Raven Press, 2011.
——. *The Unquotable Abraham Lincoln: The President's Quotes They Don't Want You To Know!* Franklin, TN: Sea Raven Press, 2011.
——. *Honest Jeff and Dishonest Abe: A Southern Children's Guide to the Civil War.* Franklin, TN: Sea Raven Press, 2012.
——. *Encyclopedia of the Battle of Franklin - A Comprehensive Guide to the Conflict that Changed the Civil War.* Franklin, TN: Sea Raven Press, 2012.
——. *The Quotable Nathan Bedford Forrest: Selections From the Writings and Speeches of the Confederacy's Most Brilliant Cavalryman.* Spring Hill, TN: Sea Raven Press, 2012.
——. *Forrest! 99 Reasons to Love Nathan Bedford Forrest.* Spring Hill, TN: Sea Raven Press, 2012.
——. *Give 'Em Hell Boys! The Complete Military Correspondence of Nathan Bedford Forrest.* Spring Hill, TN: Sea Raven Press, 2012.
——. *The Constitution of the Confederate States of America Explained: A Clause-by-Clause Study of the South's Magna Carta.* Spring Hill, TN: Sea Raven Press, 2012 Sesquicentennial Civil War Edition.
——. *The Great Impersonator: 99 Reasons to Dislike Abraham Lincoln.* Spring Hill, TN: Sea Raven Press, 2012.
——. *The Old Rebel: Robert E. Lee As He Was Seen By His Contemporaries.* Spring Hill, TN: Sea Raven Press, 2012 Sesquicentennial Civil War Edition.
——. *The Quotable Stonewall Jackson: Selections From the Writings and Speeches of the South's Most Famous General.* Spring Hill, TN: Sea Raven Press, 2012 Sesquicentennial Civil War Edition.
——. *Saddle, Sword, and Gun: A Biography of Nathan Bedford Forrest for Teens.* Spring Hill, TN: Sea Raven Press, 2013.
——. *The Alexander H. Stephens Reader: Excerpts From the Works of a Confederate Founding Father.* Spring Hill, TN: Sea Raven Press, 2013.
——. *The Quotable Alexander H. Stephens: Selections From the Writings and Speeches of the Confederacy's First Vice President.* Spring Hill, TN: Sea Raven Press, 2013 Sesquicentennial Civil War Edition.
——. *Give This Book to a Yankee! A Southern Guide to the Civil War for Northerners.* Spring Hill, TN: Sea Raven Press, 2014.
——. *The Articles of Confederation Explained: A Clause-by-Clause Study of America's First Constitution.* Spring Hill, TN: Sea Raven Press, 2014.
——. *Confederate Blood and Treasure: An Interview With Lochlainn Seabrook.* Spring Hill, TN: Sea Raven Press, 2015.
——. *Nathan Bedford Forrest and the Battle of Fort Pillow: Yankee Myth, Confederate Fact.* Spring Hill, TN: Sea Raven Press, 2015.

———. *Everything You Were Taught About American Slavery War is Wrong, Ask a Southerner!* Spring Hill, TN: Sea Raven Press, 2015.

———. *Confederacy 101: Amazing Facts You Never Knew About America's Oldest Political Tradition.* Spring Hill, TN: Sea Raven Press, 2015.

———. *The Great Yankee Coverup: What the North Doesn't Want You to Know About Lincoln's War!* Spring Hill, TN: Sea Raven Press, 2015.

———. *Slavery 101: Amazing Facts You Never Knew About America's "Peculiar Institution."* Spring Hill, TN: Sea Raven Press, 2015.

———. *Confederate Flag Facts: What Every American Should Know About Dixie's Southern Cross.* Spring Hill, TN: Sea Raven Press, 2016.

———. *Nathan Bedford Forrest and the Ku Klux Klan: Yankee Myth, Confederate Fact.* Spring Hill, TN: Sea Raven Press, 2016.

———. *Seabrook's Bible Dictionary of Traditional and Mystical Christian Doctrines.* Spring Hill, TN: Sea Raven Press, 2016.

———. *Everything You Were Taught About African-Americans and the Civil War is Wrong, Ask a Southerner!* Spring Hill, TN: Sea Raven Press, 2016.

———. *Nathan Bedford Forrest and African-Americans: Yankee Myth, Confederate Fact.* Spring Hill, TN: Sea Raven Press, 2016.

———. *Women in Gray: A Tribute to the Ladies Who Supported the Southern Confederacy.* Spring Hill, TN: Sea Raven Press, 2016.

———. *Lincoln's War: The Real Cause, the Real Winner, the Real Loser.* Spring Hill, TN: Sea Raven Press, 2016.

———. *The Unholy Crusade: Lincoln's Legacy of Destruction in the American South.* Spring Hill, TN: Sea Raven Press, 2017.

———. *Abraham Lincoln Was a Liberal, Jefferson Davis Was a Conservative: The Missing Key to Understanding the American Civil War.* Spring Hill, TN: Sea Raven Press, 2017.

———. *All We Ask is to be Let Alone: The Southern Secession Fact Book.* Spring Hill, TN: Sea Raven Press, 2017.

———. *The Ultimate Civil War Quiz Book: How Much Do You Really Know About America's Most Misunderstood Conflict?* Spring Hill, TN: Sea Raven Press, 2017.

———. *Rise Up and Call Them Blessed: Victorian Tributes to the Confederate Soldier, 1861-1901.* Spring Hill, TN: Sea Raven Press, 2017.

Sharp, Amy. *Victorian Poets.* London, UK: Methuen and Co., 1891.

Simms, William Gilmore (ed). *War Poetry of the South.* New York, NY: Richardson and Co., 1867.

Sladen, Douglas (ed.). *Younger American Poets, 1830-1890.* London, UK: Griffith, Farran, Okeden, and Welsh, 1891.

Smith, Arnold. *The Main Tendencies of Victorian Poetry: Studies in the Thought and Art of the Greater Poets.* Birmingham, UK: Saint George Press, 1907.

Stedman, Edmund Clarence, and Ellen Mackay Hutchinson (eds.). *A Library of American Literature: From the Earliest Settlement to the Present Time.* 10 vols. New York, NY: Charles L. Webster and Co., 1889.

Stephens, Alexander Hamilton. *Speech of Mr. Stephens, of Georgia, on the War and Taxation.* Washington, D.C.: J and G. Gideon, 1848.

———. *A Constitutional View of the Late War Between the States; Its Causes, Character, Conduct and Results.* 2 vols. Philadelphia, PA: National Publishing, Co., 1870.

———. *Recollections of Alexander H. Stephens: His Diary Kept When a Prisoner at Fort Warren, Boston Harbour, 1865.* New York, NY: Doubleday, Page, and Co., 1910.
Stallworthy, Jon (ed.). *The Penguin Book of Love Poetry.* 1973. Harmondsworth, UK: Penguin Books, 1980 ed.
Stedman, Edmund Clarence. *Poets of America.* Boston, MA: Houghton, Mifflin and Co., 1885.
Stevenson, Burton Egbert (ed.). *Poems of American History.* Boston, MA: Houghton Mifflin Co., 1908.
Strong, Augustus Hopkins. *American Poets and Their Theology.* Philadelphia, PA: Griffith and Rowland Press, 1916.
Strother, David Hunter. *Virginia Illustrated: Containing a Visit to the Virginian Canann, and the Adventures of Porte Crayon and His Cousins.* New York, NY: Harper and Brothers, 1871.
The Confederate War Journal: An Illustrated Magazine. New York, NY: War Journal Publishing, 1893.
Thompson, Holland. *The New South: A Chronicle of Social and Industrial Evolution.* New Haven, CT: Yale University Press, 1920.
Ticknor, Michelle Cutliff (ed.). *The Poems of Francis Orray Ticknor.* New York, NY: Neale Publishing Co., 1911.
Turner, Paul. *Victorian Poetry, Drama, and Miscellaneous Prose 1832-1890.* Oxford, UK: Clarendon Press, 1990.
Vickers, George Morley (ed.). *Under Both Flags: A Panorama of the Great Civil War as Represented in Story, Anecdote, Adventure, and Romance of Reality.* Chicago, IL: National Book Concern, 1896.
Waggoner, Hyatt H. *American Poets: From the Puritans to the Present.* Boston, MA: Houghton Mifflin Co., 1968.
Walker, Hugh. *The Greater Victorian Poets.* London, UK: Swan Sonnenschein and Co., 1895.
Wallington, Nellie Urner (ed.). *American History by American Poets.* New York, NY: Duffield and Co., 1911.
Warner, Ezra J. *Generals in Gray: Lives of the Confederate Commanders.* 1959. Baton Rouge, LA: Louisiana State University Press, 1989 ed.
———. *Generals in Blue: Lives of the Union Commanders.* 1964. Baton Rouge, LA: Louisiana State University Press, 2006 ed.
Watson, Anna Robinson. *On the Field of Honor.* Detroit, MI: Sprague Publishing, 1902.
Wharton, Henry Marvin (ed.). *War Songs and Poems of the Southern Confederacy, 1861-1865.* Chicago, IL: John C. Winston Co., 1904.
Woods, Thomas E., Jr. *The Politically Incorrect Guide to American History.* Washington, D.C.: Regnery, 2004.

INDEX

Adams, Shelby L., 576
Alexander, Phipps, 301
Allston, Joseph B., 108
Anderson, Loni, 576
Anderson, Mrs. May M., 198, 205, 251
Anderson, Richard H., 178
Andrew, Saint, 216
Archer, James J., 299
Armistead, Lewis A., 479
Arrington, A. W., 113
Arthur, King, 190, 575
Ashby, Turner, 124, 125, 129, 443, 458, 459
Atkins, Chet, 576
Attila, the Hun, 375
Augustin, John, 117
Ball, Caroline A., 186
Ballard, Sallie E., 486
Banks, Nathaniel P., 82, 443
Barrick, J. R., 519
Bayard, Chevalier de, 121, 178, 190, 458
Bealer, Gertrude E., 355
Beaufort, F. P., 428
Beauregard, Pierre G. T., 39, 68, 73, 74, 118, 179, 242, 286, 411, 422, 575
Bee, Barnard E., 178, 299
Beecher, Henry W., 82
Bell, Maurice, 450, 455
Benjamin, Judah P., 346
Bernstein, Leonard, 576
Blanchard, H. L., 164
Blunt, Mrs. Ellen K., 61
Bolling, Edith, 576
Bond, Daniel, 232
Boner, John H., 325
Boone, Daniel, 575
Boone, Pat, 576
Booty, J. A., 191
Bower, Charles, 371
Box, A. M., 421
Boyle, Virginia F., 188, 401

Bragg, Braxton, 68, 83, 346, 382, 411
Breckinridge, John C., 346, 575
Brentwood, Joe, 197
Brewster, P. H., 99
Brooke, Edward W., 576
Brooks, Preston S., 576
Brown, Dr. W. E., 334
Brown, John, 481
Brownlow, William G., 82
Brunner, J. H., 389
Bruns, John D., 103
Bryan, Susanna, 360
Buchanan, Franklin, 133
Buchanan, Patrick J., 576
Buford, Abraham, 575
Burnett, James G., 372
Burnside, Ambrose E., 83
Burroughs, Alethea S., 230
Butler, Andrew P., 576
Butler, Benjamin F., 82, 138
Byers, E. L., 310
Cameron, Anna A., 396
Campbell, Joseph, 574
Carmack, J. W., 120
Carroll, Charles, 45
Carson, Martha, 576
Carter, Theodrick, 575
Cash, Johnny, 576
Cassidy, M. A., 278
Caudill, Benjamin E., 574
Chambers, Henry, 313
Charles, the Bold, 508
Chase, Salmon P., 82
Cheairs, Nathaniel F., 576
Chesnut, Mary, 576
Clark, William, 575
Clarke, William J., 322
Clarkson, H. M., 147
Clay, Henry, 70
Cleburne, Patrick R., 202, 266, 305, 385, 417
Clifford, Ruth, 165, 166
Collins, Mortimer, 89
Combs, Bertram T., 576

Cooke, John E., 29, 85
Crawford, Cindy, 576
Crockett, Davy, 575
Croom, Mrs. Ellen R., 404
Cross, Jane T. H., 29, 201, 280, 512
Cruise, Tom, 576
Cumming, Joseph B., 77
Cunningham, Sumner A., 8
Curtin, Andrew, 82
Cyrus, Billy R., 576
Cyrus, Miley, 576
Dahlgren, John A., 83
Dangerfield, Henrietta H., 229
Dannelly, Mrs. C. O., 110
Dargan, Pegram, 23, 245
Darling, Flora A., 169
David (Bible), 425, 457
Davis, Jefferson, 19, 21, 27, 37, 39, 43, 68, 73, 90, 101, 102, 150, 158, 196, 201, 228, 302, 346, 379, 411, 426, 574, 575
Davis, Sam, 210, 211, 238, 239, 242, 288, 303, 304, 315, 387, 389
Davis, Varina A., 495
Dawson, F. W., 121
De Fontaine, Mrs. F. G., 159, 187
Dimitry, John B. S., 42, 192
Dodge, Grenville M., 335
Doles, George P., 161
Doubleday, Abner, 479
Dow, R. B., 327
Dowling, Dick, 404
Downing, Fanny, 102
Doyle, Burton T., 353
Dozier, O. T., 163
Duke, Basil W., 90
Dumas, William T., 374
Duvall, Robert, 576
Dykers, R. H., 151, 158
Early, Jubal A., 299
Edward I, King, 575
Elbert, Evan, 456
Elder, Mrs. C. D., 521
Ellinger, Esther P., 28
Elliott, Stephen, Jr., 178
Ellis, Zack, 321

Ennis, Lawrence M., 225
Everett, Edward, 82
Ewell, Richard S., 299
Fall, Philip H., 404
Farrar, Judge, 344, 345
Faxon, John W., 382, 399
Field, Charles W., 299
Fisher, W. C., 74
Flash, Harry L., 84, 413, 474
Folsom, Montgomery M., 385
Foote, Shelby, 574
Forbes, Christopher, 576
Forney, John W., 82
Forrest, Nathan B., 21, 202, 285, 299, 335-337, 381, 398, 400, 401, 574, 575
Forsee, William C., 150
Fowler, William E., 314
Frazer, C. W., 180
Freer, M. C., 74
Gabriel (Bible), 273
Garland, Samuel, Jr., 299
Garnett, Alice, 315
Garnett, Richard B., 129, 479
Gayheart, Rebecca, 576
George III, King, 20
George, Saint, 190
Gilleland, W. M., 57
Gillmore, Quincy A., 82
Gist, States R., 179, 575
Glass, Owen, 343
Goethe, Johann W. von, 407
Goodwin, G. I., 381
Gordon, George W., 575
Gorman, Ossian D., 133
Gracie, Archibald, Jr., 291, 292
Grandin, J. M., 79
Grant, Ulysses S., 83, 89, 191, 214, 446
Graves, Robert, 574
Gray, Judith, 361
Greeley, Horace, 411
Gregg, Maxcy, 252
Griffith, Andy, 576
Griggs, George B., 296
Grimk, St. Julien, 358
Guaraldi, Vince, 576
Halleck, Henry W., 82
Hampton, Wade, 55, 242, 379
Hanford, Charles, Jr., 365

Happy, John, 222
Harding, William G., 575
Hartz, Asa, 88
Hawkins, W. S., 307
Hawks, Joseph W., 111
Hay, P. D., 130
Hayne, Paul H., 29, 41, 66, 81, 475, 503, 510
Helm, Benjamin H., 375
Helper, Alexander, 275
Hempsted, Junius L., 363
Henley, William E., 391
Henry, Mrs. Dr. T. J., 298
Henry, Patrick, 23, 122
Heth, Henry, 299
Hewitt, John H., 50
Hill, Ambrose P., 111, 129, 130, 160, 299, 383, 443
Hills, Lucius P., 357
Hodgson, Mrs. Daisy, 317
Holmes, James G., 179
Holtz, Robert E., 68
Homer, 451
Hood, John B., 314, 575
Hood, Thomas B., 487
Hope, A. B. Beresford, 326
Hope, James B., 148, 463, 465
Houghton, Henry, 116
Houston, Miss Belle, 295
Houston, Sam, 295
Howard, John E., 45
Howard, W. H., 300
Hubner, Charles W., 333
Huger, Thomas B., 179
Hunter, Robert M. T., 346
Hutchen, Virginia, 375
Hutter, Lieutenant, 133
Ingraham, Duncan N., 179
Jackson, Andrew, 576
Jackson, Henry R., 429, 575
Jackson, Stonewall, 22, 51, 84, 89, 92, 111, 112, 128, 166, 169, 174, 178, 190, 192, 198, 207, 242, 263, 269, 276, 283, 285, 299, 353, 379, 382, 383, 417, 420, 443, 444, 459, 476, 494, 575
James, Frank, 576
James, Jesse, 576
Jefferson, Thomas, 23, 29, 122, 576
Jenkins, Micah, 129, 178
Jent, Elias, Sr., 575
Jervey, Mary, 482
Jesus, 154, 182, 225, 280, 310, 320, 350, 399, 410, 413, 420, 511, 534, 540, 575
John, Elton, 576
Johnson, B. J., 74
Johnson, Smith, 195
Johnston, Albert S., 39, 42, 68, 128, 139, 140, 170, 174, 285, 379, 411, 472, 482
Johnston, Annie, 171
Johnston, Joseph E., 21, 69, 70, 119, 242, 379, 382
Johnston, William P., 367
Jonas, S. A., 104, 254
Jones, Charles E., 233, 346, 417
Jones, Mrs. J. William, 196, 293, 383
Jones, S. A., 137
Jones, Sallie, 228, 239, 397, 414
Joshua (Bible), 247
Judd, Ashley, 576
Judd, Naomi, 576
Judd, Wynonna, 576
Kemper, James L., 479
Keough, Riley, 576
Ketchum, Annie C., 29, 258, 471
Keyes, Julia L., 135
Kilgour, J. M., 435
Killum, John, 523
Kyle, Ruby B., 200
La Coste, Maria, 78
Lamar, Mirabeau B., 546
Lanier, Sidney, 29, 111, 539
Latané, William, 270, 271
Le Bruni, Jack, 246
LeCand, Fred J. V., 194
Lee, Fitzhugh, 576
Lee, Frank, 287
Lee, Robert E., 39, 89, 95, 96, 107, 108, 143, 144, 146, 148, 151, 156, 164, 172, 174, 189-191, 202, 206, 208, 209, 214, 240, 242, 263, 264, 269, 275, 276, 283, 285, 289, 291, 293, 295,

299, 316, 332, 349, 357,
358, 373, 374, 376, 378,
379, 382, 411, 416, 420,
430, 434, 446-449, 451, 479,
494, 511, 575
Lee, Stephen D., 203, 575
Lee, William H. F., 576
Legaré, Elizabeth R., 349
Lewis, Meriwether, 575
Lincoln, Abraham, 19, 20, 22,
25, 27, 35, 43, 67, 73, 82,
214, 421, 422, 426, 481,
489, 544, 546
Lincoln, Joe, 405
Lomas, Henry, 527
Longstreet, James, 21, 89, 299,
443, 575
Lorrimer, Laurie, 488
Loveless, Patty, 576
Lowe, Enoch L., 45
Lucas, Daniel B., 107
M'Aulay, Allan, 94
Mackey, Franklin H., 262, 284
MaClean, Mrs. Clara D., 227
Madison, James, 23
Magruder, John B., 68, 411
Manigault, Arthur M., 575
Manigault, Joseph, 575
Manship, Luther, 342
Marion, Francis, 434
Marshall, John, 122
Martin, J. H., 492
Marvin, Lee, 576
Mason, George, 23, 122
Mason, James M., 411
Maury, Abram P., 576
McCabe, William G., 72, 94
McCarthy, Harry, 37
McClelland, Mrs. M. G., 168
McConnell, Andrew M., 231
McCullouch, Ben, 411
McDowell, Irvin, 74, 426
McDowell, James, 43
McGann, Will, 308
McGavock, Caroline E., 576
McGavock, David H., 576
McGavock, Emily, 576
McGavock, Francis, 576
McGavock, James R., 576
McGavock, John W., 576

McGavock, Lysander, 576
McGavock, Randal W., 576
McGraw, Tim, 576
McNeil, John, 70
McRae, Henry, 320
McRae, Robert, 320
Meade, Gordon G., 82
Meares, Ed, 319
Mecklin, James A., 525
Meek, Alexander B., 545
Memminger, Christopher G., 346
Mendelssohn, Felix, 446
Meriwether, Elizabeth A., 576
Meriwether, Mary W., 47
Meriwether, Minor, 576
Merrill, C. E., 140
Michael, Saint, 457
Moore, John T., 305, 337, 380
Moore, John, Jr., 203
Moore, Mrs. N. Steele, 384
Morgan, John H., 90, 129, 240,
285, 318, 378, 379, 434, 575
Morrison, D. S., 112
Morton, Albert S., 157, 177, 184,
208, 209, 211, 286
Morton, Annie B., 242, 379
Morton, John W., 576
Mosby, John S., 364, 575
Moses (Bible), 84
Mumford, William B., 138
Murat, Joachim, 121
Murphy, Jeannette R., 350
Murphy, Matt, 320
M'Aulay, Allan, 94
Nason, Reuben, 530
Noah (Bible), 201
Nugent, Ted, 576
O'Hara, Theodore, 348
Ockenden, Ida P., 265
Oliver, Thaddeus, 49
Overall, John W., 98, 491
O'Mera, Jim, 229
Page, Thomas N., 29, 237
Palmer, J. W., 444
Parton, Dolly, 576
Patterson, J. T., 273
Paul, Saint, 27, 280
Pegram, John, 129
Pelham, John, 85, 129, 209, 466
Perry, Nellie D., 354

Pettigrew, James J., 479
Pettus, Edmund W., 575
Pickett, George E., 261, 344, 479
Pickett, Mrs. LaSalle C., 345
Pierpont, James, 473
Pike, Albert, 22, 34, 142
Pillow, Gideon J., 575
Pinckney, Alfred, 129
Polk, James K., 576
Polk, Leonidas, 129, 474, 575
Polk, Lucius E., 576
Pope, John, 443
Porter, Benjamin F., 514
Porter, Ina M., 138, 409
Presley, Elvis, 576
Presley, Lisa Marie, 576
Preston, John T. L., 22
Preston, Margaret J., 22, 29, 54, 442, 459, 496, 511
Preston, Willie, 181, 182
Price, Sterling, 39, 68
Raiford, B. B., 220
Rains, James E., 299
Raleigh, Walter, 441
Randall, James R., 29, 46, 51, 118, 466
Randolph, Edmund J., 576
Randolph, George W., 346, 576
Randolph, Innis, 123
Ratigan, James E., 309
Reagan, Ronald, 576
Requier, Augustus J., 190, 437, 490
Reynolds, Burt, 576
Richardson, John M., 173
Ringgold, Samuel B., 45
Ripley, Roswell S., 178
Robbins, Hargus, 576
Robbins, Mrs. W. M., 388
Robert the Bruce, King, 575
Rockett, F. Y., 493
Rockwood, Tracy K., 318
Rodes, Robert E., 299
Rogers, Nina M., 253, 338
Rozell-Messenger, Lillian, 149
Rucker, Edmund W., 440, 575
Ryan, Abram J., 29, 115, 155, 293, 332, 390, 470
Sanders, Mary F., 321
Sansom, Emma, 335-337

Schamyl, Imam, 520
Schenck, Robert C., 82
Scott, George C., 576
Scott, Winfield, 74
Scruggs, Earl, 576
Seabrook, John L., 575
Seabrook, Lochlainn, 543, 574-577
Seddon, James A., 346
Seger, Bob, 576
Semmes, Raphael, 146, 147, 450
Seward, William H., 74, 82
Shackelford, Dan, 319
Shackelford, Theo, 319
Shelby, Joseph O., 297, 298
Shepherd, N. G., 440
Sheridan, Philip H., 167, 176
Sherman, William T., 263, 266
Signaigo, Joseph A., 39
Simmons, H. C., 199
Simms, William G., 28, 29, 467, 485
Sinclair, Miss Carrie B., 340
Skaggs, Ricky, 576
Slayback, A. W., 290
Slidell, John, 411
Smith, Gustavus W., 346
Smith, J. B. K., 235
Spotswood, Alexander, 441
Sprague, John W., 82
Stanton, Frank L., 263, 277
Stanton, Harriet, 53
Stanton, Henry T., 212, 217
Stephens, Alexander H., 19, 21, 37, 73, 575
Stevens, Clement H., 178
Stewart, Alexander P., 575
Stewart, Gabrielle T., 288
Stinson, J. B., 281, 420
Strawbridge, H. H., 533
Streight, Able D., 90, 335
Stuart, Jeb, 89, 92, 93, 129, 176, 177, 242, 257, 269, 285, 370, 371, 377, 379, 443, 575
Sumter, Thomas, 434
Taylor, Clifford M., 377
Taylor, J. C., 430
Taylor, Richard, 21, 129, 222, 575
Taylor, Sarah K., 575

Taylor, Zachary, 575
Teague, B. H., 55
Tell, William, 520
Terry, Benjamin F., 56, 57
Thomas, Olivia T., 29, 175
Thompson, Jeff, 424
Thompson, John R., 29, 63, 70, 93, 124, 126, 271, 448, 508
Thompson, Maurice, 268
Thompson, Mrs. Frank, 329
Thompson, Will H., 480
Ticknor, Francis O., 29, 64, 292, 441, 457, 472
Tilghman, Lloyd, 49
Timberlake, Fannie J. G., 269
Timrod, Henry, 29, 36, 59, 127, 145, 369, 453, 468, 501, 506, 538
Toombs, Robert A., 346
Townsend, Mary A., 256
Trenholm, George A., 346
Tucker, St. George H., 38
Tuttle, Robert, 97
Tynes, Ellen B., 576
Van Bockerlin, Johnnie, 319
Vance, Robert B., 576
Vance, Zebulon, 576
Venable, Charles S., 575
Wailes, E. Lloyd, 35
Walker, Joel P., 368
Walker, Leroy P., 346
Wallis, Severn T., 536
Walter, Carroll G., 376
Ware, Mrs. Mary, 244, 390
Warfield, Catherine A., 29, 52, 425
Washington, George, 20, 100, 122, 148, 213, 275, 283, 316, 434, 520, 526
Washington, John A., 575
Washington, Thornton A., 575
Washington, William D., 271
Watie, Stand, 299
Watson, William H., 45
Watts, Thomas H., 346
Wellburn, Drummond, 476
Wharton, Morton B., 534
Wheeler, Post, 419
Whitney, Miss Emma E., 289
Wilcox, Ella W., 29, 303, 304

Wildwood, Charlie, 522
Willis, W. H., 161
Wilson, James E., 249
Wilson, Woodrow, 576
Winder, Charles S., 576
Winder, John H., 575
Winder, Miss Nina M., 302
Witherspoon, Reese, 576
Womack, John B., 575
Womack, Lee Ann, 576
Woodcock, J. H., 423
Worsley, Philip S., 451
Wright, James A., 319
Wyeth, John A., 243
Zollicoffer, Felix K., 576
Zschokke, Johann H. D., 407

MEET THE AUTHOR

"ASKING THE PATRIOTIC SOUTH TO STOP HONORING HER CONFEDERATE ANCESTORS
IS LIKE ASKING THE SUN NOT TO SHINE." — COLONEL LOCHLAINN SEABROOK

LOCHLAINN SEABROOK, a neo-Victorian and world acclaimed man of letters, is a Kentucky Colonel and the winner of the prestigious Jefferson Davis Historical Gold Medal for his "masterpiece," *A Rebel Born: A Defense of Nathan Bedford Forrest*. A classic littérateur and an unreconstructed Southern historian, he is an award-winning author, Civil War scholar, Confederate culture expert, Bible authority, the leading popularizer of American Civil War history, and a traditional Southern Agrarian of Scottish, English, Irish, Dutch, Welsh, German, and Italian extraction.

A child prodigy, Seabrook is today a true Renaissance Man whose occupational titles also include encyclopedist, lexicographer, musician, artist, graphic designer, genealogist, photographer, and award-winning poet. Also a songwriter and a screenwriter, he has a 40 year background in historical nonfiction writing and is a member of the Sons of Confederate Veterans, the Civil War Trust, and the National Grange.

Above, Colonel Lochlainn Seabrook, "the voice of the traditional South," award-winning Civil War scholar and unreconstructed Southern historian. America's most popular and prolific pro-South author, his many books have introduced hundreds of thousands to the truth about the War for Southern Independence. He coined the phrase "South-shaming" and holds the world's record for writing the most books on Nathan Bedford Forrest: nine.

Known to his many fans as the "voice of the traditional South," due to similarities in their writing styles, ideas, and literary works, Seabrook is also often referred to as the "new Shelby Foote," the "Southern Joseph Campbell," and the "American Robert Graves" (his English cousin). Seabrook coined the terms "South-shaming" and "Lincolnian liberalism," and holds the world's record for writing the most books on Nathan Bedford Forrest: nine. In addition, Seabrook is the first Civil War scholar to connect the early American nickname for the U.S., "The Confederate States of America," with the Southern Confederacy that arose eight decades later, and the first to note that in 1860 the party platforms of the two major political parties were the opposite of what they are today (Victorian Democrats were conservatives, Victorian Republicans were liberals).

The grandson of an Appalachian coal-mining family, Seabrook is a seventh-generation Kentuckian, co-chair of the Jent/Gent Family Committee (Kentucky), founder and director of the Blakeney Family Tree Project, and a board member of the Friends of Colonel Benjamin E. Caudill. Seabrook's literary works have been endorsed by leading authorities, museum curators, award-winning historians, bestselling authors, celebrities, noted scientists, well regarded educators, TV show hosts and producers, renowned military artists, esteemed Southern organizations, and distinguished academicians from around the world.

Seabrook has authored over 50 popular adult books on the American Civil War, American and international slavery, the U.S. Confederacy (1781), the Southern Confederacy (1861), religion, theology, thealogy, Jesus, the Bible, the Apocrypha, the Law of Attraction, alternative health, spirituality, ghost stories, the paranormal, ufology, social issues, and cross-cultural studies of the family and marriage. His Confederate biographies, pro-South studies, genealogical monographs, family histories, military encyclopedias, self-help guides, and etymological dictionaries have received wide acclaim.

Seabrook's eight children's books include a Southern guide to the Civil War, a biography of Nathan Bedford Forrest, a dictionary of religion and myth, a rewriting of the King Arthur legend (which reinstates the original pre-Christian motifs), two bedtime stories for preschoolers, a naturalist's guidebook to owls, a worldwide look at the family, and an examination of the Near-Death Experience.

Of blue-blooded Southern stock through his Kentucky, Tennessee, Virginia, West Virginia, and North Carolina ancestors, he is a direct descendant of European royalty via his 6th great-grandfather, the Earl of Oxford, after which London's famous Harley Street is named. Among his celebrated male Celtic ancestors is Robert the Bruce, King of Scotland, Seabrook's 22nd great-grandfather. The 21st great-grandson of Edward I "Longshanks" Plantagenet), King of England, Seabrook is a thirteenth-generation Southerner through his descent from the colonists of Jamestown, Virginia (1607).

(Photo © Lochlainn Seabrook)

The 2nd, 3rd, and 4th great-grandson of dozens of Confederate soldiers, one of his closest connections to Lincoln's War is through his 3rd great-grandfather, Elias Jent, Sr., who fought for the Confederacy in the Thirteenth Cavalry Kentucky under Seabrook's 2nd cousin, Colonel Benjamin E. Caudill. The Thirteenth, also known as "Caudill's Army," fought in numerous conflicts, including the Battles of Saltville, Gladsville, Mill Cliff, Poor Fork, Whitesburg, and Leatherwood.

Seabrook is a direct descendant of the families of Alexander H. Stephens, John Singleton Mosby, William Giles Harding, and Edmund Winchester Rucker, and is related to the following Confederates and other 18th- and 19th-Century luminaries: Robert E. Lee, Stephen Dill Lee, Stonewall Jackson, Nathan Bedford Forrest, James Longstreet, John Hunt Morgan, Jeb Stuart, Pierre G. T. Beauregard (approved the Confederate Battle Flag design), George W. Gordon, John Bell Hood, Alexander Peter Stewart, Arthur M. Manigault, Joseph Manigault, Charles Scott Venable, Thornton A. Washington, John A. Washington, Abraham Buford, Edmund W. Pettus, Theodrick "Tod" Carter, John B. Womack, John H. Winder, Gideon J. Pillow, States Rights Gist, Henry R. Jackson, John Lawton Seabrook, John C. Breckinridge, Leonidas Polk, Zachary Taylor, Sarah Knox Taylor (first wife of Jefferson Davis), Richard Taylor, Davy Crockett, Daniel Boone, Meriwether Lewis (of the Lewis and Clark Expedition)

Andrew Jackson, James K. Polk, Abram Poindexter Maury (founder of Franklin, TN), Zebulon Vance, Thomas Jefferson, Edmund Jennings Randolph, George Wythe Randolph (grandson of Jefferson), Felix K. Zollicoffer, Fitzhugh Lee, Nathaniel F. Cheairs, Jesse James, Frank James, Robert Brank Vance, Charles Sidney Winder, John W. McGavock, Caroline E. (Winder) McGavock, David Harding McGavock, Lysander McGavock, James Randal McGavock, Randal William McGavock, Francis McGavock, Emily McGavock, William Henry F. Lee, Lucius E. Polk, Minor Meriwether (husband of noted pro-South author Elizabeth Avery Meriwether), Ellen Bourne Tynes (wife of Forrest's chief of artillery, Captain John W. Morton), South Carolina Senators Preston Smith Brooks and Andrew Pickens Butler, and famed South Carolina diarist Mary Chesnut.

Seabrook's modern day cousins include: Patrick J. Buchanan (conservative author), Cindy Crawford (model), Shelby Lee Adams (Letcher Co., Kentucky, photographer), Bertram Thomas Combs (Kentucky's 50th governor), Edith Bolling (wife of President Woodrow Wilson), and actors Andy Griffith, Riley Keough, George C. Scott, Robert Duvall, Reese Witherspoon, Lee Marvin, Rebecca Gayheart, and Tom Cruise.

Seabrook's screenplay, *A Rebel Born*, based on his book of the same name, has been signed with acclaimed filmmaker Christopher Forbes (of Forbes Film). It is now in pre-production, and is set for release in 2017 as a full-length feature film. This will be the first movie ever made of Nathan Bedford Forrest's life story, and as a historically accurate project written from the Southern perspective, is destined to be one of the most talked about Civil War films of all time.

Born with music in his blood, Seabrook is an award-winning, multi-genre, BMI-Nashville songwriter and lyricist who has composed some 3,000 songs (250 albums), and whose original music has been heard in film (*A Rebel Born*, *Cowgirls 'n Angels*, *Confederate Cavalry*, *Billy the Kid: Showdown in Lincoln County*, *Vengeance Without Mercy*, *Last Step*, *County Line*, *The Mark*) and on TV and radio worldwide. A musician, producer, multi-instrumentalist, and renown performer—whose keyboard work has been variously compared to pianists from Hargus Robbins and Vince Guaraldi to Elton John and Leonard Bernstein—Seabrook has opened for groups such as the Earl Scruggs Review, Ted Nugent, and Bob Seger, and has performed privately for such public figures as President Ronald Reagan, Burt Reynolds, Loni Anderson, and Senator Edward W. Brooke. Seabrook's cousins in the music business include: Johnny Cash, Elvis Presley, Lisa Marie Presley, Billy Ray and Miley Cyrus, Patty Loveless, Tim McGraw, Lee Ann Womack, Dolly Parton, Pat Boone, Naomi, Wynonna, and Ashley Judd, Ricky Skaggs, the Sunshine Sisters, Martha Carson, and Chet Atkins.

Seabrook lives with his wife and family in historic Middle Tennessee, the heart of Forrest country and the Confederacy, where his conservative Southern ancestors fought valiantly against Liberal Lincoln and the progressive North in defense of Jeffersonianism, constitutional government, and personal liberty.

LochlainnSeabrook.com

LOCHLAINN SEABROOK ~ 577

If you enjoyed this book you will be interested in Colonel Seabrook's other popular related titles:
- ☞ Everything You Were Taught About the Civil War is Wrong, Ask a Southerner!
- ☞ Abraham Lincoln Was a Liberal, Jefferson Davis Was a Conservative
- ☞ All We Ask is to be Let Alone: The Southern Secession Fact Book
- ☞ Everything You Were Taught About American Slavery is Wrong, Ask a Southerner!
- ☞ Confederate Flag Facts: What Every American Should Know About Dixie's Southern Cross
- ☞ Lincoln's War: The Real Cause, the Real Winner, the Real Loser

Available from Sea Raven Press and wherever fine books are sold

ALL OF OUR BOOK COVERS ARE AVAILABLE AS 11" X 17" POSTERS, SUITABLE FOR FRAMING

SeaRavenPress.com • NathanBedfordForrestBooks.com

www.ingramcontent.com/pod-product-compliance
Lightning Source LLC
Chambersburg PA
CBHW030558230426
43661CB00053B/1763